The Italian Baker

The Italian Baker

Also by Carol Field
The Hill Towns of Italy

The Italian Baker

BY CAROL FIELD

HARPER & ROW, PUBLISHERS, NEW YORK

CAMBRIDGE, HAGERSTOWN, PHILADELPHIA, SAN FRANCISCO,
LONDON, MEXICO CITY, SÃO PAULO, SINGAPORE, SYDNEY

1817

This book is for John, who has eaten it all.

THE ITALIAN BAKER. Copyright © 1985 by Carol Field. All rights reserved. Printed in the United States of America. No part of this book may be used or reproduced in any manner whatsoever without written permission except in the case of brief quotations embodied in critical articles and reviews. For information address Harper & Row, Publishers, Inc., 10 East 53rd Street, New York, N.Y. 10022. Published simultaneously in Canada by Fitzhenry & Whiteside Limited, Toronto.

DESIGN BY JOEL AVIROM

DRAWINGS BY DONNIE CAMERON

Library of Congress Cataloging in Publication Data

Field, Carol.
  The Italian baker.

  1. Baking. 2. Cookery, Italian. I. Title.
TX763.F53   1985   641.7'1   85-42565
ISBN 0-06-181266-8

When Don Abbacchio came to the reading of the gospel, he turned to us and preached us a little sermon about San Giuseppe da Copertino. We knew the story, but we always liked hearing it again. For this saint was a cafone who became a monk but never managed to learn Latin, and whenever the other monks recited the Psalms, he gave praise to our Lady by turning somersaults wherever he might be, even in church. Our Lady must have been delighted with the innocent spectacle, and to encourage and reward him she gave him the gift of levitation, and after that he had no difficulty in somersaulting all the way up to the ceiling. He died at an advanced age, after a life of severe privations, and it is said that when he appeared before the heavenly throne, God, who knew him by repute and wished him well, because Our Lady had talked about him so often, embraced him and said, "I will give you whatever you want. Don't be afraid to ask for whatever you like."

The poor saint was utterly bewildered by this offer.

"May I ask for anything?" he asked timidly.

"You may ask for anything," the Almighty encouraged him. "I give the orders here. I can do whatever I like here. And I am really fond of you. Whatever you ask for will be granted."

But San Giuseppe da Copertino did not dare confess what he really wanted. He feared that his immoderate wish might arouse the Lord to anger. Only after much insistence on the Lord's part, only after He gave His word of honor that He would not be angry, did the saint confess what he most wanted.

"O Lord," he said, "a big piece of white bread." [For the only white bread he had ever seen was in Jesus' hand in a painting on the church altar.]

And the Lord was as good as His word and did not grow angry, but embraced the cafone saint, and was moved and wept with him. And then, in His voice of thunder, He summoned twelve angels and gave orders that every day from morning till evening for all eternity, per omnia saecula saeculorum, they should give San Giuseppe da Copertino the best white bread that was baked in Paradise.

Ignazio Silone, *Fontamara*

CONTENTS

Dolci

ACKNOWLEDGMENTS

This book owes an enormous debt to so many people, both in Italy and in America. It wouldn't even exist without Carlo Veggetti, who so generously shared his formidable knowledge of Italian baking and introduced me to bakers all over Italy. And of course it owes everything to the bakers themselves. Special thanks are due to Renato Veggetti, whose generous spirit and helpfulness were endlessly tested by my requests and questions. Renato was patient and kind to an incredible degree.

I couldn't even have written this book without the boundless help of Diane Dexter, who assisted me from beginning to end. Her knowledge of baking and her extraordinary patience as we tested recipes over and over again kept me going. I don't think I could have faced so many go-arounds if Diane hadn't been as curious and as willing to keep searching for solutions as I.

When I met Joann Carmody, she was a young baker at Il Fornaio in San Francisco, who had gone to Italy to bake in Florence and Venice because she wanted to know how things were done there. She was an invaluable help, not only sharing her knowledge but actually traveling in Italy with me for her entire vacation, and baking alongside the pastry bakers.

In America, numerous friends have tasted and tested these recipes. Joyce Goldstein, then the chef at the Café at Chez Panisse, came to taste as often as she could, and was so pleased with what she found that she now serves several of the rustic breads at Square One, her restaurant in San Francisco. Her encouragement and help meant an enormous amount to me. Carol Sinton, Maxine Bloom, Marjorie Traub, Pat Berkowitz, and Leslie Freudenheim tested for me and gave me wonderful feedback. Paola Bagnatori was spectacularly helpful, tasting much that I made and even seeing bakers for me when she was in Italy, to help get answers that I needed. Francesca Vattani not only brought back special sweets from Venice, but helped me in Italy as well, and she and Alessandro were fabulously encouraging to this non-Italian admirer of their country's heritage. My father, James Hart, brought me books that I needed, and found that he loved Italian bread after all. Other special help came from Joanne Hayes, a young baker, from Barbara Winkelstein, who parted with her wonderful *panforte* recipe, from Bob and Maggie Klein, from Fred Hill, from Amanda Pope and Celeste Gainey, from Rose Scherini, from numerous Italians living in America who shared memories with me, but especially from Elisabeta Nelsen and Eugenio Pozzolini, who remembered so much of their Tuscan childhoods and the role that bread played in them, and from Loni Kuhn and Carlo Middione, who tasted my breads and discussed them with me.

In Italy, I don't know what I would have done without the friendship of Shirley and François Caracciolo in Todi and Rome, and of Gianna and Ricardo Bertelli in Tuscany. John Meis at Badia a Coltibuono, in Gaiole in Chianti, and Maria Caterina and Franco Crespi in Perugia, were wonderful sources of information and help, and Carlo Scippione at Il Collezionista in Milan was so enthusiastic and generous that I venture to guess there isn't another rare-book dealer like him anywhere. Silene Veggetti and the children—Mattia, Stefania, Alfonso, and Giulia—were wonderfully helpful and hospitable during my stays in Italy. Christian Hansen and Adolfo Veggetti are two others to whom I am very grateful for much help. Nando Tosoni bakes in Rome, but answered questions for me and baked in San Francisco as well; Agostino Di Vella was a wonderful guide to the breads and sights of Altamura and Matera. Nella Galetti showed me old-fashioned ways of baking at home.

Tom Gemelli, Joe La Bonte, and Tony Marotto at Il Fornaio in San Francisco arranged the baking of the breads and most of the sweets that are on the cover, and packed them for me to carry to New York for the photography session. I can't imagine how to thank them enough.

Barbara Ottenhoff and Helen Huckle have been unstinting in their hard work on behalf of this book, and their contributions have made a great difference. Most especially I want to thank my editor, Ann Bramson, whose belief in this book has been phenomenal. Her kindness, her caring, her sensitivity, warmth, and real dedication have been so remarkable that I marvel at my enormous good fortune in having had the opportunity of working with her.

Very special thanks go to Matthew and Alison, my children, who have endured the family kitchen being converted into a bakery and who have been enthusiastic and helpful, even though the project has meant that I was sometimes unavailable. There is no way to thank my husband, John, for all his support. He believed in me and helped with this book in every possible way. He made special trips to travel with me in Italy when it looked as if I would never survive a crazy schedule and itinerary, he ate endless breads and sweets, and he even became addicted to having his own Italian bread at home. His enthusiasm and belief and willingness to tolerate my obsession with Italian breads and baking made it all possible.

PREFACE

Bread in Italy is rough country loaves with thick chewy crusts, and flat disks of *focaccia* seasoned with the wild herbs of the fields. Their tastes and shapes are fragrant reminders of a tradition of baking that is older than the Roman monuments and Romanesque cathedrals that we rush to Europe to see. These breads are expressions of an earthy culture that still talks about its most fundamental experiences in terms of bread. In Italy, a down-to-earth man with a real heart of gold is described as *"buono come il pane"*—good, like bread. When Americans talk about being direct and straightforward, we say we're calling a spade a spade, but Italians say *"pane al pane e vino al vino,"* calling bread bread and wine wine. Bread gives us real glimpses into the complex and fascinating history of all the regions of the country. Italy wasn't even united until a little over a hundred years ago, so many of the roots have remained a little more exposed than might be true elsewhere. All the rivalries and bloody battles between neighboring cities and regions bred an intense pride in the most local expressions of place, so that just as each *paese* and city had its own bell tower looking over its fraction of countryside, ready to call citizens to arms and alert them to danger, in just the same way its breads expressed a passionate attachment to local customs and ingredients.

Bread is so fundamental to everyday eating that the Italians are forever using the word *companatico*, an all-purpose term for what one eats with bread. "What's for lunch?" *"Pane e companatico"*—bread and something that goes with it. And bread is such a basic part of life that while there are no cookbooks devoted to baking bread at home, many recipes begin: "Take 500 grams of bread dough that you've bought from your baker." Pizzas, *focacce*, enriched breads, and holiday breads often begin just that way.

Each day in Italy, more than 35,000 bakers rise early to knead their doughs and shape their loaves, and of that number 90 percent are artisan bakers, working on a small scale and dedicated to keeping a family and regional tradition alive. They are preserving the past by making it a living part of the present, but they are also showing the baker's dazzling imagination, producing "new wave" breads that turn the luscious provender of the vines and fields into tantalizing loaves.

They have taken the olive paste of Liguria, made from the first crushing of salty, aromatic olives grown near the sea, and incorporated it into a bread. They have taken pesto and sweet peppers and tomatoes dried by the sun under a dappled screen of latticework arbors, they have taken the humble potato and the most expensive aged cheeses, they have taken dark grains that once belonged to a peasant culture, and given them new companions and shapes to make a range of breads that appeal to the Italian passion for *fantasia*, in the most inventive and tantalizing tastes imaginable.

Life without bread is inconceivable in Italy, and yet if I had decided to write this book ten years ago, it would have been an elegy, a bittersweet testament to breads of another time. In the 1950s and 1960s, massive companies took over the bread baking of Italy, turning out airy white loaves like the spongy, cottony slices Americans know from our own supermarket shelves, and threatening to homogenize a tradition of breads, pastries, cookies, and pizzas that were once the culinary equivalent of Italy's numerous dialects. Gone were the indigenous specialties. The tastes and flavors of the past were interred by high-speed rollers that milled grain to a bland, highly refined flour without texture or nutrients, by huge machines that mixed and kneaded faster than the human eye could see, by automation that removed the human touch from the most basic of all human food. Suddenly giant Italian companies were making deals with American consortia to produce biscuits and crackers by the million to be eaten instead of bread. They were replacing *grissini*, the archetypal artisan-made breadstick, with pale little batons all the same color and width and length, extruded from the dies of a machine. Gone were the knobby thick breadsticks whose length was determined by the span of the baker's arms. Blandness suddenly ruled, leaving the centuries-old tradition conquered, as one writer puts it, "by the imperialism of city bread."

But just as the monks kept culture—and bread—alive during a dark time in the country's history, so there were a few bakers who refused to follow the new ways. To them—those who safeguarded tradition and perpetuated the taste of the countryside—this book owes its inspiration and its recipes.

A little less than ten years ago, Carlo Veggetti, whose family had been in the business of furnishing the interiors of bakeries for three generations, found himself increasingly discouraged by the institutionalization of baking in Italy. The handmade regional specialties that had been baked for hundreds of years were disappearing with alarming speed. So he set himself to create a network of bakers and bakeries that would preserve traditional breads from every region of Italy and bring them back to the public. By now, a full-scale revolution has been achieved and over five hundred of his Il Fornaio bakeries exist in Italy, with several other chains visible as well across the landscape. It was Carlo Veggetti, an expansive and energetic man—the Fellini of Italian bread—who opened the doors of his bakeries to me. I baked with his bakers in Como and Milan, in Florence and Rome, in Palermo and Lecce, in Venice and Lugano, in small towns and big cities. His feeling for these breads and the artisans who are masters of their trade is contagious. He talks about eating bread with the eyes as well as the mouth. He speaks of bread as the ultimate art form: "Imagine any work of art with such variety in form, color, aroma, and taste. A work of art that you eat!" There's even music involved in the eating. "Listen: cric-crac, cric-crac."

Through Veggetti I met Giancarlo Grignani, a Milanese baker and a scholar of bread who reads anything he can find on his chosen subject, and even has a clipping service that saves everything relevant in the Italian newspapers. He has recreated the breads of Pompeii as they were baked in Roman times and has made numerous twentieth-century versions of breads of the Lombard countryside from much earlier times—breads made with corn flour, crunchy crusted loaves of Como, and earthy regional breads baked with organically grown flours produced as they were before 1900. He even put together an exhibition of regional Italian breads in the main piazza of Milan.

Other Il Fornaio bakers include Giorgio Gobbi in Lugano and Giovanni Pesenti in Florence, who makes pictures using baked doughs as his medium and creates whole landscapes out of *grissini*; Luca Cucumazzo, a baker from Puglia, and Salvatore Sacco, who dreamed up the *picce calabresi* and showed me secrets of some breads of southern Italy.

Giovanni Galli in Florence, both a pastry and a bread baker, is giving life again to the Tuscan specialties that were once part of country life and tradition. He has put the tastes of this extraordinary landscape into oil-drizzled *schiacciate* and *pizzette* with elegant slices of vegetables and fine powderings of herbs, into festival specialties like sweet rosemary-scented buns and breads bursting with fat golden zibibbo raisins. Gianfranco Anelli makes 100 kilos of pizza a day in his wood-burning ovens in Rome, renders the rustic loaves of tiny towns like Genzano and larger cities like Terni, and has created a *coccodrillo* (crocodile) bread that people in Rome travel far across the city to get. Giorgio Puppola has been baking in Venice since he was a very young boy. His skill with pastry is phenomenal and his flights of imagination created the *ossa da mordere*, the *focaccia* laced with zabaglione cream, and the *bolzanese* in this book. In Venice too, Severino Scarpa shared forty years of baking experience and showed me how breads and rolls were made before machines had such a large part in the cutting and shaping of doughs. Also in Venice, Carlo Cavaliere and Ferruccio Bellemo and Renato Milanese all showed me secrets of bread and pastry baking. Sergio Saturnino in Genoa makes the true *focaccia* of the region, crammed with the pungent tasty olives of Liguria and the fresh herbs of the hillsides.

I have learned the special shaping of the myriad forms in the region of Emilia Romagna from Margherita Simili, the rare woman baker in a world dominated by men. Vito Forte in Altamura has an extraordinary bakery where some loaves are produced industrially— no human hand touches the dough from its mixing to its baking— and others are made by simpatico and knowing artisans, who shape them to look like a woman's pompadour. Truckloads of his breads fan out across the countryside, to Milan and Turin in the north and to tiny *paesi* deep on the heel of the boot. I have shaped and dimpled pizza doughs in Naples, watched bakers in Palermo make calzones and cassatas, and eaten their brioches filled with ice cream, as all the Palermitani do for breakfast. The brothers Spinnato in Palermo took me under their collective wing, taught me about *mafalda* and *sfuncini*, the bread and pizza specialties of the city, and wouldn't hear of my leaving without tasting everything on the premises. Pino Micoli taught me about *rustici* in Lecce, where Avvocato Marangio made sure that I felt and smelled all the flours, learned about the variables of baking in the heat of a southern Italian summer, and introduced me to the bakers of *calzone* and *puccia* and other Pugliese specialties. Carla Schucani of the famous bakery Sandri in Perugia was very gracious, inviting me in to watch the Easter baking, and allowing me to witness everything from the cutting of a wheel of three-year-old Parmigiano-Reggiano to the mixing of Umbrian specialties. In San Francisco, Luciano Pancalde, who comes from Ferrara, shared secrets and recipes with me, tasted what I baked, and gave me more pointers. He was my link to Italy in this country.

These and many more are the sources of the recipes and folklore of Italian bread, and they are the ones who day after day make the breads and sweets that bring these tastes to the fortunate Italians who eat them at breakfast and dinner, over coffee and aperitifs in the *trattorie* and restaurants, coffee bars and *piazze*, where the people of Italy live out their lives.

The revival of bread and a new pride in its myriad forms has led real aficionados to wonder why a different bread isn't served with each course, in the same spirit as wine. Giancarlo Grignani is undoubtedly avant-garde in designing a bread menu for the restaurant Malatesta in Milan, where it is possible to choose one loaf to go with the appetizer, a second for the main course, and a third for the salad. At a quite ordinary restaurant in the Galleria in Milan, I was surprised to find a basket with five very different breads automatically set on the table. Angelo Albini, a baker from Cividale, whose *gubana* is one of the great discoveries of my travels, talks about breads much as winemakers talk about wine. "Smell it," he said to me, "taste it, put it on the back of your throat, and taste it again." It is his dream to achieve a D.O.C. classification for such regional breads just as winemakers have their *Denominazione di Origine Controllata*. D.O.C. on a wine label means that the wine was made under carefully controlled and specified conditions in accordance with traditional procedures; it verifies the authenticity of the character of the wine and indicates quality. If wine is made by transforming grapes, yeast, and water, and bread is made by the alchemical fusion of flour, water, yeast, and salt, why not confirm its regional authenticity with some special highly respected authority?

Seeing really good bakers at work can be eye-opening. When they roll out the dough, their touch can be as delicate as a lover's caress, and when they knead, their authority can almost command the dough to respond. They can take an inert and colorless piece of dough and with their fingers give it form, elasticity, and vitality. The pale white dust that sifts over everything, and the sounds—the slapping and banging of the dough, the thud as it hits the table right out of the mixer, the thunk of the canvas carrier being snapped into the oven and then retracted—the smells, and the sights make the bakery a special world of its own.

Knowing the story and tastes of the regional breads that come out of these ovens is like taking a trip through the Italian countryside. Saving and honoring them is like preserving the stone villages on the hillsides or their churches and frescoes, for saving the taste of the past keeps it alive in the present. The bakers who are committed to rediscovering the past and creating new ways of eating in the present do honor to the oldest of man's foods and to authentic Italian tradition, for bread is one of the most persuasive images of man's struggle to survive. No wonder baking is called *l'arte bianco*, the white art, for the mystical life-giving magic of yeast creates nourishment that sustains a people and keeps alive memories connecting the collective past to the world of today.

BREAD IN ITALY

Bread is merely flour, water, yeast, and salt as the world is merely earth, water, fire, and air. These four elemental ingredients—grain from the fields, water from rivers and mountain streams, leavening from the wild yeasts of the air, and salt from the sea—have been combined since Roman days to make the breads of Italy. In a country where the family is the primary source of physical and emotional sustenance, bread celebrates the richest and simplest pleasures of daily living. It is the single inevitable presence at the table during all three meals of the day, for no Italian would contemplate a meal without bread.

Bread is such a basic part of life in Italy that every restaurant automatically sets it on the table and imposes a cover charge (*coperto*) to cover its cost. Almost every street in Italy's large and middle-sized cities seems to have at least one *panificio* (bakery) and *pasticceria* (pastry shop), and even tiny towns without bread ovens have a grocery store where bread is delivered warm in the mornings. It is calculated that Italians eat almost half a pound of bread a day, the highest consumption in all of Europe, a statistic that translates to 4.5 billion pounds of bread a year.

Under the circumstances, it is not surprising that Italians express many of their most intensely felt sentiments through sayings and proverbs that use bread as their common metaphor.

Buono come il pane—As good as bread (said of a bighearted, down-to-earth person).

Senza il pane tutto diventa orfano—Without bread, everyone is an orphan.

I miei parenti son i soldi in tasca e il pane nella casa—My family is money in my pocket and bread at home.

Issu este unu cantu de pane—He is a piece of bread (he is a good and reliable man, a man who can be trusted).

Uscire di pane duro—To leave behind hard bread (to have a change for the better).

Dire pane al pane e vino al vino—To call bread bread and wine wine (to call a spade a spade).

La prima parola della guerra è pronunciata dal cannone ma l'ultima è sempre detta dal pane—The announcement of war is given by cannons, but bread always has the last word (when there is no more bread, the war is lost).

Trovar pane per i propri denti—To find bread for one's very teeth (to meet one's match).

Se non è zuppa è pan bagnato—If it isn't soup, it's moistened bread (it's six of one or half a dozen of the other).

Nutrirsi a pan bianco—To eat white bread all the time (to live on easy street).

Avere per un pezzo di pane—To get it for a piece of bread (to get it very cheap).

Essere pan e cacio—To be like bread and cheese with someone (to be thick as thieves).

Distinguere pane dai sassi—To know the difference between bread and rocks (to know what's what).

Render pane per focaccia—To give bread for *focaccia* (to give tit for tat).

E tanto pane!—It's so much bread (said upon seeing rain where there's real need of water).

Il pan di casa stufa—Homemade bread makes you fed up (the grass is always greener on the other side).

Meglio nero pane che nera fame—Better dark bread than the dark despair of hunger.

Mangiar pan a tradimento—To eat unearned bread (to be a sponger).

Riuscire meglio a pane che a farina—To succeed more with the bread than with the flour (to have more success than expected).

Per il vecchio e il neonato, il pancotto è prelibato—Bread soup is the food of the old and the newborn (who have no teeth).

Chiurugo come il pane, medico come il vino—Look for a surgeon like bread (young) and a doctor like wine (well aged).

Non è pane per i suoi denti—It is not bread for his teeth (it's not his cup of tea).

Even the academic body that serves to maintain the purity of the Italian language is called Accademia della Crusca—the Academy of Bran—for it sees itself as sifting the wheat from the chaff. Its symbol is an agricultural flour sifter.

Walk past a bakery and you'll often see displays of grains set in the window so people can learn about what they are eating. Go inside and you'll notice that every bread is labeled not only with its name but with every ingredient, as well as the price per kilo. Bread is so basic to a sense of well-being that local governments regulate the prices of the traditional breads of the *commune*, keeping it affordable for anyone with but a few hundred lire in a pocket. The saltless bread of Tuscany, which is very cheap in Florence and Siena, can be sold for any price outside regional limits—though most of the people of, say, Milan and Rome have no cravings for or childhood ties to saltless bread. Anyone from the countryside around Chianti, however, or from the little hill towns that have sat in this landscape since the Etruscans first sited them, will tell you that saltless bread is part of a heritage that stretches back long before Dante.

A Tuscan would no more choose to eat a Roman *pagnotta* or a Milanese *michetta* than he would expect to find Wiener schnitzel on his dinner plate. So how could it come as a surprise that each region boasts variations on its breads and ingredients and makes its local tastes into breads that define a small geographical area.

When I was in Altamura, a town in the south of Italy famous for its golden durum-flour bread, I went to talk to a baker, watch the bread being made, and to taste it, of course. Later in the day at a restaurant about fifteen kilometers away, a big basket of golden bread with a chewy crust and a porous interior was brought to our table. I exclaimed to my host with pleasure, "Oh, wonderful—more bread from Altamura." A disgruntled look fleeted across his face and disappointment clouded his eyes. "Well," he said grudgingly, "more or less." I had insulted the tradition. We were a little less than ten miles from Altamura, but no matter, we might as well have been five hundred. The bread of Altamura comes from *its* bakers and *its* grains and *its* tradition. Although the bread on our table was similar, it just wasn't the same.

I should have known better. How could it be otherwise in a country that has a dial-a-message service for regional recipes? Each day, the recording gives a new recipe for a dish from each of the regions of Italy. And how could it be otherwise in a country scarred in medieval times by cities that chose to fight ferociously with their closest neighbors to prove their supremacy, their dedication to local alliances finally leading them to stamp their own identity not only on the landscape but on the foods as well? This rich, complex, and combative heritage influences Italian baking and is embellished by the reality that everyone from the Saracens to the Austrians conquered different regions and left their culinary signature behind. The porous and crunchy crusted Pugliese bread of the south is a legacy of the brown country loaf brought by the Turks who long ago walked the streets of Apulia; and the famous *michetta* roll of Milan was born of the *Kaiser Semmel* of Vienna, which was brought to Milan by the Austrian cavalry in the late 1800s.

In the country at large, there are more names for the shapes of bread than Eskimos have words for snow. This is a very fragmentary list: *azzimo* (unleavened), *casareccio* (homemade), *ciabatta* (slipper), *ciambella* (wreath), *corolla* (crown), *manini* (little hands), *mattone* (brick), *pagnotta* (round loaf), *panino* (roll), *piadina* (flat disk), *quattrocorni* (four horns), *ruota* (wheel), *schiacciata* (flattened), *sfilatino* (long, thin thread), *stella* (star), *tegola* (tile), *treccia* (braid). Italian bakers say there may be somewhere between one thousand and two thousand different breads in the national repertory, although "only" a few hundred are commonly available, and while there are numbers of typical regional breads—*biove* from Piedmont, *ciopa* from Venice, *crocetta* from Ferrara, *michetta* from Milan, and saltless loaves from Tuscany—each type may have slight variations attributable to the individual bakers. The taste of bread is so much a product not only of local ingredients, of the humidity of the air and the quality of the water, but even of the fingers and hands of the baker, that people know immediately when a local baker has died, because the bread suddenly tastes different.

Secrets and techniques for making bread have been handed down from baker to baker over the years, and they belong to an oral tradition like folk tales and peasant wisdom. Apprentices learn by watching and asking and doing, since this is a tradition that relies not on specific recipes but on formulas that are expressed in proportions. I once asked a baker how he made the chewy, crunchy crusted bread of his region and he told me: "Use 2 percent yeast, 2 percent salt, 60 percent water, to 100 percent flour." Of course the baker understood exactly what he meant, but his answer left a few loose ends for me. How long did he mix the ingredients? Did the dough rise twice or three times its original size to produce the special texture? Was the water cool or warm? The bakers' formulas are merely guidelines, for knowledgeable baking depends on touch, taste, sight, smell, and experience—knowing when to add a little water or when to work the dough a little longer. Clearly, the flexible formula leaves room for the baker's individuality, his personal touches and the flashes of imagination that put his stamp on the bread and make it his own. These recipes do not exist anywhere in written form. Unlike the French, who make numerous regional breads and sweets according to quantified recipes and a codified tradition, Italian bakers are forever experimenting and dreaming up new interpretations. If forty bakers at Lake Como are making *ciabatta*, you can be sure there will be forty slightly different tastes.

These breads of Italy have their fragrance, their color, and their flavor, but most also have their raison d'être. Most Italian breads are soft, but the tradition of hard breads is rooted with a people who needed their basic nourishment to keep for a long time. Sardinian shepherds carry wafer-thin *carasau* bread, big flat crackly disks also called *carta da musica* (sheet music bread), for its parchment color and fine veining of horizontal lines. The *frisedde* of Puglia, the *gallette* of seagoing sailors, and the *ciambelle valtelline* of the cold north, where snow isolates regions for weeks at a time, are all hard breads made to last for months. When eaten, they are dipped into water or broth, or moistened with slices of tomato, flavored with oil, salt, pepper, and herbs like oregano that grow wild in the countryside, then perhaps topped with slices of cheese, which might come from the milk of the sheep the shepherds of Sardinia tend. The standard Venetian *pani biscotti*, biscuits that are rather like hardtack, were a perfect provision for sailors or even businessmen who went to sea for months at a time. They were made, as their name implies, by being twice cooked (*bis cotto*) to draw off almost all the moisture and produce a very light, long-lasting biscuit that couldn't possibly mold or go bad. It is said that both Marco Polo and Christopher Columbus relied on *biscotti* on their long voyages.

There are many rituals and elements of etiquette connected with bread. In Tuscany and Puglia, big rounds of crusty rustic loaves are always held in the crook of the elbow and sliced toward the chest. Knowing how to cut bread is as important to an Italian man as learning how to carve meat is to an American.

In Italy, bread is an object of respect, a sign of the grace of providence which is treated with almost sacramental reverence. Mothers teach their children that no one is allowed to waste a crumb of bread. Should a single bit accidentally fall to the floor, it must be picked up, immediately cleaned off, and eaten. It is said that anyone wasting bread will be condemned to Purgatory for as many years as there were crumbs and will be compelled to collect each little bit upon the eyelids, one at a time. Bread placed upside down on a table will bring bad luck. No one should ever leave a knife plunged into the crust of bread because it is like the flesh of the Lord and the person responsible will never again partake of grace. Bakers always make the sign of the cross over the oven and often make it in the dough itself before baking, as many peasants do before taking a first bite of freshly baked loaves. Bread is so powerful that even the smell of it is believed to have healing powers.

Some forms of bread have roots in prehistory, and are charged to this day with symbolic significance. Round *pan di morte* (bread of the dead) appears in late October, and cookies called *ossa di morte* and *fave di morte* are eaten in honor of the dead on the Day of the Dead and All Souls Day. On those days families participate in ceremonies meant to prove to the dead that they have not been forgotten and continue to share in the life of the family. The tibia-shaped *ossa di morte* are eaten all over Italy, from Lombardy to Sicily, and are known, regionally, as *ossa da mordere, oss de mord, ossi da morto,* or *stinchetti.* Outsiders may find these little nougats a bit strange, as Paul Valéry did on a trip to Italy in 1834, when he made it very clear that he didn't care for "this horrible confection," to which he attributed the ancient reputation of the Umbrians for ferocity. He had a point—Umbrian history is nothing short of hair-raising before the seventeenth century—but the bone-shaped cookies seem a bit more abstract than the serpent-shaped cakes of Perugia and Umbria, which are bristling with primitive associations.

In Calabria for the feast day of San Rocco, whose specialty is protecting against contagious diseases, bakers shape *panpepati,* which are like spicy Italian gingerbread cakes, into ex-votos that represent various parts of the body. A parade of local pilgrims winds through the city streets on its way to a statue of the saint, where they offer these baked arms, legs, heads, and various organs decorated with all the imagination of the local baker. They are collected the next day in a huge basket and sold at an auction to support the singers and comics, puppeteers, actors, band players, and makers of fireworks whose art furnishes the ceremonies for the saint's day.

In three of the most rustic regions of Italy, Puglia, Lucania, and Calabria, where the poor generally eat only the darker, lesser grains, wheat bread is given only to the dying ("he has arrived at the bread" is the local proverb) and to women about to give birth.

In some remote mountain communities in the Alto Adige, the Val d'Aosta, and the Trentino, far in the north of Italy, superstitions surround the choice of which days are most propitious for the baking of bread. It is universally agreed that bread must never be made on days when the furrows of the earth are open for the sowing of the wheat, for then the bread would mold. Some say that the moon must be rising, others that it should be in its last quarter, but there is no question that the worst time for making bread is at the first sign of the new moon, which would surely bewitch the loaves. Some folk wisdom maintains that bread must be baked in the early morning, for it swells in the oven in harmony with the ascension of the sun. In the same spirit, breads in their round shapes are seen as being like the sun, which appears anew every day to keep away darkness and make the earth grow.

Braided breads, which surfaced in the late Middle Ages, are also richly symbolic. In ancient days, women were expected to join their dead husbands in their tombs, but over time human sacrifice was replaced by the symbolic sacrifice of the woman's hair. When women were finally allowed to keep their hair, the symbol was replaced by a loaf of bread plaited like a braid, which was given to the poor instead of being placed in the grave.

Some breads are literally meant to carry the blessings of home and church. Traditional rolls made only for Calabrians who are leaving their native countryside are stamped with an image of the Madonna and then blessed by a priest before they are entrusted to the departing family.

Breads created to celebrate New Year's Day, Easter, or marriage ceremonies are hard to tell apart because all three deal with beginnings, which must be nourished with the most affirmative symbols. Votive breads in south and central Italy take the form of wheat sheaves, clusters of swollen grapes, and doll-like figures called *pupazze*. All three have overtones of fertility and religion. The *pupazze* made for Easter always have a red egg tucked under each arm. Red is the color of fertility and an egg represents renewal in both pagan and church terms. These breads celebrate birth and rebirth and new beginnings in physical, emotional, and religious connotations, and celebrate as well the sensuality inherent in the stalks of wheat that are planted and plowed in the warmth of mother earth.

The simple aromatic breads of the countryside are more than the flavors and smells of an ancient culture. They are rife with sexual symbolism. The *banana* and *barlino* from the Emilia Romagna region and various Venetian breads are rolled into unmistakably phallic shapes or curved into a round *ciambella* with a hole in the center. The high swollen shapes of softer *pagnotta pasquale* (Easter bread) are as round as breasts or pregnant bellies. Some breads, such as the *coppiette* of Ferrara, are barely disguised images of coupling, which were once made to propitiate the forces of nature and encourage the fertility of the fields. Bakers in some small towns in Lazio still make breads in the form of women with three cone-shaped breasts, recalling Diana of Ephesus who had 100 breasts and represented the mythic ferocity of fertility.

The sweets and breads of Sicily are especially rich with sexual imagery. Little almond treats called "breasts of the virgin" (*mammelle di vergine*) are shaped just as you might imagine and are surprisingly prized most by the nuns who created them. Don Fabrizio in Lampedusa's *The Leopard* asks for the "virgin's cakes" at a huge sumptuous party in Sicily. As he looks at them on his plate, he sees a profane caricature of St. Agatha and exclaims, "Why didn't the Holy Office forbid these cakes when it had the chance? St. Agatha's sliced-off breasts sold by convents, devoured at dances! Well, Well!" To this day, phallic babas and plump round brioche cakes with a squish of cream and the crown of a single fat berry, succulent images of sexuality, line the glass cases of bakeries all over Palermo.

Italy is a landscape of hundreds of small protected valleys enclosed within mountain chains and dramatic seacoasts. Its valleys and soft open plains are etched with pale ribbons of rivers and stone walls and punctuated with silvery olive trees, rows of grapevines, and ancient stone villas. Even today, much of it looks as it did in the Renaissance paintings from which we still preserve our image of the country. In this countryside, the historical roots of bread are no less significant than the geography that produced the regional tradition and the peasant culture that gave it its flavor.

The Romans learned to bake from the Greeks, who followed the victorious Roman armies back to Rome in 170 B.C. and revolutionized the practice of bread baking, which had belonged to housewives for centuries. The Greeks were great bakers who made more than fifty kinds of bread, milling their grain to a very fine flour. They actually worshiped bread, which was intimately tied to religious rituals that centered on Demeter, goddess of grain and abundance. Demeter originally made the earth dry and infertile while she searched for her daughter Persephone, who had been kidnapped by Pluto and taken to the underworld. She pleaded with Zeus for the girl's release, but only after she refused to allow grain to grow was the god forced to restore Persephone to her mother for half the year, the period corresponding to the sowing, ripening, and threshing of the fields. The famous Eleusinian mysteries which revolve around Demeter celebrate the force of feminine fertility that is profoundly tied to the fertility of the earth. In Sicily to this day, an annual holiday in honor of Demeter and Persephone includes offerings of sesame-and-honey *focacce* shaped like women's sexual organs. They are intended to make the goddess laugh and to distract her from the sadness brought on by her daughter's disappearance.

Before they ever tasted or made bread, the Romans ate *puls,* a kind of mush of grains boiled in water, a predecessor of polenta. It was made of millet or, more commonly, spelt, a grain called *farro* in Latin, from which comes *far,* the root for *farina,* which is the Italian word for flour. By 147 B.C., the Greek slaves who tended the ovens in Roman bakeries had taught the Romans their trade, and those Romans had become so important that they were given social status and rank and had formed a professional corporation that had very strict rules about the quality and ingredients used in making bread. Bakery owners were generally freed slaves—the second mayor of Pompeii was one—but once a man became a baker, he could never change work, and his sons and sons-in-law after him were obliged to follow the trade as well.

Bread baking reached its greatest moment around 25 B.C. in the time of Emperor Augustus, when there were 329 public bakeries in Rome alone. The bakers leavened bread by using a bit of dough from the baking of the day before or by adding beer yeast, which they had learned about from the Gauls and the Germans. They made saltless sponges, which were called *biga*—as they still are today—by fermenting wheat flour with grape must, sprouted barley, or bran soaked in white wine. They also made enriched breads with milk, eggs, oil, honey from Greece and Asia Minor, anise, poppy seeds, nuts, cheese, and sesame seeds. They even developed some baking forms, such as the long, thin sandwich bread mold, that are still in use today.

The big central bread market in Rome boasted round breads; breads notched into eight sections, which were easy to break off into individual pieces; breads shaped like keys, cubes, or braids; breads that looked like mushrooms; and breads that looked like wreaths. There was a bread for each social class—senators' bread, knights' bread, citizens', people's, and peasants' bread. White bread was already a status symbol, even though some writers knew that darker, coarser loaves were healthier and gave sustenance to hard-working peasants and farmers. The rich ate *siligo*, the finest wheat flour, which was so white that the women of Rome powdered their faces with it. Pliny noted that "in some places bread is named after the dishes eaten with it, such as oyster bread, in others from its special delicacy, as cake bread, in others from the short time spent making it, as hasty bread, and also from the method of baking, as oven bread, or tin loaf, or baking pan bread."

In those days, breads were made with wheat, millet, and rye. Bran was usually baked into loaves that were tossed to the dogs; oats were fed to cattle. A clever Roman baker dreamed up a labor-saving mechanical kneader that was powered by a horse or donkey trudging in circles, churning the water, flour, and leavening inside its big basin—the Kitchen Aid mixer of its day. Animals eventually took over from men to provide the power for mills as well. Whereas flour was originally made by crushing grain with a mortar and pestle, then sifting it through a fine cloth, it was now ground between two hourglass-shaped stones that were rotated by mules. The word that defined the grinding action was *pistor*, a term still used today in Venice to define a baker; elsewhere in Italy, a baker is called a *fornaio* or *panettiere*, from the words for oven and bread.

Bakers' brick and stone ovens insulated hot air in a hollow square space set within an arched opening; wood from tree branches provided the heat, and there was even a container for water so that humidity would make crisp crusts. The Romans celebrated June 9 as the festival of Fornax, goddess of the ovens, by decorating oven mouths with flowers and hanging wreaths from the necks of the mules who turned the mills.

Wheat and bread shaped the destiny of Rome and were intimately tied to its rise and fall. In early Roman days, all land belonged to the state, except for small parcels of acreage given to soldiers returning home from the wars. The state protected the farmers, but as its ambitions grew, its need for more capital led to the decision to let land to the rich. These wealthy landlords, who forced small farmers to abandon their fields, were able to combine parcels of land into vast estates. Rather than grow wheat, they turned their farmland into pasturage, which was more profitable. Wheat-growing was virtually abandoned, and the small farmers were forced to the city, where they melted into the growing mass of the dispossessed and unemployed. Caesar, Augustus, and Nero provided free grain to keep the restive unemployed from rebelling, hoping that bread and circuses would distract them, but each ruler was forced to import ever greater amounts. The constant search for more and more grain was partially responsible for the expansion of empire. While Trajan established the first bakers' school in A.D. 100, and the architect Vitruvius discovered hydraulic milling, which could produce much more flour from the same amounts of grain, Rome continued to swallow up territory until the empire stretched from Britain to the deserts of Africa and grew too large to be controlled by a single ruler. When the empire was divided between east and west, Rome lost control of the vast wheat fields of Egypt and Africa, which fed its population. The end of the wheat supply coincided almost precisely with the fall of the empire. Barbarian tribes plunged across the borders and virtually dismembered the state. The once rich arable land, which had been given over to pasturage, reverted to swamp. Bread, as the Romans knew it, disappeared from Rome and the farther reaches of Italy. For a while, whatever bread there was was baked at home and was contrived of roots, beans, acorns, and minor grains.

Surprisingly enough, even the barbarian conquerors knew bread. The brilliant Byzantine general Belisarius built mills at the edge of the Tiber, and produced enough grain to fill the needs of sixth-century Rome. But it was at the monasteries that earth was cultivated and bread first baked again, under the watchful eyes of the monks. To get on with their work and studies, these monks needed every labor- and time-saving device they could find. The powerful hydraulic milling machines they put to work again were major forces behind the rebirth of baking. Bread making became more important after 800, when Charlemagne came to power. Mills multiplied and eating became more than keeping body and soul together. In the years that followed, rich lords with great castles and estates took control of much of the countryside. What grain wasn't collected for these great landholders went to the monasteries, whose huge tracts of land gave them substantial clout. Farmers and peasants were compelled to take whatever grains were left to make their daily bread. People collected in cities once again—in self-defense as much as anything else, since they needed security against those nobles who were decimating the landscape with their power struggles. As urbanization proceeded, bakers organized guilds as they had in Roman times.

The breads of the Middle Ages were as stratified as Roman bread.

There was a bread for the pope, bread for knights and pages, bread for the cavalry, bread for canons and priests, and bread for soldiers, as well as the little loaves of rye and wheat meant for everyday eating. Bread was so basic to daily nourishment and survival that whenever a battle was fought—and in these crisis-ridden centuries there were many battles—a bread baker always rode off with the soldiers, bringing his iron oven and his grains to bake *gallette* and loaves for the army.

These medieval centuries were the years of a new spirit of independence, when regional identities were being forged. Just as each area had its own currency and customs (imagine having to clear customs several times on a trip between Milan and Florence, and you begin to get the picture), each region had its own ingredients, and its own attitudes about bakers and bread. Verona and Padua had baking corporations before 1200, which made them avant-garde for the times. In Venice, where bakers had already been at work in the first years of the eleventh century, there were strict laws about quality control. If bread was discovered to be short weighted, it was distributed free to the poor; if the quality was below standard, it was crumbled into pieces and tossed off the Rialto Bridge. By 1280, artisan bakers in Florence had already collected in professional guilds and were baking breads and sweets in the city's 146 ovens. Although Florence's sumptuary laws prohibited serving more than three courses per meal, some bakers got around the problem by layering all kinds of meats and vegetables in a single dish, wrapping them in pastry, and cooking them all under the embers. What they pulled out of the fire were meat and vegetable tarts, born as a strategy of having one's cake, so to speak, and eating it too.

Things were entirely different in Rome, where bread making, like everything else, had fallen into a deplorable state when the popes decamped for Avignon. When they returned in 1378, there were only 30,000 people in the city. The popes knew that they had to do something to revive urban life, so they imported a number of foreigners, including German bakers. We know that bread was the basic food of the city, either by itself or with a *companatico* (something to eat with bread), because carefully kept records show that bakers used 85–90 percent of the grain that came into the city. Pasta was barely eaten at all and bread baked at home by individuals was extremely rare. White breads were made and sold only in special separate luxury shops. Dark loaves accounted for the vast majority of what was baked and eaten.

And what of Milan, the city that now symbolizes urban sophistication? Milan didn't have a single independent baker in the Middle Ages because the bakers were all under the thumb of the powerful ruling Visconti family until the end of the sixteenth century. Which isn't to say that bread didn't have a powerful position. On the contrary. The only people in the city who could be elected to the medieval parliament of Milan had to produce their own bread and wine, which says a lot about who the producers were as well as the position of bread. Please understand that we're not talking about white bread here. The Milanese ate a millet bread called *pan de mei*, the ancestor of today's corn loaves, or they ate breads that were either totally dark or made of mixed grains.

Progress was substantially set back by the plagues of the fourteenth century. The Black Death marched across the cities of Italy, decimating as much as 40 percent of their populations, and bringing with it famine and hunger. For many Italians, bread became a mere memory. The high cost of wheat compelled some bakers to come up with whatever substitutions they had at hand. Many of them found themselves mixing rye, corn, and millet or grinding acorns, using hard wheat instead of soft, or even baking with elm leaves and roots mixed in. Some bakers resorted to mixing in clay from the earth to make their loaves look whiter. Many of the best bakers gave up their ovens. To cope with the shortage, the pope effectively municipalized bread by opening numerous bread ovens in Rome. Still, as late as the eighteenth century, the poor were rioting around the famous fountains in the Piazza Navona with placards lettered "Let these cobblestones turn into bread."

Although cooks in Renaissance Italy devised sophisticated techniques of bread baking, the Italians lost their supremacy as bakers to the Viennese, who opened their first coffeehouses in 1782, offering the phenomenal sweets and pastries that made Vienna the capital of elegant baking. New high-speed roller mills turned out the cheap and plentiful white flour that was the basic material not only for these sweets but for bread.

The French shared honors with the Viennese in the field of baking. While white bread had once been reserved for the rich, the soldiers of Napoleon's army introduced it to the masses as they made their way across the continent. French bread became synonymous with bread. When Napoleon sold Venice to the Austrians in 1797, the Hapsburgs brought with them an army of inhabitants whose gastronomic traditions were enthusiastically accepted. They made the *Kipfel*, a croissant-like pastry that is still a great favorite at breakfast, and a century later the Austrian cavalry brought the *michetta*, the quintessential roll of Milan. The contribution of other cultures made an impact in Italy as well. America contributed her ingredients: the tomato, which eventually made a perfect marriage with Neapolitan pizza; the potato; the pimento; vanilla; the chocolate that transformed the pastries of Turin; and the corn that was milled and then baked into delicate pound cakes and heartier breads. Much earlier gifts from the Saracens—citrus fruits, grappa, and distilled spirits—and the Arab contributions of anise, nuts, almond paste, spices, and sugar gave special inflections to the cooking of Sicily and the south. The culinary signatures of invaders, conquerors, and explorers are all part of the heritage that remains today.

It wasn't until the beginning of the twentieth century that Pellegrino Artusi, a Florentine, rekindled Italian culinary pride by writing a cookbook that preserved genuine Italian cooking and gave respect to the regional tradition of middle-class food in the north. The book is chatty and amusing, and a fair number of its recipes are based on bread.

It could be said that an undercurrent common to these centuries was a class struggle between the *bocche da pane*, bread eaters who had white breads on their tables, and *bocche da biada*, literally fodder eaters, peasants and members of the rural and urban poor who ate only dark breads made of whatever grains and beans the land offered up. In Italy, bread has always been a symbol of quality of life (a meal without it is unthinkable), and the quality of bread has always been a statement of social distinction. The privileged ate white bread even in Roman times. Until the last decade, dark breads have been identified with deprivation and hunger in the collective memory of Italy. The identification was particularly intense during the years when scarcities forced people to rely on *pane selvaggi*, breads made of whatever seeds and grains could be harvested from the countryside. (For centuries, scarcity has been the mother of invention in Italian baking. A baker in Venice told me that as recently as World War II, he mixed sawdust with whatever grain he had, and used water straight from the sea to compensate for a scarcity of salt.)

Today it is rare to find many people baking at home—with a bakery on every block or in every neighborhood, there's scarcely a need to—but there are still pockets where the old ways prevail, among both the poor and the more privileged. In these places, which are almost always in the countryside, bread is baked in wood-burning ovens every few days by women who keep a nugget of natural yeast from one baking to the next. In the south, women share the yeast, passing it from household to household. Where once there were numerous communal ovens, today there are very few, where women of the community still take turns baking the breads, with hours assigned on the basis of seniority. These women know the temperature of the interior of the brick oven as it changes during the day, know where the hot spots are and where to put the breads so they will bake correctly. In the heyday of communal ovens, when there were numerous loaves being baked together, women would score their doughs with a special identifying mark on the top.

The old and honorable bakery tradition, with its roots that reach deep into the Roman past, changed with the advent of high-speed machinery, but things really took a turn for the worse in the 1950s and 1960s, when huge machines were introduced that mixed and kneaded practically at the speed of light and produced cottony breads and bland *grissini*. To many people they were a denial of the art of the Italian baker, which was nourished by an agrarian past and by a passionate attachment to local ingredients and customs. The counter-revolution of the past several years is again changing the face of baking. It is not that industrial methods have been banished, but that the conformity and lack of imagination connected with them are being challenged by artisan bakers. These men (and a tiny number of women) have touched a profoundly sensitive nerve in Italians who remember the true tastes of breads, pizzas, *focacce*, and sweets. They are restoring a real taste to bread, and bringing back a tradition that offers the best of genuine fragrant tastes that have given pleasure to Italians for centuries.

A NOTE ON ITALIAN USAGE

Terms and spellings for breads and sweets vary from region to region, and the same term can have different meanings in different regions.

BAKING BASICS

About the Recipes

In these recipes I have tried to recreate the breads and pastries, the *focacce, biscotti,* and cakes that I have lingered over in Italian cities, towns, and those tiny entities of geography which are called *fraz.,* for *frazione* (fraction), because they contain only a handful of buildings and really are splinters of the larger nearby community. The recipes are meant to bring the tastes of the Italian countryside to the American table and evoke memories of a way of life in which bread and the food it accompanies are shared among friends and family. As many of the recipes come from small towns that are off the beaten track or are baked for special holidays or to commemorate ancient regional practices, only travelers who have strayed from the usual hotel and restaurant route will have found them. No matter: try the breads and pastries this way first, then go to the country and sample them in context.

I have tried to keep these baked goods tasting as they do in Italy. I haven't sweetened the breads or added ingredients that would please the American palate, though I have reduced the amount of sugar in a few of the desserts and cookies—the Italian sweet tooth didn't get its fame undeservedly. Occasionally I have made an ingredient or two optional; the Italian passion for candied fruit is not reciprocated in America, so I have used candied orange peel as a substitute from time to time and required candied fruit only when a recipe truly couldn't do without it. When I have made an ingredient optional, I have often noted how the Italians would use them. I have specified the best-quality ingredients, using butter where some bakeries use vegetable fats or oils (if your preferences run to margarine or safflower and/or corn oil, however, you can certainly use them, especially in the breads). In light of the current national preoccupation with reducing our intake of animal fats, you may prefer to use olive oil in place of lard, although it is lard that gives some of these breads and *focacce* their special taste and texture. I do suggest that Americans try to use whatever Italian ingredients are available here.

The recipes in this book are all Italian. They began in huge quantities—20 kilos of flour is not an uncommon starting point—but they have been scaled down, reworked, and tested so that they can be made in an ordinary American kitchen, using American ingredients that most closely approximate their Italian counterparts. I've given weight as well as volume for measures of all dry ingredients because it is a much more accurate way of measuring—4 cups of flour can vary by as much as 100 grams, depending on how the flour is scooped and packed into the measuring cup. I much prefer weighing ingredients, for just that reason. I have given all measurements for active dry yeast in teaspoons, using 2½ teaspoons per packet as a general rule of thumb. Many of these recipes, especially those calling for a starter, use much less yeast than traditional American recipes, and as a result bring out the mellow, nutty flavor of the grain. Italian bakers never use sugar to activate yeast, and neither do I. Where sugar is called for, it is part of the recipe's ingredients. Italian bakers have used mixers since a baker designed the first automatic kneading machine in ancient Rome, and things have only grown bigger and faster since that time. I have given instructions for making the breads by hand as well as with an electric mixer such as Kitchen Aid or Kenwood. (Please don't even think of using a hand-held mixer; it doesn't have the power to engage these bread doughs, and all you'll get for your trouble is a burned-out motor.) I decided to convert a number of the recipes for the food processor as well, because so many people are delighted by the speed and ease with which this new miracle machine can handle bread dough.

On the following pages, you will find descriptions of the various ingredients and equipment called for in the full range of these recipes, and a review of the basic steps of bread baking and pastry making. Please read these sections carefully, and refer to them whenever you need a bit of clarification. The one ingredient and technique not specifically listed in this chapter is patience. Rome wasn't built in a day and some of its breads need a little time to let their character mature. Should your plans change after you've embarked on a bread, and your presence be required somewhere other than the kitchen, just leave the dough in a cool spot or in the refrigerator. Please don't let bread baking dictate your day.

The Ingredients

The regional breads of Italy are made only with flour, water, yeast, and common salt, because that is the law of the land. "Special bread," another category entirely, may be enriched with milk, oil, or lard and flavored with the dazzling products of the countryside, including myriad types of olives, vegetables and grains from the earth, spices, herbs, fruits, raisins, nuts, and various essences and aromas. But it is the basic four ingredients that become the traditional rustic bread of the country, and to trace their flavors from Lugano in the north to Sicily at the toe of the boot is to make an odyssey in history and tastes. It is how they are measured and mixed, and in what proportions, how they are left to rise and be shaped, that determine their ultimate texture and taste, for these are the variables that give each bread its individual personality.

Flour
Farina

Flour in Italy. Bakers in Italy think it's impossible to find flour in America that isn't wonderful. I can't count the number of times during my work with Italian bakers that I heard the word "Manitoba," which becomes *Mahn-ee-TOE-ba*, four liquid syllables, in an Italian accent. It's a code word for fine flour, since the powerful wheats of the American and Canadian prairie absorb considerably more water and produce larger and more expansive doughs than common Italian grain. Bakers spoke of it with admiration and a tone of distant longing, for the Italian earth, which remains so hospitable to grapes and olives, has been so consistently exploited that today it produces weak grains that lack the strength and flavor of the grain of the past. Some Italian flours may have as much gluten as ours, but they are unable to absorb the water and then free it when the baking process requires. Many Italian bakers give a boost to their doughs by mixing in some of the higher-gluten, stronger American flour they admire, to approximate our all-purpose flours.

To capture the true taste of bread as it used to be made, some impassioned professionals, like Giancarlo Grignani of Milan, have gone in search of grain cultivated as it was in earlier centuries, before chemicals and industrial fertilizers were introduced, and they have found millers who stone-grind it to a coarse texture that retains some of its bran. But of course most bakers make do with the common flours of the country and are able to prepare wonderful breads with them.

Flour in Italy comes commonly from the species *Triticum aestivum*, which is divided into two major varieties—soft wheat and hard wheat (*grano tenero*)—and from which almost all bread is made. Durum hard grain (*grano duro*), or *Triticum durum*, a different species, is the hardest wheat grown, and is usually milled into semolina. It is a golden grain that has a higher protein and gluten content and is used almost exclusively for pasta production. The creamy, silky golden durum flour makes wonderful bread, used alone or in combination with unbleached or all-purpose flour, but it does need to be mixed and kneaded for a longer time. The Italian baker has five grades of *grano tenero* to choose from, although they are classified not by strength and protein content like ours but by how much of the husk and whole grain have been sifted away. The whitest flour has the least fiber; the lower the number, the more refined and whiter the flour, so that of the five categories, "00" is the whitest and silkiest flour, "0" a bit darker and less fine, since it contains about 70 percent of the grain, "1" even darker; "2," darker and coarser yet, has almost entirely disappeared from Italy. *Integrale*, or whole wheat, contains the whole wheat berry—husk, wheat germ, and all—and varies only depending on how it is milled. If you were intent on reproducing Italian "00" flour, you could mix about one part pastry flour with three parts all-purpose; to make "0" flour, mix one part cake flour with four parts all-purpose. The color of the flour is determined by the amount of bran present, but ironically, the white flours, which have the fewest nutrients and vitamins, are very expensive since the refining process is so costly. Unfortunately, it doesn't follow that healthier whole-wheat flours are cheap, because most mills have been adapted to produce the refined flours; bran is taken out in an industrial process and used frequently for feeding animals. For all the talk of the prevalence of whole grain in the healthy Mediterranean diet, only about 2 percent of Italian breads are made with whole wheat. The health revolution is only beginning. And in one of the stranger twists in the contemporary story of flour, I have heard of millers who simply take refined white flour, stir in a quantity of bran, and pronounce it whole wheat.

Flour in America. In America, we are used to thinking of flour in terms of its strength, which is measured by the amount of gluten-forming protein, although there is enormous variation in flours from region to region. The hard winter wheat produces strong bread flour with a high 13–15 percent gluten-forming content, and it must be kneaded longer and harder than other flours. Soft wheat, grown in the hot months between spring and autumn, when it is harvested, is much lower in gluten—usually 4–9 percent—and it is generally used for cake and pastry flours.

Most of the recipes in this book can be made with all-purpose flour, which is a blend of the two, although at 11 or 12 grams of protein per cup, which is how we determine the percentage of gluten, it is slightly stronger than its Italian counterpart. If you can find stone-ground flour that hasn't lost its natural qualities from a speeded-up milling process, I'd encourage you to use it. I generally use unbleached flour, which is confusingly misnamed, as it is in fact bleached by the aging process, a characteristic it shares with Italian flours. No chemicals, however, give it its color. Our flours are enriched with thiamine, riboflavin, niacin, and iron and have a small amount of added malt. (Italians add malt as a grain extract to their doughs to encourage their rising and the golden bloom of their crusts; they are also allowed a tiny addition of ascorbic acid, a form of vitamin C, intended to mature the dough.)

Many of the major brands of all-purpose flour note on the package that the flour has been pre-sifted. Actually, once a bag of flour has left the miller, been trucked to a grocery store, put on the shelf, and then brought home with you, it couldn't possibly still be sifted. Just treat it like unsifted flour and, if possible, weigh it on a scale to measure it correctly. Never sift flour for bread; always sift it for pastries and cookies. If you weigh your ingredients, sift the flour after measuring; if you use cup measures, sift before measuring.

Go to any supermarket these days and you can find not only the basic flours—all-purpose, unbleached, high-gluten bread flour, whole-wheat and rye—but you'll probably find semolina too, although it may be in the pasta section. It is sometimes a bit trickier to find a few of the more exotic flours, like pastry, graham, or durum, but even they may appear in small packages, or in the big bins of loose ingredients in today's supermarkets and groceries that hark back to the general stores of the last century.

In addition to these most basic flours, other grains include:

Bread Flour. All the bread baking going on in this country has impelled large flour companies like Pillsbury and Gold Medal to market their own high-gluten bread flour with 13–14 percent protein content. Very few recipes in this book call for its use. Please do not substitute it for all-purpose flour, even if you are tempted by the promise of its more expansive doughs, because it is much too powerful for traditional Italian breads.

Corn Flour. Corn first appeared in Europe when Christopher Columbus brought it back from America, but the first boatload didn't reach Italy until the eighteenth century. And then, against all evidence, it was called *grano turco* (Turkish grain), on the theory that such a strange import must come from an exotic eastern locale such as Turkey. Corn became the grain of the poor, for whom polenta to this day replaces bread in some areas, but it was used particularly widely in Lombardy, where it grows in profusion and is made into wheels of fairly dense, but delicious, corn bread. Corn flour is essentially a finely ground version of golden cornmeal, and it can be stone ground, so that it retains a bit of its grittiness, or water ground, for a silkier texture. Since it has no gluten, it must be combined with wheat flour, unless it is being used for an unleavened bread like *pan meino.*

Cornmeal. Cornmeal is used for baking and for dusting baking stones. When it is an ingredient in a bread or cake, I recommend using stone-ground golden cornmeal, which retains a bit of its traditional gritty texture. Do not buy the degerminated variety for baking, because you'll get a lot of starch without any food value. Be sure to store the stone-ground variety in the refrigerator, so that the oils in it don't go rancid.

For dusting a baking stone or sheet, degerminated cornmeal is just fine. It costs less, can be stored at room temperature in a cupboard, and all the starch dries out the bottom of the dough and keeps it from sticking.

Durum Flour. Durum flour is a creamy, silky fine golden flour milled from durum wheat, which is different from the hard wheats that are used for almost all bread making. It grows in very cold climes, such as Montana and Manitoba, as well as the great Tavoliere plain in Puglia, on the heel of the boot in southern Italy. Durum flour is the hardest kind of wheat. It is very high in gluten and, contrary to general opinion, makes wonderful bread, either alone or in combination with all-purpose flour.

Graham Flour. Graham flour is actually whole-wheat flour from which the bran and wheat germ were extracted, finely powdered, and then reincorporated. It is named for Sylvester Graham, a militant nineteenth-century reformer from Boston who crusaded against the lack of nutritional value in white flour and was such an ardent advocate of the entire wheat grain that his name has become synonymous, in some parts of Italy at least, with whole wheat. You wouldn't expect to find such a flour in Italy, but it has become rather stylish recently and it makes a wonderfully rich, nutty-tasting bread that has a decidedly lighter and flakier texture than whole wheat.

Oat Flour. Oats are the grains richest in proteins and minerals, but since they have minimal gluten, they must be combined with wheat flour to make a risen bread. Oat flour is used to add flavor and fat to bread dough as well as helping it to last longer, since it prevents fats from becoming rancid. If you can't find oat flour, you can grind rolled oats to a fine powder in your blender or food mill.

Pastry Flour. Pastry flour is made from soft wheat that produces a flour lower in gluten than all-purpose flour. It is perfect for baking pastries, tarts, and cakes. Although figures vary from brand to brand, pastry flour tends to have 8 or 9 percent protein, or gluten, content while cake flour has 7 percent. If you are unable to find pastry flour, you can approximate it by mixing 60 percent cake flour with 40 percent unbleached all-purpose flour.

Rice Flour. Rice produces a fine silky flour that has less gluten but more starch than wheat flour. Regular rice flour is made only of the interior of the rice, while brown rice flour comes from the entire grain, including the bran and the germ, and it lends its nutty rich taste and smooth, if somewhat dense, texture to multi-grain breads. These are having a small boom in some parts of Italy, where a strong interest in health and nutrition has become a real concern. *Cinque* and *sette cereali* breads (five and seven grain) are where these special grains are most in evidence.

Rye Flour. The truest indigenous rye tradition in Italy comes from Lombardy's far northern valley of the Valtellina, which is wedged tightly up against the beginning of the Alps, and from Alagna Valsesia at the foot of Monte Rosa on the Swiss border. The rye is dark and the flour contains the bran of the grain. Rye breads were common in Italy in the Middle Ages and today are found extensively in the Trentino and Alto Adige, which were part of the South Tirol until the end of World War I, so that they essentially represent an Austrian tradition. A little grappa is still added to the rye bread of

Venice in memory of days when slices of rye were flavored with aquavit. Rye has a low percentage of gluten, so it is combined with wheat in various proportions to help it rise effectively. Always make a rye starter to give a boost to the fermentation process and to add a lovely sour taste. Rye makes a dough sticky, so it is usually easier to handle if you use a dough scraper as an extension of your hand in the kneading process. When kneading dark rye in a mixer, keep it on low speed so that the delicate gluten strands don't break.

Semolina. Coarse, grainy cream-colored particles of semolina, milled from the hearts of durum wheat berries, are perfect for dusting your baking stone or sheet. The starch will keep your bread dough from sticking. Don't, however, substitute semolina granules for semolina flour; they simply won't make bread.

Semolina Flour. Semolina flour is made from the amber-colored granular grain that comes from grinding the heart of the durum wheat berry. If you read most imported pasta packages, you'll notice that they list *semolino di grano duro* as the major ingredient; this hard, high-gluten wheat flour is the basis of the best industrially made pastas, as it cooks firmly and absorbs less water than softer flour products.

In Italy, semolina is ground especially for bread making, but here it is hard to find and never quite as silky as its Italian counterpart. If you can find the fine-grind semolina, wonderful; otherwise, you'll have to grind the slightly gritty semolina with some unbleached white flour in your blender. Or you can use pale golden durum flour, which comes closest to the Italian equivalent.

Yeast
Lievito

Yeast is considered the soul of the bread, the source of its life and its character. A bread made without it ends up as flat as the *piadina* of Emilia, a thin disk that looks very much like a Mexican tortilla. Virtually every bread in this book is made with an infusion of yeast.

Yeast is a living product suspended in a dormant state until it is reactivated by being completely dissolved in water. Although Italian bakers chunk half-kilo bars of fresh compressed yeast into their doughs, we Americans can use much smaller cubes of creamy fresh yeast, which come foil wrapped in two sizes—the smaller weighing about ½ ounce (18 grams) and the larger 2 ounces (70 grams)—or active dry yeast, fawn-colored granules packed in small (7 gram) sealed envelopes. Since fresh yeast is perishable and keeps only about a week under refrigeration, I find that I use active dry yeast almost exclusively. It is much easier to store and can be kept at cool room temperature; it stays fresh in the refrigerator for as long as three years. It's important to know that active dry yeast is about twice as potent in relation to its weight as the fresh, so that an envelope of the former is the equivalent of a small cube of the latter. If you are going to buy individual packets, I would recommend El Molino, Fleischmann's, or Red Star. The new high-speed yeasts work in a miraculously short time, but speed is achieved at the noticeable expense of flavor. Better yet, if you do much baking, I strongly recommend buying yeast in bulk. Not only does it come without preservatives, but the money you save is absolutely astonishing: a pound bought in bulk for $1.20 can cost $14.00 in individual packets.

Now that yeast is successfully standardized, I never proof it to verify its freshness. I have baked hundreds and hundreds of loaves of bread for this book and never had the yeast fail me. But if you are uncertain, simply dissolve the yeast in warm water along with a pinch of sugar and wait about ten minutes to see that it foams.

Starters. Before yeast was manufactured industrially, bakers' choices of leavening were rather limited. Many used a piece of dough left over from the previous day to ferment a new dough. Numbers of the best bakers do essentially the same thing today, using *biga* (page 100), a simple saltless mixture of flour, water, and a minute amount of commercial yeast left to ferment at cool room temperature for five to sixteen hours. It is essentially the same as a fermented day-old chunk of saltless Tuscan bread dough, left to triple and bubble with vigorous activity (don't worry if it then collapses) before it is added to the ingredients of the new dough, which is then left to rise again before it is shaped. In some of the recipes that follow, yeast is mixed with water and a small amount of flour and allowed to stand for an hour or two to form an unfermented sponge (so called because of the spongy texture of the resulting dough). The remaining flour and all of the flavorings are then kneaded in. Yeast breads made by the sponge method or with the added tang of the fermented *biga* have a special dimension of texture and flavor. These forms of leavening that create new life are known as *la madre*, the mother, in northern Italy and as *il babbo*, the father, in Tuscany and farther south.

Natural Yeasts. Relatively few bakers still go to the trouble of making yeast from natural fermentation, as the process is as complicated as it is splendid. It begins with a batter of flour and water left to sour at room temperature by collecting the wild yeasts of the air, or by feeding on natural yeasts such as those that cling to the skins of the grape. That's only the beginning: the original mixture has to be refreshed with several additions of flour and water. It is a time-consuming and difficult art that is referred to as a "wild horse," since there's no knowing when it will act up on its own and do whatever it pleases.

I have made so much bread in my kitchen for so long that all I have to do is mix up some flour and water and leave the uncovered bowl out at room temperature, and within forty-eight hours all sorts of magical bubbling begins. Imagine what a feast of wild yeast spores are dancing in the air, like submicroscopic motes, waiting for the chance to fertilize two of the simplest elements on earth and start the whole life process again. And it does happen, time and time again. The Romans used must from the skins of grapes as a natural source of wild yeast, but if you want to try your hand, you can just take 1½ cups of flour and 1 cup of warm water and a small portion of mashed overripe banana, and mix well. Leave the mixture out to collect the yeasts of the air for a day or two, stir in 2 cups each of flour and water, and after three similar infusions—after seven days even bakers can rest—you'll have a natural yeast. If you're lucky. Natural yeasts are very tricky. Then use it instead of commercial active dry or fresh cake yeast called for in any recipe, substituting in the amount of 20–35 percent of the weight of the flour; for instance, a recipe of 3¾ to 4 cups of flour (500 grams) would use 100 to 175 grams of the starter, ¾ cup or a bit more. Add it last, just before finishing the mixing of the dough, and you'll be amazed at what flavorful and aromatic breads you can make. They'll last longer and stay tastier than breads made with a single addition of yeast. The quantity you use is something you'll have to experiment with, although you can be sure you will need more for a fruit-filled panettone than for a rustic regional bread. You can also make a starter that is close to a natural yeast by combining a cup of *biga* with 2 cups of flour and 2 cups of water. Proceed as above.

Bakers, who have noses like doctors or pharmacists, insist you can cut into the yeast and smell if it's right. The really expert say that if you set your ear right next to it, you can hear the little "tic-tac" of its growing.

Water
Acqua

Water is the one ingredient in bread baking that we tend to take for granted, since we can simply turn the tap and draw out what we want. Or so I thought until several Italian bakers looked somewhat dubious when I talked about making their breads in America. It wasn't the flour they were concerned about but the water. "Too many chemicals," said one. "Too much chlorine," said another. "The water's too hard," volunteered a third. Hard water can be a real problem, even in Italy, where bakers sometimes use a filter, and you can do the same if you get really involved in making these breads. Some breads are said to owe their ineffable taste to the water of their towns, and obviously we can hardly hope to duplicate the flavor of water fresh from cool mountain springs, although I admit that I have made some of these regional breads with the bottled waters of their areas. True, it's an expensive way to search out the authentic taste of one of the most basic foods in the world. Still, would I recommend it? If your water is heavily chlorinated or full of chemicals, I'd certainly tell you to give it a try. Or at the least to boil and cool your water before baking with it.

Salt
Sale

Salt in Italy comes in two forms, the coarser sea salt that is used in the kitchen and the fine grains that appear only at table. The fatter grains, which still taste a bit of the sea, are considerably cheaper there and are what Italian bakers always use in their breads.

The best sea salt comes from Europe, and still has all its natural nutrients. In America, the FDA requires that all the magnesium and trace minerals be washed off table salt; many companies go further and use an additive that allows it to pour freely, for salt is naturally moist and tends to clump. Still, I hesitate slightly to tell you to use imported finely ground sea salt, because it is so expensive. After all, this is bread, which has nourished the poor for centuries; it is as basic a food as exists, and is made of the most earthy ingredients. But let's face it: the salt of Italy is pulled right from the sea and hasn't been washed free of its nutrients, so it's a question of how much you value the natural qualities and taste of real sea salt. Please understand that I am talking about fine sea salt crystals, not the coarse fat ones that I use to sprinkle the top of *panmarino* bread, or big crystals of kosher salt. I personally use fine sea salt from the Mediterranean, which can be bought at health-food and gourmet stores; it tastes saltier than any other salt, while kosher salt tastes the mildest. Two teaspoons of kosher salt are equal in weight and taste to 1 teaspoon of fine sea salt.

Salt is a state monopoly in Italy, a national product of such importance that in the old days you could tell whether a region was doing well simply by the price of its salt, rather as we can judge countries today on the price of their oil. Salt has only recently appeared on supermarket and grocery shelves in Italy, after centuries of being available solely at the *tabacchi* where other state-regulated items, such as stamps and tobacco, are sold.

Salt not only gives flavor to bread and adds to the elasticity of the gluten, but it retards the action of the yeast, so that many bakers add it to the dough only at the very end of the mixing process. If, for some reason, you forget to add the salt, don't worry; you can dissolve it in a little water and mix it in slowly even after the dough has come together. If the amount of salt seems somewhat high, remember that Italians never put butter on their bread and Americans, who almost always do, predominantly use salted butter.

ADDITIONAL INGREDIENTS, ESSENTIALLY FOR BREAD

Luigi Barzini was once asked to contribute an introduction to an Italian cookbook. In it he wrote that "every recipe should begin by advising readers to buy a small estate in Tuscany so they can produce their own cheese, olives and oil, and raise their own chickens for eggs." The editors ended up deleting the section, "because," they said, "it was not practical and readers would be discouraged."

Barzini was perhaps a bit extreme in his approach, although it is hard to disagree with his sentiments, given the Italian reverence for food. It is a rare conversation that doesn't sooner or later turn to the subject of eating, so maybe it is not an exaggeration to conclude that the DNA of Italians must include a special gene predisposing them to care passionately about the quality of their food. Italians won't tolerate indifferent ingredients or dishes. They continue to rely on natural products, and enough people live on the land or maintain a closeness to nature for many products even now to live up to the high expectations created by centuries of good taste. Colors and flavors are clear and clean: bright green basil, darker glossy rosemary, fat red tomatoes, golden and scarlet peppers, rich green olive oil that comes from the first pressing of the fruit. The yolks of Italian eggs are almost orange-gold because the chickens are fed daily rations of corn. The tastes are as clear and clean as the colors, and they embody an attitude about life that is as Italian as Fra Angelico frescoes and the Renaissance palazzi that we identify as the cultural patrimony of the country.

Anchovies
Acciughe

Anchovies are tasty tiny fish that are a wonderful source of flavor. They are preserved in olive oil—filleted and in small convenient tins or jars—or in salt. The anchovies packed in salt come in large one- or two-pound tins and have more taste, but since they are not filleted, you should clean them under running water and slip out their central backbone, a simple procedure. *Anchovy paste* comes in a tube, and while a fresh paste tastes better, there is a lot to be said for the convenience of having mashed anchovies on hand.

Capers
Capperi

Capers are the small unripe buds of a plant that grows wild, anchoring itself in the fissures and cracks of stone walls and cliffs around the entire Mediterranean. I have seen them climbing ruins in Sicily and on walls of ancient buildings in small Italian towns. Capers come in two sizes: plump and fat, and the smaller variety, called nonpareils, which are considered finer. Both sizes are sold in vinegar brines and may need to be rinsed before they are used; if you manage to find capers preserved in salt in an Italian market, be sure to rinse them before proceeding.

I drain capers by putting them in a strainer over a bowl. I save the liquid and return it to the caper jar; after I've measured out the capers that I need, I put the unused ones back in the jar along with the reserved brine.

Cheeses
Formaggi

Caciocavallo. This hard cooked cheese from southern Italy and Sicily has a smooth and firm pale-yellow interior. It is made by warming the curd so that it can be stretched and kneaded into its idiosyncratic shape resembling an elongated flask with a small knob on top. The knob has a purpose: it allows the cheese to be tied in pairs, as if to be slung over the back of a horse (*caciocavallo* means "cheese on horseback"). The more mature caciocavallo, aged for six months to a year, is meant for grating. It is piquant and tangy and adds pungency to the southern pizzas and calzones. If you can't find fresh caciocavallo, mild provolone is an excellent substitute.

Crescenza. A fresh, semi-soft, medium-fat rindless cheese that comes from the countryside around Milan, crescenza is made with fresh cow's milk. White or very pale golden cream in color, it is especially gentle and delicate. *Crescenza* means "growth," and the cheese is so named because when left in a warm place, it begins to expand, as if it were dough rising.

Fontina. One of the most distinctive cheeses of Italy. Named for Mont Fontin near Aosta, it is an Alpine cheese synonymous with the Val d'Aosta of Piedmont. It should only be made of milk from that region, which produces a rich, aged, firm cheese that is golden in color and very lightly dotted with holes inside, rather like a Gruyère. Its slightly nutty, buttery taste is so delicious that fontina is considered at least as much a table as a cooking cheese. There are a variety of Italian fontinas, but the finest has on its brown-gold rind the purple-ink trademark of the producing Fontina corporation.

Gorgonzola. A rich semi-soft blue cheese made from the milk of the cows of Lombardy, gorgonzola was once aged in caves that were home to the mold that invaded its creamy interior and gave it its distinctive blue veins and wonderful taste and smell. Today, quantities of gorgonzola are made in factories by injecting the cheese with bacteria to encourage the growth of its blue veins; the aging process is speeded up but the taste is still glorious. You can choose from two kinds of gorgonzola: *gorgonzola dolce,* as sweet and buttery as a blue cheese can be, or *gorgonzola piccante,* which has a more pungent flavor and aroma. Be sure the cheese you buy is fresh and moist. If you can't find an Italian gorgonzola, you may substitute a mild Oregon blue cheese, as long as it is still creamy and fresh.

Grana. Grana is a grating cheese made in a number of northern Italian locations. The cow's milk differs from place to place and the aging fluctuates between one and two years.

Groviera. This cheese is similar in all ways to French Gruyère except that it began life in Italy and has an Italian name. Gruyère is a perfect alternative.

Mascarpone. This is a fresh thick cheese made from sweet cream, although it sometimes tastes as if it were whipped cream made of fine cheese. What we get in America has been pasteurized so that it isn't as fluffy or delicate as the fresh Italian product, but it is still a lovely dessert cheese that can be flavored and tucked between layers of cake for *tiramisù*. In its place you can use the freshest possible cream cheese made without stabilizers or preservatives, or you could beat a half-pound of ricotta with a cup of whipping cream until the mixture is very, very smooth. Both would be more than adequate replacements for the highly perishable snowy-white cheese. Depending on whose story you believe, mascarpone may be named for the Lombard dialect word for ricotta, *marcherpe*, or for the response of a high Spanish official in the seventeenth century who tasted the cheese and exclaimed, "*¡Más que bueno!*"—"Delicious!"

Mozzarella. The classic pizza cheese because it melts to such a lovely creamy consistency, Italian mozzarella is ideally made from the milk of the buffalo that still roam the marshy plain of Campania outside Naples. More and more frequently, however, the familiar egg-shaped ovals or spheres are made with some, if not all, cow's milk. Both varieties are flown to America, so should you decide to buy them, be sure they are fresh, creamy, and still sitting in their own milky brine. The real product bears almost no relationship to the rubbery ball that Americans know as mozzarella, which is made of skim milk and must be grated to be used. If you are fortunate enough to live in a city where a cheesemaker produces whole-milk mozzarella, leap at the opportunity to use it. Otherwise, you may either make do with the American equivalent or use Bel Paese as a fine substitute.

Parmigiano-Reggiano. This is undoubtedly the most famous of all Italian cheeses. It belongs to a group of hard grating cheeses (*grana*) of which there are many produced in northern Italy. Like fine French *appellation controlée* wines and D.O.C. wines in Italy, Parmigiano-Reggiano is produced only in strictly controlled areas under very specific conditions. Production begins with the high-quality milk of summer on April 1 and ends on November 11 and can only take place in the provinces of Parma, Reggio Emilia, and Modena, in Mantua on the right bank of the Po and Bologna on the left bank of the river Reno. The cheese is made entirely by hand in a centuries-old artisan tradition and is left to age for a minimum of two years. What is produced at the end of this long process is a straw-colored cheese with an extremely attractive flavor that is clean and somewhat salty. It is slightly crumbly in texture. You can know that you are buying the real thing if the rind is etched with the words Parmigiano-Reggiano around the entire circumference. Lesser Parmesans include *grana padana*, which simply means that the cheese comes from the plain of Lombardy. Domestic Parmesan is bland; Argentinian Parmesan has some bite to it. Both are infinitely preferable to pre-grated American Parmesan, which has no real taste at all. Buy a whole chunk of Parmesan and grate just before using it, so that the taste and perfume of the Parmesan truly become part of the bread or pizza you are making.

Parmesan knife

Pecorino. What Parmesan cheese is to the north, pecorino is to the south of Italy, where it has the most widespread popularity of all hard grating cheeses. Though there are a variety of pecorini, all are made of sheep's milk (*pecora* means sheep) and all are sharp-tasting medium-fat cheeses. They look similar to Parmesan with their compact gold-colored interiors. The difference comes on the tongue; pecorino is saltier, tangier, and sharper-tasting, clearly meant only for grating and not for eating at table. The best pecorino to use for these recipes is pecorino romano, the most widely imported of all pecorini, although you may try an aged pecorino sardo as well. Be sure they are still moist and crumbly enough to grate. Buy the cheese in a chunk and grate it only when you are ready to use it. You will notice that recipes sometimes call for a mixture of the piquant pecorino and the milder parmigiano, or for pecorino alone.

Provolone. Even people who know very little about Italian cheese seem to recognize the long bulbous provolone, which is divided into sections by the strings that hold it. It also comes in less picturesque shapes, and can be conical or round, in sizes ranging from as small as two pounds to gigantic. When well aged, it is always a hard cow's-milk cheese with a smooth golden-yellow rind. Both the sweet, mild provolone dolce and the more mature piquant variety are specialties of the south of Italy and can be used interchangeably with caciocavallo.

Stracchino. A rindless fresh cheese produced in the plain of Lombardy, stracchino is made from two milkings: the fresh milk of the morning is mixed with that from the night before. It gets its name from the dialect word for "tired," because the best cheese is said to have come from the evening milking, after the cows have grazed all day in good alpine pastures and have returned home exhausted. Stracchino is creamy in both color and texture and has a slight tang when it is fully mature.

Tallegio. This is another pale golden whole-cow's-milk cheese from Lombardy, rich and semi-soft. It is compact, smooth, and buttery, although it gets a delicate aromatic flavor as the cheese ages and grows stronger. Tallegio, stracchino, and crescenza may be used interchangeably. If your taste buds remember them from Italy, where they are farmhouse cheeses of wonderful smooth and creamy texture, you may detect a bit of difference when you sample them in America, because the government requires that all cheeses under sixty days old must be pasteurized to be imported into this country.

Herbs
Erbe

Basil

Buy a window box or planter to grow your own or convince your local market to carry fresh herbs. I don't mind sounding like a fanatic: The taste that fresh herbs give to doughs and pizzas is so fragrant and lovely that it's a shame to miss their aromatic seasoning. Dried rosemary and oregano are fine in any of these recipes, but dried basil isn't even a distant relation of its fresh self and there's no hope of making pesto with it.

Basil/Basilico. The aroma of fresh basil is so enticing that I think it must imprint itself on our sense memories forever. It is what makes pesto so fragrant, what gives the wonderful taste of summer to tomatoes and mozzarella, to zucchini and other vegetables. The green leafy herb doesn't grow all year long, but it can be preserved in any of three ways. Pick the leaves and pat them clean with a damp paper towel; you can then pack them in plastic bags for the freezer, layer them in coarse salt in Mason jars, or cover them with olive oil. The olive oil method is particularly successful in retaining the bright green color of the leaves.

There are a number of prepared pestos on the market, and if you choose to buy one, be sure it is still green from fresh basil and is made with authentic Italian cheese, fine olive oil, and pine nuts.

Oregano/Origano. This good, hardy herb grows wild in Italy and is a sturdy perennial that grows in America without demanding anything other than a bit of land, sun, and water. It is characteristic of southern Italian cooking and appears frequently dusting the tops of pizzas. It is considerably milder in its fresh state, so you should use it accordingly.

Parsley/Prezzemolo. Italian parsley is dark green and flat-leaved and has a much more tantalizing flavor than the curly-leaved variety Americans know. If you look in Italian markets or specialty shops, you'll see that it is appearing more frequently among the herbs. In its absence, substitute regular parsley.

Italian parsley

Rosemary

Rosemary/Rosmarino. Rosemary grows wild in many parts of Italy, in thickets and hedges and dense low ground cover. The glossy dark leaves look rather like pine needles and have a strong taste. They will take root easily in most gardens and pots. Rosemary is so often used with roasts and chickens in Italy that the butcher frequently includes free branches with your order, since it is taken for granted that the herb belongs in your roasting pan. Fresh rosemary is preferable to dried, but should you use the dried, be sure to use smaller quantities, since the taste is concentrated. When adding fresh rosemary to bread, cut the leaves with a sharp knife to release the fragrance and strong flavor.

Lard
Strutto

Italy is a country full of pigs—hence all the salamis, sausages, prosciutto, and *pancetta*. Good pork lard, cheap and plentiful, gives a smooth, moist, creamy texture to doughs and is commonly used in any number of breads, pizzas, *focacce,* and *grissini.* In diet-conscious America, where high-cholesterol animal fat is frowned upon, good lard is difficult to find. There is inexpensive lard on some grocery shelves, but I strongly urge you to buy the best pork fat you can and render it at home. Try to get leaf lard, the creamy fat around pork kidneys, or use pork back fat, which can be found in cities with Chinese markets. My butcher, who is usually extremely accommodating, has to sell me leaf lard in ten-pound lots, so I have one busy afternoon rendering it and then can keep it refrigerated in small lots for months. To render it, just cut the pork fat into smallish pieces, put them in a large heavy-bottomed saucepan, and set it over a very low flame. Let it cook until it has become a transparent liquid. Skim off the little pork cracklings—they taste delicious added to bread— pour the lard into an earthenware container, and leave at room temperature until it cools completely and hardens to a creamy white substance. Keep it in the refrigerator or freezer. If you have to substitute for lard, olive oil makes an acceptable alternative in non-sweet bread doughs. I think Crisco leaves a cottony taste and coating on the tongue, so I would never use it.

Liqueurs and Wines
Liquori e vini

Grappa. An aquavit, the distillation of the residue of pressed grapes, grappa can have a strong, fiery bite and be a little rough around the edges unless it has been adequately aged. Grappas are not easily found in this country, although wineshops with a strong Italian stock and some big liquor stores do carry them. You can certainly use slivovitz or marc as a substitute.

Maraschino. This is a favorite of Italian bakers, who use it in remarkable quantities. It is distilled from marasca cherries, but is neither sweet nor viscous.

Marsala. A fortified Sicilian wine that is essentially the Italian equivalent of Madeira in French cooking, Marsala was originated in 1773 by an Englishman who wanted to improve the staying power of good Sicilian wine. Use Marsala Superiore or Fine, not the egg (al'Uovo) or cream variety.

Sambuca. The liqueur of Civitavecchia, the port of the city of Rome, sambuca is made from aniseed and sugar and has a distinct licorice flavor.

Malt Extract
Malto

Italian bakers use malt as a yeast food to improve the dough in a variety of ways: It encourages the growth of a loaf, retains moisture in the dough, and is definitely responsible for a lovely golden crust. Malt extract is a grain product in syrup form, made usually of barley, or of barley and corn mashed and malted, and it should be used in such tiny amounts that its taste is almost entirely hidden. Lately it has been getting harder and harder to find a good source of malted grain extract, but Premier Malt Company of Milwaukee makes malt extract that can be found in supermarkets and health food stores. Be sure to get the type that is *not* flavored with hops. If you can't find malt extract, you can omit it without changing the results drastically.

Dried Wild Mushrooms
Funghi Secchi

Porcini Mushrooms. These wild mushrooms, which are the same as French cèpes, are the most highly prized mushrooms in Italy, where they still grow in abundance. During the season, markets are full of the huge-capped fresh mushrooms, but they can be found all year long in a dried version. Their rich earthy taste flavors dishes with a pungent fragrance of the woods. They are traditionally added to numerous risottos, pastas, and main dishes, but I think that adding them to bread is an imaginative new use of one of Italy's most fragrant ingredients. Dried porcini mushrooms are expensive, although a little goes a long way. They are always soaked in warm water for at least half an hour, and the soaking liquid should be strained and saved, since it is so flavorful. Be sure to ask for *Italian* porcini mushrooms. I once had the unfortunate experience of being sold an Argentinian variety that looked and smelled the same but had a taste so pallid as to be imperceptible.

Nuts
Noci

Almonds, Walnuts, and Hazelnuts. Mandorle, noci, and *nocciole* constitute the great triumvirate of nuts frequently used in sweet breads and desserts. They all arrive toasted at Italian bakeries, but you will have to toast your own by spreading them on a baking sheet and setting them in a 350° F oven for about ten minutes.

Almonds may be purchased whole or slivered, with skins or blanched. If you need to blanch your own almonds, drop them into boiling water and after about two minutes remove them with a slotted spoon or skimmer. Lay them on a tea towel and let them cool briefly. Then just squeeze each one between your fingers and let it pop out of its skin.

Hazelnuts have much tighter skins than almonds and it takes a bit more work to remove them. Lay the hazelnuts in a single layer on a baking sheet and bake them at 350° F for about ten minutes, until the skins crack, shrivel, and flake. Remove from the oven, wrap in a tea towel, and let them steam and cool off for about five minutes. While they are still in the towel, rub them vigorously en masse in your fingers; while this won't get all the nuts to shed their skins, it will make a good start. Then you'll need to take the nuts individually and rub them between your fingers to encourage them to shed the rest of the still clinging skin. Unless the nuts are being used for decorative purposes and must look perfect, feel free to use nuts with some skin still apparent.

The lazy way to remove hazelnut skins is to put the toasted nuts into a food processor with the plastic blade in place and pulse. This ingenious solution does work, but the drawback is that you lose a third of the nuts this way.

Pine Nuts. Tiny *pignoli* come from the seeds of pine cones and must be individually shelled and extracted, which explains their great cost. Their rich, creamy flavor is unique and they are folded into any number of sweet breads and fillings as well as desserts. They are as well the traditional nut in pesto, although walnuts may be substituted there. Pine nuts used to be served regularly in Liguria during Lent, when clever people skirted the prohibitions of ecclesiastical authorities by adding them to give taste and substance to otherwise rather thin dishes. Italian bakeries have their pine nuts already toasted; you will need to toast your own, where noted, in a 350° F oven for ten minutes. They are expensive, no matter how you buy them, although little cellophane bags holding fractions of an ounce of this precious cargo are even more so. There really isn't a good substitute for the unique taste of pine nuts.

Olives
Olive

Were there but world enough and time, we could talk of olives almost indefinitely. Olives in Italy are a world unto themselves, for 95 percent of the world's olives are cultivated on Mediterranean shores and many of the most prized come from central Italy. Olives for eating and cooking are either picked green or are tree ripened until they are mahogany or purple-black in color. They may be cured in salt, oil, or brine. Those most commonly used in these recipes are:

Gaeta Olives. Grown in the Campania region around Naples, these are succulent reddish-purple olives with a wonderfully salty, mildly bitter flavor, somewhat like Kalamata olives from Greece.

Ligurian Olives. These come from the Italian Riviera, the region that wraps around Genoa like a boomerang and extends from the border of southern France to the northernmost edge of Tuscany. Benedictine monks first introduced olives to the area, but now many hillsides are silvery gray with olive trees that are nourished by fertile earth, warm sun, and salt water from the Mediterranean, whose moisture is drawn in by the roots of the trees. Black *ponentine* olives are tiny and mild, while fat, flavorful *Ardoino* are saltier and more pungent; both are purplish black and are perfect for using in pizza or bread. Pitting them takes a bit of time. Tiny black Niçoise olives from Provence are an excellent substitute, since they are the same type of olive, cured slightly differently.

Sicilian-Style Olives. Crisp, big, fleshy green olives that are cured in brine, these are somewhat salty tasting. The easiest variety to find come from California and are cured in the Sicilian style. They are perfect for use in green olive bread, although I have also used cracked green Greek olives with splendid results. Please don't use canned California green or black ripe olives; they simply haven't enough taste. They are so mild, I would say, as to lack all flavor when baked into a bread. What makes the Sicilian-style olive different is that it ferments in a salt brine cure for up to six months. Its pungent, salty taste and crisp texture give the bread the strong personality of a full-flavored, well-aged olive.

Olive Oil
Olio d'oliva

Bread, *focacce*, and pizza doughs flavored with olive oil are richer and longer-lasting than regular rustic breads. Use a well-made cold-pressed olive oil, but that doesn't mean you need a fruity, expensive oil that you purchased at a double-digit figure. The flavor should be mild and delicate, not heavy. The oil gives lightness, springiness, and moisture to the dough and makes it supple and easy to work with. Since oil is a preservative, some of the focacce and breads made with it tend to last several days. Don't forget to brush pizzas hot out of the oven with a glaze of oil.

Olive Paste
Polpa d'oliva

Olive pastes, such as the wonderful Olivada San Remo imported from Liguria, are rich and strong salty mixtures made of pulverized olives that are preserved in extra virgin olive oil and flavored with herbs. They make wonderful *crostini*, especially on Tuscan bread, which is a perfect foil for the salty mixture. The *Chiavari* bread dough (page 140), which incorporates olive paste, can very simply be treated like *focaccia* dough by spreading it in a *focaccia* pan and baking it according to *focaccia* instructions. And Genoese *focaccia*, in a turnabout, can be topped with a liberal washing of the olive paste. Olive paste is known in Italy as *caviale nero*, black caviar.

Pancetta

Pancetta is unsmoked Italian bacon that has been preserved in salt, seasoned with pepper, and rolled up like a fat salami. Good *pancetta* is a nice balance of creamy fat and lean meat with a salty taste and a peppery crunch. It should be easy to find in Italian markets or delicatessens. If you can't find any, don't use smoked bacon; instead, substitute salt pork to which you have added some pepper.

Prosciutto

In Italy, *prosciutto* means simply ham. If you want cooked ham, ask for *prosciutto cotto*; to obtain raw, air-dried ham cured with salt and seasonings, specify *prosciutto crudo*. Since Italian prosciutto is only beginning to be imported into this country, you may need to find a high-quality American product, such as Citterio brand. Don't buy thinly sliced prosciutto in plastic packages if you have a chance to go to a delicatessen or specialty shop, where you'll simply get better value and better taste.

Raisins
Uva Passa

Raisins are concentrated grapes. The Romans were such connoisseurs that they made distinctions between grapes to be eaten at table, grapes to be made into wine, and grapes that would be dried for raisins, usually the biggest and sweetest white grapes. Several types of raisins are used in Italy, for which counterparts are readily available here.

Malaga. These raisins from Pantelleria, the island off Sicily, are a big seedless variety that tastes almost as rich as a fig. Muscats can be substituted.

Sultanina. These seedless blond raisins from Turkey and Sicily have a wonderful sugary taste. Substitute either a golden or dark seedless raisin.

Uvette. Very sweet tiny raisins, always used in plum cake, these are much like our currants.

Zibibbo. These big, fat raisins are both amber and chestnut colored, are sometimes as much as an inch long, and have just enough seeds inside to be slightly crunchy. The best American equivalent is a golden raisin.

Our golden seedless raisins have achieved their color by being bleached in sulfur dioxide; the trick is never to soak them in hot water, which will bring out the strongly sulfur flavor. Plump raisins in cool water or in something stronger, like rum or Marsala.

Sesame Seeds
Sesamo

These pale little seeds that give the slightest hint of a peanut taste are often used in Sicily. Buy them in bulk in ethnic markets or health-food stores and you will be staggered at how much money you save in contrast to what you spend buying them in little spice jars. Store them in the refrigerator in a tightly closed jar to keep their oils from becoming rancid. To bring out their nutty flavor, you can roast them in a dry iron skillet over medium heat for five minutes.

Spices
Spezie

Many of the imaginatively spiced breads you can now buy all over Italy sound like wonderful creations of an innovative new breed of baker, but the breads of the Roman Empire were flavored with just such unusual combinations. The bakers of ancient Rome made loaves with fennel seeds, anise, raisin juices, and poppy seeds, and even perfumed one variety with maidenhair. By the time of Augustus, when a real bread-baking industry was thriving, there were three hundred bakeries in Rome alone, white bread had taken on class distinction as a status symbol, and there existed a long and astonishing list of the variety of breads available. Breads had even taken on special functions: there was a bread for keeping a beautiful complexion, a bread for sailors to eat on the high seas, a bread meant to be eaten with oysters, and even a bread for dogs, made mostly of bran. Spices were familiar components in these years of the empire. Then in 410, Alaric, leader of the Visigoths, seized and plundered Rome. The darkness that fell in his wake shadowed all of Italian life in the early Middle Ages, and bread making lost its virtuosity.

Spices fell into disuse until the Venetians went to sea and brought back pepper, cinnamon, cloves, nutmeg, mace, and ginger from the exotic East. Some flavorings sat on the tables of the poor to pep up monotonous dishes, and by the twelfth century spices gave strength and taste to a whole range of foods, including the still popular *panforte*, a fruitcake-like confection bursting with dried fruits and nuts and flavored with coriander, cloves, cinnamon, ginger, mace, and even white pepper. Spices were much in demand as symbols of conspicuous consumption because they were so expensive and hard to get ("as dear as pepper" was a common saying); some of them were considered aphrodisiacs; and of course, they also served to preserve fish and meat and masked the smells of rotting food. The

Ligurians' preference to this day for fresh greens and herbs can be traced to the reaction of Genoese sailors subjected to the powerful odors of spices collected in ships' holds. But the spice merchants profited mightily: Spices were so important to Venice that an entire stock market based on their value was set up on the Rialto. Speculation gave pepper and cinnamon a value way beyond what they were worth, and all kinds of secret deals based on fluctuating prices were made until the bubble of this craze for kitchen spices inevitably burst, or at least leaked and then declined dramatically once Vasco da Gama broke the Venetian monopoly. Cinnamon and ginger ceased to be such great rarities. All the historic spices continued to be used in Italian baking. Nowadays they aren't tossed into the doughs and mixtures with quite so free a hand, but they do lend their flavors to any number of breads and desserts.

Anise Seeds/Semi di Anice. Anise seeds, according to mythology, have a magical effect on the digestive system, which probably explains why they turn up at the end of the meal in so many desserts. They taste of licorice and are part of an entire tradition of spicing that ranges from the Udine far in the north to Sardinia, Sicily, and Calabria in the south. They are what gives a special flavor to the *brigidini* of Tuscany and the *biscotti anici* of Sicily and Sardinia.

Cinnamon/Cannella. Cinnamon, in stick form and powder, is utilized in a number of Italian sweets and breads, but it has nothing like the popularity it enjoys in American baking. It is, in fact, usually one of several spices blended together.

Clove/Chiodi di Garofano. Part of the arsenal of spices from medieval and Renaissance spicing that remains today, cloves are used frequently in desserts.

Mace/Macis. The filament covering the nutmeg is ground and used in only a few Italian desserts.

Nutmeg/Noce Moscata. Ever since the Venetians brought spices back from the East, nutmeg has had a prominent place in the cooking of Italy. It is used in both sweet and savory dishes, often bringing out the flavors of spinach and cheeses. Better flavor is achieved by grating the whole nutmeg each time you use it. Ground nutmeg is hard to find in Italy because good cooks know that most of the flavor and aroma is lost as it sits in the tin or bottle.

Pepper/Pepe. Black peppercorns are called for in all these recipes. They should always be ground freshly at the time of cooking. The only exception is *panforte*, in which white pepper is traditional; you don't even know that it's there, but it wouldn't be *panforte* without it.

Tomatoes
Pomodori

Canned Tomatoes/Pomodori in scatola. Even Italians, who live in the land of the sun-ripened tomato, must use canned tomatoes for their sauces in the deep of winter. Like them, you should look for canned plum tomatoes from San Marzano. Failing this, canned tomatoes from America, although less ripe and less sweet, are a good second choice.

Sun-Dried Tomatoes/Pomodori secchi. These are tomatoes allowed to ripen on the vine, and then dried out of direct sunlight. You may find them covered with extra virgin olive oil and spiced with Ligurian herbs. A less expensive alternative is loose dried tomatoes, which you should steep in boiling water for a minute to soften, then either use straightaway or cover with oil. Jo Bettoja and Anna Maria Cornetto give a simple and direct recipe for drying your own in *Italian Cooking in the Grand Tradition.*

Tomato Paste/Concentrato di pomodoro. Tomato paste is a concentrate of tomatoes, and you don't need much to get the desired taste. Don't expect twice as much to give you twice as much taste of tomato; it will only tend to drown out other flavors. I am particularly fond of the clean, rich tomato flavor of Pagani Brothers brand, but no matter which you buy, I recommend the type that comes in a tube as toothpaste does, since it can be closed and easily stored in the refrigerator, and eliminates waste.

ADDITIONAL INGREDIENTS ESSENTIALLY FOR PASTRY AND COOKIES

These few extra ingredients, found mainly in pastries and cookies, are part of a long tradition of *dolci* in Italy.

Almonds
Mandorle

Almond Paste/Pasta di Mandorle. Without almond paste there would be no *amaretti, brutti ma buoni, torta deliziosa,* or any number of Italian desserts to requite the famous Italian sweet tooth. You may either make your own (see page 345), which will have lots of flavor but never be as smooth as the commercial product, or you can buy almond paste, a very fine, flavorful mixture of blanched almonds, sugar, and glucose to which almond extract may be added. Odense and Blue Star are good brands.

Bitter Almonds/Ermelline. Bitter almonds are used in the making of *amaretti* because they concentrate the powerful flavor of almonds. They grow freely in the Mediterranean basin, but since they are toxic in their natural state, they are outlawed in the United States. Substitute kernels from peach or apricot pits, but it is recommended that you blanch them and then toast them in a low 250° to 275° F oven for about ten minutes, until they are a pale golden color. I find them easily in Chinese markets as almond kernels, but they are also available in some Middle European specialty markets.

Marzipan/Pasta di Marzapane. This is essentially almond paste which has been rolled even finer and sweetened more. Its name is said to come from *marci panis,* Latin for St. Mark's bread, and that's what *marzapane* is actually called in Venice, the city of which St. Mark is patron saint. It is said to have been invented in the early fifteenth century during a grain shortage, when a clever baker made "flour" by grinding almonds to a powder, adding sugar, and kneading to make a kind of bread.

Wild Cherries
Amarena

These ripe wild cherries preserved in syrup (preferably) or brandy are moist and fleshy. The Fabbri brand is imported from Italy.

Ammonium Carbonate

A leavening agent like baking soda, known also as hartshorn, this makes very crisp cookies. Use only a little, since it has a pronounced ammonium smell, and be sure to crush the crystals well. It works best for thin cookies, helping a drop cookie spread smooth and fine on a cookie sheet. Some drugstores still carry it, but if you can't find it, it can be ordered from H. Roth or Maid of Scandinavia (see Appendix). Store in a cool, dark, dry place.

Butter
Burro

Italian butter is sweet, so that all the pastry recipes are written to unsalted butter. If you use butter with salt, be sure to cut down on the salt called for in the list of ingredients.

Candied Citron
Cedro Candito

Citron, a citrus fruit that grows in the Mediterranean, is as big as a quince and has a bumpy thick rind. It is often candied and used in sweet breads and desserts, and many specialty shops carry it.

Slicing candied citron

Candied Orange and Lemon Rind
Arancia Candita e Limone Candito

Among the revelations that come with eating in Italy is the chance to taste all kinds of candied fruits and the candied rinds of Sicilian oranges, lemons, and citrons that are used in numerous sweet breads and desserts. "They are like cinnamon in American baking," someone told me. "They are in everything." The rinds are fat and full of flavor, and the fruits have a concentrated sweetness and clean fresh taste that is irresistible. And the colors: the deep red-orange of Sicilian oranges is as seductive to the eye as it is to the tongue. Because I can't find any preparation close to them in America, I buy the best fruit I can and candy it myself. The next-best alternative is to search out fine candied fruit and rinds in specialty shops, where they are most likely to appear during the holidays. Sometimes cottage industries pop up, offering wonderful examples of the art. And sometimes you'll find them in health-food stores. Do try to stay away from the tubs of mixed candied fruit sold in supermarkets, which have lots of preservatives and very little taste.

Chocolate
Cioccolata

Chocolate doesn't appear as frequently in Italy as it does in other European countries, but that isn't to say that it isn't delicious when it does turn up. The secret is to use a good-quality chocolate, such as Perugina, Tobler, Lindt, or Callebaut. Most of the chocolate called for in this book is bittersweet and should have a rich, deep flavor and silky texture.

Cocoa
Cacao

Italian bakeries use cocoa fairly frequently to give the flavor of chocolate to cookies and pastries. Use Dutch-process cocoa, which is the pure unsweetened powder of cocoa beans that have been roasted, their oils extracted, and then ground very fine. The style is darker and mellower tasting than regular cocoas. If you want to add cocoa to a recipe to give it a chocolate taste, subtract 7 ounces (200 grams) of flour for every 3½ ounces (100 grams) of cocoa that you add.

Eggs
Uova

All the eggs used in these recipes are size large and they should be at room temperature when they are used. If you've forgotten to take them out of the refrigerator or decided to make a recipe at the last minute, soak the eggs in a bowl of warm water for about 10 minutes to warm them up.

Essences and Aromas
Essenze e Aromi

The Italians flavor all sorts of sweets and sweet breads with highly potent, concentrated essences. They include essence of panettone (just take the top off one of the bottles and you are transported directly into the center of the panettone) and aroma of *colomba*, special mixtures of the combinations of spices that give these sweet breads their taste signatures. There are also aromas of lemon, of sweet orange, orange flower, and bitter orange, as well as an essence of bitter almond, which is wonderfully bracing to smell. No one in Italy really expects to make panettoni or *colombe* at home, so their essences aren't easy to find, but all the others are widely available in several brands of small jars. The concentration of Italian essences and aromas is considerably stronger than equivalent American extracts, and these recipes have been adjusted with that in mind. The important thing with orange and lemon extracts is to look for "pure" liquid flavorings, since that indicates the contents are from a plant substance. Lemon and orange oils are extracted from the peels, and in the best ones the harsh volatile oils are removed to leave true fruit flavors. If you don't have an extract available, you can do what some of the best Italian bakers do: substitute grated lemon and/or orange rind. If you choose to use a lemon extract, be sure to use one like Dittman's or Cook's. Almond extract is made of oil of bitter almonds, alcohol, and water in varying proportions. A little goes a long way. (See also the remarks under Vanilla, opposite.)

Potato Starch
Fecola

A starch-like flour made from grinding potatoes, potato starch is extremely fine and makes a lovely silky *pasta frolla* for elegant tarts and tortes. Sometimes it can be found in supermarkets; otherwise, potato starch is often carried by health-food stores and ethnic markets.

Rice
Riso

More than fifty kinds of rice are produced in Italy, but only one is really important for pastries. *Originario*, the most common and least expensive type, is a round-grain rice that cooks in twelve to sixteen minutes and absorbs about three times its weight in liquid. Use it for *torte di riso*. If you don't have *originario*, use long-grain rice.

Turbinado Sugar
Zucchero

The Italians use baking sugar on top of any number of their sweet breads and cakes to give them a wonderful crunch and lightly sweetened taste. Alas, the ordinary sugars we buy at the supermarket melt under high temperatures, but turbinado sugar, the raw unrefined sugar crystals washed with steam, keeps its texture even when put in roaring-hot ovens. It is available at health-food and specialty stores and I notice it turning up more and more frequently at supermarkets. My other solution—much more expensive—has been to buy coarse-cut cubes of French sugar and flatten them with the side of a cleaver only enough to make them chunky granules.

Vanilla
Vaniglia

The strong sweet smell in Italian *pasticcerie* comes from vanilla sugar, which flavors cakes and cookies and has its own very special qualities. Italian housewives use little packets of vanilla sugar and bakers have a very very fine powder, like superfine granulated sugar made with vanilla flavor. There are now some fine crystallized vanilla sugars, very delicately flavored, available in America, but since we are so used to using vanilla extract, the trick is to find a really good one that gives the delicate lovely flavor of vanilla. I prefer Nielsen-Massey because it starts with the real pod and ends up with a pure essence suspended in an alcohol solution. You can, of course, make your own vanilla sugar by burying a vanilla bean in a canister of sugar, but these recipes have been written with vanilla extract in mind.

Equipment

On one of my stays in Italy, I was introduced to a wonderful peasant woman named Nella who dwelt in the tiny town of Cordigliano in the Umbrian countryside, just outside Todi. Nella lived in one of several houses clustered among olive and fruit trees, and every ten days she made an enormous batch of breads to feed her family, her close neighbors, and several families for whom she did housework. When I was invited to watch her make bread, in the same way that her mother and grandmother once had, I was immediately impressed that she had almost no equipment. She used a *madia,* a deep chest on legs with a sizable interior trough, made to hold crockery, but in which she kept a big mound of flour on one side and her natural yeast on the other. She used the trough to mix and knead the dough, which she then covered with a well-worn blanket to let it rise. When the time came to shape the dough, she placed it on a big board on her dining room table, cut it in twelve pieces, formed huge ovals, and set them on a long piece of well-floured canvas so the loaves wouldn't stick to the cloth or each other. The blanket went back over the top and the bread rose again until it was time to set the loaves in the wood-burning outdoor oven. The total of her equipment: a bucket to measure the water, the *madia* in which to mix and knead, the board on which to cut and shape, the cloth on which to set the loaves, and the dough scraper. Bread baking is one of the most basic and enduring activities in human history, and I do not want to suggest that readers rush out and stock up on unusual equipment for the process. You probably have in your kitchen almost all the basics that you need, and if you choose to make some of the regional specialties, you may need to buy (or borrow or invent) a few of the special traditional forms or molds.

THE BASIC THREE

If it were up to me, I would insist on only three things: a scale, a dough scraper, and a porous baking stone or quarry tiles.

Scale

I prefer a scale that is calibrated in both metric grams and American ounces and pounds, so that ingredients can be accurately weighed for measurement.

Dough Scraper

This is simply a rectangular piece of stainless steel with a rolled steel or wooden handle and a sharp edge. As far as I am concerned, it is one of the great inventions of modern life, since it can be used for everything from lifting and kneading the dough to cutting it and cleaning the surface on which you have been working.

Porous Baking Stone or Quarry Tiles

These effectively replicate the brick floor of a baker's oven. Made of natural clay stoneware fired at extremely high temperatures, they distribute high heat evenly and absorb the moisture of the dough, thereby producing heavier, crisper crusts. I prefer a single stone, for quarry tiles don't always fit together perfectly and tend to jiggle and bounce a bit when you're aiming a round of wet dough onto their surface. Baking stones come in rectangular and round shapes, for breads and pizzas, and I like to use the largest ones I can find so I can bake more than one loaf at a time.

Whether I am baking pizzas or cookies, pastries or bread, and whether or not the bread is in loaf pans or on baking sheets, I leave the stones in place to promote even distribution of heat, as in the professional baker's brick oven. Of course, you don't have to have baking stones when you are making cookies or many desserts. Puff pastry and croissants, for instance, are best baked without them. Be sure to preheat the stone or tiles for at least 30 minutes in a hot 400° or 425° F oven, and to sprinkle them with a dusting of cornmeal or semolina just before you slide the doughs on them.

Excellent sources of baking stones are listed in the Appendix.

OTHER ESSENTIALS

Bowls for Mixing

You will probably want several different sizes, ranging from a small one in which to dissolve the yeast to big-scaled wide-mouthed bowls that can be used for both mixing and kneading the doughs. They can be earthenware, stoneware, ceramic, glass, plastic, or stainless steel, and you can find them at humble hardware and restaurant supply stores as well as in fancier kitchenware emporia. It is a good idea to have a straight-sided container that allows the dough to rise easily. If it fits conveniently into the refrigerator, for slowing down the action of the yeast when necessary, so much the better.

Surface on Which to Knead

I love my butcher-block table, which is 24 × 30 inches, big enough to hold a scale and basic tools, but any wooden or Formica surface will do handsomely as long as it is at least 2 feet square and is high enough for you to work comfortably with your palms extended and your back straight. Stooping or stretching will make it hard to knead correctly and can give you a backache—hardly desirable, since one of the reasons for baking is pleasure in the process as well as in the wonderful loaves and tastes that ultimately appear. Be sure that your work surface is easy to scrape down and clean after each batch of dough.

Electric Mixer

I can't imagine life without my heavy-duty solid-state Kitchen Aid mixer. It can do everything a human baker could wish—stirring, mixing, kneading, whipping—and demands almost nothing in return except that it is sometimes necessary to stop the machine and scrape down doughs that tend to creep up the collar of the hook. I use the paddle to mix doughs and the dough hook to knead them and the whisk for making pastries and cakes and for beating egg whites (there is even a copper bowl for the task). It is a big, solid, old-fashioned maternal presence in my kitchen that I can always depend upon, although I invariably finish kneading by hand because I am convinced that the dough responds to the warmth of the human touch and comes to life beneath my palms and fingertips.

Electric mixer with dough hook, whisk, and paddle

Food Processor

So much has been written in praise of food processors that I scarcely need to add to the verbiage. Although it is rare to find such machines in Italian bakeries, there is no reason not to use them in American kitchens for mixing and kneading bread, pizza, and pastry doughs in a fraction of the time it takes to perform the same processes by hand. The larger-capacity machines are more useful than the smaller, but you should be aware that many inexpensive food processors are not strong enough to process yeast doughs. Be certain to check whether yours is up to the task before you start work on a recipe. The processor is useful for any number of other operations as well: for making pesto, grating cheeses, grinding soaked whole-wheat grains, and turning nuts into pastes. Because the motor is so powerful and heats up the contents as it whirs at almost supersonic speeds, you must be careful to use *cold* water for almost all the liquid called for in bread and pizza recipes.

Instant-Reading Thermometer

Lots of cookbooks tell you to dissolve yeast at specified temperatures—active dry at 105° to 115° F, fresh cake yeast at 90° to 95° F—and suggest that you will know lukewarm from hot just by touch, rather as mothers do baby formulas. When I started baking, I never guessed right and spent untold nervous minutes waiting for thermometers to steer me where I belonged. Now no one need worry: instant-reading thermometers like Bio-Therm and Cuisinart can be put into water or the dough itself and they register the internal temperature immediately. It is important not to get a liquid too hot—the yeast is killed above 140° F—or too cool, since that will retard its development, but dormant yeasts are reactivated in a wider range of temperatures than the instructions on their little packets would have you believe. Lower temperatures may take a bit longer, but any number of Italian bakers regularly dissolve yeast at room temperature, especially in the heat of summer.

Baking Sheets

If you're not baking on stones, you'll need baking sheets, and the heavier the better, especially since these breads bake at such high temperatures that flimsy or tin ones will warp. If you don't have a baking stone, preheat a heavy baking sheet and use it like a stone. Dark carbon steel absorbs and retains heat and produces crisp crusts; heavy aluminum sheets retain heat as well. The traditional half-sheet pan, about 11½ × 17½ inches, is a very useful size, but use anything as long as it leaves an inch of clearance on all sides so that hot air can circulate freely around it in your oven. When setting shaped breads to rise before they are baked, use either rimless baking sheets or the backs of baking sheets with raised edges and you'll find it easier to get them on and off.

Bread Molds

Most of the breads in this book are free-form hearth loaves shaped by your hands and baked directly on a stone or baking sheet, but a few need loaf pans or pie tins or traditional molds such as:

Covered Pullman Loaf Pan. There is no way to make the Italian equivalent of sandwich bread without this long, narrow closed rectangular mold with its sliding top. It is designed to produce close-textured almost crustless bread used for such dishes as *mozzarella in carrozza* as well as for the *tramezzini* that fill the glass cases of Italian caffè bars. Do not forget to butter the underside of the lid before letting the bread have its final rise inside; otherwise you'll have a devilish time getting the loaf out in one piece.

Pandoro Mold. To make the authentic sweet Christmas bread of Verona, you must have the tinned-steel five-sided star mold that gives it its traditional shape. Otherwise, you may substitute any high-sided tall mold with an eight-cup capacity.

A pandoro mold and round and oval bannetons

Panettone Mold. A tall, thin cylindrical mold allows the panettone to expand and grow into the lightly porous sweet bread that comes from Milan at Christmastime. You can substitute a two- or three-pound coffee can or a charlotte mold with its sides built up with aluminum foil, and I have even seen a panettone mold with a central shaft, rather like a narrow angel food cake pan, which may not be traditional but certainly bakes a good panettone.

Banneton. This coiled reed basket is made in a round or oval shape which turns out a rustic-looking loaf with a beehive pattern of flour etched on the surface of the bread. Flour the form well, then put the dough inside for its second and final rise; when it has doubled, and the time has come for baking, simply turn it upside down directly on the baking stone or sheet, being careful to dislodge it gingerly from its heavily floured basket. If you don't have a banneton, you can easily make one by lining any basket you have with a coarse tea towel or some heavy canvas fabric.

Charlotte Molds. These tinned steel pans with heart-shaped handles come in one- and two-quart sizes and serve as wonderful molds for various breads as well as for tortes, cakes, and such dishes made with leftovers as apple charlotte. Soufflé dishes of the same capacity and springforms can be used the same way.

Ring Mold. A flat-bottomed ring mold or tube pan 9 inches in diameter, with a 3-inch-diameter hole in the center, becomes an excellent form for breads baked in a wreath shape.

La Cloche

La Cloche, which bills itself as an instant bread oven, is an unglazed stoneware dome that fits over a 2-inch-deep stoneware base, and it truly does bake wonderful crusty country loaves. I like to soak the top in water for 15 to 30 minutes, while the bread is rising in the base with an inverted bowl over it. The humidity given off by the dome at the high oven temperature really crisps the crust. You may also leave the dough to rise under the domed top until it has doubled, then simply set it in a very hot oven. I get my best results when I preheat the stone base at 450° F, allowing the bread to rise elsewhere.

Razor Blade

To slash the characteristic cuts on top of rustic and traditional loaves, you'll need a razor-sharp edge. Italian bakers use a single-edge razor blade, but I prefer a much safer gadget called a Widget, which costs about two dollars at the hardware store and is essentially a razor blade inserted in a plastic carrying case that functions as a handle and greatly reduces the danger of cutting yourself instead of the bread. If you are very nimble, you can simply score the tops of loaves with a sharp knife or the metal blade of your food processor.

Baker's Peel

In Italy there are two ways that bakers set their breads in the oven. For much of the production they use an extremely long stretcher-like apparatus slung with canvas. As many as twenty loaves rise on it, and when they are fully ready, it is thrust all the way into the oven, the canvas is snapped back and retracted—something like the revolving cloth towel in some public washrooms—leaving the loaves to bake on the oven floor or shelves. Clearly, there's no such equipment for American home ovens, but we can use the alternative, a peel, or wooden paddle, the long-handled version of which is traditionally used for dropping in and scooping up pizzas and breads. A short-handled peel is easy to find in cookware stores. Just sprinkle it with cornmeal or flour so the dough won't stick, let the loaves rise on it, and with a couple of expert stiff shakes, free the loaf or pizza onto the cornmeal-sprinkled baking stone or baking sheet. Pizza peels come in sizes that vary from small—perfect for a single loaf or a small pizza—to as large as 16 × 18 inches, scaled to a giant pizza. A convenient alternative for shifting dough from rising surface to oven could be a rimless cookie sheet, a thin wooden cutting board or a sturdy piece of cardboard, all of which work very well even if they don't have quite the same authenticity.

Loaves rising on a dusted peel

Cooling Rack

You will need a rack made of wire, coated metal, wood, or even bamboo, on which the loaves of bread can cool with air circulating freely around them. Be sure to remove any breads baked in loaf pans or pie forms immediately and set them on the rack so steam doesn't collect around them. Do the opposite with delicate cakes or highly risen sweet breads, which must be cooled completely in their forms before you set them gingerly on a rack. I have known people who took them carefully out of their molds and allowed them to cool on pillows; there they recline elegantly as the heat dissipates into the air, the absence of steam preventing the formation of moisture on the bottoms. I have found that the high sweet breads like *pandoro* or *Veneziana* are less likely to crack or crumble if laid on their sides.

Rolling Pin

Only a few breads demand the attentions of a rolling pin—*pane in cassetta* and *pasta dura* are two—but all croissants, puff pastries, and a number of sweets have no hope of coming to life without one. Use either the French variety, which is a thin, heavy cylinder of wood, or the thicker American kind, which has handles and is mounted on ball bearings. Whichever you choose, I recommend that it be at least 15 to 18 inches long, and have the kind of heft that gives you authority over the dough. Country women use a wine bottle, and you'd be surprised how well it works in a pinch.

Bread Knife

Please do not go to all the trouble of making a wonderful loaf of bread and then not have a sharp, well-made serrated knife with wide teeth to cut it. A good knife also cuts delicate *pan di spagna* and *maddalèna* cakes in half horizontally with grace.

OPTIONAL BUT DEFINITELY NICE TO HAVE

Hammarplast Bowl

This straight-sided plastic bowl, invented by a Swedish chemist familiar with the properties of yeast, works wonderfully in helping breads to rise. Four tiny feet elevate the bowl, allowing easy air circulation around the form, and the clear plastic top, which fits very tightly, allows you to peek in and follow the progress of the dough in its risings. I particularly like the large 5½ quart size, which can easily handle large quantities of dough, as in Pugliese bread, which starts with a kilo of flour and has to triple in its expansion.

Parchment Paper

Sometimes I am afraid that I sound like a spokesman for the parchment paper industry, if there is such a thing, because I think parchment paper one of the great products of the century. Use a piece on baking sheets or peels, and sticky doughs suddenly become manageable and cookies no longer stick. When you are baking breads, you can slide the bread and the parchment paper right onto the baking stone, wait about twenty minutes, and then pull out the parchment and leave the loaves or pizzas baking directly on the stone. I have even lined high-sided molds that might be tricky to get breads out of, and had them come out in a single lovely, airy loaf.

ESPECIALLY FOR PIZZA

Baking Pans

Black steel bakeware is the best choice for pizza making because it absorbs and retains heat and distributes it evenly to turn out crisp pizza crusts. Brush the pan lightly with vegetable oil to season it before each baking session, and don't be disconcerted by the mottling and discoloration that are inevitable with these pans. They come in 10-inch, 12-inch, and 15-inch rounds, and in 12-inch and 16-inch square and deep-dish pans, as well as a 12 × 16-inch rectangular pan for *focaccia*. (If you have a baking stone in the oven, you can omit the pan and bake the pizza on the stone.)

Mezzaluna

If you want to be authentically Italian, you might want to do all your chopping and mincing with a *mezzaluna,* a half-moon-shaped knife with two handles that works by rocking the blade back and forth over the parsley, garlic, herbs, or raisins in question.

Cutting Wheel

A heavy-duty, finely honed cutting wheel cuts through a pizza with ease. The Dexter is sturdy and has a replaceable blade, which makes it more than worth its price. I have often used a good pair of kitchen scissors to cut *focaccia* and some thick pizzas as well.

Oilcan

The Tin Woodman wasn't the only person to depend on an oilcan. Pizza bakers brush doughs with oil before and after baking, bakers lightly coat forms with oil, and you can be sure that the fine spout of an oilcan allows just the right few drops to take care of the problem.

SPECIAL EQUIPMENT FOR PASTRY BAKING

Nut Grinder

Nothing works as well as a real nut grinder—not a food processor, which tends to separate out the oils, not a well-aimed knife, not a blender. The grinder can make a delicate flour out of nuts for pastry and for nut pastes, and can chop chocolate in lovely fine even flakes.

Grater

For all the lemon and orange zest that appear in pastries and breads, I much prefer using the flat fine-tooth grater with one size hole to the four-sided boxy version. It is much easier to handle and is just right for laying directly over the bowl, grating the lemon or orange right into the dough without having to transfer it and risk losing some of the essential oils and zest.

Tart Pans

Tart pans with removable bottoms significantly reduce the risk of breaking a crust. They come in heavy tinned steel and in black steel, which absorbs heat quickly and retains it; they can be found in a variety of sizes, including 8-inch and 9½-inch diameter, individual 4¼-inch tartlets, 2-inch-deep 9-inch tart pans, and 11 × 7-inch rectangles. Springform pans function similarly, although they are almost always deeper than tart pans and never have fluted edges.

Cookie Cutters

These come oval and round, fluted and smooth, range from 1¼ inches to 3¾ inches, and should have fine sharp edges so they cut cleanly through the dough. In a pinch, you can use the top of a spice jar.

Pastry Brushes

There really isn't a substitute for a brush that will dust flour onto or off the surface of dough; a brush that lets you glaze the tops of tarts, cookies, and even breads; a brush that washes the interior edges of cookies or *calzoni* so they stick together during the baking.

Saddle of Venison Cake Pans

Also called *Rehrücken* molds—literally, saddle of venison—these are long rectangular loaf pans with raised ridges along the sides that are traditionally used for *amor polenta*, the cornmeal tea cakes from Italy's Veneto region.

Saddle of venison pan

Pastry Bag with Tips

Treat yourself to a plastic-coated cloth pastry bag with a sizable capacity, which is easy to fill and easy to clean. You will need several basic tips, along with a plastic coupler and nut for the special long-nosed nozzle used to inject zabaglione cream into Focaccia Veneziana. (Otherwise, just slice the cake carefully into three horizontal layers, lace each with zabaglione cream, and put it back together.)

Flour Sifter

You should never sift flour for bread and always sift it for pastries. If you don't have a sifter, simply use your wide-mouthed fine mesh sieve, which works perfectly for the task. It will do the same for sifting powdered sugar over the tops of tarts, cakes, and cookies.

Plastic Dough Scraper

This arcs along the contours of a bowl and gets out every last drop of filling or dough.

Techniques for Baking Bread

Dissolving the Yeast

Those little packets of active dry yeast or small cubes of fresh compressed yeast that you buy at the store give life to bread, but they must be reactivated to do their work. If you read pages 39–41, you will understand how yeast works. Almost every recipe begins by telling you to dissolve the yeast in a small amount of warm water. Compressed cake yeast is best stirred into water that is 90° to 100° F, while active dry yeast returns to life at a slightly higher 105° to 115° F. Don't worry too much about getting the temperature precisely right; just make sure that it is warm to the touch—neither hot nor cool. If you are using dry yeast, sprinkle it over the water in a bowl and stir in the granules with a small whisk. Cake yeast should be crumbled directly into the water and stirred to dissolve it. Let the mixture stand for about 10 minutes, when it will look creamy, then whisk it briefly to mix it all up.

Measuring the Ingredients

Italian bakers weigh all their ingredients. They have never heard of measuring cups or spoons, and for the purposes of cooking these breads and pastries, I wish Americans hadn't either. I'd like to persuade everyone to use a scale—at least for the flours, which vary amazingly, depending on how much moisture they contain and how they have been handled. Many of these recipes begin with 500 grams of unbleached all-purpose flour, which can measure anywhere from 3¼ to 4½ cups, depending on how they are scooped and whether they were sifted or packed down. If you don't have a scale, this is the most accurate way to measure flour consistently: First stir the flour to aerate it, then scoop it into a measuring cup and level it off with a knife. Never sift the flour for bread making. And never pack it down into the cup. Measure sugar the same way. I like to measure my eggs as well. A large egg should weigh 2 ounces or about 60 grams, but there will be some variation; for perfect measurement, break an egg, two if necessary, into a bowl and use what you need.

Temperature of Other Ingredients

Warm water is used to dissolve the yeast, but other ingredients should be at room temperature, with one exception: In the case of the food processor, which works with such speed that it heats up the contents of the bowl in no time, cold water is used for almost all the liquid called for in the bread and pizza recipes. Italian bakers consider 75° F the ideal temperature for the water and insist that successful bread is best made with the average of all the ingredients—water, flour, and room temperature—at that same 75° F. This means that if you are baking in the cold of winter, you may need to heat up the water and warm the flour in the oven, while in summer you should use cool, or even cold, water to keep the same balance.

Mixing the Dough

Mixing the dough itself is straightforward. Dissolve the yeast in the water as directed, add whatever other wet ingredients are called for— olive oil, milk, lard—and mix them in well with a wooden spoon, if you are working by hand, or with the paddle of the mixer. When you mix in the flour, please reserve a bit of it until the end; the dough may come together and you might not need it all. If you are mixing the dough by hand, you may want to use a big widemouthed bowl—I have a set that I bought at the hardware store and have seen similar ones at restaurant supply shops—so that you can knead in it as well as spare yourself the inevitable crusty counter that has to be cleaned.

By Hand. Stir the flour, which is often first mixed with the salt, into the yeast-liquid mixture, one cup at a time. I sometimes use a whisk to mix in the first cup or two, because it virtually assures a lump-free mixture, but I wouldn't want you to think that there is anything traditionally Italian about that particular method. There isn't. In fact, I never saw anything remotely like it in Italy. It just works well, so I've adopted it. After that, you'll want to use a wooden spoon to mix in the rest of the flour, a cup at a time, beating thoroughly after each addition. Should the dough become too dense to continue easily, just plunge in with your hands and continue mixing until you have a consistent dough. It will be shaggy and rough and in some cases quite sticky, but that's to be expected. The process usually takes 4 or 5 minutes.

By Mixer. I have made every single one of the breads and pizzas, to say nothing of the pastries, cakes, and cookies, in this book in my Kitchen Aid mixer. It's easy, quick, and tidy. I use the paddle to mix doughs and the dough hook to knead them, although I invariably finish kneading by hand. Just dissolve the yeast in the bowl of the mixer until it's creamy, add the rest of the water and any other wet ingredients, and mix them all together using the paddle. I set a bit of the flour to the side and add the rest all at once, but I would caution you that this is only a good idea when you have weighed the flour, so that your amounts are sure to be correct. If you're using dry measures, set aside a larger portion just to be safe. It takes to 1 to 3 minutes for the ingredients to become combined into a rough dough; it's easy to tell that the flour has been absorbed when there are no dry patches of it left in the bottom of the bowl.

By Food Processor. Making bread with the processor is incredibly easy, but it works very differently than a mixer or your hands. Some recipes specify more liquid and both liquid ingredients and butter must be cold. You should begin by setting the steel blade in the processor bowl with the flour and salt, and process with several pulses to sift and mix. Sometimes you will want to change to the dough blade and other times you may not; the recipes vary and your procedure depends in great part on the capacity of the processor bowl. The dough blade adds to the capacity of the bowl. A standard machine with a 6½-inch-diameter bowl will process 3¾ cups flour (about 500 grams) and 1½ cups water. The larger machines with larger work bowls accept from 8 cups flour and 2½ cups water to huge quantities professionals need. Please note that not all processors have motors powerful enough to mix and knead bread dough, so read the instructions of your machine. If your processor slows down during the mixing, stop it and take out half the dough. You can always combine the two pieces when you finish, kneading them together on a lightly floured surface. Once you have mixed the ingredients in the processor by pouring the wet ingredients and dissolved yeast through the feed tube, process until the dough gathers into a rough mass.

Kneading

When I started baking bread, kneading seemed the most mysteriously appealing process because it transformed a shaggy clump into silky, elastic dough. I love my Kitchen Aid, but I always finish kneading by hand, because I am convinced that the warmth of human touch communicates itself and makes a real difference to the responsiveness and final feel of the dough. I hope you'll do the same; machines are wonderful, but it's you, not they, that are really making these breads.

By Hand. If you are kneading by hand, choose a work surface that allows you to knead the dough with a straight back. Sprinkle the surface lightly with flour. Pick up the dough from its mixing bowl, put it on the table, and flatten it gently into a disk. Curl your fingertips under the opposite side, lift it, and fold it toward you. With the heel of your hand, roll and push the dough away under your hand, staying parallel to the counter. Press out, not down. Give the dough a quarter turn and do it again. If it looks shredded, you're working too hard; just repeat the motions, but slowly, gently, and

1. Transfer the dough to lightly floured work surface.

2. Sprinkle with flour.

3. *Fold dough toward you.*

4. *Roll and push away with the palm of your hand.*

5. *Give dough a quarter turn.*

with a lighter touch. Sprinkle flour on the work surface and over the dough so that it moves easily on the table without sticking. If a piece does stick, scrape it off with the dough scraper and toss it away. If you sprinkle flour over the ragged dough on the work surface, it will continue to collect more of your dough, and pretty soon you'll be making one loaf instead of two. With wet, sticky doughs, like ryes or the rustic regional loaves, be sure to have your dough scraper handy. You can use it as an extension of your hand, turning and folding the dough with it and working in a little of the flour on your work surface. Keep kneading for the time called for in the recipe or until the dough is silky and elastic, or whatever consistency is described. One Italian baker told me it should feel as soft as a baby's bottom. Try not to mix in much extra flour as you knead, for it changes the texture of the bread you are making. Please note that when substantial amounts of flour are called for in kneading, amounts are given in the method; if no specific amount is mentioned, you can assume that sprinkles will be sufficient.

Firmer doughs, when they no longer stick to your hands or the work surface, can be lifted up and banged down hard against the surface, to develop the gluten. In many cases—although not in the big porous regional breads—you are aiming for a supple, silky dough that may show definite air bubbles beneath the surface when fully kneaded and spring back when you flatten it with your palm.

If you are kneading in a bowl, follow the same instructions, adding sprinkles of flour as you knead.

By Mixer. Once your ingredients have come together to form a consistent dough, change from the paddle to the dough hook for the actual kneading. Begin by kneading at a low speed, but be sure to follow the recipe instructions; some call for subsequent kneading at a higher speed. The mixer does all the work, but please keep an eye on it. I once turned my back to finish kneading another dough on my worktable, and I didn't notice that the mixer was working so hard on a big batch of dough that it began to move with the exertion, literally walking from the back of my counter to the front and then falling to the floor. Needless to say, the dough was a mess; as for the mixer, it spent the next few days at a repair shop. Otherwise, the only effort you'll exert is when you push down any dough that climbs up the collar of the dough hook. Be sure to turn off the motor before you do. When the dough is all kneaded and feels the way the instructions describe, scoop it out of the mixer bowl and knead it briefly by hand on a lightly floured surface.

By Food Processor. In a food processor, kneading is simply processing for the additional time called for in the recipe—usually between 25 and 40 seconds—although some recipes will ask you to process briefly, then finish kneading by hand. Even if it is not specifically called for, I recommend that you finish kneading with your hands briefly on a lightly floured surface; bread whirled into being in this high-speed machine needs the consolation of human warmth.

Rising

Dough set to rise in a covered Hammarplast bowl

Like wine or cheese, bread is a natural product that needs to mature at its own pace in an undisturbed spot where it can rise slowly. When the yeast comes back to life and begins to breathe, it emits carbon dioxide bubbles that become trapped in the elastic gluten network built up in the kneading, and they leaven and lighten the dough, pushing it up so that it rises to double or triple its original size. These breads all have at least two rises, and a few have three. The rises allow the flavor of the wheat to mature so that the full taste of the grain permeates the finished loaves. They also encourage the chewy country loaves with big holes in the interior to develop their character. Be sure to choose a bowl large enough to permit this astonishing transformation. Lightly oil its interior so the dough won't stick to it. (I use olive oil, but any vegetable oil will do.) Cover tightly with a plastic top or plastic wrap secured with a rubber band, so the heat and moisture generated by the process are contained in the bowl; you'll be able to watch it all happening as the steamy moisture is trapped on the plastic wrap. Italian bakers let their doughs rise at room temperature, about 75° F, which is quite a bit cooler than the usual American practice, and I encourage you to do the same. It will take a bit longer, in some cases, but the final flavor of the bread is well worth it.

Professional bakers work on an enormous scale, of course, using containers the size of garbage cans, with tight-fitting lids. I use any number of things: large ceramic and earthenware bowls, the Hammarplast bowl (see page 73), or the domestic equivalent of bakers' equipment, which I have found in hardware and restaurant supply stores in the form of outsize refrigerator containers with tight-fitting lids. If you use a straight-sided translucent plastic or glass container, like a large Pyrex measuring cup, you can monitor the process. Otherwise you might want to put a mark on the outside of the container, indicating where the dough started in volume so that you can accurately gauge when it has doubled or tripled, as the recipe requires. That's one way to tell if the dough has risen enough; the other is to poke your finger gently into the dough and see if the impression remains; if it does, you can be sure that it has risen sufficiently.

Monitoring the rising process: mark shows original level of dough

Timing

If you find that things are simply not moving along with the speed you want, you can set the bowl with your dough in a larger bowl containing warm water, and cover it well. If you find the rise is going too fast—maybe you have to go out and don't want to take the chance of the dough overrising—you can always put it in a cool place or, even better, in the refrigerator, and let it rise very slowly there. Cold doesn't ever kill yeast; it just slows its action. When you are ready, take the dough out, let it warm to room temperature, which will take between 2 and 3 hours, and proceed with the recipe. You can do this for the first rise, the second rise, after the bread has been shaped, or even the third rise, if the dough gets that many.

Breads with Starters

Many of these doughs fit wonderfully into a busy contemporary life because they begin with a starter that is essentially a dough made with a bit of yeast and water and a goodly amount of flour. Please look at the *Biga* recipe (page 100) for a fuller explanation. A small amount of yeast is dissolved in water, and enough flour is beaten in to make a soft batter. The bowl is covered and the starter is allowed to ferment. It gives a boost to the true dough, which is made with a new infusion of flour, water, and yeast, and it allows the flavor of the grain to mature and the texture to develop. It's a system that has been used in Italy since Roman times, and it fits perfectly into an American life-style because you can make the initial starter anywhere from 6 to 24 hours before you put the dough together for the bread.

Make it anytime the day before you plan to bake—first thing in the morning or after dinner—and then let it rise overnight. The next day, make the dough and let it rise according to your plans. I keep starters on hand all the time. The contents of my refrigerator and freezer are definitely not the typical American vision, for sometimes there are more inedible than edible contents, should you start counting starters, flours, yeasts, grains, dried mushrooms, and any number of containers of lard. Still, I can decide to make a *pane pugliese* or a *ciabatta* in the morning and have them for dinner without bending my schedule dramatically. You can do the same. Should your plans change after you've embarked on a bread, set the dough in the refrigerator and let it rise more slowly. Just be sure to bring your dough back to room temperature before proceeding. And don't worry if you leave your dough in a very cool spot and let it rise for a long time. I got the same advice from bakers all over Italy: Give the dough long, cool rises to develop its fragrance and texture. In the same spirit, use very little yeast and rely instead on a starter or dough from the day before to get the intense taste of the grain and the texture that makes these such satisfying breads.

Shaping

In 1½ to 2 hours, in most cases, the dough will have doubled in volume. It will look soft and spongy. Punch down the dough only if the recipe says so. Turn it out on a lightly floured surface, divide it into the requisite number of pieces by cutting them with a dough scraper, and flatten them (if directed) a bit more to release the carbon dioxide. Now the yeast can begin to work again, after the loaves have been shaped, and the bread can rise a second time before being baked. Because almost all of these loaves are freestanding—unlike most American breads, which are baked in loaf pans and molds—it is very important to give them enough structure in the shaping so they can keep their form. Start by taking the piece of dough and flattening it, and then, using your thumbs as a guide in the center, roll it up toward you into a fat cylinder. Roll it up once again until you have a thick sausage shape. The real secret in shaping the dough into a firm ball is to roll the dough tightly across the surface of the table with cupped hands, then pull it back firmly against the work surface, always using your cupped hands to help form and maintain its firm round shape. Repeat several times until you have the desired taut ball. What you have really done is to pull the gluten net tight and given the dough the shape it will ultimately take. Professional bakers have a learned ambidexterity and can shape two small round loaves or rolls at the same time, one in each hand, so quickly that you can hardly comprehend what you're watching.

Every loaf of bread has a smooth side and a rough wrinkled side, where the dough being pulled downward in the shaping process is collected. Once you have your shaped dough, you will place it with the smooth or the rough side up. Often the attractive veining of flour on the top of rustic country loaves comes from a bread's having risen smooth side down in a light bed of flour; then, when the dough is inverted onto the baking stone or baking sheet, the smooth surface is up, with a pattern of flour on top and the rough seam side on the bottom.

1. *Flatten dough and roll into fat cylinders.*
2. *Roll up once again.*
3. *Shape into balls using cupped hands.*

Second Rising

The dough now gets a second rise, during which most will again double in volume, but in considerably less time than the first rise—within 45 minutes to 1¼ hours. A very few even get a third rise, but they are exceptions.

Read the recipe carefully for each particular bread. If it is to have its second rise on a baker's peel, or a piece of cardboard or wood, be sure to have sprinkled the surface with semolina, cornmeal, or flour; if the dough is to bake on a baking sheet, be sure it is oiled before placing the dough on it to rise. If it is to bake on a preheated heavy baking sheet, be sure to sprinkle it with semolina or cornmeal just before baking. Parchment paper is a real friend, especially with many of the moist, delicate doughs. Shape the loaf and set it on parchment paper that has been floured and put on a peel or the back of a baking sheet, and cover it with a towel. When the time comes for baking, you can slide the parchment paper right onto the baking stone and slip the paper out 15 to 20 minutes later, when the dough has set.

Some of the breads are set in oiled or buttered molds or baking tins. They will look small and somewhat unpromising—doughs should fill only half the mold or tin—but in no time they will have risen to the top. Be sure to cover the top of the shaped dough to keep it from developing a skin, which would be the end of its expansion. Sometimes I use a moist (not wet) kitchen towel dampened with water that's at room temperature, and sometimes a heavy bath towel; both work fine. For any slow-rising or delicate breads, I prefer a heavy towel. To slow down the rise, a baker in Rome taught me to oil the tops of some sticky moist doughs and gently lay plastic wrap over them. When the circulation of air is cut down dramatically by this method, the dough rises slowly and helps develop flavor. If you want to stop the rise altogether, cover the dough well and refrigerate it.

Covering shaped dough

To speed the rise, you can do what Italian women have done for centuries: place the shaped dough in a bed still warm from a sleeping body. Pull the blanket up over it and wait until it has risen. I have given this a twentieth-century twist by using an electric blanket at a low setting in the middle of winter, protecting the dough well with a towel. Bakers use proofers—warm, moist chambers—at this stage, and you may want to utilize the low heat of a gas pilot light or a briefly warmed electric oven (turn it on at 150° F or its lowest setting for 3 minutes, then turn it off again) to help your loaves to rise; on a cold day you can even set a pan of steaming water on the bottom shelf of the oven to provide the warm moist atmosphere that will encourage the dough to rise. This works particularly well with rich, sweet bread and doughs bursting with fruits and nuts.

Slashing

Some breads have a pattern slashed on their tops before they are set in the oven. The secret of slashing is to hold the razor at a diagonal slant to the dough and to slash quickly with a firm motion that slices deep. You can always go back and slash again if you are not happy with your first effort, but the single definite gesture is much more successful.

Slashing the top

Baking

The last transformation takes place in the oven, where the doughs get their final rise. Italian bakers slide the risen loaves directly onto a hot brick floor while jets of steam are shot into the oven for the first few minutes of baking. All that vapor lets the yeast work a little longer, giving the loaves an extra burst of volume while delaying the setting of the crust.

You don't need a brick-lined oven that heats to 750° F to make outstanding bread, as long as you take advantage of several secrets of the Italian baker. It makes no real difference whether your oven is gas or electric; what matters is the brick interior. I like to use baking stones or quarry tiles because they distribute the heat evenly, absorb moisture from the bottom of the loaves, and produce crunchy crusts. If you own a La Cloche, which is a wonderful replica of a baker's oven, you will find it perfect for any regional or rustic bread. I wouldn't use it for a sweet or fruit bread, but it is superior for any bread that needs a good crust. If you prefer a golden crunchy crust, be sure to take the top off for the last 15 minutes of baking, or you'll get a softer, paler crust. If you have neither baking stones, quarry tiles, nor the *cloche*, you still have good options. The easiest is to let the dough rise and bake directly on a heavy baking sheet. Alternatively, you can set a heavy baking sheet or even a ⅜-inch-thick griddle in the oven, heat it for 30 minutes, then transfer the dough to it. Unless it is Teflon coated, sprinkle it with cornmeal or semolina just before sliding the dough on top. If you have baked the breads in a form or special pan, you might want to unmold them for the last 10 to 15 minutes, to let them bake directly on a stone and take some color.

Getting the Doughs in the Oven

Italian bakers often use a long-handled peel to set the dough in the oven. They stick it in and, with a single expert motion, jerk it back, leaving the dough on the oven floor. You can slide your risen doughs onto a baking stone in the oven with a peel, a piece of cardboard, or a wooden board, depending on what they have risen on, or you may choose to deposit a dough that has risen on the back of one baking sheet onto a second, hot baking sheet. Or you may simply bake on the baking sheet that the bread dough rose on, although I prefer the preheated baking sheet. If your dough has risen on parchment paper, you'll find it especially easy to get it onto a baking stone, because it can be transferred paper and all. I always dust the stone with cornmeal or semolina, whether or not I'm using parchment, partly from sheer habit and partly because I usually remove the paper after about 20 minutes, and if the loaf is a little moist, I know that I don't have to worry that the dough will stick.

Adding Moisture

There are several ways to get steam into the oven. You can place a broiler pan with 1½ cups boiling water on the floor of a gas oven or the bottom shelf of an electric oven 10 minutes before you put in the loaves. Set the bread inside, close the door, and the steam will continue to mist the interior for about 10 minutes. By the time the crust has set, the water will have evaporated, and the rest of the baking will be done in a hot, dry oven. If you prefer, toss several handfuls of ice cubes into a broiler pan as you place the loaves in the oven; they will melt and emit steam for about 10 minutes. The easiest solution is to fill a plant atomizer with cold water and spray the loaves three times during the first 10 minutes of baking. Whatever you do, don't toss ice cubes on the oven floor—it will warp—and be certain not to spray the oven light while you're doing all this humidifying, because it might explode.

Spraying the loaf

When Are the Loaves Done?

The traditional method of determining when loaves are done is to knock on the bottom of the loaf and listen for the resonant hollow ring that indicates they have cooked through. If you are uncertain, you can stick an instant-reading thermometer into the center of the loaf; by constant checking I have discovered that breads are done between 200° and 210° F, although the crust reaches temperatures of about 325° F.

Cooling

Cool the bread on a rack so that steam doesn't soften the bottom. Cookbooks always specify wire racks, but I have a wonderful Teflon-coated rack that I like to use, and my butcher-block table, which was designed for pasta making, has natural wood racks that work just fine.

Storing

Breads made with only flour, water, yeast, and salt are best eaten the day they are baked. Age—just a few hours sometimes—does in fact cause them to go stale. If you make more than you can consume quickly or give away to friends, you can freeze bread with very good results. The best-keeping breads are those made with starters and those made with a little milk, olive oil, or butter. They seem to stay fresh longer than their plainer, earthier relatives and can be stored in a paper (not plastic) bag in a cool, dark spot. It is true that breads keep a bit longer in a refrigerator, but American frost-free refrigerators draw out the moisture in a loaf, and that doesn't seem a good trade-off to me.

Many of these breads—the *ciabatta*, *pugliese*, *genzano*, and *coccodrillo*, for instance—make spectacular toast, as well as wonderful croutons to be sautéed in butter and oil and set in the bottom of a bowl of Italian soup. Italian folklore is full of warnings about the horrible fate in store for anyone who wastes a single crumb of bread, so it is hardly surprising that there are numerous dishes based on leftover breads (see pages 180–197).

Freezing and Refreshing

To freeze the breads, wrap them up tightly, first in aluminum foil, then in plastic wrap, and set them in the freezer. I don't let them thaw at all, but set them in a 350° F oven for 15 to 30 minutes, depending on how thick they are. *Ciabatte,* for instance, are ready in 15 to 20 minutes, while *pugliesi* or any of the higher-domed breads, such as *panmarino* or sweet breads, take about 30 minutes.

Beginner Breads and Harder Breads

If you are new to baking, start with one of the vegetable or herb breads, like the pesto bread, the sweet pepper or rosemary bread; try the *focacce,* the *grissini,* or any of the whole-grain breads. You can also try the rolls—both savory and sweet—that are a vital part of the social life in this most social of all countries. Try the *maritozze* or the spinach rolls or the *ciambelle* with oil and salt. These breads are straightforward and uncomplicated, and the proportion of flour to water makes them easy to mix and knead.

The big regional breads with chewy, porous interiors tend to be more difficult to prepare, because they are made with starters and because the doughs are uncommonly moist, which takes some getting used to. Italian bakers toss great blobs of them onto the worktable and shape them with ease, but I have to admit to fantasies of someone plunging in to knead or shape one of these wet doughs, only to find herself trapped in great sticky masses and having to wait for a friend to come by and rescue her. Actually, there is nothing tricky about these doughs as long as you are psychologically and physically prepared with a mound of flour nearby for your work surface, your hands, and even your tools. These wet doughs may sound somewhat formidable, but they make spectacular breads. They are survivors of a rustic tradition that remains alive in pockets of Italy today, and they more than repay in taste what they demand in effort. Often all it takes is an extra tablespoon or two of flour to bring an unmanageably soft dough under control.

Other difficult doughs tend to demand more time than anything else. The addition of butter, which coats the gluten strands of the sweet doughs, slows down the rises, as do the fruit and nut fillings, handfuls of cheese, and chunks of salami. Make sure you've allowed for the hours that the rises will take and the extra few minutes that rolling in the fillings demand. Follow the instructions carefully, and you won't have any problems.

Most of the recipes in this book are traditional or variations on the traditional. But what makes this a spirited romp in the fields of the baker is the fact that tradition is constantly being modified by the creative instincts of the very bakers who dreamed up the variations in the first place. More times than I'd like to count, I've gone back to a bakery, drawn by memories of a wonderful bread, only to discover that they're making it slightly differently. Someone's *fantasia* has added a little durum flour or shaped it into a braid or an extravagant big wheel. These bakers start with flour, water, yeast, and salt, but by the time they're finished, they've added color, fragrance, new flavors and aromas, and dusted a surface with a handful of fresh herbs or tiny crunchy seeds. So while you must follow the recipes and learn from the bakers' techniques, once you've conquered the technique you may decide to follow their lead and invent your own variations. You might make a long, thin baguette of the *pugliese* dough or put salty olives in one of the salt-free doughs, add herbs from your garden or a bit of Marsala or rum to a lightly sweetened dough.

A FEW USEFUL HINTS

□ The rule of thumb: The slower and longer the rise, the greater the flavor. But if the dough is left so long that it overrises and slumps, as the carbon dioxide bubbles begin to burst, don't worry. Dough is very forgiving. Knead it, shape it, and set it to rise once more; you will find that it reaches its desired size rather quickly.

□ The more yeast, the quicker the rise.

□ The less mixing or kneading used in working the dough, the longer the rise will take.

□ Dough with less water is more substantial and compact than softer, moister dough, which will need more mixing and kneading, and longer rising times.

□ Lower temperatures encourage the formation of acetic acids, which give breads a more aromatic taste.

□ Many of the rustic regional breads should triple in the first rising and can take three risings nicely, in case you need more flexibility than the recipes indicate.

□ At the second rise, after they have been shaped, you can lightly oil the tops of the sticky wet doughs and gently lay plastic wrap over them. The circulation of air is cut down dramatically by this method, so the dough rises slowly and develops more flavor.

□ Add fruits and nuts after the first rise by flattening the dough and spooning part of the mixture onto the dough in two or three additions. Fold the dough, flatten again, and repeat until all the filling is in the dough. Knead until the filling is evenly distributed.

Techniques for Baking Tarts, Cakes, and Cookies

Putting ingredients together for Italian sweets is much easier than for breads. First of all, no yeast, no starters, no rises are involved. Secondly, many of these desserts are based on *pasta frolla*, a sweet short pastry dough that is a snap to make. Even the shaping is simple once you get the hang of it.

A Few Basic Rules

Always have your butter and eggs at room temperature. If you're baking on the spur of the moment and don't have any eggs at 70° F, set your refrigerated eggs in a bowl of warm water for about ten minutes and they'll be ready for you. Always weigh your flour (or measure it) before sifting. Always sift the flour before incorporating it. If you are using baking powder, sift it along with the other dry ingredients. Most of the recipes depend on the few following basic processes.

Making Dough for Tart Shells

By Hand. First place the flour, salt, and sugar in a mixing bowl and stir them briefly to blend. Cut the butter into small pieces and scatter them over the top. Using a pastry cutter or two knives, cut in the butter until the mixture looks like coarse meal. Beat egg, egg yolk and flavorings until smooth. Drizzle the mixture over the flour and work until the dough comes together.

By Mixer. Cream the butter and sugar until they are light and fluffy, about 4 minutes at medium speed. Add the egg and egg yolk, one at a time, mixing in the first before adding the second. Beat in the flavorings last. Sift the flour and salt over the mixture and work them in by hand with a wooden spoon or rubber spatula just until blended.

By Food Processor. The processor has this tart dough together almost before you've started. Set the steel blade in place, put the flour, salt, and sugar in the bowl, and scatter the cold butter in small chunks on top. Process with several pulses until the mixture looks like coarse meal. Combine the egg, egg yolk, and flavorings and, with the machine running, pour them through the feed tube. Process just until the dough comes together on top of the blade. If you wait for the dough to gather into a ball, it will be too tough. Finish by kneading the dough briefly on a lightly floured surface until it is no longer sticky.

Shaping the Dough

Bring the dough together with your hands and knead it briefly on a lightly floured surface until it forms a single mass. Transfer it to a piece of plastic wrap, flatten it to a round disk, and refrigerate it until cold, at least 1 hour but no longer than a day.

Rolling with a Rolling Pin

Place the cold dough on a surface that you have dusted lightly with flour, and sprinkle the top of the dough with just enough flour to keep it from being sticky. The point of the rolling is to make an even, thin circle of dough, so start from the center and roll evenly and smoothly away from you about 3 inches in each direction. Don't try to roll it very far—2 to 3 inches is fine—and don't press down hard. Lift up the dough, give it a half-quarter turn, sprinkle a very little bit of flour underneath it if it shows any tendency to stick, and repeat the process, always rolling away from the center. Don't roll over the edges or you might damage them. Keep rolling to the dimensions you need; if your dough sticks at any point, be sure to scrape the offending particles off your work surface with the dough scraper and flour the surface lightly.

Transferring the Dough to the Tart Pan

Simply lay your rolling pin lightly on the top quarter of the dough, pick up that piece of the dough, and lay it back over the rolling pin. Gently roll the pin toward you, collecting the remaining dough around it. Lift the rolling pin and set it over the tart pan, rolling the dough away from you and allowing it to drape into the pan. With practice, it gets easier to judge how to center it; if you miss the first few times, just pick up the dough gently and set it where you want it. Delicately press the dough into the contours of the pan, then gently push the sides up toward the rim. If you accidentally tear it, patch it by using a little of your leftover dough or by collecting the two edges of torn dough and pinching the edges together.

Setting dough into pan

Shaping the Edges

Once the dough has been fitted into the pan, take the rolling pin and roll it gently over the top edges to cut the pastry dough neatly. Once again I push the dough gently upward toward the rim with my thumb, pressing the overflow with my other thumb to make a slightly thicker edge. The pastry-lined pan is usually refrigerated for 20 to 30 minutes to reduce shrinking while it bakes.

Prebaking a Pastry Shell

Many of the tart shells in this book need to be prebaked, which simply means that before it is filled, the pastry must be baked until it can hold its shape. Line the chilled tart shell with aluminum foil fitted to the bottom contours, and spread 2½ to 3 cups dried beans in the foil. Fold the edges of the foil in slightly so they are easy to grasp later. Bake as directed, usually 12 to 15 minutes at 350° F. The dough should have cooked enough so that it won't feel tacky or sticky. Then, depending on the recipe instructions, either take it out of the oven to cool after removing the beans, or remove the beans, prick the bottom of the pastry all over with a fork, and finish baking.

Making Dough for Cakes and Some Cookies

Creaming Butter and Sugar. Although it is possible to cream butter and sugar by hand with a wooden spoon, I'd certainly recommend that you use an electric mixer. It's much easier, less time-consuming, and it produces a cake as professional as a baker's. Creaming the butter and sugar means beating the two ingredients (butter at room temperature, please) until they are light and fluffy.

Adding Eggs. Add the eggs, one at a time, being sure to incorporate each completely before adding the next. If the mixture looks as if it is curdling, speed up the mixer, beat until the batter is smooth again, and then reduce the speed to that called for in the recipe.

Sifting In Dry Ingredients. Add the dry ingredients by hand. Flour for sweets is always measured, sifted, and sifted again right into the butter, sugar, and egg base. Use a rubber spatula to fold in the ingredients, so that the batter stays airy and light.

Alternating Liquid and Dry Ingredients. Stir the first portion of the liquid ingredients into your initial mixture, always working from the center out. Alternate liquid and dry ingredients, making sure each addition is smoothly blended before continuing. Always end with the flour.

Grinding Nuts. You can grind nuts in a nut grinder, a spice grinder, or a food processor fitted with the steel blade. With all these methods, you must take care that the nuts are ground just until powdery and fluffy. If you overprocess the nuts they will be oily and ruin your pastries. If you are using a food processor, add a little of the sugar called for in the recipe to the nuts and process with repeated pulses just to a powder—be sure to keep checking.

Whipping Eggs and Sugar Together. Beat the sugar and eggs at medium speed until pale and about tripled in volume. Usually, about half the sugar is added initially, the rest is added by bits as the eggs get lighter. If, when you lift the beaters or whisk, the ribbon that falls from the beaters onto the surface remains for ten seconds or so, the eggs and sugar are sufficiently mixed.

Whipping Egg Whites. To whip egg whites to their full volume, be sure that they are at room temperature and that you have a clean, grease-free bowl and beaters. If you are at all in doubt, just wipe the bowl and beaters with a little vinegar before beginning. A balloon whisk and a copper bowl are wonderful if you are beating by hand, but electric mixers work fabulously and save time and energy. Begin by beating at medium-low speed for about 30 seconds, then increase the speed to medium-high and beat until the whites are stiff but not dry, and hold smooth peaks.

Using the Pastry Bag and Piping. I'll try to explain the process, but a little hands-on experience and practice is worth a thousand words. To begin, insert the tip in the bag, fold a third of the top down over your hand, fill the bag about two-thirds full, and twist it closed at the top to push the contents down into the tip. Hold the tip between your thumb and index finger at a 45 to 90 degree angle to the baking sheet and squeeze firmly but gently at the top of the bag with your other hand. Hold the bag gently to create a smooth, steady pressure that will pipe a line the width and size of your tip. Squeeze a bit harder and faster, and you'll get a thicker, larger flow.

Dusting with Powdered Sugar. Use a wide-mouthed fine sieve to sprinkle an even layer of powdered sugar over the top of tarts or tortes.

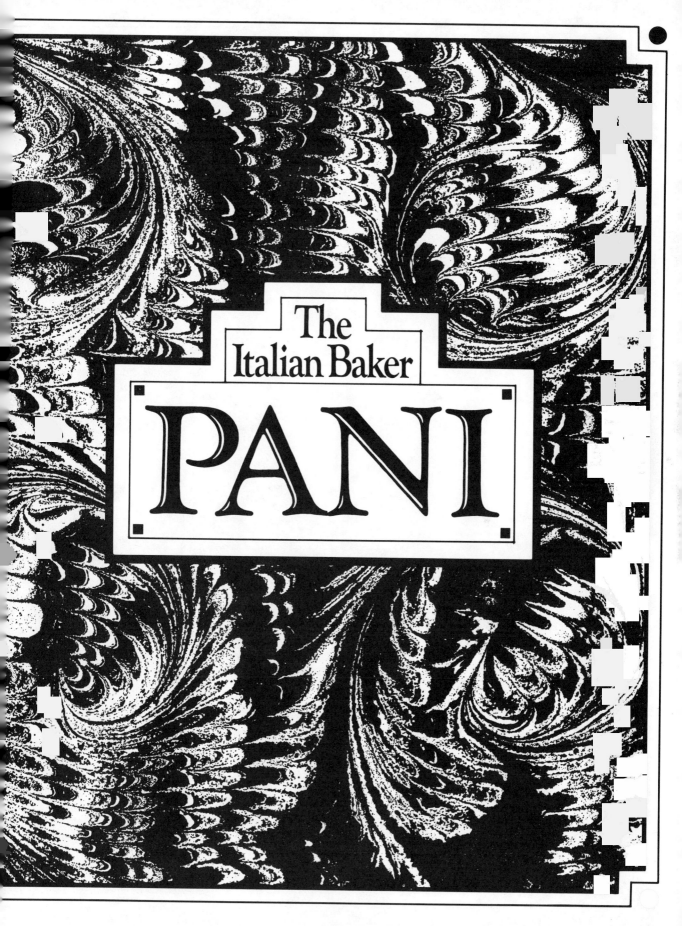

The Italian Baker

PANI

PANI REGIONALI E RUSTICI
Regional and Rustic Breads

D o they really exist, those mahogany-colored wheels of country bread with creamy interiors, crackly crusted chewy loaves that still taste intensely of the grains of the fields? The question can only be answered both yes and no. For many people, those fragrant loaves belong to a fleeting moment in the golden past when life was slower and simpler, when breads were made by hand and eaten with a glass of wine and a few slices of good local cheese. Today those breads can still be found, but you must look for them. For all their satisfying flavor, their continued existence was severely endangered during the 1950s and 1960s, when mass production and industrialization centralized baking and threatened to do away with these more complicated breads. Fortunately, they have been revived by artisan bakers all over the country, so that their tastes remain part of another generation's patrimony.

These are the traditional regional breads of Italy, made with only flour, water, yeast, and salt. Most get their taste from a starter that has been allowed to mature and grow slightly sour, so that the loaves will have the deep mellow taste of the grain itself. You will need to start these breads a half-day or day before you plan to bake, by making a starter. I often make more starter than the recipe calls for and freeze what's left, for frozen starter can be revived within a few hours. The doughs for these rustic breads will be a new experience for American cooks who are accustomed to firm bread doughs. The biggest challenge is that they are wet and sticky. When I traveled from bakery to bakery in Italy, watching experts shape, with swift, dexterous motions, doughs that fell off the beaters like buttercream, I knew I would have to explain the procedure carefully. Many of the doughs will seem impossibly wet—a couple even ooze right out of their containers after the first rise—but all it takes is a tablespoon or two of flour to make them easy to shape. *Do not punch them down.* Be ready with a small mound of flour nearby to sprinkle on the sticky doughs, and be sure to keep the work surface floured and your dough scraper handy. Scrape the surface clean so that the little ragged pieces of dough that stick do not tear away at your dough. Parchment paper on baking sheets or peels makes turning these doughs over or sliding them onto the baking stone so much easier than shaking them off a peel.

Classic Tastes of Italy

Biga (or Bighino in small amounts)

Universal Starter

Many of the recipes for the classic regional breads begin with a starter dough made from small amounts of flour, water, and yeast allowed an initial fermentation and then used to infuse the actual bread dough. The starter, known as *biga* in Italy, not only gives strength and force to what in Italy are weak flours, but also produces a secondary fermentation from which come the wonderful aroma, natural flavor, and special porosity of the final loaves and wheels of bread.

I keep some *biga* on hand at all times—the contents of our refrigerator and freezer are definitely not the typical American vision with more inedible than edible contents. Still, by having it on hand, I can decide to make *pane pugliese* or *ciabatta* in the morning and have it for dinner that night.

In Italy, bakers save saltless dough from the previous day's bake to start a new dough. Because the first *biga* must come from somewhere, you may make it following the instructions below. This *biga* is remarkable. It freezes very well and needs only about three hours at room temperature until it is bubbly and active again. It can be refrigerated for about a week; after that, it gets a bit strong. When using it in recipes, it is best to weigh it, rather than measure it, for it expands at room temperature. The bakers I admire most advise ten to eleven hours for the first rise and then another three hours after adding more flour and water, but others are very happy with the twenty-four hours it takes for dough to become truly yesterday's dough. If you like sour bread, allow your *biga* to rest for twenty-four to seventy-two hours. The important point about a starter dough is that it is very close to natural yeast and the breads made with it develop a wonderful taste because their risings are long and bring out the flavor of the grain. Another benefit is that the loaves remain fresher and taste sweeter than those made with large amounts of commercial yeast.

Makes 2⅓ cups (about 585 grams) Biga

¼ teaspoon active dry yeast or ¹⁄₁₀ small cake (2 grams) fresh yeast
¼ cup warm water
¾ cup plus 1 tablespoon plus 1 teaspoon water, room temperature
2½ cups (about 330 grams) unbleached all-purpose flour

Makes 3½ cups (about 750 grams) Biga

½ teaspoon active dry yeast or ⅕ cake (3 to 5 grams) fresh yeast
¼ cup warm water
1¼ cups plus 2 tablespoons water, room temperature
3¾ cups (500 grams) unbleached all-purpose flour

Stir the yeast into the warm water and let stand until creamy, about 10 minutes. Stir in the remaining water and then the flour, 1 cup at a time.

BY HAND   Mix with a wooden spoon for 3 to 4 minutes.

BY MIXER   Mix with the paddle at the lowest speed for 2 minutes.

BY PROCESSOR   Mix just until a sticky dough is formed.

Rising. Remove to a lightly oiled bowl, cover with plastic wrap, and let rise at a cool room temperature for 6 to 24 hours. The starter will triple in volume and still be wet and sticky when ready. Cover and refrigerate until ready to use. When needed, scoop out desired amount.

Both recipes can easily be cut in half.

Pane di Como
Como Bread

This is a spectacularly delicious white bread with a crunchy dome and a feathery floury top that tastes of the sweetness of wheat. It is excellent for breakfast. The loaf is engraved with the delicate pattern of the basket in which it is given its final rise and the interior is honeycombed with irregular holes.

The breads of Como are more than slightly confusing. Both the *ciabatta* and the *pane francese* (recipes follow) are also breads from Como, but this Como bread is what is made and eaten there today.

Makes 2 round loaves

STARTER
1 teaspoon active dry yeast or ⅓ small cake (6 grams) fresh yeast
1 scant teaspoon malt syrup
⅓ cup warm water
⅔ cup milk, room temperature
1 cup (135 grams) unbleached all-purpose flour

Stir the yeast and malt into the water; let stand until foamy, about 10 minutes. Stir in the milk and beat in the flour with a rubber spatula or wooden spoon about 100 strokes until smooth. Cover with plastic wrap and let stand until bubbly, at least 4 hours but preferably overnight.

DOUGH
2 cups water, room temperature
6¼ cups (860 grams) unbleached all-purpose flour
1 tablespoon (15 grams) salt
Cornmeal

BY HAND

Add the water to the starter; mix and squeeze it between your fingers until the starter is fairly well broken up. Mix the flour and salt and stir 2 cups at a time into the starter mixture. When the dough is too stiff to mix with a wooden spoon, just plunge in with your hands. Mix until well blended, 4 to 5 minutes. Knead on a well-floured surface until elastic but still moist and tacky. Once it has come together nicely, crash it down vigorously on the work surface to develop the gluten.

BY MIXER

Mix the starter and the water with the paddle until the starter is well broken up. Add the flour and salt and mix for 2 to 3 minutes at low speed. The dough will be smooth but won't pull away from the side of the bowl. Change to the dough hook and knead at medium speed, scraping down the side of the bowl as necessary, until the dough is elastic but still slightly sticky, 3 to 4 minutes. Finish kneading by hand on a floured work surface.

BY PROCESSOR

Refrigerate the starter until cold. Unless you have a large processor, make the dough in two batches. Place the flour and salt in a food processor fitted with the dough blade and process with several pulses to sift. Place the starter on top of the flour mixture. With the machine running, pour 2 cups cold water through the feed tube and process until the dough comes together and gathers into a ball. Process 30 to 45 seconds longer to knead. Finish kneading on a well-floured surface with well-floured hands. The dough will be tacky and moist.

First Rise. Place in a well-oiled bowl, cover tightly with plastic wrap, and let rise until doubled, about 1½ hours. The dough is ready when it is very bubbly and blistered.

Shaping and Second Rise. Cut the dough in half on a floured surface and shape into 2 round loaves. Place in oiled and floured 8-inch round bannetons or in baskets lined with generously floured kitchen towels. Cover with towels and let rise until fully doubled and risen to the tops of the bannetons, about 1 hour.

Baking. Thirty minutes before baking, heat the oven with a baking stone in it to 400° F. Sprinkle the stone with cornmeal. Very carefully invert the loaves onto the stone and bake until the loaf sounds hollow when the bottom is tapped, about 1 hour. Cool on racks.

Pane di Como Antico o Pane Francese

Como Bread of the Past, Known Today as French Bread

It is said that the legendary taste of Como bread owes a lot to the air and water of the famous lake, but even without those particular ingredients, this bread is a remarkable and delicious loaf with a big-holed chewy interior and a crunchy crust. Today it is known all over Italy as *pane francese*, or French bread. When it was still called Como bread, it was the only food that brought about a rapprochement of sorts between the contentious regions of Lombardy and Piedmont. Each was fiercely proud of its culinary specialties, creating quarrels over every dish and gastronomic tradition, but they did relax their differences long enough to speed this bread from the Paduan plain

Pane di Como Antico (continued)

where it was baked to the far reaches of both areas. I am told that it reached its pinnacle of tastiness on the Sunday bicycle ride from Milan to Como when it was served as a snack after about 25 miles of pedaling.

I based this recipe on one from Giancarlo Grignani, a scholar and master baker in Milan, who researched the bread as it tasted in earlier centuries. He uses a complicated natural yeast for which I have substituted a starter made with a minuscule amount of yeast and mixed with a little whole-wheat flour into the unbleached flour to give it the authentic taste of a time when flours were less refined than today. I have often made this dough and refrigerated it overnight for the second rise; it only gets better with the long cool development of the yeast.

Serve it with stews and meats with rich sauces, with green salads, fresh cheeses, sliced salami, and smoked meats.

Makes 2 long loaves

¾ cup (180 grams) *Biga* (page 100) made with half the yeast
1½ cups water, room temperature
½ cup (65 grams) whole-wheat flour
3 to 3¼ cups (435 grams) unbleached all-purpose flour
2 teaspoons (10 grams) salt
Cornmeal

BY HAND

Cut the starter into small pieces in a large mixing bowl. Add all but 1 to 2 tablespoons of the water and mix until the starter is in fine shreds and the liquid is chalky white. Stir in the whole-wheat flour and most of the all-purpose flour, 1 cup at a time. When the dough is a fairly rough and shaggy mass, stir in the salt dissolved in the remaining water. Knead on a floured surface, sprinkling with up to ½ cup additional flour and using the dough scraper to scrape up the fine film of dough that will accumulate on the work surface, as well as to turn and lift the dough. After about 5 minutes of kneading, slam the dough down hard several times to help develop the gluten. Continue kneading until the dough is smooth, a total of 8 to 12 minutes. The dough should still be soft, moist, and sticky.

BY MIXER

Mix the starter and all but 1 to 2 tablespoons of the water with the paddle in a large mixer bowl. Mix in the flours and then the salt dissolved in the remaining water. Change to the dough hook and knead at medium speed until soft, moist, and sticky but obviously elastic, about 4 minutes. Finish kneading by hand on a floured surface, sprinkling with additional flour, until smooth but still soft.

BY PROCESSOR

Refrigerate the starter until cold. Process the starter and 1½ cups cold water with the steel blade and remove to another bowl. Change to the dough blade and process the flours and salt with 2 or 3 pulses to sift. With the machine running, pour the starter mixture through the feed tube as quickly as the flour can absorb it. Process 30 to 45 seconds longer to knead. The dough will be moist and sticky. Finish kneading by hand on a floured surface, sprinkling with additional flour, until the dough is smooth but still soft.

First Rise. Place the dough in a lightly oiled bowl, cover with plastic wrap, and let rise until doubled, 1½ to 2 hours. The dough is ready when it has numerous bubbles and blisters under the skin.

Shaping and Second Rise. Divide the dough in half on a floured surface without kneading it. Shape into 2 round loaves. Let them relax under a cloth for 20 minutes. Line baking sheets or peels with parchment paper and flour the paper generously. Roll each ball into a fat cylinder and place seam side down on the paper. Dimple the loaves all over with your fingertips or knuckles, as for *focaccia,* to keep the dough from springing up. The dough should feel delicate but extremely springy. Cover the loaves and let rise until doubled, with many visible air bubbles, 1¼ to 1½ hours.

Baking. Thirty minutes before baking, heat the oven with a baking stone in it to 425° F. Sprinkle the baking stone with cornmeal. Carry the peel or baking sheet to the oven and very gently invert the dough onto the stone. Gently remove the parchment paper. (See illustration in *Ciabatta* recipe, page 107.) Immediately reduce the heat to 400° F and bake until golden, 35 to 40 minutes. Cool on racks.

Ciabatta

Slipper-Shaped Bread from Lake Como

I can't think of a way to describe the fabulous and unusual taste of *ciabatta* except to say that once you've eaten it, you'll never think of white bread in the same way again. Everyone who tries this bread loves it. *Ciabatta* means slipper in Italian; one glance at the short stubby bread will make it clear how it was named. *Ciabatta* is a remarkable combination of rustic country texture and elegant and tantalizing taste. It is much lighter than its homely shape would indicate, and the porous chewy interior is enclosed in a slightly crunchy crust that is veiled with flour. Eat for breakfast or slice an entire *ciabatta* horizontally and stuff it with salami and cheese.

This dough should be made in the mixer, although it also works in the processor. I have made it by hand but wouldn't recommend it unless you are willing to knead the wet, sticky mass between your hands—in mid-air—turning, folding, and twisting it rather like taffy, your hands covered with dough. You can't put it on the table because the natural inclination is to add lots of flour to this very sticky dough and pretty soon you wouldn't have a *ciabatta*. Resist the temptation to add flour and follow the instructions. The dough will feel utterly unfamiliar and probably a bit scary. And that's not the only unusual feature—the shaped loaves are flat and look definitely unpromising; even when they are puffed after the second rise, you may feel certain you've done it all wrong. Don't give up. The loaves rise nicely in the oven.

Makes 4 loaves, each about the width of a hand and the length of the arm from wrist to elbow

1 teaspoon active dry yeast or ⅓ small cake (6 grams) fresh yeast
5 tablespoons warm milk
1 cup plus 3 tablespoons water, room temperature
1 tablespoon olive oil
2 cups (500 grams) *Biga* (page 100), made 12 hours before
3¾ cups (500 grams) unbleached all-purpose flour
1 tablespoon (15 grams) salt
Cornmeal

BY MIXER

Stir the yeast into the milk in a mixer bowl; let stand until creamy, about 10 minutes. Add the water, oil, and starter and mix with the paddle until blended. Mix the flour and salt, add to the bowl, and mix for 2 to 3 minutes. Change to the dough hook and knead for 2 minutes at low speed, then 2 minutes at medium speed. Knead briefly on a well-floured surface, adding as little flour as possible, until the dough is velvety, supple, very springy, and moist.

BY PROCESSOR

Refrigerate the starter until cold. Stir the yeast into the milk in a large bowl; let stand until creamy, about 10 minutes. Add 1 cup plus 3 tablespoons cold water, the oil, and starter and mix, squeezing the starter between your fingers to break it up. Place the flour and salt in the food processor fitted with the dough blade and process with several pulses to sift. With the machine running, pour the starter mixture through the feed tube and process until the dough comes together. Process about 45 seconds longer to knead. Finish kneading on a well-floured surface until the dough is velvety, supple, moist, and very springy.

First Rise. Place the dough in an oiled bowl, cover with plastic wrap, and let rise until doubled, about 1¼ hours. The dough should be full of air bubbles, very supple, elastic, and sticky.

Shaping and Second Rise. Cut the dough into 4 equal pieces on a well-floured surface. Roll up each piece into a cylinder, then stretch each into a rectangle, about 10 × 4 inches, pulling with your fingers to get it long and wide enough. Generously flour 4 pieces of parchment paper on peels or baking sheets. Place each loaf, seam side up, on a paper. Dimple the loaves vigorously with your fingertips or knuckles so that they won't rise too much. The dough will look heavily pockmarked, but it is very resilient so don't be concerned. Cover loosely with dampened towels and let rise until puffy but not doubled, 1½ to 2 hours. The loaves will look flat and definitely unpromising but don't give up for they will rise more in the oven.

Baking. Thirty minutes before baking, heat the oven with baking stones in it to 425° F. Just before baking, sprinkle the stones with cornmeal. Carefully invert each loaf onto a stone. If the dough sticks a bit, just work it free from the paper gently. Bake for 20 to 25 minutes, spraying 3 times with water in the first 10 minutes. Cool on racks.

1. Pulling and stretching the dough

2. Dimpling the dough

3. Turning the ciabatta *off parchment onto stone*

Pane all'Olio
Olive Oil Bread

A little good olive oil makes a tasty white bread, especially when the top is sprinkled with granules of sea salt. I am charmed by this shape—little rolls connected in a wreath, each roll broken off and eaten individually. I've also seen the bread made into *manini*, little hands, made by crossing two narrow cylinders of dough at a slight angle, so that it looks like a four-fingered hand. Serve with sliced salami, sausages, smoked meats, roast veal, ham, or *antipasti*.

Makes 2 rings of 6 or 7 rolls each or 12 to 14 individual rolls

2½ teaspoons (1 package) active dry yeast or 1 small cake (18 grams)
   fresh yeast
1 cup plus 3 tablespoons warm water
3 tablespoons plus 1 teaspoon olive oil
2 to 3 teaspoons lard, room temperature
3¾ cups (500 grams) unbleached all-purpose flour
2 teaspoons (10 grams) salt
Sea salt

BY HAND

Stir the yeast into the water in a large mixing bowl; let stand until creamy, about 10 minutes. Stir in the oil and lard, and then the flour and salt until well blended. Knead on a floured surface until elastic and velvety, 8 to 10 minutes.

BY MIXER

Stir the yeast into the water in a mixer bowl; let stand until creamy, about 10 minutes. Stir in the oil and lard with the paddle; then mix in the flour and salt. Change to the dough hook and knead about 5 minutes, half at low and half at medium speed. Scrape down the sides of the bowl as necessary. The dough should be elastic and velvety.

BY PROCESSOR

Stir the yeast into ¼ cup warm water; let stand until creamy, about 10 minutes. Place the flour and salt in a food processor fitted with the steel blade and process with several pulses to sift. Place the lard on top of the flour. With the machine running, pour the 1 cup cold water, the oil, and dissolved yeast through the feed tube and process until the dough gathers into a ball. Process about 40 seconds longer to knead. Finish kneading briefly by hand on a lightly floured surface. The dough should be elastic and velvety.

First Rise. Place the dough in a lightly oiled bowl, cover with plastic wrap, and let rise until doubled, about 2 hours. The dough should be very moist and velvety.

Shaping and Second Rise. Divide the dough into 12 to 14 equal pieces, each about the size of a lime, and shape into small balls. Arrange the balls about 1½ inches apart in 2 free-form circles on oiled or parchment-lined baking sheets, or place in oiled ring molds that have been sprinkled with sea salt. Cover with plastic wrap and then a towel and let rise until doubled, about 1¼ to 1½ hours.

Baking. Heat the oven to 400° F. If you have made the free-form rings, brush the tops of the rolls with olive oil and then sprinkle lightly with sea salt. Bake 35 minutes for the wreath, 20 minutes for individual rolls. Cool on racks.

Balls set in circle prior to baking

The finished rolls baked in a wreath

Variation. To make *manini*, divide dough into 12 to 14 pieces, each about the size of a lime. Roll out each piece lengthwise with a rolling pin into a thin strip, ⅜ to ½ inch thick. Curve 1 strip into a bent half-circle. Arrange another strip across the first so that their centers meet, and curve the strip as you did the first. Roll each piece so that it looks like a four-fingered hand. Bake 20 minutes.

Pane all'Olio shaped as manini

Pane Toscano o Pane Sciocco

Saltless Tuscan Bread

Some cookbook authors insist a bread made without salt could only be flat and insipid, but the Tuscans have been making this saltless bread for many centuries. Dante referred to it in the Paradiso of *The Divine Comedy*: Foreseeing the difficulties of his exile from Florence, he speaks of them figuratively, "You shall learn how salty is the taste of another's bread." The big flat rounds scored in tic-tac-toe patterns or the smaller crusty ovals of bread are sometimes rough and somewhat coarse, sometimes more compact inside, but they are always mellow and bland.

One explanation of the saltless bread is that the Tuscans, well known for being tightfisted, couldn't bear to pay the government salt tax and chose instead to make bread without it. Perhaps, but gastronomes point out that the Tuscan bread is perfectly suited to their cuisine, which is full of strong flavors. Tuscans eat thick slabs of a local prosciutto that is much stronger and saltier than that of other regions, and their *finocchiona* sausages are more highly flavored than other Italian varieties; the saltless Tuscan bread is a perfect foil for both. The sauces for Tuscan meats and stews are extremely spicy and flavorful, and the saltless bread sets a perfect balance when steeped in the gravies. Use Tuscan breads as the Tuscans do: for *fettunta*, a slice of bread grilled or broiled, rubbed with garlic, and then brushed with a fruity olive oil of the first pressing; for *crostini* with chicken livers or game; for highly flavored Tuscan salami and prosciutto; for spicy sauces and gravies with meat. The bread dries out very quickly, but it is very tasty soaked in a dressing or liquid for a salad or soup, such as *panzanella* or *ribollita*.

Makes 1 large ruota *or wheel, or 2 oval loaves*

STARTER
¼ teaspoon active dry yeast or ¹⁄₁₂ small cake (about 1½ grams) fresh yeast
⅔ cup warm water
About 1⅓ cups (175 grams) unbleached all-purpose flour

Stir the yeast into the water in a small bowl; let stand until creamy, about 10 minutes. Add the flour and stir with about 100 strokes of a wooden spoon, or stir with the paddle of an electric mixer for about 1 minute. Cover with plastic wrap and let rise until tripled, 6 hours to overnight.

DOUGH
1¼ teaspoons active dry yeast or ½ small cake (9 grams) fresh yeast
⅓ cup warm water
1 cup water, room temperature
3¾ cups (500 grams) unbleached all-purpose flour
Pinch salt (optional)
Cornmeal

BY HAND

Stir the yeast into the warm water in a large bowl; let stand until creamy, about 10 minutes. Add the starter and 1 cup water and mix well, squeezing the starter between your fingers to break it up. Beat in the flour, 1 cup at a time, and continue beating until the dough is thoroughly mixed, about 4 to 5 minutes. Stir in the salt, if desired, in the last minutes. Turn out onto a well-floured surface and knead, using a dough scraper to begin with, until elastic, resilient, and somewhat velvety, 8 to 10 minutes.

BY MIXER

Stir the yeast into the warm water in a small bowl; let stand until creamy, 10 minutes. Add the dissolved yeast and 1 cup water to the starter in a large mixer bowl and mix with the paddle. Beat in the flour and continue beating until thoroughly mixed, 1 to 2 minutes. Add the salt, if desired, and beat 1 more minute. Change to the dough hook and knead until the dough is elastic, resilient, and somewhat velvety, about 4 minutes. Finish kneading by hand on a floured surface.

BY PROCESSOR

If the capacity of your food processor is 7 cups or less, process this dough in 2 batches. Refrigerate the starter until cold. Stir the yeast into the warm water; let stand until creamy, about 10 minutes. Process the dissolved yeast, cold starter, and 1 cup cold water with the steel blade to the consistency of lumpy pancake batter. Pour the mixture into another container and change to the dough blade without cleaning the bowl. Add the flour and salt, if desired, to the bowl and process with 2 or 3 pulses to sift. With the machine running, pour the starter mixture through the feed tube as quickly as the flour can absorb it and process until the dough gathers into a ball. Process 20 seconds longer to knead. Don't worry if the dough never truly forms a ball, but it should hold its shape and not ooze. Finish kneading by hand on a lightly floured surface until elastic, resilient, and somewhat velvety.

First Rise. Place the dough in an oiled bowl, cover with plastic wrap, and let rise until doubled, about 1 hour.

Pane Toscano (continued)

Shaping and Second Rise. Turn the dough out onto a floured surface and lightly dust the top with flour. The dough will be very moist and soft, but don't punch it down. Flatten it with your hands and shape into a large flat round loaf, or cut it in half and shape each half into an oval. Place on a well-floured baking sheet or peel and gently turn the loaf over to collect some of the flour onto its surface. Turn it again, smooth side up, cover with a towel, and let rise until doubled, 45 minutes to 1¼ hours.

Baking. Thirty minutes before baking, heat the oven with a baking stone in it to 450° F. If you have shaped the dough into a single large wheel, score a tic-tac-toe pattern on top with a razor or sharp bread knife. Just before baking, sprinkle the stone with cornmeal and slide the loaf onto it. Bake 15 minutes. Reduce the heat to 400° F, and bake 20 minutes for the smaller ovals and 25 to 30 minutes for the large *ruota*. Cool on a rack.

Pane Toscano Scuro

Dark Tuscan Bread

A very common variation of the traditional saltless Tuscan bread is made with whole wheat. This recipe comes from Giovanni Galli, a wonderful Florentine baker, who showed me how Tuscan housewives made this bread. This is not a wet, sticky dough of the bakeries but a typical country loaf.

When it gets stale—and it will very quickly—use it for *panzanella*, the bread salad which starts with bread soaked in oil and vinegar, and for *pappa al pomodoro*, the vegetable soup thickened with bread and served in Tuscany in place of pasta.

Makes 1 large ruota *or* wheel, *or 2 oval loaves*

STARTER
1 teaspoon active dry yeast or scant ⅓ small cake (6 grams) fresh yeast
⅔ cup warm water
1⅓ cups (175 grams) unbleached all-purpose flour

Stir the yeast into the water; let stand until creamy, about 10 minutes. Add the flour and stir with 100 strokes of a wooden spoon, or stir with the paddle of an electric mixer for 1 minute. Cover with plastic wrap and let rise until tripled, 6 hours to overnight.

DOUGH

1¼ teaspoons active dry yeast or ½ small cake (9 grams) fresh yeast
⅓ cup warm water
1 cup water, room temperature
¼ cup (30 grams) unbleached all-purpose flour
3¾ cups (475 grams) stone-ground whole-wheat flour
Cornmeal

BY HAND

Stir the yeast into the warm water in a large mixing bowl; let stand until creamy, about 10 minutes. Add 1 cup water and the starter. Stir vigorously or squeeze the mixture between your fingers to break the starter up. Stir in the flours, 2 cups at a time, and continue stirring until thoroughly mixed. Flour a work surface well with all-purpose flour and knead the dough on the surface until firm and resilient, 8 to 10 minutes.

BY MIXER

Stir the yeast into the warm water in a mixer bowl; let stand until creamy, about 10 minutes. Add 1 cup water and the starter and mix with the paddle until the starter is broken up. Add the flours and mix until the dough comes together. Change to the dough hook and knead until firm and elastic, 3 to 4 minutes. Finish kneading briefly by hand on a surface floured with all-purpose flour.

First Rise. Place the dough in a lightly oiled bowl, cover tightly with plastic wrap, and let rise until doubled, 1 to 1½ hours.

Shaping and Second Rise. Turn the dough out onto a floured surface, flatten it gently to expel some of the air, and then shape into a flat round loaf or 2 oval loaves. Place on a cornmeal-sprinkled peel or an oiled baking sheet. Dust the top lightly with flour, cover with a very lightly dampened towel, and let rise until doubled, 45 minutes to 1 hour.

Scoring the pattern

Baking. Heat the oven to 450° F. If you are using a baking stone, turn the oven on 30 minutes before baking, and sprinkle the stone with cornmeal just before sliding the loaf onto it. Score the top of the single large loaf in a tic-tac-toe pattern with a razor or sharp bread knife. Bake 15 minutes. Reduce the heat to 400° F and bake the smaller loaves 20 minutes and the large *ruota* 25 to 30 minutes. Cool on a rack.

Variation. For a lighter loaf, use 1 scant cup (125 grams) whole wheat flour and 2¾ cups (375 grams) all-purpose unbleached flour.

Pane di Terni
Terni Bread

This wonderful rustic bread from Terni, a largish city in southern Umbria, is in such great demand that quantities of it are rushed to Rome daily. Traditionally a saltless bread, it tastes delicious with a bit of salt added. This is yet another exceptionally good country bread with a light crunchy crust, but the interior of the *pane di Terni* is a bit different from most because its close texture is honeycombed with larger holes. *Pane di Terni* makes wonderful toast and can be used in such Umbrian soups as *acquacotta* and *pancotto*.

Makes 4 round loaves

$^1\!/_2$ teaspoon active dry yeast or $^1\!/_{10}$ small cake (2 grams) fresh yeast
$^1\!/_3$ cup warm water
1 cup water, room temperature
3$^1\!/_2$ cups (750 grams) *Biga* (page 100), made with half the amount of
   yeast
1$^1\!/_2$ cups (180 grams) whole-wheat pastry flour
2$^1\!/_4$ to 2$^1\!/_2$ cups (320 grams) unbleached all-purpose flour
4 teaspoons (20 grams) salt (optional)
Cornmeal

BY HAND

Stir the yeast into the warm water; let stand until creamy, about 10 minutes. Add 1 cup water and the starter; stir with a rubber spatula or wooden spoon or squeeze the mixture between your fingers to break up the starter. Stir in the whole-wheat flour. Add the all-purpose flour and the salt, if desired, and mix first with a spoon and then with your hands until the dough comes together. Knead on a floured surface until firm and elastic, about 8 to 10 minutes.

BY MIXER

Stir the yeast into the warm water in a large mixer bowl; let stand until creamy, about 10 minutes. Add 1 cup water and the starter and mix with the paddle until the starter is fairly well broken up. Add the flours and salt, if desired. Mix until the dough comes together and then for 1 minute longer. Change to the dough hook and knead until the dough is firm and elastic, about 3 minutes. Finish kneading briefly by hand on a floured surface.

BY PROCESSOR

If your work bowl is 7 cups or smaller, process the dough in 2 batches. Refrigerate the starter until cold. Stir the yeast into the warm water; let stand about 10 minutes. Place the flours and salt, if desired, in a food processor fitted with the steel or dough blade and process with 3 pulses to sift. Mix the dissolved yeast and 1 cup cold water. With the machine running, quickly pour the yeast mixture and then the starter through the feed tube. Process 30 seconds longer to knead. Finish kneading by hand on a floured surface until firm and elastic, 1 to 3 minutes.

Rising. Place the dough in an oiled bowl, cover tightly with plastic wrap, and let rise until doubled, 2 to 3 hours.

Shaping and Second Rise. Divide the dough into 4 equal pieces on a floured surface and shape each piece into a round loaf. Cut 4 pieces of parchment paper and place on baking sheets; flour the paper. Place the loaves, rough side up, on the paper. Cover loosely with towels and let rest for 30 minutes. Dimple the loaves with your fingertips or knuckles; then oil the tops lightly and cover with plastic wrap. Let rise until very blistered with sizable air bubbles visible, about 2 hours. Remove the plastic wrap for the last 10 to 15 minutes of rising time to allow the loaves to develop a slight skin.

Baking. Thirty minutes before baking, heat the oven with baking stones in it to 400° F. Just before baking, sprinkle the stones with cornmeal. Very gently invert each loaf onto a stone and remove the parchment paper. Bake until golden brown, 35 to 40 minutes, spraying the loaves with water 3 times in the first 10 minutes. Cool on racks.

Oiling the dimpled tops

Coccodrillo
Crocodile Bread

This bread, named for its shape, was dreamed up about thirty years ago by Gianfranco Anelli, a baker in Rome. It is his favorite bread and, judging from the numbers of people who come from all over the city to buy it, it may be his most popular as well. At the bakery it takes two days to make; I suggest that you start it in the morning, work at it again for ten minutes in the evening, and finish the next day. I actually prefer to stretch the process over three days because the flavor is even better. Three days may seem formidable, but the working time of the first two days is only 5 to 10 minutes.

This is one dough that you will find difficult to make without an electric mixer, for it requires thirty minutes of continuous stirring for the final dough—of course you could enlist help. The result is an extremely light bread with a crunchy dark-speckled crust and a very chewy interior. The bread stays fresh for an amazing number of days.

Makes 2 large loaves

FIRST STARTER
$\frac{1}{2}$ teaspoon active dry yeast or $\frac{1}{6}$ small cake (3 grams) fresh yeast
1 cup warm water
$\frac{1}{4}$ cup (35 grams) durum flour
$\frac{3}{4}$ cup (90 grams) unbleached stone-ground flour

The morning of the first day, stir the yeast into the water; let stand until creamy, about 10 minutes. Add the flours and stir with a wooden spoon about 50 strokes or with the paddle of an electric mixer about 30 seconds. Cover with plastic wrap and let rise 12 to 24 hours. The starter should be bubbly.

SECOND STARTER
1¼ teaspoons active dry yeast or ½ small cake (9 grams) fresh yeast
¼ cup warm water
1¼ cups water, room temperature
½ cup (70 grams) durum flour
1½ cups (180 grams) unbleached stone-ground flour

The evening of the same day or the next morning, stir the yeast into the warm water; let stand until creamy, about 10 minutes. Add the water, flours and dissolved yeast to the first starter and stir, using a spatula or wooden spoon or the paddle of the electric mixer until smooth. Cover with plastic wrap and let rise 12 to 24 hours.

DOUGH
¼ cup (35 grams) durum flour
1 to 1¼ cups (120 to 140 grams) unbleached stone-ground flour
1½ tablespoons (25 grams) salt

BY MIXER

The next day, add the durum flour and 1 cup unbleached flour to the starter in a mixer bowl; mix with the paddle on the lowest speed for 17 minutes. Add the salt and mix 3 minutes longer, adding the remaining flour if needed for the dough to come together. You may need to turn the mixer off once or twice to keep it from overheating.

BY HAND

If you decide to make this dough by hand, place the starter, durum flour, and 1 cup unbleached flour in a widemouthed bowl. Stir with a rubber spatula or wooden spoon for 25 to 30 minutes; then add the salt and remaining flour if needed and stir 5 minutes longer. The dough is very wet and will not be kneaded.

First Rise. Pour the dough into a Hammarplast bowl or a widemouthed large bowl placed on an open trivet on legs or on a wok ring so that air can circulate all around it. Loosely drape a towel over the top and let rise at about 70° F, turning the dough over in the bowl every hour, until just about tripled, 4 or 5 hours.

Shaping and Second Rise. Pour the wet dough onto a generously floured surface. Have a mound of flour nearby to flour your hands, the top of the oozy dough, and the work surface itself. This will all work fine—appearances to the contrary—but be prepared for an unusually wet dough. Make a big round shape of it by just folding and tucking the edges under a bit. Please don't try to shape it precisely; it's a hopeless task and quite unnecessary. Place the dough on well-floured parchment or brown paper placed on a baking sheet or peel. Cover with a dampened towel and let rise until very blistered and full of air bubbles, about 45 minutes.

Make the final cut just before baking.

Baking. Thirty minutes before baking, heat the oven with a baking stone in it to 475° F. Just before baking, cut the dough in half down the center with a dough scraper; a knife would tear the dough. Gently slide the 2 pieces apart and turn so that the cut surfaces face upward. Sprinkle the stone with cornmeal. If you feel brave, slide the paper with the dough on it onto the stone, but the dough can also be baked directly on the baking sheet. When the dough has set, slide the paper out. Bake for about 30 to 35 minutes. Cool on a rack.

Pane di Genzano

Genzano Bread

When this bread is baked in the brick ovens of Genzano, a small city in the once castle-filled countryside just south of Rome, it has an almost black crust. Baked at home in a conventional oven, the fine dusting of bran that coats the dough gives it a golden to deep brown color. This is one of those good country breads made with a wet Italian dough, which is best left to the mixer, although you can use a food processor. Be sure to flour everything that comes in contact with the dough: the work surface, the dough scraper, and especially your hands. "The wetter the dough, the better the bread," one of the best bakers I know told me. Also, the longer the rise, the better the taste—let this bread develop slowly at a cool (70° F) room temperature. *Pane di Genzano* is wonderful toasted, as well as served with salads, cheeses, and smoked meats.

Makes 1 round loaf

1 teaspoon yeast or ⅓ small cake (6 grams) fresh yeast
⅓ cup warm water
1⅓ cups minus 1 tablespoon water, room temperature
About 3 cups (400 grams) unbleached all-purpose flour
¾ cup plus or minus 1 tablespoon (100 grams) pastry flour, white
  or whole wheat
2 teaspoons (10 grams) salt
½ cup bran

BY MIXER

Stir the yeast into the warm water in a mixer bowl; let stand until creamy, about 10 minutes. Stir in the remaining water. Add the flours and salt and mix with the paddle for 2 to 3 minutes. Change to the dough hook and knead for 5 to 6 minutes, half at low speed, then half at medium. You'll probably have to stop the machine and scrape down the dough from the collar of the hook several times. The dough should be extremely soft, velvety, and moist. You can pour the dough directly into an oiled bowl for the first rise, or first knead the dough briefly with well-floured hands and a dough scraper on a well-floured surface.

BY PROCESSOR

Stir the yeast into the warm water; let stand until creamy, about 10 minutes. Place the flours and salt in a food processor fitted with the dough blade and process with 2 or 3 pulses to sift. With the machine running, pour the cold water and the dissolved yeast through the feed tube as quickly as the flour can absorb it and process until the dough comes together. Process 45 seconds longer to knead. Finish kneading with well-floured hands and a dough scraper on a well-floured surface. The dough should be extremely soft, velvety, and moist.

First Rise. Place the dough in a lightly oiled bowl, cover with plastic wrap, and let rise until tripled, 3 to 5 hours. While the dough is rising, grind the bran extremely fine in a blender. Lightly oil an 8- or 9-inch pie plate with sloping sides and coat the bottom with ¼ cup of the bran.

Shaping and Second Rise. Flour the work surface and your hands very well and pour the sticky dough onto the surface. Shape the dough loosely into a round loaf; don't worry if it is not perfectly or tightly shaped. Place the dough in the prepared pie plate and gingerly pat the remaining bran around the sides and over the top of the dough so that it is completely covered. Cover the dough with a towel and let rise at a cool room temperature until at least doubled, 1½ to 2 hours. Even when the dough has more than completely filled the pie plate and risen to a dome, it will shake like jello when you jiggle it.

Baking. This is a perfect bread to bake in Sassafras's La Cloche if you have one. Thirty minutes before baking, heat the oven with the *cloche* top and bottom or a baking stone in it to 425° F. If you are using the *cloche,* place the pie plate in the bottom and cover it with the top; if not, place the pie plate on the baking stone. Bake for 40 to 45 minutes. Remove the top for the last 10 to 15 minutes so the crust can brown. Because the bran makes it so difficult to test the bread for doneness (tapping the bottom gets you a handful of loose bran), try using a cake tester to see if it comes out clean or insert an instant-reading thermometer and check if the bread in the middle has reached 210° F. Immediately turn the loaf out of the plate onto a rack to cool.

Pane Tipo Altamura

Durum-Flour Bread from Altamura

The golden bread of Altamura, a handsome town in the region of Puglia on the heel of the Italian boot, is famous all over Italy. Made of the high-gluten durum wheat that grows across the Tavoliere plain, the bread is typically rustic with a hard crust but chewy interior that exudes the intense, pungent smell and taste of the wheat.

Initially a baker from Puglia who was working in Florence taught me this version, which must be called *tipo Altamura*, or Altamura type, and has a delicate, fine-textured interior. When I ate the bread in Altamura, however, I discovered a much chewier and more rustic loaf. There Vito Forte makes a starter that becomes essentially natural yeast after three refreshings. I'm not sure any but the most impassioned bakers would go to the trouble of making it, but it is certainly popular in Italy—Forte uses 10,000 kilos of flour for each day's baking.

Durum flour, the golden hard wheat used for making pasta, can be found in specialty food shops and some health food stores, which carry it for home pasta makers. You can also order it by mail from the sources listed on page 421.

This bread keeps wonderfully and is splendid toasted. Eat it simply spread with butter or serve it with fish or vegetable soups or meat with gravies or sauces.

Makes 2 oval loaves

1¼ teaspoons active dry yeast or ½ small cake (9 grams) fresh yeast
¼ cup warm water
1¾ cups water, room temperature
1½ cups (375 grams) Biga (page 100)
About 5½ cups (750 grams) durum flour
1 tablespoon (15 to 20 grams) salt
Unbleached all-purpose flour for kneading

BY HAND

Stir the yeast into the warm water; let stand until creamy, about 10 minutes. Mix the dissolved yeast, remaining water, and the starter in a large mixing bowl, squeezing the starter between your fingers to break it up and stirring vigorously with a wooden spoon. Mix the durum flour and salt and stir 2 cups at a time into the yeast mixture; plunge in with your hands when the mixture becomes too stiff to stir. Knead on a surface sprinkled with all-purpose flour until the dough is smooth, elastic, slightly moist, and very blistered, about 10 minutes. Slam the dough on the surface while kneading to develop the gluten.

BY MIXER

Stir the yeast into 2 cups warm water in a large mixer bowl; let stand until creamy, about 10 minutes. Add the starter and mix with the paddle until the starter is broken up and the liquid is chalky white. Add the durum flour and salt and mix until the dough pulls away from the side of the bowl, about 2 minutes. Don't add extra water, although you will be tempted, for this flour absorbs moisture slowly. If after mixing for 2 minutes it still seems dry, mix in 1 teaspoon water at a time. Change to the dough hook and knead 2 minutes on low, then 3 to 4 minutes on medium speed. The dough should be smooth to the touch but very blistered on top. It will feel like Silly Putty and be slightly tacky even when fully kneaded. Knead lightly by hand on a surface floured with all-purpose flour.

BY PROCESSOR

If the capacity of your food processor is 7 cups or less, process this dough in 2 batches. Refrigerate the starter until cold. Stir the yeast into the warm water; let stand until creamy, about 10 minutes. Process 1¾ cups cold water and the starter with the steel blade to mix. Remove the starter mixture to another bowl. Change to the dough blade and process the flour and salt with 2 or 3 pulses to sift. With the machine running, pour the dissolved yeast and starter mixture through the feed tube as fast as the flour can absorb it and process until the dough comes together. Process 45 seconds longer to knead. Finish kneading on a surface floured with all-purpose flour. The dough should be elastic, slightly moist, and very blistered.

First Rise. Place the dough in a lightly oiled bowl, cover with plastic wrap, and let rise until doubled, about 1¾ to 2 hours.

Shaping and Second Rise. Turn out onto a lightly floured work surface and cut the dough in half. Shape each piece first into a round, then to an oval that is higher and plumper in the center and slightly tapered at the ends. Make a deep slash down the middle of each loaf with a razor. Let rise, cut side down and covered with a towel, on a well-floured board or peel until doubled, 45 minutes to 1 hour.

Cutting a deep slash

Baking. Thirty minutes before baking, heat the oven with a baking stone in it to 400° F. Turn the dough over and cut the slash again if it has closed during the rise. Sprinkle the stone with cornmeal and gently slide the loaf, cut side up, onto the stone. Bake 35 minutes. Cool on a rack.

Pane Pugliese
Bread of Puglia

These big, crusty wheels of country bread originated from much darker loaves, a legacy of Turkish conquerors who baked their chewy porous bread in wood-burning stoves. In Italy, today, they still bow to tradition by making these loaves with less refined flours. To me they are the best of all possible rustic breads, perfect for picnics and informal eating. Baked in huge one- or two-kilo rounds, they are then held against the chest and sliced towards the body with a sharp knife. The sizable hunks are dropped into soup or flavored with oil, salt, strong ricotta, and tomatoes. Because this is the bread of the poor, it is served with the typical food of the region: greens, fish from the sea, cheese, and fruit. More prosperous Italians eat it with stews and meats with strong-flavored sauces and gravies, steaks, and even *carpaccio*. Reverence for this bread still persists, as does the Pugliese legend that one who wasted even crumbs of this loaf would be condemned to Purgatory for as many years as there were crumbs. One embellishment insists that the sinner would spend the time collecting the crumbs with his eyelids.

This bread is best made in the mixer, for the wet dough takes incredible skill and an extraordinary amount of flour when done by hand. Once you've made it—and please don't be daunted by the advice about the oozing doughs; it is just meant to guide you realistically through the process—you'll find that it isn't difficult if you keep enough flour at hand.

Makes 2 large round flat loaves or 3 smaller round loaves

1¼ teaspoons active dry yeast or ½ small cake (9 grams) fresh yeast
¼ cup warm water
3 cups water, room temperature
⅘ cup (200 grams) *Biga* (page 100)
7½ cups (1000 grams) unbleached all-purpose flour
1 tablespoon plus 1 teaspoon (20 grams) salt

BY MIXER

Stir the yeast into the warm water in a large mixer bowl; let stand until creamy, about 10 minutes. Add 3 cups water and the starter and mix with the paddle until well blended. Add the flour and salt and mix until the dough comes together and pulls away from the side of the bowl, 1 to 2 minutes. You may need to add another 1 to 2 tablespoons flour. Change to the dough hook and knead at medium speed for 3 to 5 minutes. The dough will be very soft and elastic but will never pull entirely away from the bottom of the bowl. If you want, finish kneading by hand on a floured surface with floured hands until the dough loses its stickiness and is soft and velvety, about 1 minute.

First Rise. Place the dough in a lightly oiled large bowl or plastic tub, cover tightly with plastic wrap, and let rise until tripled, about 3 hours. Do not punch down.

Shaping and Second Rise. Flour your work surface generously, flour a dough scraper, and have a mound of flour nearby for your hands. Pour the dough out of the bowl, flour the top, and cut into 2 or 3 equal pieces, depending on how many loaves you are planning. Flatten each piece of dough and roll it up lengthwise, using your thumbs as a guide for how tight the rolls should be. Turn the dough 90°, pat it flat, then roll up again still using your thumbs as a guide. Shape each piece into a ball by rolling the dough between your cupped hands and using the surface of the work table to generate tension and pull the dough taut across the skin of the dough. Place the loaves on floured parchment paper set on baking sheets or peels, cover with a heavy towel or cloth, and let rise until doubled, about 1 hour.

1. *Roll dough lengthwise, using thumbs.*

2. *Give 90° turn, pat flat, then roll again.*

3. *Shape into taut, springy rounds.*

Baking. Thirty minutes before baking, heat the oven with baking stones in it to 450° F. Five to ten minutes before baking, flour the tops of the loaves and dimple them all over with your fingertips. The imprints will disappear but will keep the bread from rising crazily in the oven. Let stand 5 to 10 minutes. The loaves will feel as soft as a baby's bottom when ready to bake, although you will notice a bit of resistance in the dough. Sprinkle the stones with cornmeal. Italian bakers turn the doughs over into the oven very carefully with a swooping motion that scoops up some of the flour on the peel. You may prefer to slide the loaves onto the baking stones without turning them over, or, if they are on baking sheets, the loaves can be baked directly on the pans. Bake until golden brown and crusty, about 50

Pane Pugliese (continued)

to 60 minutes for the larger loaves, 30 to 35 minutes for the smaller ones. Check by knocking on the bottom of each loaf and listening for the hollow ring that indicates it is cooked through, but, if you're in doubt, bake for the longer time indicated. Cool on racks.

Variation. To make *puccia,* the traditional olive-studded bread of Puglia, knead a scant 8 ounces pitted small salty black olives into the dough after it has been mixed. Let the dough rise until tripled. Divide into pieces the size of a lemon (7 ounces or 200 grams) and roll each piece into a ball. Let rise again covered until doubled and bake at 425° F for 20 to 30 minutes.

Pane Siciliano
Sicilian Bread

One of my favorite memories of Sicily is of the hill town of Erice, which is perched so far above the sea that the weather changes three times on the way up. We first found it on a fog-shrouded night when the only person visible was an ancient hunter carrying an even more ancient blunderbuss. Next morning the sun came out and people appeared in the shops and *piazze.* At breakfast we had the most wonderful golden semolina bread sprinkled with sesame seeds. We ventured on to the bakery, where we found that the bread came in an extravagant variety of forms. *Mafalda,* the most common, looks like a snake curled back and forth over itself with a baton laid across it; made without the baton, it's called a *scaletta,* or little ladder. The shape that looks like a slightly askew pair of eyeglasses is actually in homage to Santa Lucia, the patron saint of vision.

All the loaves have a golden crust with crunchy sesame seeds that give a faint peanutlike taste to the bread. The Sicilians make it with a semolina flour milled especially for the bread, but because our semolina is coarser than theirs, I use durum flour. If you can't find any durum flour, pulverize fine semolina processed specifically for pasta making and all-purpose flour in your blender to a silky flour. Don't use the coarse semolina, for it simply won't make bread. This bread is especially good with sausages, salami, oysters, and mussels.

Makes 2 loaves

2½ teaspoons active dry yeast or 1 small cake (18 grams) fresh yeast
¼ cup warm water
1 tablespoon olive oil
1 teaspoon malt syrup
1 cup water, room temperature
About 2½ cups (350 grams) durum flour or very fine semolina for pasta
1 cup plus 1 tablespoon (150 grams) unbleached all-purpose flour
2 to 3 teaspoons (10 to 15 grams) salt
⅓ cup sesame seeds

BY HAND

Dissolve the yeast in the warm water in a large mixing bowl; let stand until creamy, about 10 minutes. Whisk in the oil, malt, and 1 cup water. Mix the flours and salt and whisk 1 cup at a time into the yeast mixture. Beat vigorously with a wooden spoon until smooth. Knead on a floured surface 8 to 10 minutes, occasionally slamming the dough down vigorously to develop the gluten.

BY MIXER

Stir the yeast into 1¼ cups warm water in a large mixer bowl; let stand until creamy, about 10 minutes. Stir in the oil and malt with the paddle; then add the flours and salt and mix until smooth. Change to the dough hook and knead on medium speed until the dough is firm, compact, and elastic with lots of body, 4 to 5 minutes. Finish kneading by hand on a lightly floured surface.

BY PROCESSOR

Stir the yeast and malt into the warm water; let stand until foamy, about 10 minutes. Place the flours and salt in a food processor fitted with the steel blade; process with 2 or 3 pulses to sift. Mix 1 cup cold water and the oil. With the machine running, pour the yeast and water mixtures through the feed tube as quickly as possible and process until the dough comes together. Process 45 seconds longer to knead. Finish kneading briefly by hand on a lightly floured surface.

First Rise. Place the dough in a lightly oiled bowl, cover tightly with plastic wrap, and let rise until doubled, about 1½ hours. The dough should be springy and blistered but still soft and velvety.

Pane Siciliano (continued)

Shaping and Second Rise. Punch the dough down, knead it briefly, and let it rest for 5 minutes. Flatten it with your forearm into a square. Roll it into a long, fairly narrow rope, about 20 to 22 inches long. The dough should be so elastic that it could almost be swung and stretched like a jump rope. Cut the dough in half and shape each half into a loaf, choosing from the following shapes:

To form the classic Mafalda:

1. Curl rope back and forth on itself; leave a 5-inch tail for the baton.

2. Lay the baton over the top without stretching. Do not tuck it under or the loaf will not rise.

To form into the shape of an eye:

1. Roll the dough into a 1½-inch-thick rope, then coil into a figure that looks like an inverted "S."

2. Continue the coiling from each end until ends meet.

To form into a crown or corona:

1. Flatten the dough into a rectangle and score three times at equal intervals.

2. Pull apart slightly.

Place the loaves on floured parchment paper, peels sprinkled with cornmeal, or oiled baking sheets. Brush the entire surface of each loaf lightly with water and sprinkle with sesame seeds; pat the seeds very gently into the dough. Cover with plastic wrap and then a kitchen towel, and let rise until doubled, 1 to 1½ hours.

Baking. Thirty minutes before baking heat the oven with baking stones to 425° F. Sprinkle the stones with cornmeal just before sliding the loaves onto them. Bake 10 minutes, spraying 3 times with water. Reduce the heat to 400° F and bake 25 to 30 minutes longer. Cool on racks.

The baked Mafalda

The baked Occhi di Santa Lucia

The baked Corona

Tastes of the Countryside

Pan Bigio

Whole-Wheat Bread

When I hear bakers reminisce about rustic country bread before the flour became weak and overly refined and the water was treated with chemicals, this is the bread I think of. Big-holed and chewy with a porous interior and a good firm crust, *pan bigio* is the classic bread of peasants. It is wonderful with everything from green salad to soft fresh cheeses, from a handful of good salty olives to fresh tomatoes drizzled with olive oil and sprinkled with herbs. The brownish color comes from the whole wheat and its good earthy smell and taste from the long, slow maturing of the dough. This wet dough is better left to the mixer but is not impossible to do by hand.

Makes 2 large or 3 smaller round loaves

1¼ teaspoons active dry yeast or ½ small cake (9 grams) fresh yeast
¼ cup warm water
2½ cups water, room temperature
1 cup (250 grams) *Biga* (page 100)
Scant 2 cups (250 grams) whole-wheat flour, preferably stone ground
3¾ cups (500 grams) unbleached all-purpose flour
1 tablespoon (15 grams) salt (1 teaspoon more, optional)

BY MIXER

Stir the yeast into the warm water in a mixer bowl; let stand until creamy, about 10 minutes. Add 2½ cups water and the starter and mix with the paddle until the water is chalky white and the starter is fairly well broken up. Add the flours and salt and mix until the dough comes together. You may need to add up to 2 tablespoons more flour, but the dough will never pull clean away from the side and bottom of the bowl. Change to the dough hook and knead a full 5 minutes at medium speed. Finish kneading the sticky, wet dough by hand on a well-floured surface, sprinkling the top with about 3 to 4 more tablespoons of flour.

BY HAND

Stir the yeast into ¼ cup warm water in a large mixing bowl; let stand until creamy, about 10 minutes. Add 2½ cups water and the starter; squeeze the starter between your fingers to break it up and stir vigorously. Mix the flours and salt and stir 2 cups at a time into the yeast mixture; beat with a wooden spoon for 4 to 5 minutes. Flour your work surface generously, flour a dough scraper, and have a mound of flour nearby for your hands. Turn the dough out onto the floured surface and, with the help of the dough scraper and extra flour, turn and knead the dough until it gradually loses its stickiness, although it will remain wet.

First Rise. Place the dough in a lightly oiled large bowl, cover tightly with plastic wrap, and let rise until tripled and full of air bubbles, about 3 hours. Do not punch down.

Shaping and Second Rise. Turn the dough out onto a well-floured surface and shape into 2 big flat rounds or 3 smaller ones, pulling tight on the surface of the dough with your cupped hands to make a taut loaf. Place the loaves, rough side up, on well-floured baking sheets, peels, or parchment paper set on baking sheets. Cover with a towel and let rise until there are lots of air bubbles under the skin, about 1 hour.

Baking. Thirty minutes before baking, heat the oven with baking stones in it to 450° F. You can also use a cast-iron or aluminum griddle that is at least ⅜ inch thick or preheated heavy baking sheets. Dimple the tops of the loaves all over with your fingertips or knuckles, and let rest for 10 to 15 minutes. Just before baking, sprinkle the stones or griddle with cornmeal. Gently invert the loaves onto the stones. The bread will look deflated when you initially put it in, but it will puff up like a big pillow in no time. Bake for 45 to 55 minutes. Cool on racks.

Pan Giallo o Pan di Mais

Corn Bread from Lombardy

This Italian corn bread is not at all like the crumbly rich bread of the American South, which is sweetened with sugar, enriched with butter, and leavened with baking powder. The Italian bread is dense and firm and is traditionally eaten with soups or rich broths after it has dried out for 3 to 4 days. Long ago, it was made in huge wheels of one and one-half or two kilos, but now, even in Lombardy, where it is still popular, the dough is baked in much smaller loaves. Corn grows in the northern sections of Italy—the Veneto, Piedmont, and Lombardy—and corn breads, like polenta, are quite heavy and rich with the taste of the corn. For a slightly less dense bread, the Italians use half cornmeal and half flour. This bread is often cut in big slices and dipped in beef broth with lots of Parmesan cheese or spread with Gorgonzola, warmed in the oven, and served with an aperitif.

Makes 2 round loaves

5 teaspoons (2 packages) active dry yeast or 2 small cakes (36 grams) fresh yeast
2 cups minus 2 tablespoons warm water
½ cup olive oil
3¾ cups (600 grams) cornmeal, preferably stone ground and not degerminated
About 3 cups (400 grams) unbleached all-purpose flour
1 tablespoon (15 grams) salt

This bread is just not worth the effort of making by hand, although it can be done if you have enormous patience. You must keep breaking the dough into little pieces, adding flour, then letting it rest, because it exudes water as it relaxes. Because it can take as long as 30 minutes, I strongly recommend the electric mixer.

BY MIXER Stir the yeast into the water in a large mixer bowl; let stand until creamy, about 10 minutes. Stir in the oil; then mix in the cornmeal, flour, and salt with the paddle until the dough comes together. Change to the dough hook and knead for 3 to 4 minutes. Finish kneading briefly by hand on a lightly floured work surface.

BY PROCESSOR Process this dough in 2 batches. Stir the yeast into ¼ cup warm water in a small bowl; let stand until creamy, about 10 minutes. Place the cornmeal, flour, and salt in a food processor fitted with the dough blade and process with several pulses to sift. Mix the oil and 1¾ cups minus 2 tablespoons cold water. With the machine running, pour the dissolved yeast and cold water mixture through the feed tube as fast as possible. Process 45 seconds to knead. Finish kneading by hand on a lightly floured surface. The dough should be soft but not wet; it will stick to your hands a bit.

First Rise. Place the dough in a lightly oiled bowl, cover tightly with plastic wrap, and let rise until doubled, about 1 hour.

Shaping and Second Rise. Cut the dough in half on a floured surface and shape each piece into a round loaf. Place in buttered 4-cup charlotte molds or soufflé dishes, sprinkle the tops lightly with flour, cover with a towel, and let rise about 45 minutes. It must not double in volume or it will collapse in the oven.

Baking. Heat the oven to 400° F. Just before baking, cut a pattern, either a tic-tac-toe or 3 parallel lines, on top of the loaves. Bake for 30 minutes. (It will be slightly underdone but corn dries out as it cools.) You may bake the loaves out of the molds on a baking sheet or stone for the last 5 to 10 minutes to brown the bottoms and sides. Cool on racks.

Pane Nero
Rye Bread from Bolzano

You can taste a strong German influence in the dark rye of Bolzano, just as the city, tight against the high Alps near the border of the country, is still at least as Middle European as it is Italian. Street signs and shop names are in both German and Italian, and the alpine look of the architecture is a continual reminder that the city was part of the south Tirol of Austria before World War I. Rye thrives in these cold northern regions where wheat cannot grow. This bread is traditionally flavored with caraway seeds and put to rise in bannetons.

Rye breads are always made with some wheat flour so that they will rise nicely, for there isn't much gluten in rye flour to hold the bubbles of fermenting gases. Because rye always makes sticky doughs, be prepared with your dough scraper at hand. The traditional four holes poked in the top of the dough let the loaf expand without cracking, as well as give it an interesting and characteristic look.

Italians serve rye breads with butter, fresh cheeses, game, mushrooms, caviar, smoked salmon, oysters, and other mollusks.

Makes 2 oval loaves

SPONGE
4¼ teaspoons active dry yeast or 1⅔ small cakes (30 grams) fresh
  yeast
1½ cups warm water
2 cups plus 2 tablespoons (250 grams) rye flour

Stir the yeast into the water in a large mixing bowl; let stand until creamy, about 10 minutes. Stir in the flour until blended. Cover with plastic wrap and let rise at room temperature at least 3 hours or overnight. The longer it is left, the stronger its taste will be.

DOUGH
1 cup water, room temperature
1 tablespoon malt syrup
2 cups plus 2 tablespoons (250 grams) rye flour
3¾ cups (500 grams) unbleached all-purpose flour
1 tablespoon (15 grams) salt
2½ teaspoons caraway seeds or 1½ teaspoons fennel seeds, crushed

BY HAND

Add the water and malt to the sponge and stir thoroughly. Stir in 1 cup of the rye and then the all-purpose flour, 1 cup at a time, until the dough is too stiff to stir. Using your hands, mix in the remaining all-purpose flour, then the remaining rye, the salt, and caraway or fennel seeds. When the dough is no longer impossibly sticky, turn it out onto a well-floured surface and knead for 8 to 10 minutes. The dough will be dense and sticky at first, but, as kneading proceeds, it will become more workable. Use the dough scraper and sprinkle with additional all-purpose flour as needed. When you are almost finished, slam the dough down hard 4 or 5 times while you are working it to help develop the gluten.

BY MIXER

Add the water and malt to the sponge in a large mixer bowl and mix well with the paddle. Add the flours, salt, and caraway or fennel seeds and mix until the dough pulls away from the side of the bowl. Change to the dough hook and knead 3 to 4 minutes at low speed, then 2 at medium. Finish kneading briefly by hand on a floured surface.

BY PROCESSOR

Process this dough in 2 batches. Refrigerate the sponge until cold. Place the flours, salt, and caraway or fennel seeds in a food processor fitted with the dough blade; process with several pulses to sift. Mix the cold starter, 1 cup cold water, and the malt. With the machine running, quickly pour the mixture through the feed tube. If the dough seems too dry, add up to 2 tablespoons cold water to each batch to get a workable dough. Process 45 seconds longer to knead. Finish kneading briefly by hand on a floured surface.

First Rise. Place the dough in a lightly oiled bowl, cover tightly with plastic wrap, and let rise until doubled, about 1½ to 2½ hours. It will soften considerably and feel a bit like taffy.

Shaping and Second Rise. Cut the dough in half on a floured surface. Shape each half into a long oval loaf that is plump in the center and tapered at the ends. Place the loaves on lightly oiled baking sheets or peels sprinkled with cornmeal and let rise covered until doubled, about 1¼ to 1½ hours.

Baking. Heat the oven to 425° F. If you are using a baking stone, turn the oven on 30 minutes before baking and sprinkle the stone with cornmeal just before sliding the loaves onto it. Just before baking, poke 4 holes down the center of each loaf with the end of a cooking thermometer or a chopstick. Bake 45 minutes. Cool on racks.

Other Shapes. Shape pieces of the dough, each the size of a lemon, into rolls. Bake for 20 minutes.

L'Otto di Merano

Rye from Merano

This moist and slightly tangy rye gets its name from its shape: two balls of bread connected at the center look like a figure eight. Eat it with smoked meats, game, smoked salmon, caviar, fresh cheeses, or oysters.

Makes 1 large loaf

SPONGE
2½ teaspoons (1 package) active dry yeast or 1 small cake (18 grams) fresh yeast
1 tablespoon malt syrup
1½ cups warm water
Scant cup (100 grams) stone-ground rye flour
¾ cup (100 grams) unbleached all-purpose flour

BY HAND

Stir the yeast and malt into the water in a large mixing bowl; let stand until foamy, 5 to 10 minutes. Stir in the flours. Cover tightly with plastic wrap and let rise until bubbly, 3 hours.

BY PROCESSOR

Dissolve the yeast and malt in the water as described above. Place the flours in the food processor fitted with the steel blade and process with several pulses to sift. With the machine running, pour the yeast mixture through the feed tube as quickly as the flour can absorb it. Process 10 seconds longer and remove to a bowl. Cover tightly with plastic wrap and let rise for 3 hours.

DOUGH
2 tablespoons (30 grams) lard
About 3 cups (400 grams) unbleached all-purpose flour
2 teaspoons (10 grams) salt
1¼ teaspoons caraway seeds

BY HAND

Stir the lard into the sponge. Combine the flour, salt, and caraway seeds and mix 1 cup at a time into the sponge. Stir until the dough comes together. Knead on a lightly floured surface until firm and elastic, 8 to 10 minutes.

BY MIXER

Add the lard to the sponge in a mixer bowl; mix with the paddle until blended. Add the flour, salt, and caraway seeds; mix until the dough comes together. Change to the dough hook and knead until firm and elastic, 3 to 4 minutes. If you want, finish kneading briefly by hand on a floured surface.

BY PROCESSOR
(larger machines only)

Refrigerate the sponge until cold. Place the flour, salt, and caraway seeds in a food processor fitted with the dough blade. Place the lard in small bits on top of the dry ingredients. With the machine running, quickly pour the sponge through the feed tube and process until the dough gathers into a ball. Process 40 seconds longer to knead. Finish kneading by hand on a floured surface.

First Rise. Place the dough in a lightly oiled bowl, cover tightly with plastic wrap, and let rise until doubled, about 2 hours.

Shaping and Second Rise. Cut the dough in half on a floured surface and shape each piece into a round loaf. On a lightly oiled baking sheet or on floured parchment paper placed on cardboard or a peel, place the loaves next to each other so that they look like a figure 8. Cover with a towel and let rise until doubled, about 1 hour.

Baking. Heat the oven to 400° F. If you are using a baking stone, turn the oven on 30 minutes before baking. Slide the parchment paper with the loaf on it onto the stone and remove the paper after the dough has set. Bake until the loaf sounds hollow when tapped, about 40 minutes. Cool on a rack.

Ciambelline Valtelline
Little Rye Rounds from the Valtellina

High in the province of Sondrio in the farthest reaches of Lombardy lies the Valtellina, a valley that is usually covered with snow in the long months of winter. There people still make the rustic and charmingly uneven rings of rye bread that look like big flat doughnuts. They were once all baked in the communal wood-burning ovens and scored with marks that were so individual that each family could find its own baked rings. Today the necessity to bake bread at the beginning of winter that will last the entire season is not so great, but these little rye rounds are still made in every part of the area. Preserved in the cool, dry winter climate for months, the *ciambelline* are hung on long strings in the houses. When the need arises, they are snatched down, cracked on the table, and eaten like hard tack or dipped in soup to soften them. Long before the rounds become so hard, they are crisp and crunchy and eaten as a snack with salami, sausages, aged cheese, and wine from local cellars. Somewhat larger

Ciambelline Valtelline (continued)

rings of rye are also known as *brazadei* because the bread, is served at the table slipped onto the right arm while the left serves the local wine.

Makes 10 to 12 rings

SPONGE
2½ teaspoons (1 package) active dry yeast or 1 small cake (18 grams) fresh yeast
2 cups warm water
2½ cups (300 grams) dark rye flour or 225 grams dark rye and 75 grams buckwheat flour

Stir the yeast into the water in a mixing bowl; let stand until creamy, about 10 minutes. Stir in the rye flour with a wooden spoon or the paddle of an electric mixer (it will be a very sticky mass). Cover tightly with plastic wrap and let rise about 2 hours.

DOUGH
3¾ teaspoons active dry yeast or 1½ small cakes (27 grams) fresh yeast
1½ cups warm water
3¾ cups (500 grams) bread flour
Scant 2 cups (200 grams) dark rye flour
⅓ cup (25 grams) bran
1 tablespoon (15 grams) salt

BY HAND

Stir the yeast into the water in a large mixing bowl; let stand until creamy, about 10 minutes. Stir in the sponge, then the flours, 2 cups at a time, the bran, and salt. Continue stirring until the dough is soft and light. Flour your work surface generously, flour a dough scraper, and have a mound of flour nearby for your hands. Turn the very sticky dough out onto the floured surface and knead until the dough is the color of gingerbread and sticky inside but velvety against your palm on the outside.

BY MIXER

Stir the yeast into the warm water in a small bowl; let stand until creamy, about 10 minutes. Add the dissolved yeast to the sponge in a mixer bowl and mix with the paddle. Add the flours, bran, and salt and mix until the dough is soft and light. Change to the dough hook and knead until the dough is velvety to the touch but still sticky inside, about 5 minutes.

First Rise. Place the dough in a lightly oiled bowl, cover tightly with plastic wrap, and let rise until puffy, about 45 minutes.

Shaping and Second Rise. Divide the dough on a lightly floured surface into 10 to 12 equal pieces. Roll each piece into a 12- to 14-inch rope and join the ends to make a circle. Flatten the tops of the dough circles with little karate chops delivered with the side of your hand. Place the dough circles on parchment paper set on baking sheets or on lightly oiled baking sheets (the rising will take longer). To capture the heat generated by the fermentation, prop up plastic wrap above the dough with juice glasses or herb jars and cover with a towel. You can heat the oven at 150° F for 2 to 3 minutes, turn it off, and place the *ciambelline* inside to rise. These rye rings should rise ½ to ¾ inch high and 10 inches in diameter.

Baking. Heat oven to 425° F. If you are using baking stones, turn the oven on 30 minutes before baking and sprinkle the stones with cornmeal just before sliding the rings onto them. The rings can be baked on the parchment paper until set and then the paper can be slipped out. Place the rings in the oven and reduce the heat to 375° F. Bake 15 to 20 minutes, spraying with water 3 times in the first 10 minutes. Cool on racks.

1. Join the ends in a circle.

2. Use karate chops to flatten.

Pane alle Olive
Olive Bread

Along the coast of the Italian Riviera near Genoa, the hillsides are covered with endless ranks of silvery green olive trees interrupted only by tile-roofed pink villas, sharp outlines of palm trees, and flashes of brilliant geraniums. The strong sun and warm earth of the region produce the exceptional olives that find their way into the bread. In the past sailors took the bread to sea because the rich olive oil kept it fresh and the tiny pungent black and sweeter green olives gave it its flavor.

There are two ways to make this bread: Mix Sicilian-style green olives, which are easy to find, into the dough so that their moisture becomes part of the dough, or knead in half tiny black Ligurian olives with the green olives by hand. Serve with *carpaccio*, green salads, *antipasti*, and lamb. This bread makes wonderful sandwiches.

Makes 2 oval loaves or round rings

3½ teaspoons active dry yeast or 1⅓ small cakes (24 grams) fresh yeast
¾ cup warm water
¼ cup olive oil
12 ounces (340 grams) Sicilian-style green olives, pitted; or 6 ounces (170 grams) tiny black Ligurian olives, such as Ardoino or Crespi Olivelle, and 6 ounces (170 grams) green olives, also pitted; reserve several whole olives for garnish
3¾ cups (500 grams) unbleached all-purpose flour, ⅓ cup reserved for kneading
1½ teaspoons (8 grams) salt

This bread is difficult—if not impossible—to make by hand, because the olives must be broken down enough to provide some of the liquid for the dough. The mixer and the food processor do the job nicely.

BY MIXER

Stir the yeast into the water in a large mixer bowl; let stand until creamy, about 10 minutes. Add the oil, pitted olives, flour, and salt. Mix with the paddle for 2 minutes on low speed; then change to the dough hook and mix 4 to 5 minutes until the olives are well broken down. The olives will exude their liquid, which will give the dough enough moisture. If necessary, add up to 1½ tablespoons additional water. Finish kneading briefly by hand on a lightly floured surface, adding the reserved flour as needed, until the dough is firm. The dough will feel soft but never smooth.

BY PROCESSOR

Stir the yeast into ¼ cup warm water; let stand until creamy, about 10 minutes. Stir the oil and ½ cup cold water into the yeast mixture. Place the flour and salt in a food processor fitted with the steel blade; process with several pulses to sift. With the machine running, pour the yeast mixture through the feed tube in a steady stream. The flour will be moistened but will not yet make a dough. Sprinkle the olives over the top and process until the dough gathers into a ball and pulls away from the side of the bowl. Process 30 seconds longer to knead. Knead briefly by hand on a floured work surface.

First Rise. Place the dough in an oiled bowl, cover with plastic wrap, and let rise until doubled, 1½ to 2 hours.

Balls set in circle prior to baking

Shaping and Second Rise. Cut the dough in half for 2 oval loaves or 16 to 18 equal pieces for the rings. To make the oval loaves, flatten each half of the dough and fold into thirds, like a business letter. Roll the dough towards yourself, using your thumbs to guide the dough and create tension in the rolling process. Roll with both hands to a cigar shape that is plumper in the middle and tapered at the ends. Place the loaves on oiled baking sheets or peels sprinkled with cornmeal. To make the rings, roll each piece of the dough into a ball and arrange 1½ inches apart in 2 rings on oiled baking sheets or in 2 oiled ring molds. Press the reserved olives *hard* into the tops. Cover with a towel and let rise in a warm spot for about 1 hour. The dough should relax and the skin should not be tight when it goes into the oven.

Baking. Heat the oven to 450° F. If you are using a baking stone, turn the oven on 30 minutes before baking and sprinkle the stone with cornmeal just before sliding the loaves onto it. Place the loaves in the oven and reduce the heat to 400° F. Bake 35 to 40 minutes. Cool on racks.

Pane di Chiavari

Bread of Chiavari

The unusual dark color of this bread comes from the shiny black olives of the Ligurian Riviera, where Chiavari is located. The olives have been ground into a paste, seasoned with herbs and salt, and left for six months to develop their full flavor. A mound of this paste in the dough creates a subtle, distinctive bread that is marbled with purplish black highlights and speckles. The bread keeps very well and seems to improve with age. It is especially good with lamb, chicken dishes, and fresh cheeses.

Makes 1 loaf

2½ teaspoons (1 package) active dry yeast or 1 small cake (18 grams) fresh yeast
1 cup plus 3 tablespoons warm water
Scant ½ cup (100 grams) olive paste
3¾ cups (500 grams) unbleached all-purpose flour
1 teaspoon (5 grams) salt
10 to 12 black olives (garnish)
1 egg white, beaten
Cornmeal

BY HAND

Stir the yeast into ¼ cup of the water in a large mixing bowl; let stand until creamy, about 10 minutes. Stir in the remaining water and the olive paste. Mix the flour and salt and stir into the yeast mixture in 2 additions. Knead on a lightly floured surface, sprinkling with 2 to 4 tablespoons additional flour as needed, until shiny, elastic, and velvety, 5 to 7 minutes.

BY MIXER

Stir the yeast into the water in a large mixer bowl; let stand until creamy, about 10 minutes. Stir in the olive paste with the paddle. Combine the flour and salt and mix into the yeast mixture until well blended. Change to the dough hook and knead until shiny, elastic, and velvety, about 2 minutes. If you want, finish kneading by hand on a lightly floured surface.

BY PROCESSOR

Stir the yeast into ¼ cup warm water in a medium-size bowl; let stand until creamy, about 10 minutes. Stir in the olive paste and ¾ cup plus 3 tablespoons cold water. Place the flour and salt in a food processor fitted with the dough blade and process with several pulses to sift. With the machine running, pour the yeast mixture through the feed tube as quickly as the flour can absorb it. Process 45 seconds longer to knead. Finish kneading briefly by hand on a lightly floured surface.

First Rise. Place the dough in a lightly oiled bowl, cover tightly with plastic wrap, and let rise until doubled, about 1½ hours.

Shaping and Second Rise. Turn the dough out onto a lightly floured surface, punch it down, and knead briefly. Shape the dough into one of the following: a large round loaf; an oval loaf, with both ends twisted so that it looks a bit like a large olive; a ring made by rolling the dough into a long thin rope and connecting the ends; 2 wreaths of 6 or 7 rolls each. The ring or wreath can be baked free form or placed in an oiled ring mold. Place the shaped dough on a peel lightly sprinkled with cornmeal or on a lightly oiled baking sheet. Cover loosely with a towel and let rise until doubled, about 45 minutes.

Baking. Heat the oven to 450° F. If you are using a baking stone, turn the oven on 30 minutes before baking and sprinkle the stone with cornmeal just before sliding the loaf onto it. Just before baking, press the whole olives hard into the loaf and brush the top with the egg white. Bake 10 minutes. Reduce the heat to 400° F and bake for 35 minutes more (10 minutes for rolls). Cool on a rack.

Twisting the ends in opposite directions to resemble an olive—use crossed arms (it's easier)

Piccia Calabrese

Calabrian Bread

I don't think there is a single southern Italian ingredient that hasn't found its way into this bread. To make it you can practically work your way through your pantry, opening jar after jar and chunking bits and pieces into this dough. If you don't have everything, just double an ingredient you do have or leave out an ingredient or two; it doesn't seem to make a big difference. The bread has a beautiful golden crust and an interior fragrant with all the tastes of the south, but it isn't nearly as overwhelming as the list of ingredients would lead you to believe. It tastes particularly good with fresh mozzarella, ricotta, Monterey Jack, or another smooth fresh cheese.

Makes 1 large or 2 smaller loaves

2½ teaspoons (1 package) active dry yeast or 1 small cake (18 grams) fresh yeast
¼ cup warm water
1¼ cups (300 grams) *Biga* (page 100)
2 tablespoons (30 grams) lard
2 tablespoons sliced mushrooms
1 tablespoon olive oil
3 tablespoons chopped canned tomato with juices
½ large or 1 small anchovy, boned and chopped
1 tablespoon capers, drained and chopped
6 little cocktail onions, chopped
2 tablespoons chopped tiny artichoke
3 gherkin pickles, chopped
2 strips roasted sweet red pepper, fresh or canned, chopped
1 tablespoon dried oregano
About 2¼ cups (300 grams) unbleached all-purpose flour
1 teaspoon (5 grams) salt
¾ teaspoon freshly cracked pepper

BY HAND

Stir the yeast into the water in a large mixing bowl; let stand until creamy, about 10 minutes. Add the starter and mix, squeezing the starter through your fingers to break it up. Stir in the lard until well blended. Sauté the mushrooms briefly in the oil and let cool. Stir in the mushrooms, tomato, anchovy, capers, onions, artichoke, pickles, red pepper, and oregano thoroughly. Mix the flour, salt, and pepper and stir into the starter mixture, 1 cup at a time. When the dough is too stiff for stirring, plunge in with your hands. Using a dough scraper and sprinkling with ½ to ⅔ cup additional flour as needed, knead the dough on a well-floured surface until velvety, moist, and elastic, 8 to 10 minutes.

BY MIXER

Stir the yeast into the water in a large mixer bowl; let stand until creamy, about 10 minutes. Add the starter and mix with the paddle until well blended. Add the lard and mix. Sauté the mushrooms briefly in the oil and let cool. Add the mushrooms, tomato, anchovy, capers, onions, artichoke, pickles, red peppers, and oregano and mix thoroughly. Add the flour, salt, and pepper, and mix slowly until the dough comes together. Change to the dough hook and knead at medium speed until velvety, moist, and elastic, about 3 minutes. If you want, finish kneading by hand on a floured surface, sprinkling with ½ to ⅔ cup additional flour as needed.

BY PROCESSOR

Refrigerate the starter until cold. Stir the yeast into the water in a small bowl; let stand until creamy, about 10 minutes. Sauté the mushrooms briefly in the oil and let cool. Roughly chop the tomato, mushrooms, anchovy, capers, onions, artichoke, pickles, and red peppers in a food processor fitted with the steel blade. Remove to another bowl. Process the oregano, flour, salt, and pepper with 5 or 6 pulses to mix. Place the cold starter and the lard over the dry ingredients. With the machine running, pour the dissolved yeast through the feed tube as quickly as the flour can absorb it. Add the vegetable mixture and process just until combined. Finish kneading by hand on a well-floured surface, sprinkling with ½ to ⅔ cup additional flour as needed, until elastic, moist, and velvety.

First Rise. Place the dough in an oiled bowl, cover with plastic wrap, and let rise until doubled, 1 to 1½ hours.

Shaping and Second Rise. Shape the dough on a floured surface into 1 large or 2 smaller round loaves by rolling the dough first into a fairly taut log, then shaping it into a round loaf. The dough will be slightly sticky; sprinkle the dough and the work surface with flour while shaping it. Place each loaf on a peel sprinkled with cornmeal, cover with a slightly dampened towel, and let rise until doubled, about 50 minutes.

Baking. Thirty minutes before baking, heat the oven with baking stones in it to 425° F. Just before baking, cut an even slash around the shoulder of the loaf or 3 slashes across the top with a razor. Sprinkle the stones with cornmeal and slide the loaves onto the stones. Bake, spraying 3 times with water in the first 10 minutes, for 45 minutes. Cool on racks.

Casatiello

This spicy cheese bread, flecked with chunks of salami and freshly ground pepper, was originally made for Easter in the countryside of Naples, but now it is eaten year round except during the steamy months of summer. The traditional *casatiello* was a peppery rustic bread, shaped like a large doughnut and with eggs still in the shell held in place on top with two crossed bands of dough. This version can certainly be made with eggs set on the top, but as the eggs cook during the baking they will sink into the bread. The Roman baker who taught me this variation has given it some of the richness of the *pizza pasquale* that Romans ate for lunch on the Saturday before Easter.

Makes 2 round loaves

SPONGE

4¼ teaspoons active dry yeast or 1⅔ small cakes (30 grams) fresh
   yeast
1 tablespoon plus 1 teaspoon (20 grams) sugar
1¼ cups warm water
4 egg yolks
About 2¼ cups (300 grams) unbleached all-purpose flour
1¼ teaspoons (7 grams) salt

Stir the yeast and 1 teaspoon sugar into the water in a mixing bowl; let stand until foamy, about 10 minutes. Add the egg yolks and remaining sugar and stir until smooth. Stir in half the flour and beat until smooth. Add the remaining flour and the salt and stir until a soft dough is formed. Knead gently on a lightly floured surface for 3 to 4 minutes, or with the dough hook of an electric mixer at low speed for 1 to 2 minutes. Cover tightly with plastic wrap and let rise 45 minutes to 1 hour.

DOUGH

4 eggs
½ cup plus 1½ tablespoons (120 grams) sugar
1⅓ teaspoons (7 grams) salt
About 4¼ cups (550 grams) unbleached all-purpose flour
2 sticks plus 2 tablespoons (250 grams) unsalted butter, room
   temperature
2 ounces (60 grams) Pecorino Romano cheese, grated
2 ounces (60 grams) Parmesan cheese, grated
1 ounce (30 grams) Gruyère cheese, grated

2 ounces (60 grams) Provolone, cut into small cubes
3½ ounces (100 grams) Milano salami, thinly sliced and finely
 chopped
1 teaspoon coarsely ground pepper
1 egg white, beaten

BY HAND

Beat the eggs, sugar, and salt together in a large mixing bowl. Add 1 cup of the flour and stir until smooth. Chop the sponge into small pieces and add it to the egg mixture. Beat it together; then add the remaining flour and mix with your hands to a shaggy mass. Mix in the butter. Sprinkle the dough with the grated Pecorino, Parmesan, and Gruyère and knead it in with your hands. When the dough has come together but is still fairly rough, knead it on a floured surface until elastic, supple, and fairly smooth, 5 to 7 minutes.

BY MIXER

Beat the eggs, sugar, and salt together with the paddle in a large mixer bowl. Add the sponge and mix until blended. Add the flour and mix to a shaggy mass. Add the butter and continue beating with the paddle until a rough dough is formed. Sprinkle the grated Pecorino, Parmesan, and Gruyère over the dough and mix until it is roughly blended. Change to the dough hook and knead at medium speed until elastic, supple, and fairly smooth, 3 to 4 minutes.

First Rise. Place the dough in a lightly oiled bowl, cover with plastic wrap, and let rise until almost tripled, 1 to 1½ hours.

Shaping and Second Rise. Turn out onto a lightly floured surface and pat and roll the dough out to a large rectangle, ¾ inch thick. Sprinkle half the Provolone, salami, and pepper over the surface. Fold into thirds, like a business letter; then roll the dough out again ¾ inch thick. Sprinkle the dough with the remaining Provolone, salami, and pepper, and fold again into thirds. Gently knead for 2 to 3 minutes to distribute the cheese and salami evenly. Cut the dough in half and, with the cut side up, knead each half gently into a round ball by rolling the dough between cupped hands on the work surface and pulling the skin of the dough taut. Place each ball in a buttered 2-quart charlotte mold or soufflé dish. The dough should fill about half the mold. Cover with a towel and let rise to the tops of the molds, 1 to 1½ hours.

Baking. Heat the oven to 400° F. Brush the top of each loaf with egg white. Bake for 45 minutes; remove from molds and cool on racks.

Crescia al Formaggio

Easter Cheese Bread

This is the bread that traditionally opens Easter lunch in Umbria. Eggs and cheese are beaten together to make a rich briochelike dough that has an intensely cheesy, lacy interior. When I watched it being made at Sandri in Perugia, the bakers cut right into a fifty-pound wheel of three-year-old Parmigiano-Reggiano, the finest cheese the country offers. If you want the authentic bread, bake it in terra-cotta flowerpots (plug any holes in the bottom), and you'll see where the bread gets its name. *Crescia* refers to the sudden dramatic doming of the dough above the pots.

To season flowerpots, coat them with oil and set in a preheated 400° F oven for 20 minutes. Oil them again, then set them back in the 400° F oven for 20 minutes more. Cool them and be sure to grease them well before putting the dough inside.

Makes 2 tall round loaves

4¼ teaspoons active dry yeast or 1⅔ small cakes (30 grams) fresh yeast
1 tablespoon sugar
5 tablespoons warm water
4 eggs, room temperature
4 egg yolks, room temperature
About 2 cups (250 grams) unbleached all-purpose flour
1½ sticks (170 grams) unsalted butter, room temperature
About 2 cups (250 grams) bread flour
1 teaspoon (5 grams) salt
2 cups (200 grams) freshly grated Parmesan
1 cup (100 grams) freshly grated Pecorino Romano
1 egg white, beaten

BY HAND

Stir the yeast and sugar into the water in a large mixing bowl; let stand until foamy, about 10 minutes. Beat the eggs and egg yolks together and beat into the yeast mixture. Add 1 cup of the all-purpose flour and beat until smooth. Add the butter in small pieces and mix well. Reserve ¼ cup of one of the flours for kneading. Stir in all the remaining flour and the salt. Knead on a floured surface, sprinkling with the reserved flour, 8 to 12 minutes; add the cheeses in sprinkles in the last minutes of kneading. It will take a while, but it is the only way to get this much cheese evenly distributed.

BY MIXER

Stir the yeast and sugar into the water in a large mixer bowl; let stand until foamy, about 10 minutes. Mix in the eggs, egg yolks, and butter with the paddle. Add the flours and salt and mix until the dough comes together, about 2 minutes. Change to the dough hook and knead at medium speed for about 5 minutes, adding up to 2 tablespoons more flour, until the dough pulls away from the side of the bowl. If the dough climbs up to the collar, turn off the motor and push the dough down. Spread the dough out on a floured surface and gradually knead in sprinkles of cheese. The dough should be rich, springy, golden, and slightly gritty.

First Rise. Place the dough in a lightly buttered bowl, cover with plastic wrap, and let rise until doubled, 2 to 2½ hours.

Shaping. Turn the dough out onto a lightly floured surface and cut into 2 pieces, one twice as large as the other. Shape each piece into a tight ball and let rest under a towel for about 10 minutes. Reshape the balls firmly. Place the large ball, seam side down, in an oiled 2-quart terra-cotta flowerpot or charlotte mold, and the smaller ball in an oiled 1-quart pot or mold. The dough should fill the pots about halfway. Cover with plastic wrap held by a rubber band and let rise to the tops of the pots, 2 to 2½ hours.

Baking. Heat the oven to 425° F. Brush the tops of the dough with the egg white. Bake until the tops have risen dramatically above the pots and are deep golden brown, about 45 minutes. Let breads cool 10 to 15 minutes before unmolding. Cool on racks.

PANI NUOVI
New Breads

In Italy, where *fantasia* is the rule and bakers are artists, there has been a real revolution in bread baking in the last ten years. Bakers have given their imaginations free rein and simply started kneading all the best products of the country's markets right into their doughs, making "new-wave" tastes in the world's oldest food. Mounds of sweet peppers, fat bunches of basil, wheels of aged Parmesan cheese, nuts, and exotic grains have all found new homes in unusual loaves.

And that's not all. The Mediterranean diet has become the latest rage and is being touted as the healthiest way to eat, because it is rich in grains and vegetables, olive oil, and fresh fruit. Suddenly the Italian concern with *la bella figura* has reached beyond an obvious eye for the waistline, and a rush is on for tasty meals that keep dread cholesterol far from the door. The irony is that the best example of a healthy diet is probably what the poor people of Naples have always eaten—a diet of vegetables and grains (what are pizzas after all?), which they put together with dazzling colors and an abundant variety of flavors. Ten years ago you could not find whole-wheat or graham flour or multi-grain breads at all, and bran was more likely fed to animals than to humans. Now bakers are really hitting their stride and are talking about a bread for every course and a course for every bread, hinting at a kind of culinary refinement and richness we Americans can hardly imagine.

Vegetable and Herb Breads

Pane al Pesto
Pesto Bread

Let's sing the praises of the unknown baker who first stirred fresh pesto into bread dough. When I was living with my family on the coast of Liguria in a tiny town above Lerici, the lady who helped us keep house was a wonderful cook who often arrived with bouquets of basil so recently picked that the leaves were still warm from the sun. She ground pine nuts and garlic with the basil leaves, then stirred in Parmesan cheese and beat in olive oil by drops, as if she were making mayonnaise. We ate it on fat ribbons of *trenette* pasta (our friends just over the border in Tuscany, not more than 30 kilometers away, served it on *fusilli,* which caught the sauce in its twists and turns), on potatoes, on grilled fresh fish, and sometimes just on our fingers, which we dipped surreptitiously into the bowl.

This recipe for pesto is stronger and more concentrated than most because it must retain its fragrance and taste even through the process of being baked into bread. And it does!

You must use fresh basil for the pesto; neither dried basil, which bears almost no relationship to the fresh, parsley, nor spinach will do. You may, however, substitute walnuts for the pine nuts.

Makes 2 round loaves

PESTO
1 cup (75 grams) fresh basil leaves
¾ cup (75 grams) grated Parmesan cheese
½ cup olive oil
2 tablespoons pine nuts or chopped walnuts
1½ teaspoons minced garlic
⅛ teaspoon salt
⅛ teaspoon pepper

Purée all ingredients in a food processor fitted with the steel blade or a blender. Measure ½ cup (100 grams) for this recipe.

DOUGH
2½ teaspoons (1 package) active dry yeast or 1 small cake (18 grams) fresh yeast
1 cup plus 2 tablespoons warm water
Scant 2 tablespoons olive oil
3¾ cups (500 grams) unbleached all-purpose flour
2 teaspoons (10 grams) salt
Cornmeal

BY HAND

Stir the yeast into the water in a mixing bowl; let stand until creamy, about 10 minutes. Stir in the oil and ½ cup pesto thoroughly. Mix the flour and salt and add to the yeast mixture. Stir until the dough comes together. Knead on a floured surface until soft, velvety, and elastic, 8 to 10 minutes.

Pane al Pesto (continued)

BY MIXER

Stir the yeast into the water in a mixer bowl; let stand until creamy, about 10 minutes. Stir in the oil and ½ cup pesto thoroughly with the paddle. Mix the flour and salt and add to the yeast mixture. Mix until well moistened. Change to the dough hook and knead until the dough is velvety and medium soft, 3 to 4 minutes. Finish kneading briefly by hand on a lightly floured surface.

BY PROCESSOR

Stir the yeast into ¼ cup warm water in a small bowl; let stand until creamy, about 10 minutes. Place the flour and salt in a food processor fitted with the dough blade and process 10 seconds to sift. With the machine running, pour ½ cup pesto, the dissolved yeast, and 1 cup cold water through the feed tube as quickly as the flour can absorb it. Process 45 seconds longer to knead. Finish kneading by hand on a lightly floured surface for 1 minute.

First Rise. Place the dough in an oiled bowl, cover tightly with plastic wrap, and let rise until doubled, about 1¼ hours.

Shaping and Second Rise. Cut the dough in half on a lightly floured surface. Punch each piece down and knead briefly to expel the air. Shape each piece into a round loaf. Place each loaf, seam side down, on an oiled baking sheet or a peel sprinkled with cornmeal. Cover with a towel and let rise until doubled, about 45 minutes to 1 hour. The dough must be very relaxed and fully risen before it should be baked, so don't rush it.

Baking. Heat the oven to 450° F. If you are using baking stones, turn the oven on 30 minutes before baking and sprinkle the stones with cornmeal just before sliding the loaves onto them. Place the loaves in the oven and immediately reduce the heat to 400° F. Bake 35 to 40 minutes, spraying 3 times with water in the first 10 minutes, if you want. Cool completely on racks.

Basil

Ciabatta ai Funghi

Mushroom Bread

The two secrets of getting the most flavor into this bread are using the soaking water from the *porcini* and allowing the flavor to develop over long rises. You may find the bread growing powerfully in its second rise; if so, just dimple it gently to deflate it slightly, and allow the rise to go the full three hours.

Makes 2 large oval loaves

4 to 6 dried *porcini*
1¾ cups warm water
8 ounces (225 grams) fresh mushrooms, sliced
1 teaspoon minced garlic
1 to 2 tablespoons olive oil
1¼ teaspoons active dry yeast or ½ small cake (9 grams) fresh yeast
3¾ cups (500 grams) unbleached all-purpose flour
1 tablespoon (15 grams) salt
Cornmeal

Soak the *porcini* in the warm water at least 1 hour; drain but save the liquid. Strain the liquid through cheesecloth 2 or 3 times and measure 1½ cups. Roughly chop the *porcini* and pat dry. Sauté the fresh mushrooms and the garlic in as little of the oil as possible and set aside to cool. Warm the *porcini* liquid to 105° to 115° F. If you are using the food processor, refrigerate 1¼ cups of the liquid until cold and warm the remaining ¼ cup.

BY HAND

Stir the yeast into the warm *porcini* liquid in a large mixing bowl; let stand until creamy, about 10 minutes. Mix the flour and salt and stir into the yeast mixture in 3 additions; add the chopped *porcini* with the last of the flour. When the dough is too stiff to stir, plunge in with your hands. Knead on a lightly floured surface until the dough is as velvety as a baby's bottom, 5 to 7 minutes.

BY MIXER

Stir the yeast into the warm *porcini* liquid in a mixer bowl; let stand until creamy, about 10 minutes. Mix the flour and salt and add to the yeast mixture. Mix with the paddle until the flour is absorbed. Change to the dough hook and knead for 2 minutes at low speed and 2 minutes at medium. You will have to stop several times to adjust the dough in the bowl. Finish kneading briefly by hand on a floured surface, adding the *porcini* and a little extra flour to bring the dough together.

Ciabatta di Funghi (continued)

BY PROCESSOR

Stir the yeast into ¼ cup warm *porcini* liquid in a small bowl; let stand until creamy, about 10 minutes. Place the flour and salt in a food processor fitted with the steel blade and process with 2 or 3 pulses to sift. Pour the dissolved yeast over the flour. With the machine running, pour the cold *porcini* liquid through the feed tube and process until the dough gathers into a ball. Process 45 seconds longer to knead. Finish kneading briefly by hand on a floured surface, adding the *porcini*. The dough should be soft, velvety, and very resilient.

First Rise. Place the dough in a lightly oiled bowl, cover tightly with plastic wrap, and let rise for 3 hours.

Shaping and Second Rise. Pour the dough onto a floured surface, punch it down, and knead briefly. Divide the dough in half and shape each half into a big flat oval. Scatter the sautéed mushroom over both ovals and roll the dough up, tucking in the ends. Pat each loaf flat, roll it up again, and shape into an oval. The loaves will be compact and quite small initially, but they will rise. Dimple each loaf with your fingertips or knuckles, being careful not to expose the mushrooms. Place on a baking sheet or peel sprinkled with cornmeal, cover with a dampened kitchen towel or a heavy towel, and let rise for 3 hours.

Baking. Thirty minutes before baking, heat the oven with baking stones in it to 400° F. Just before baking, sprinkle the stones with cornmeal. Slide the loaves onto the stones and bake 50 minutes to 1 hour, spraying 3 times with water in the first 10 minutes. The loaves can also be baked on an oiled baking sheet, if you prefer. Cool completely on wire racks.

Pane di Patate
Potato Bread

It's the rare person who even connects potatoes and Italy, but, in fact, they grow all over Puglia and Basilicata, two of the southern regions of Italy. It seems everyone there has enough potatoes in their gardens to make into dough for bread, *focaccia*, or pizza. This bread needs to be prepared by a machine, either a processor or a mixer, because of its minimal water content. Because potatoes have a lot of starch, the bread browns quickly and you must keep an eye on it. It will split open dramatically as it bakes and come out looking like a big, crusty rosette. Potato bread is particularly good with stews or rich meat sauces into which slices of the bread can be dipped.

Makes 2 round loaves

1½ pounds (675 grams) baking potatoes
5 teaspoons (2 packages) active dry yeast or 2 small cakes (36 grams)
  fresh yeast
3 tablespoons warm water
1½ to 2 tablespoons olive oil
3¾ cups (500 grams) unbleached all-purpose flour
1½ teaspoons (8 grams) salt
Cornmeal

Boil the potatoes in water to cover until tender; drain. Peel and press the potatoes through a ricer or mash until very smooth and free of lumps. Use while still warm.

BY MIXER

Stir the yeast into the warm water; let stand until creamy, about 10 minutes. Place the potatoes, dissolved yeast, oil, flour, and salt in a mixer bowl. Beat with the paddle at low speed 2 to 3 minutes. The dough will initially be very fine, like cornmeal, and then it will start to clump together. Add up to 1 tablespoon water if necessary for the dough to come together. If you make a small ball of the dough between your fingers, it should feel very slightly sticky. This is a hard dough that never gets very smooth. Knead by hand on a lightly floured surface 3 to 4 minutes.

BY PROCESSOR

Stir the yeast into 4 tablespoons warm water; let stand until creamy, about 10 minutes. Place the potatoes, flour, and salt in a food processor fitted with the dough blade, and process with several pulses to mix. With the machine running, pour the dissolved yeast, oil, and additional ¼ cup cold water through the feed tube and process until the dough comes together. Process 45 seconds longer to knead. This is a hard dough that never gets very smooth. If you want, finish kneading briefly by hand.

First Rise. Place the dough in a lightly oiled bowl, cover tightly with plastic wrap, and let rise until doubled, 1 to 2 hours. The processor dough is sticky and delicate because of the extra water, and the mixer dough is slightly tacky and looks chunky.

Shaping and Second Rise. Cut the dough in half on a lightly floured surface and shape each half into a round loaf, using very light tension in the shaping. Flatten slightly with the palm of your hand to encourage it to spread just a bit. Place the loaves, seam side down,

Pane di Patate (continued)

on heavily floured peels or rimless baking sheets. Flour the tops lightly and cover with dampened kitchen towels. Let rise until doubled, about 45 minutes. When fully risen, the dough will feel somewhat soft.

Baking. Thirty minutes before baking, heat the oven with baking stones in it to 450° F. Just before baking, sprinkle the stones with cornmeal. Very carefully invert the loaves onto the stones (the seam side will open dramatically in the baking). Bake 35 to 40 minutes, spraying 3 times with water in the first 10 minutes. Cool completely on racks.

Pane al Pomodoro
Tomato Bread

There is no question that this is an extravagant bread, but imagine an American hamburger on it or slices of soft fresh cheese. You can throw caution to the wind and buy Italian sun-dried tomatoes packed in wonderful Ligurian olive oil, or you can be somewhat more restrained and buy the sun-dried tomatoes by the ounce. You can even dry and pack the tomatoes in oil yourself. The amount of tomatoes you use is up to you.

Makes 1 round loaf

1 clove garlic, minced
2 tablespoons finely chopped onion
1 tablespoon oil from the sun-dried tomatoes
2½ teaspoons (1 package) active dry yeast or 1 small cake (18 grams) fresh yeast
¼ cup warm water
1 cup water, room temperature
⅓ cup to ½ cup coarsely chopped sun-dried tomatoes (packed in oil)
3¾ cups (500 grams) unbleached all-purpose flour
2 teaspoons (10 grams) salt
1 egg white, beaten

Lightly sauté the garlic and onion in the oil; let cool to room temperature.

BY HAND

Stir the yeast into the warm water in a large mixing bowl; let stand until creamy, about 10 minutes. Stir in 1 cup water and the garlic and onion with the oil; then stir in the tomatoes. Mix the flour and salt and stir 1 cup at a time into the yeast mixture. Knead on a lightly floured surface, sprinkling with 2 to 3 tablespoons additional flour as needed, until the dough is soft, velvety, and slightly moist, 8 to 10 minutes.

BY MIXER

Stir the yeast into the warm water in a mixer bowl; let stand until creamy, about 10 minutes. Using the paddle, stir in 1 cup water and the garlic and onion with the oil; then stir in the tomatoes. Stir in the flour and salt. Change to the dough hook and knead until soft, velvety, and elastic, about 3 minutes. The tomatoes will be distinct chunks.

BY PROCESSOR

Stir the yeast into ¼ cup warm water in a small bowl; let stand until creamy, about 10 minutes. Place the flour and salt in a food processor fitted with the steel blade or dough blade and process briefly to sift. Place the garlic and onion with the oil and the tomatoes on top of the flour. With the machine running, pour the dissolved yeast and the 1 cup cold water through the feed tube as quickly as the flour can absorb it. Process until the dough comes together. Process 30 seconds longer to knead. The dough will be velvety, elastic, and salmon colored. Finish kneading briefly by hand on a floured surface, if you want.

First Rise. Place the dough in a lightly oiled bowl, cover with plastic wrap, and let rise until doubled, about 1 hour.

Shaping and Second Rise. Punch the dough down on a lightly floured surface and knead briefly. Shape the dough into a ball. Place on a lightly oiled baking sheet or a peel sprinkled with flour, cover with a towel, and let rise until doubled, about 45 to 55 minutes.

Baking. Heat the oven to 425° F. If you are using a baking stone, turn the oven on 30 minutes before baking and sprinkle the stone with cornmeal just before sliding the loaf onto it. Make 3 parallel slashes on the top of the loaf with a razor. Brush the top with the egg white. Bake 10 minutes, spraying 3 times with water. Reduce the heat to 375° F and bake 25 to 30 minutes longer. Cool completely on a rack.

Pane agli Spinaci
Spinach Bread

I watched bakers in Venice turn out hundreds of little spinach rolls all destined for elegant *antipasti* or the Italian variant of sandwiches for lunch. Why not make a loaf of bread of these beautiful marbled green interiors, I wondered, and then proceeded to turn *panini* into *pane*. The bread is wonderful with roast chicken or lamb and tastes as good as it looks. Be certain to thaw the frozen spinach without cooking it further. Squeeze the spinach dry but save the liquid for the bread dough.

Makes 1 round loaf or 12 to 14 rolls

2 cloves garlic, minced
Scant 2 tablespoons olive oil
¾ cup reserved spinach liquid
2½ teaspoons (1 package) active dry yeast or 1 small cake (18 grams) fresh yeast
¼ teaspoon sugar
2 packages (10 ounces, 285 grams, each) frozen spinach, thawed, squeezed dry, but liquid reserved
¼ teaspoon freshly grated nutmeg
3¾ cups (500 grams) unbleached all-purpose flour
2½ teaspoons (12 grams) salt

Lightly sauté the garlic in the oil and cool to room temperature. Warm ¼ cup of the reserved spinach liquid to 105° to 115° F (90° to 100° F for fresh yeast).

BY HAND

Stir the yeast and sugar into the warm spinach liquid in a mixing bowl; let stand until foamy, about 10 minutes. Add the remaining ½ cup spinach liquid, which should be at room temperature, the garlic with the oil, the spinach, and nutmeg and stir thoroughly. Mix the flour and salt and stir into the spinach mixture. Knead on a floured surface, sprinkling with additional flour to absorb the moisture from the spinach, until the dough is well marbled, soft, and velvety, 8 to 10 minutes.

BY MIXER

Stir the yeast and sugar into the warm spinach liquid in a mixer bowl; let stand until foamy, about 10 minutes. Add the remaining spinach liquid, which should be at room temperature, the garlic with the oil, the spinach, and nutmeg and mix with the paddle. Add the flour and salt and mix until the flour is absorbed. Change to the dough hook and knead until the dough is well marbled, soft, and velvety, 2 to 3 minutes.

BY PROCESSOR

If the capacity of your food processor is 7 cups or less, process this dough in 2 batches. Stir the yeast and sugar into the warm spinach liquid in a small bowl; let stand until foamy, about 10 minutes. Place the flour, salt, and nutmeg in a food processor fitted with the steel blade and process with 2 or 3 pulses to sift. Place the spinach in clumps on top of the flour mixture. Stir ½ cup cold spinach liquid, the garlic with the oil, and 1 tablespoon additional cold water into the dissolved yeast. With the machine running, pour the yeast mixture through the feed tube and process until the dough comes together. Add up to 1 tablespoon more water if needed for the dough to come together. Process 40 seconds longer to knead. Finish kneading briefly by hand on a lightly floured surface, if you want.

First Rise. Place the dough in an oiled bowl, cover tightly with plastic wrap, and let rise until doubled, 1¼ to 1½ hours.

Shaping and Second Rise. The dough will be even wetter after rising, because the spinach will have exuded more liquid. Pour the dough onto a floured work surface and flour the top of the dough. Don't punch it down or try to knead it. Shape into a round loaf or rolls the size of a fat lemon and place on a lightly oiled baking sheet. Cover with a towel and let rise until doubled, about 45 minutes.

Baking. Heat the oven to 425° F. Slash a big V on top of the loaf with a razor. Bake for 10 minutes. Reduce the heat to 400° F and bake the rolls 20 minutes and the loaf 30 to 35 minutes. Cool completely on a rack.

Slashing a big V on top of the loaf

Pane ai Peperoni

Sweet Pepper Bread

Once bakers started letting their imaginations run free and using the whole range of ingredients the land produced, it was only a question of time before sweet red peppers would find their way into the avant-garde loaves of today. After all, slices of peppers have been baked on *focacce* and *schiacciate* for years. This bread is unexpectedly delicious and particularly appealing with its brilliant red color and the sweet bite of peppers, and it is very easy and straightforward to make. Serve this bread with soft and semisoft cheeses, roast chicken, lamb, or pork. It is easily made into rolls and makes a splendid vehicle for a sandwich.

Makes 2 long, thin loaves

1 large sweet red pepper
2 tablespoons olive oil
1¾ teaspoons active dry yeast or ⅔ small cake (12 grams) fresh yeast
1¼ cups warm water
3¾ cups (500 grams) unbleached all-purpose flour
2 teaspoons (10 grams) salt

Broil the pepper 2 inches from the heat until the skin on the exposed side is blackened and puffed. Turn the pepper and continue to broil until the pepper is blackened all over. While it is still warm, cut the pepper in half and scrape out the seeds. Cut into wide strips and pull off the blackened skin. Roughly chop the pepper and sauté in the oil over low heat for 4 to 5 minutes, but don't let it brown.

BY HAND

Stir the yeast into the water in a large mixing bowl; let stand until creamy, about 10 minutes. Stir in the pepper with the oil. Mix the flour and salt and stir 1 cup at a time into the yeast mixture. When the dough has roughly come together, knead on a lightly floured surface until soft and elastic, 8 to 10 minutes.

BY MIXER

Stir the yeast into the water in a mixer bowl; let stand until creamy, about 10 minutes. Stir in the pepper with the oil, then the flour and salt with the paddle. Mix until the dough comes together, about 2 minutes. Change to the dough hook and knead at medium speed 2 to 3 minutes. Finish kneading briefly by hand on a floured surface. The dough should be soft and elastic.

BY PROCESSOR

Stir the yeast into ¼ cup warm water in a small bowl; let stand until creamy, about 10 minutes. Drain the oil from the pepper and add the oil to the dissolved yeast. Place the flour, salt, and pepper in a food processor fitted with the dough or steel blade and process 10 seconds to mix. With the machine running, pour the dissolved yeast mixture and 1 cup cold water through the feed tube; process until the dough gathers into a ball. Process 45 seconds longer to knead. Finish kneading briefly by hand on a lightly floured surface. The dough should be soft and elastic.

First Rise. Place the dough in an oiled bowl, cover with plastic wrap, and let rise until doubled, about 1 hour.

Shaping and Second Rise. Punch the dough down on a floured surface and knead it briefly. Cut the dough in half. Shape each half into a long, round log, and then curve one end so that it looks like a J. Place the loaves on an oiled baking sheet or a peel sprinkled with cornmeal or flour, cover with a towel, and let rise until doubled, 45 minutes to 1 hour.

1. *Roll the dough into a log.*

2. *Shape into a J.*

Baking. Heat the oven to 450° F. If you are using a baking stone, turn the oven on 30 minutes before baking and sprinkle the stone with cornmeal just before sliding the loaves onto it. Place the loaves in the oven and immediately reduce the heat to 400° F. Bake 35 minutes, spraying 3 times with water in the first 10 minutes. Cool completely on a rack.

Pane al Formaggio
Cheese Bread

Take two of Italy's best cheeses—aged Parmesan and the saltier, more pungent *pecorino*—fold them into a dough enriched with eggs and a little olive oil, and you have a superb cheese bread to eat with smoked meats, soups, green salads, and even fresh fruit.

Makes 2 round or long, thin loaves

2½ teaspoons (1 package) active dry yeast or 1 small cake (18 grams) fresh yeast
1 cup warm water
2 eggs, room temperature
2 tablespoons olive oil
3¾ cups (500 grams) unbleached all-purpose flour
2 teaspoons (10 grams) salt
¾ cup (75 grams) grated Parmesan cheese
½ cup (50 grams) grated *pecorino* cheese
Cornmeal
1 egg white, beaten

BY HAND

Stir the yeast into the water in a large mixing bowl; let stand until creamy, about 10 minutes. Whisk in the eggs and oil. Mix the flour and salt and stir half into the yeast mixture; stir in the remaining flour with the cheese. Knead on a lightly floured surface, sprinkling with 2 to 3 tablespoons additional flour as needed, until firm, elastic, and silky, 8 to 10 minutes. The texture may be slightly gritty from the cheeses.

BY MIXER

Stir the yeast into the water in a mixer bowl; let stand until creamy, about 10 minutes. Mix in the eggs and oil with the paddle, and then the flour, salt, and cheeses. Change to the dough hook and knead until firm, velvety, and elastic, 3 to 4 minutes. The texture may be slightly gritty from the cheeses.

BY PROCESSOR

If the capacity of your food processor is 7 cups or less, process this dough in 2 batches. Stir the yeast into ¼ cup warm water in a small bowl; let stand until creamy, about 10 minutes. Place the flour, salt, and cheeses in a food processor fitted with the dough blade and process with several pulses to mix. Break the eggs and pour the oil on top of the flour mixture. With the machine running, pour the dissolved yeast and ¾ cup plus 2 tablespoons cold water through the feed tube as quickly as the flour can absorb it and process until the dough gathers into a ball. Process 45 seconds longer to knead. Knead briefly by hand on a lightly floured surface until elastic and silky.

First Rise. Place the dough in a lightly oiled bowl, cover with plastic wrap, and let rise until doubled, about 2 hours.

Shaping and Second Rise. Punch the dough down on a lightly floured surface and knead it briefly. Cut the dough in half and shape each piece into a round loaf or a log that is fatter in the middle and tapered at the ends. Place on a baking sheet or peel sprinkled with cornmeal, cover with a towel, and let rise until doubled, about 1 hour.

Baking. Thirty minutes before baking, heat the oven with a baking stone in it to 425° F. Just before baking, brush the loaves with the egg white. Slash the long loaves with 3 parallel cuts, using a razor. Sprinkle the stone with cornmeal and slide the loaves onto it. Bake 40 minutes, spraying 3 times with water in the first 10 minutes. Cool completely on a rack.

Panmarino
Rosemary Bread

The lovely pungent flavor of rosemary is often kneaded into the breads of Tuscany and Liguria, but this *panmarino* comes from Ferrara, the invention of an ebullient, mustachioed baker named Luciano Pancalde, whose surname aptly translates as "hot bread." Years ago, while reading a biography of the d'Este family who once ruled Ferrara, he discovered that one of the numerous spectacular court banquets featured a rosemary bread with a crust described as sparkling with diamonds. Luciano baked and baked again before he came up with this wonderful dome-shaped bread that is aromatic with fresh rosemary. But there's no need to go to Tiffany's for any of the ingredients. Just before baking, he slashes the top in the pattern of a star and sprinkles chunky crystals of sea salt into the crevices. The salt really does sparkle like diamonds.

I make this bread all the time, not only because it is so easy and takes relatively little time from beginning to end, but also because it goes well with so many foods. It is wonderful with roast pork, chicken, or lamb and has an affinity with white fish, especially swordfish. Because the recipe makes two loaves, the second usually ends up sliced for sandwiches or a platter of cold meat.

If you use the electric mixer, you will have to stop the motor several times to push down the dough because the recipe proportions are just at the edge of the machine's capacity. Be sure not to let the

Panmarino (continued)

dough fully double in its second rise or it won't spring to its full height in the oven. And there's no sense in not having a spectacular-looking bread to bring to the table.

Makes 2 round loaves

3¾ teaspoons active dry yeast or 1½ small cakes (27 grams) fresh
    yeast
1 cup warm water
1 cup milk, room temperature
⅓ cup less 1 tablespoon olive oil
3½ to 4 tablespoons finely chopped fresh rosemary or 1½ tablespoons
    dried
1 tablespoon plus 1 teaspoon (20 grams) salt
About 6¾ cups (900 grams) unbleached all-purpose flour
1 to 1½ teaspoons coarse sea salt

BY HAND

Stir the yeast into the water in a large mixing bowl; let stand until creamy, about 10 minutes. Stir in the milk and oil. Combine the rosemary, salt, and flour and stir into the yeast mixture in 3 or 4 additions. Stir until the dough comes together. Knead on a floured surface until velvety, elastic, and smooth, 8 to 10 minutes. It should be somewhat moist and blistered.

BY MIXER

This recipe is slightly large for the mixer, so that you'll have to stop and push the dough down frequently while the mixer is kneading it. Stir the yeast into the water in a mixer bowl; let stand until creamy, about 10 minutes. Stir in the milk and oil with the paddle. Combine the rosemary, salt, and flour and add to the yeast mixture. Mix until the flour is absorbed, 1 to 2 minutes. Change to the dough hook and knead on medium speed until velvety, elastic, smooth, and somewhat moist, about 3 minutes. Finish kneading briefly by hand on a lightly floured surface.

BY PROCESSOR

Make sure your food processor can handle the volume of this dough. Even when done in 2 batches there will be about 3½ cups flour plus liquid to be processed. If you have a large-capacity machine, use the dough blade. Stir the yeast into ¼ cup warm water in a small bowl; let stand until creamy, about 10 minutes. Place the rosemary, salt, and flour in a food processor fitted with the dough or steel blade and process briefly to mix and chop the rosemary. Stir the oil into the dissolved yeast. With the machine running, pour the yeast mixture, cold milk, and ¾ cup cold water in a steady stream through the feed tube and process until the dough gathers into a ball. Process 45 seconds longer to knead. Finish kneading by hand on a lightly floured surface until smooth, velvety, elastic, and slightly moist, 2 to 3 minutes.

First Rise. Place the dough in an oiled bowl, cover tightly with plastic wrap, and let rise until doubled, about 1½ hours.

Shaping and Second Rise. Gently punch the dough down on a lightly floured surface, but don't knead it. Cut the dough in half and shape each half into a round ball. Place the loaves on a lightly floured peel or a lightly oiled baking sheet, cover with a towel, and let rise 45 to 55 minutes (but not until truly doubled).

Baking. Heat the oven to 450° F. If you are using a baking stone, turn the oven on 30 minutes before baking and sprinkle the stone with cornmeal just before sliding the loaves onto it. Just before you put the loaves in the oven, slash the top of each loaf in an asterisk with a razor blade and sprinkle half the sea salt into the cuts of each loaf. Bake 10 minutes, spraying 3 times with water. Reduce the heat to 400° F and bake 30 to 35 minutes longer. Cool completely on racks.

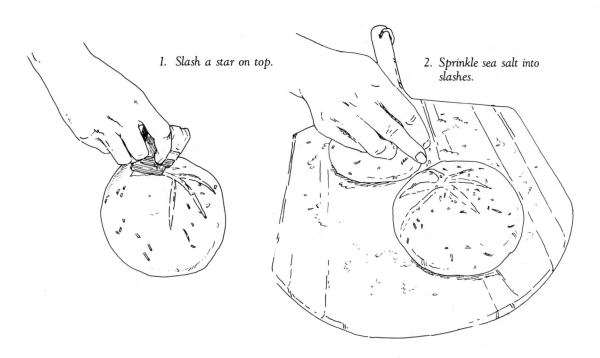

1. *Slash a star on top.*

2. *Sprinkle sea salt into slashes.*

Pane all'Erbe
Herb Bread

The first time our family lived in Italy, we rented a house in a tiny community where we were the sole foreigners. All the shopping was done in the five or six shops set along the only street in town. Every morning our children went to the grocery to get the bread that was delivered still hot from the nearby ovens, and later in the morning, I would appear for the real shopping of the day with the other ladies, who gossiped, admired each other's children, and talked as the line moved sluggishly toward the reward of wonderful fresh fruits and vegetables. On one of our first days in town, I asked at the market for some parsley, only to feel the lady behind me tap me on the shoulder and ask me to save her place in line. "I'll be right back," she said, and she was, in a flash, with a lovely handful of parsley from her garden. In small Italian towns it seems that everyone grows aromatic parsley with its flat green leaves. Elsewhere it is sometimes presented free with vegetables at the grocery or with meat at the butcher shop when it seems appropriate. If you can find Italian parsley with its full-flavored taste, please use it in this bread; otherwise, the curly-leaf American variety will do just fine. The piquant taste of the garlic, onions, and herbs give this bread a robust and earthy character, making it a particularly good choice to serve with roast meats and fish.

Makes 2 round loaves

½ cup tightly packed fresh parsley leaves
3 tablespoons minced onion
1 large clove garlic
2½ teaspoons (1 package) active dry yeast or 1 small cake (18 grams) fresh yeast
1 cup plus 2 tablespoons warm water
1 tablespoon olive oil
3¾ cups (500 grams) unbleached all-purpose flour
2 teaspoons (10 grams) salt
Cornmeal

Using a sharp knife or a food processor fitted with the steel blade, chop the parsley, onion, and garlic together until finely minced.

BY HAND

Stir the yeast into the water in a mixing bowl; let stand until creamy, about 10 minutes. Stir in the minced parsley mixture and the oil. Mix the flour and salt and stir 1 cup at a time into the yeast mixture. Stir until the dough comes together. Knead on a lightly floured surface, sprinkling with additional flour as needed, until silky and elastic, 8 to 10 minutes.

BY MIXER

Stir the yeast into the water in a mixer bowl; let stand until creamy, about 10 minutes. Mix in the oil and then the parsley mixture with the paddle. Mix the flour and salt and mix 1 cup at a time into the yeast mixture. Mix until the dough pulls away from the sides of the bowl. Change to the dough hook and knead until silky, elastic, and resilient, 2 to 3 minutes.

BY PROCESSOR

Stir the yeast into ¼ cup warm water in a small bowl; let stand until creamy, about 10 minutes. Place the flour and salt in a food processor fitted with the steel blade and process with 2 or 3 pulses to sift. Spoon the parsley mixture on top of the flour. With the machine running, pour the dissolved yeast and ¾ cup plus 2 tablespoons cold water through the feed tube and process until the dough comes together. Process 40 seconds longer to knead. Finish kneading briefly by hand on a lightly floured surface.

First Rise. Place the dough in a lightly oiled bowl, cover tightly with plastic wrap, and let rise until doubled, about 1½ hours. The dough should be soft and pillowy.

Shaping and Second Rise. Punch the dough down on a lightly floured surface and knead it briefly. Cut the dough in half and shape each half into a round loaf. Place the loaves on a peel lightly sprinkled with cornmeal or on a lightly oiled baking sheet. Cover with a towel and let rise until doubled, about 45 minutes.

Baking. Heat the oven to 400° F. If you are using a baking stone, turn the oven on 30 minutes before baking and sprinkle the stone with cornmeal just before sliding the loaves onto it. Bake until the loaves sound hollow when you tap the bottoms, 40 to 45 minutes. Cool completely on racks.

Italian parsley

Pane al Pepe Verde

Green-Peppercorn Bread

Italian bakers with their artisan ways lose no time in incorporating new ingredients into their breads. This bread belongs to the new wave of imaginative combinations, but it is surprisingly delicate and smooth and much less overwhelming than it sounds. Use green peppercorns from Madagascar, if you can find them. The bread goes well with mild cheeses, roast chicken, and vegetable salads.

Makes 1 long or round loaf

1¾ teaspoons active dry yeast or ⅔ small cake (12 grams) fresh yeast
1 cup warm water
1¼ to 1½ tablespoons green peppercorns (packed in brine), well drained
2 teaspoons olive oil
2¾ to 3 cups (375 grams) unbleached all-purpose flour
1 teaspoon (5 grams) salt

BY HAND

Stir the yeast into the water in a large mixing bowl; let stand until creamy, about 10 minutes. Finely chop the peppercorns. If the peppercorns are not well chopped, they have an annoying way of popping out of the dough as you knead it. Stir the oil into the dissolved yeast; stir in the flour, salt, and peppercorns. Stir until the dough comes together. Knead on a floured surface, sprinkling with additional flour as needed, until moist, velvety, and elastic, 8 to 10 minutes. The dough should feel faintly like Silly Putty.

BY MIXER

Stir the yeast into the water in a large mixer bowl; let stand until creamy, about 10 minutes. Lightly chop the peppercorns. Stir the oil into the dissolved yeast with the paddle. Add the flour, salt, and peppercorns and mix until the dough comes together. Change to the dough hook and knead at medium speed until the dough is elastic and velvety but still moist, 3 to 4 minutes. Finish kneading briefly by hand on a floured surface.

BY PROCESSOR

Stir the yeast into ¼ cup warm water in a small bowl; let stand until creamy, about 10 minutes. Stir in the oil and ¾ cup cold water. Place the flour, salt, and peppercorns (drained but not chopped) in a food processor fitted with the steel blade and process with 2 or 3 pulses to lightly chop the peppercorns. With the machine running, pour the yeast mixture through the feed tube as quickly as the flour can absorb it. Process 45 seconds longer to knead. Finish kneading briefly by hand on a lightly floured surface.

First Rise. Place the dough in a lightly oiled bowl, cover with plastic wrap, and let rise until doubled, about 1½ hours.

Shaping and Second Rise. Punch the dough down on a lightly floured surface and knead it briefly. Shape the dough into a long thin or a round loaf. The dough will be slightly moist. Place the loaf on a peel sprinkled with cornmeal or on a lightly oiled baking sheet. Cover with a towel and let rise until doubled, about 45 minutes to 1 hour. Flatten the bread slightly by pressing down firmly with the palm of your hand. Using a razor, slash 3 parallel wavy lines or, in the top of the round loaf, a star-shaped pattern.

Baking. Heat the oven to 500° F. If you are using a baking stone, turn the oven on 30 minutes before baking and sprinkle the stone with cornmeal just before sliding the loaf onto it. Place the loaf in the oven and immediately reduce the heat to 400° F. Bake 35 minutes, spraying 3 times with water in the first 10 minutes. Cool completely on a rack.

Slashing wavy lines on top

Various-Grain Breads with New Tastes

Segale con Pancetta

Rye Bread with Pancetta

This is a dense, dark rye that is moist and velvety in texture. The *pancetta* gives it a slight bite, wonderful aroma, and good strong taste, but you can certainly substitute bacon or bake it as a regular rye without the *pancetta*. It is wonderful with cheese.

Makes 2 round loaves

SPONGE
5 teaspoons (2 packages) active dry yeast or 2 small cakes (36 grams) fresh yeast
3½ cups warm water
3¾ cups (500 grams) bread or unbleached all-purpose flour

Stir the yeast into the warm water in a large mixing bowl or mixer bowl, depending on your method; let stand until creamy, about 10 minutes. Stir in the flour and let stand until bubbly, 15 to 20 minutes.

DOUGH
¼ cup extra virgin olive oil
4 to 4½ cups (500 grams) rye flour, preferably stone ground
1 tablespoon plus 1 teaspoon (25 grams) sea salt
6 to 7 ounces (180 to 200 grams) *pancetta*, cut into small cubes
Cornmeal

BY HAND

Stir the oil into the sponge. Mix the rye flour and the salt; stir 1 cup at a time into the sponge. The dough should come together easily. Flour your work surface generously, flour a dough scraper, and have a small mound of flour nearby for your hands. Knead the dough 8 to 10 minutes, using the dough scraper and sprinkling with ¼ to ⅓ cup additional bread or all-purpose flour as needed. Although it hardly seems possible at the beginning, the dough will become firm, elastic, and consistent by the time you are through. Knead in the *pancetta* in 2 additions by sprinkling over the flattened dough, rolling up the dough, and repeating.

BY MIXER   Stir the oil into the sponge with the paddle. Add the rye flour and salt and mix until the dough comes together and is velvety to the touch. Change to the dough hook and knead at low speed until firm, consistent, and elastic, about 4 minutes. Knead in the *pancetta* in 2 additions as directed for mixing by hand.

BY PROCESSOR   Make sure your food processor can handle the volume of this dough. Even when done in 2 batches, there will be 4 cups flour to be processed. Refrigerate the sponge covered at least 30 minutes. Place the salt and rye flour in a food processor fitted with the dough blade and process with 2 or 3 pulses to sift. Stir the oil into the sponge. With the machine running, pour the yeast mixture through the feed tube as quickly as the flour can absorb it and process until the dough gathers into a ball. Process 40 seconds longer to knead. Knead in the *pancetta* in 2 additions as directed for mixing by hand.

First Rise. Place the dough in an oiled bowl, cover tightly with plastic wrap, and let rise until doubled, about 1 hour.

Shaping and Second Rise. Turn the dough out onto a floured surface. Without kneading, cut the dough in half and shape each half into a round loaf, handling the dough gently. Place each loaf, seam side up, in an oiled and well-floured round banneton or basket lined with a tea towel that has been oiled and floured. Cover the loaves with heavy towels and let rise until the dough has doubled and thoroughly filled the baskets, about 1 hour. Like all ryes, the risen loaf will feel slightly tacky.

Baking. Thirty minutes before baking, heat the oven with baking stones in it to 400° F. Just before baking, sprinkle the stones or baking sheets with cornmeal. Very gently invert the loaves onto the stones. Bake 40 to 45 minutes. Cool completely on racks.

Pan Completo o Pan Graham
Graham Bread

Ten years ago it was almost impossible to find a loaf of whole-wheat bread or a sack of whole-wheat flour in Italy. But that was before the rediscovery of the highly prized Mediterranean diet, which is rich in whole grains, and it was certainly before the appearance of graham flour, which is actually whole-wheat flour from which the bran and wheat germ have been extracted, finely powdered, and then reincorporated.

Graham flour is named for the nineteenth-century reformer who was such a fanatic crusader for the benefits of whole grain that his name has become synonymous with whole wheat in some places. Graham bread is enjoying a vogue in the big cities of Italy, not only for obvious reasons of health but also because it is a rich, nutty-tasting loaf with a lighter texture than might reasonably be expected. It is wonderful toasted. Variations of whole-wheat breads made at Gianfornaio in Milan include *pan graham* baked with yogurt, linen seeds, herbs, or soy flakes, which combine with the grain in a synergistic way so that the bread has the protein value of a sizable beef steak. If you can't find graham flour, substitute fine stone-ground whole-wheat flour. Eat the bread with salami and smoked meat, mushrooms, or sliced salmon.

Makes two 9 × 5-inch loaves

STARTER
¾ teaspoon active dry yeast or ¼ small cake (4 grams) fresh yeast
¼ cup warm water
1¾ cups water, cool room temperature
3¾ cups (500 grams) graham or stone-ground whole-wheat flour

Stir the yeast into the warm water in a mixing or mixer bowl; let stand until creamy, about 10 minutes. Stir in 1¾ cups water and then the flour. Cover with plastic wrap and let rise overnight. The dough will initially be stiff, but it will have relaxed by morning.

DOUGH
½ teaspoon active dry yeast or ⅛ cake (2 grams) fresh yeast
1 tablespoon warm water
About 2 cups (250 grams) graham or stone-ground whole-wheat flour
1 teaspoon (5 grams) salt
About ⅓ cup unbleached all-purpose flour for kneading

BY HAND

Stir the yeast into the water in a small bowl; let stand until creamy, about 10 minutes. Stir the dissolved yeast into the starter. Mix the graham flour and salt and stir ¼ cup at a time into the starter, using strong strokes to work the stiff dough. Generously flour a work surface with all-purpose flour and knead the dough for 10 to 12 minutes. You will need to use about ⅓ cup all-purpose flour in the kneading. Use a dough scraper to remove the film left on the work surface. Slam the dough down hard several times towards the end of the kneading time to help develop the gluten.

BY MIXER

Stir the yeast into the water in a small bowl; let stand until creamy, about 10 minutes. Stir the dissolved yeast into the starter with the paddle. Mix the graham flour and salt and add to the starter. Mix until the dough comes together. Change to the dough hook and knead for 3 to 5 minutes at medium speed. Finish kneading briefly by hand on a floured work surface, sprinkling with all-purpose flour, until the dough is no longer sticky.

First Rise. Place the dough in a lightly oiled bowl, cover tightly with plastic wrap, and let rise until doubled, about 1¾ hours.

Shaping and Second Rise. Punch the dough down on a floured surface and cut it in half. Knead briefly and shape each half into an oval loaf to fit into a 9 × 5-inch loaf pan. Place the loaves, seam sides down, in the oiled loaf pans and cover with a towel. Let rise to one-and-a-half times its volume, about 40 minutes.

Baking. Heat the oven to 375° F. Make several parallel slashes on top of each loaf so that the sides won't split during baking. Bake 40 minutes. If you want, bake the last 10 minutes out of the pans on a baking sheet so that the bottom and sides brown. Cool completely on racks.

Pane Integrale con Miele

Whole-Wheat with Honey

The taste of whole wheat and a drizzle of honey makes a wonderful full-flavored bread. Try it as delicious small dinner rolls, as well as a perfect breakfast or sandwich loaf.

Makes 1 round loaf

STARTER (*optional*)
¼ teaspoon active dry yeast
⅔ cup warm water
1½ cups (200 grams) unbleached all-purpose flour

Stir the yeast into the water in a medium-size mixing bowl; let stand until creamy, about 10 minutes. Stir in the flour with 70 to 100 strokes of a wooden spoon. Let rise covered 6 to 24 hours. Measure ¼ cup (50 grams) for this recipe.

DOUGH
1¾ teaspoons active dry yeast or ⅔ small cake (12 grams) fresh yeast
1 tablespoon plus 2 teaspoons honey
1½ cups warm water
3¾ cups (500 grams) whole-wheat flour
1½ teaspoons (8 grams) salt

BY HAND

Stir the yeast and honey into ¼ cup of the water in a large mixing bowl; let stand until foamy, about 10 minutes. Chop the starter into small pieces and add to the dissolved yeast. Pour in the remaining 1¼ cups water and squeeze the starter between your fingers until the starter is in little shreds and the water is chalky. Mix the flour and salt and stir 1 cup at a time into the yeast mixture. Stir until the dough comes together. Knead on a floured surface, sprinkling with additional whole-wheat flour, until the dough is fairly smooth and has lost most of its stickiness, about 8 to 10 minutes.

BY MIXER

Stir the yeast and honey into the water in a mixer bowl; let stand until foamy, about 10 minutes. Chop the starter into small pieces and add to the dissolved yeast. Stir with the paddle until the starter is in little shreds. Add the flour and salt and mix until the dough comes together. Change to the dough hook and knead 2 minutes at low speed and 2 minutes at medium speed. The dough should be fairly smooth and have lost most of its stickiness. Finish kneading briefly by hand on a floured surface, if you want.

First Rise. Place the dough in an oiled bowl, cover tightly with plastic wrap, and let rise until doubled, about 2 hours.

Shaping and Second Rise. Turn the dough out onto a well-floured surface and shape into a round loaf without punching the dough down. Place the loaf on a lightly oiled baking sheet or a peel sprinkled with cornmeal. Cover with waxed paper or a towel or lightly oil the top and cover with plastic wrap. Let rise until doubled, 45 minutes to 1 hour.

Baking. Heat the oven to 450° F. If you are using a baking stone, turn the oven on 30 minutes before baking and sprinkle the stone with cornmeal just before sliding the loaf onto it. Bake 10 minutes, spraying 3 times with water. Reduce the heat to 400° F and bake 25 minutes longer. Cool completely on a rack.

Pane Rustico
Rustic Whole-Wheat Pillows

These pillow-shaped breads have a crisp crust and a nutty, crunchy interior with a robust flavor. They are wonderful sliced in half for sandwiches, but you can also make them much, much smaller for tiny hors d'oeuvres. The longer you soak your wheat berries, the more flavorful they will be, but if you find they smell sour, add a little baking soda to the water and everything will be fine.

Makes 8 large rolls

½ cup (100 grams) cracked hard wheat berries
¾ cup (100 grams) unbleached all-purpose flour
2½ teaspoons (1 package) active dry yeast or 1 small cake (18 grams) fresh yeast
1 cup warm water
About 2¼ cups (300 grams) whole-wheat flour
1 tablespoon (15 grams) salt
Unbleached all-purpose flour for kneading

Soak the wheat berries in cold water for 1 to 3 days or pour boiling water over the berries and let stand 6 to 8 hours. Drain the wheat berries and process the berries and all-purpose flour in a food processor or blender just until coarsely chopped. If too finely chopped, the berries won't be crunchy.

Pane Rustico (continued)

BY HAND

Stir the yeast into the warm water in a mixing bowl; let stand until creamy, about 10 minutes. Stir in the berry mixture. Mix the whole-wheat flour and salt and stir 2 cups at a time into the yeast mixture. Stir until the dough is stiff and sticky. Knead on a surface floured with all-purpose flour until firm, elastic, but still slightly tacky, 8 to 10 minutes.

BY MIXER

Stir the yeast into the warm water in a mixer bowl; let stand until creamy, about 10 minutes. Stir in the berry mixture with the paddle and then the whole-wheat flour and salt. Mix until the dough comes together and is stiff and sticky. Change to the dough hook and knead until firm, elastic, but still slightly tacky, 3 to 4 minutes. If you want, finish kneading briefly by hand on a surface floured with all-purpose flour.

BY PROCESSOR

Stir the yeast into ¼ cup warm water in a small bowl; let stand until creamy, about 10 minutes. Place the berry mixture, whole-wheat flour, and salt in a food processor fitted with the steel blade. With the machine running, pour the dissolved yeast and ¾ cup cold water through the feed tube as quickly as the flour can absorb it and process until the dough comes together. Process 40 seconds longer to knead. Finish kneading briefly by hand on a surface floured with all-purpose flour until firm, elastic, but still slightly tacky.

First Rise. Place the dough in a lightly oiled bowl, cover tightly with plastic wrap, and let rise until doubled, about 2 hours.

Shaping and Second Rise. Punch the dough down on a lightly floured surface and knead briefly. Shape into a long rectangle by flattening it with your forearm. Cut into eight 5-inch squares. Place on a lightly oiled baking sheet, cover with a towel, and let rise until well puffed and almost doubled, about 1¾ hours.

Baking. Heat oven to 450° F. Bake 10 minutes. Reduce the heat to 350° F and bake 15 minutes longer. Cool completely on racks.

Pane Integrale alle Erbe

Whole-Wheat Bread with Herbs

"Spiritoso," said the Roman baker, describing this bread—meaning it's witty and spirited, a bit out of the ordinary with its clever counterpoint of herbs played against the whole wheat. It's also straightforward and honest, with a crunchy top and soft interior, and it tastes wonderful with hearty beef and lamb dishes.

Makes 2 rings of 10 to 12 rolls each or 24 individual rolls

3¼ teaspoons active dry yeast or 1⅓ small cakes (24 grams) fresh
  yeast
¼ cup warm water
Scant ¼ cup olive oil
2¾ cups water, room temperature
2 tablespoons chopped fresh rosemary or 2 teaspoons dried
⅔ cup chopped fresh parsley
About 6 cups (800 grams) whole-wheat flour
1½ cups (200 grams) unbleached all-purpose flour
1 tablespoon plus 1 teaspoon (20 grams) salt

BY HAND

Stir the yeast into the warm water in a large mixing bowl; let stand until creamy, about 10 minutes. Stir in the oil and 2¾ cups water. Stir in the rosemary and parsley. Mix the flours and salt and stir 1 cup at a time into the yeast mixture. Stir quickly to work into a dough. Knead on a lightly floured surface until firm and elastic, 8 to 10 minutes.

BY MIXER

Stir the yeast into the warm water in a mixer bowl; let stand until creamy, about 10 minutes. Stir in the oil and 2¾ cups water with the paddle. Add the rosemary, parsley, flours, and salt and mix until the dough pulls away from the side of the bowl. Change to the dough hook and knead until firm and elastic, 2 to 3 minutes.

BY PROCESSOR

If the capacity of your food processor is 7 cups or less, process this dough in 2 batches. Stir the yeast into ¼ cup warm water in a small bowl; let stand until creamy, about 10 minutes. Place the rosemary, parsley, salt, and flours in a food processor fitted with a steel blade and process with 1 or 2 pulses to mix. Pour the dissolved yeast and oil over the flour. With the machine running, pour 2¾ cups cold water through the feed tube as quickly as the flour can absorb it. Process until the dough gathers into a ball. Stop and then process 45 seconds longer to knead. Finish kneading briefly by hand on a lightly floured surface.

Pane Integrale alle Erbe (continued)

First Rise. Place the dough in a lightly oiled bowl, cover with plastic wrap, and let rise until doubled, about 1 hour 20 minutes.

Shaping and Second Rise. Punch the dough down on a lightly floured surface. Cut the dough in half and cover the piece you are not working on with plastic wrap to keep the dough from drying out. Shape each piece into 10 to 12 balls and cover the shaped dough as you finish. Arrange 10 to 12 rolls about ½ to ¾ inches apart in a ring on a lightly oiled or parchment-lined baking sheet or in a ring mold. Cover with plastic wrap propped up on juice glasses or spice or herb jars. Place a towel over the plastic wrap and let dough rise until doubled, about 1¼ hours. The risen rolls should look like big Swedish meatballs flecked with little pieces of parsley. You may make individual rolls instead of arranging them in rings, if you prefer.

Baking. Heat the oven to 400° F. If you are using baking stones, turn the oven on 30 minutes before baking and sprinkle with cornmeal just before sliding the rolls onto them. Bake the rings 20 minutes and individual rolls 20 minutes. Cool completely on racks.

The baked Pane Integrale alle Erbe

Pane ai Cinque Cereali con Noci

Five-Grain Bread with Walnuts

Walnuts are the brilliant touch in this bread. I've had more than my share of several-grain breads and have never been particularly knocked out by their taste. But when I bit into this and let the crunch and rich flavor of the toasted nuts race across my tongue, I knew I had left the world of health food for something a good deal more intriguing. Multi-grain breads are experiencing a surge of popularity in Italy, confirming what people living close to the earth have always known—the more genuine and natural the food, the better for the body. These natural grains may be tonic for the body, but it's those lovely nuts that make a particularly tasty bread. Serve with smoked meats, smoked salmon, oysters and mussels, and sharp cheeses.

Makes 2 9 × 5-inch loaves

1¼ cups (300 grams) walnut pieces

3¾ teaspoons active dry yeast or 1½ small cakes (27 grams) fresh
  yeast

¼ cup warm water

3 cups water, room temperature

3¾ cups (500 grams) unbleached all-purpose flour

1¼ cups (125 grams) oat flour or finely ground rolled oats

1 cup plus 2 tablespoons (125 grams) rye flour

1 cup less 1 tablespoon (125 grams) whole-wheat flour

¾ cup (125 grams) brown rice flour

1 tablespoon plus 1 teaspoon (20 grams) salt

Toast the walnuts for 10 minutes in a 400° F oven; then chop in a
food processor fitted with the steel blade or with a sharp knife to the
size of a fat rice kernel. Do not grind them finely.

BY HAND   Stir the yeast into the warm water in a large mixing bowl; let stand
until creamy, about 10 minutes. Stir in 3 cups water. Mix the walnuts,
flours, and salt and stir 2 cups at a time into the dissolved yeast,
stirring vigorously with a wooden spoon or rubber spatula. The
dough should come together easily. Knead on a floured surface,
sprinkling with additional all-purpose flour as needed, until firm,
elastic, and no longer sticky, 8 to 10 minutes.

BY MIXER   Stir the yeast into the warm water in a mixer bowl; let stand until
creamy, about 10 minutes. Stir in 3 cups water. Stir in the flours,
walnuts, and salt with the paddle. Mix until the dough comes
together. Change to the dough hook and knead for 3 to 4 minutes
at medium speed until firm and elastic but still slightly sticky. Finish
kneading briefly by hand on a surface floured with all-purpose flour.

BY PROCESSOR   Make sure your food processor can handle the volume of this dough.
Even when done in 2 batches, there will be 4 cups flour to be
processed. Stir the yeast into the warm water in a small bowl; let
stand until creamy, about 10 minutes. Place the flours and salt in a
food processor fitted with the dough blade and process with several
pulses to sift. With the machine running, pour the dissolved yeast
and 3 cups cold water through the feed tube as quickly as the flours
can absorb it; process until the dough gathers into a ball. Process 40
seconds longer to knead. Knead in the walnuts by hand on a surface
floured with all-purpose flour.

Pane ai Cinque Cereali con Noci (continued)

First Rise. Place the dough in a lightly oiled bowl, cover with plastic wrap, and let rise until doubled, about 1 hour.

Shaping and Second Rise. Turn the dough out onto a lightly floured surface. The dough should be moist, firm, and noticeably elastic, if slightly sticky. Cut the dough in half and shape each half into an oval loaf to fit a loaf pan. Place the loaves in the oiled pans (preferably glass), cover with a heavy towel, and let rise until truly doubled and fully above the tops of the pans, 1 to 1¼ hours.

Baking. Heat oven to 400° F. Slash a pattern in the top of the loaves. One baker in Milan cuts the shape of a stalk of grain on the top; elsewhere bakers make 3 parallel slashes. Bake 40 to 45 minutes; bake the last 5 to 10 minutes out of the pans on a baking stone or baking sheet to brown the bottoms and sides. Cool completely on a rack.

Campagnolo
Country Bread with Bran

There are Italians who jog and Italians who diet, and now there are more and more Italians who appreciate the importance of natural foods to health. Inspired by research extolling bran as an aid to digestion, a country baker dreamed up this bread, which gets its nutty crunch from the bran but maintains a lovely balance between heartiness and delicate flavor. Serve it with fresh cheeses.

Makes 2 loaves

2½ teaspoons (1 package) active dry yeast or 1 small cake (18 grams) fresh yeast
⅓ cup warm water
2⅔ cups water, room temperature
2 tablespoons olive oil
About 5½ cups (750 grams) unbleached all-purpose flour
2 cups (150 grams) bran
2¼ teaspoons (12 grams) salt

BY HAND

Stir the yeast into the warm water in a large mixing bowl; let stand until creamy, about 10 minutes. Stir in all but 2 tablespoons of the 2⅔ cups water (you probably won't need it) and the oil. Mix the flour, bran, and salt and stir 2 cups at a time into the yeast mixture, reserving ¼ to ½ cup of the flour mixture. When the dough is too stiff to stir, plunge in with your hands. Knead on a floured work surface, sprinkling with the reserved flour as needed, until firm and elastic but still slightly sticky, 8 to 10 minutes. Slam the dough down several times towards the end of the kneading to help develop the gluten.

BY MIXER   Stir the yeast into the warm water in a large mixer bowl; let stand until creamy, about 10 minutes. Stir in 2⅔ cups water and the oil. Mix the flour, bran, and salt and reserve ¼ to ½ cup for kneading. Add the remaining flour mixture to the yeast mixture and mix with the paddle for 2 to 3 minutes. Change to the dough hook and knead 3 to 4 minutes, half at low speed and half at medium. The dough should be creamy beige and feel stiff but elastic. If the dough is very stiff, let it rest a couple of minutes and then continue kneading. The dough will be sticky even when fully kneaded because of the bran. Finish kneading by hand, sprinkling with the reserved flour as needed, for 1 to 2 minutes.

BY PROCESSOR   Make sure your processor can handle the volume of this dough. Stir the yeast into the warm water in a small bowl; let stand until creamy, about 10 minutes. Place the flour, bran, and salt in a food processor fitted with the steel blade and process with 2 or 3 pulses to mix. Pour the oil and dissolved yeast over the flour mixture. With the machine running, pour 2⅔ cups plus 1 tablespoon cold water through the feed tube and process until the dough comes together. Process 45 seconds longer to knead. Finish kneading very briefly by hand on a floured surface.

First Rise. Place the dough in a lightly oiled bowl, cover with plastic wrap, and let rise until doubled, about 1½ hours.

Shaping and Second Rise. Turn the dough out on a lightly floured surface. Cut the dough in half and shape each piece into a ball and then into an oval loaf. Dip the flat edge of your hand, from little finger to wrist bone, into a bit of flour, and press it down the center of each loaf to make a lengthwise cleft. Pinch the ends of the loaf tightly together and make a deep impression with your thumb at each end. It should resemble a pair of lips. Place the loaves, cleft sides down, on heavily floured peels or baking sheets. Cover with a towel and let rise for about 45 minutes. The dough will feel slightly less resilient than other doughs even when it is ready.

Baking. Thirty minutes before baking, heat the oven with baking stones or oiled baking sheets in it to 425° F. If you are using baking stones, sprinkle the stone with cornmeal just before baking. Invert and firmly press the cleft again with the edge of your hand and emphasize the thumb impressions. Place the loaves onto the hot stones or baking sheets and bake 20 minutes. Reduce the heat to 375° F and bake 20 to 25 minutes longer. Cool on racks at least 30 minutes.

GLI AVANZI
Using Leftover Breads

Some of the best dishes in all Italy are the simplest and most rustic. They are the spontaneous creations of a peasant culture that has taken the tastiest ingredients of the countryside and turned them into comforting country food. Most of them begin with breads, those fat wheels and crusty ovals that are served at the table three times a day. These rustic dishes are a prime example of making a virtue of necessity; because these regional breads go stale rather quickly, frugal peasants and thrifty housewives and cooks have dreamed up a whole poor people's cuisine that uses up every last crumb.

Many of these dishes are essentially moist breads turned into soups with the addition of a bit of broth and an egg or two or a handful of greens, or into salads with slices of tomato, bits of chopped onion and garlic, perhaps a sprinkling of herbs and a few gratings of pepper. These homey regional recipes—such as they are, for every household has its own variation—are savory and satisfying, the quintessential Sunday night supper. Some of them are absolutely basic to the region—*mozzarella in carrozza* is unmistakably Neapolitan and *pappa al pomodoro* is totally Tuscan—and others are generic—you'll find bread puddings in more than one region—but all are the best of simple regional Italian cuisine, mixing leftover and stale bread with the freshest ingredients to make filling, tasty dishes.

Savory Dishes

Bruschetta o Fettunta

Garlic Bread

Good chewy peasant bread grilled over a wood fire and drizzled with olive oil, sometimes rubbed with a clove of garlic and sometimes not, is known as *bruschetta* in Rome, *fettunta* in Tuscany, and *soma d'ai* in Piedmont. In all three places, it is the perfect way to taste rich, fruity olive oil just after it has been pressed.

Makes 6 servings

6 slices country bread, or *Pane Toscano* (Saltless Tuscan Bread, page 110) for *fettunta*
1 or 2 large cloves garlic, cut in half
Salt
Freshly ground pepper
¼ cup best-quality extra virgin olive oil

Toast or grill the bread. When the slices are still warm, rub one side with the garlic clove so that the flavor permeates the bread. Sprinkle with salt and pepper, and then drizzle with the oil. Serve immediately.

Variation. For *Bruschetta Pugliese*, cook 2 chopped seeded ripe tomatoes in 3 to 4 tablespoons olive oil in a sauté pan over medium-low heat to a rich concentrate, about 10 minutes. If you want, cook 1 minced garlic clove with the tomatoes. Spread 6 slices of *bruschetta* made from Altamura Bread (page 120) with the tomato concentrate.

Crostini

These traditional hors d'oeuvres are nothing more than croutons of saltless Tuscan bread topped with a particularly tasty chopped liver spread. The anchovies and capers are the perfect salty, piquant foil to the mellow but bland bread of the region. There are endless variations of *crostini*, but you can be sure that any antipasto you encounter at a Florentine restaurant will include one of them.

Makes 6 to 8 servings

8 ounces (225 grams) chicken livers
2 tablespoons (30 grams) unsalted butter
1 tablespoon olive oil
¼ cup chopped onion
2 bay leaves
¼ cup Marsala
2 anchovies, drained
2 teaspoons capers, drained
8 slices (¼ inch thick) *Pane Toscano* (Saltless Tuscan Bread, page 110)

Rinse the chicken livers and cut away any yellow spots. Heat the butter and oil in a sauté pan over medium-low heat. Add the livers

Crostini (continued)

and onion and sauté 3 to 5 minutes. Stir in the bay leaves and Marsala and cook over medium-high heat until the Marsala is almost evaporated. Remove the chicken livers to a cutting board. Very finely chop the chicken livers, anchovies, and capers with a mezzaluna or a chef's knife. Don't use a food processor or blender, for the mixture will be too fine a paste for true Tuscan *crostini*, which should have a bit of texture to it. Return the liver mixture to the pan and cook 1 to 2 minutes.

Meanwhile, cut the bread into 2-inch squares or slightly larger rectangles for hors d'oeuvres or cut the slices in half for antipasto. Toast the bread lightly in the oven or butter one side lightly and sauté, buttered side down, briefly in a skillet. Let the bread cool completely; then spread with the liver mixture or spoon it into a small bowl and let everyone spread his or her own. The chicken liver mixture is often served warm or at room temperature.

Crostoni con Taleggio o Gorgonzola

What are *crostoni?* They are the perfect solution to a really quick first course or antipasto on a cold winter evening. Toast country bread, make a simple cheese topping, warm them together, and you have a splendid hors d'oeuvre that uses up your stale bread as well.

Makes 6 servings

3 to 3½ tablespoons (50 grams) unsalted butter, room temperature
6 thick slices slightly stale country bread
6 ounces (180 grams) Taleggio or Gorgonzola cheese, crumbled
4 to 6 teaspoons water or milk
1 garlic clove, finely slivered (optional)
Salt
Freshly ground pepper

Heat the oven to 425° F. Using 2 tablespoons of the butter, spread one side of each slice of bread with butter. Place buttered sides up on a baking sheet and bake until lightly browned.

Meanwhile, place the cheese, 4 teaspoons water, 1 tablespoon butter, and the garlic, if desired, in a small saucepan; heat over very low heat, mashing the cheese with a wooden spoon, until melted and creamy. Add the remaining water and butter if the cheese mixture is too thick to spread.

Spread the cheese mixture on the lightly toasted bread and heat very quickly in the oven until golden. Season and serve immediately.

Mozzarella in Carrozza
Mozzarella in a Carriage

In Naples this sandwich of *mozzarella di bufala*, sitting handsomely in its carriage of bread, is almost as famous as pizza and is made in the same rustic pizzerias, for it is a simple and unsophisticated dish. It almost seems silly to write a recipe for two slices of bread enclosing a bit of mozzarella, which is dipped into egg and flour and fried in hot oil. I particularly like this with a sliver or two of anchovy so that the saltiness of the fish plays against the crunch of the fried bread and the soft melting cheese.

Makes 4 servings

4 thick slices (about ½ inch) fresh mozzarella
8 slices (½ inch) *Pane in Cassetta* (Sandwich Bread, page 258), crusts
 trimmed
4 anchovy fillets, drained, cut into thin slivers (optional)
Milk
2 eggs
Pinch salt
About 2 tablespoons unbleached all-purpose flour
Olive oil for frying

Place 1 slice of the mozzarella on each of 4 slices of bread, making sure that none of the cheese overlaps the bread. Place 1 or 2 anchovy slivers on the cheese, if you want. Top with the remaining bread. Pour milk onto a platter and quickly dip both sides of each sandwich into it, just to moisten it. Beat the eggs with the salt in a wide bowl; soak each sandwich to absorb the eggs for 2 to 10 minutes a side. Place 2 tablespoons flour on a plate and dip each side of the sandwiches very lightly onto the flour to coat the bread very thinly with flour. Shake off excess flour.

Heat ⅜ inch olive oil in a large skillet over medium-high heat. When the oil is hot, add the sandwiches and fry until golden on both sides, turning once. Drain on paper towels and serve immediately.

Panzanella

Panzanella is one of the humblest Tuscan dishes, made merely of stale dark saltless bread moistened with water and turned into a salad with slices of tomato, chopped basil leaves, a few vegetables, and the best fruity olive oil. It is the perfect picnic food on a hot summer day and is a dish that you can make on the spur of the moment. That's why there really aren't any recipes, just lists of ingredients. The bread should be rough and mellow—a good chewy *Toscano*—and the oil, the best peppery one you can find.

No one knows where the name for this salad comes from, although some say that *pan* (bread) and *zanella* (a little soup tureen) are easily enough deciphered. We do know that it has been popular for a long time, for, in the middle of the sixteenth century, the mannerist painter Bronzino wrote a little rhyme in praise of a bread salad with chopped onion, cucumber, basil, the herb *porcellana*, which is now out of fashion, and *ruchetta*, an aromatic green which we know as arugola. The tomato hadn't yet made its debut in Italy, but there are words of praise for the pleasures of life enhanced by this lovely combination.

Makes 6 to 8 servings

6 to 8 thick slices *Pane Toscano* (Saltless Tuscan Bread, page 110)
6 ripe medium-size tomatoes, finely sliced
3 cucumbers, peeled and finely sliced
2 red onions, finely sliced
2 ribs celery, finely sliced
10 to 12 fresh basil leaves
½ cup olive oil
2 tablespoons red wine vinegar
Salt
Freshly ground pepper

Soak the bread in cold water to cover until very moist, about 15 minutes. Squeeze each bread slice dry between your hands and then tear into small chunks.

Place the bread in a large bowl and add the tomatoes, cucumbers, onions, celery, and basil leaves. Mix the oil, vinegar, and salt and pepper to taste and pour over the salad. Toss to combine. Serve at room temperature.

Variation. The Romans like their *panzanella* spicier and add chopped capers, parsley, anchovies, garlic, and sometimes hard-cooked eggs.

Pappa al Pomodoro

Tomato and Bread Soup

Here's a common enough Tuscan sort of soup: soften stale bread in good broth, whisk it all up, flavor it with a good peppery Tuscan oil and salt and pepper to taste, and add a bit of Tuscan *pecorino* cheese. There are countless recipes for *pappa al pomodoro*, because every Florentine considers it his heritage and has vivid memories of how it tasted at home. There are two schools of thought on how it should be cooked: either all the ingredients go in the pot cold and get boiled together or the bread, garlic, and tomato are tossed into the hot broth. This recipe uses the traditional ingredients with a bit of extra garlic; it is full of flavor but isn't heavy or gummy.

Makes 6 servings

¾ to 1 cup olive oil, plus additional for garnish
2 large cloves garlic, chopped
1 teaspoon tomato paste
Scant 2 pounds (850 grams) fresh ripe tomatoes, peeled, seeded, and chopped (2 cups)
8 to 10 fresh basil leaves, torn into 3 or 4 pieces
6 cups chicken broth, preferably homemade
Salt
Freshly ground pepper
1 pound stale *Pane Toscano Scuro* (Dark Tuscan Bread, page 112) or *Pane Toscano* (page 110), thinly sliced or broken into small chunks

Heat the oil in a heavy 10-inch skillet over medium heat. Add the garlic and lightly sauté. Stir in the tomato paste and then the tomatoes and basil. Simmer over low heat for 5 minutes.

Heat the broth and salt and pepper to taste in a large saucepan to a boil. Stir in the bread and the tomato mixture. Cook over medium heat 2 to 3 minutes. Remove from the heat and let stand uncovered 1 hour.

Just before serving, stir thoroughly. Serve hot, at room temperature, or cold. Drizzle a thin ribbon of olive oil over the top. *Pappa* is never eaten with cheese.

Basil

Ribollita
Tuscan Bean Soup

These days, simple is sophisticated and rustic is chic. All over Tuscany, trattorie are full of the most delicious peasant soups, which were initially created from simple necessity. Some say that *ribollita* was made from the bread that was used as a trencher for roasts in medieval times. After it had served its purpose, it was given to the hungry servants, who put it in a big pot of water with vegetables and spices and turned it into *ribollita*. I've also heard that it was a soup prepared in the country on a Friday; therefore it is meatless and doesn't even have the hint of a *prosciutto* bone or a bit of *pancetta*. It is made of the most basic ingredients—bread, potatoes, kale, a few handfuls of cabbage. When it was *ribollita*, or reboiled, it turned up again at lunch on Saturday as a wonderful leftover that has now become a staple soup of the region. Nowadays most *ribollite* in Tuscany are tasty vegetable soups made with Tuscan beans, a civilized bit of cuisine created from rougher beginnings.

Makes 6 servings

8 ounces (225 grams) dried white *cannellini* beans or 1½ cups canned *cannellini*
¾ cup olive oil
2 medium-size yellow onions, finely chopped
3 ribs celery, diced
4 carrots, peeled and chopped
1 teaspoon tomato paste
2 teaspoons warm water
3 ripe medium-size tomatoes, chopped
3 bunches Swiss chard (about 3 pounds, 1⅓ kilograms), stems trimmed, leaves chopped
1 bunch kale, stems trimmed, leaves chopped
½ Savoy cabbage, finely shredded
4 medium-size potatoes, peeled and chopped
1 fresh small chile, seeded and chopped
2 cloves garlic, minced
2 teaspoons chopped fresh thyme or 1 teaspoon dried
Salt
Freshly ground pepper
5 to 6 cups cold water
12 to 16 slices stale *Pane Toscano Scuro* (Dark Tuscan Bread, page 112) or *Pane Toscano* (page 110)
Best-quality Tuscan olive oil for garnish

If you are using dried beans, soak the beans overnight in water to cover, then drain. Heat the beans and fresh water to cover over high heat to a boil. Reduce heat to medium-low and simmer covered until tender, about 1½ hours. Drain the beans but reserve the cooking liquid. Purée three quarters of the cooked beans with a little of the cooking liquid or three quarters of the canned beans in a little of their liquid in a food processor fitted with the steel blade or in a blender. Reserve the remaining whole beans.

Heat ½ cup oil in a heavy large pan or Dutch oven over medium high heat. Add the onions, celery, and carrots and sauté until the onions are soft, about 5 minutes. Thin the tomato paste with the 2 teaspoons water and add the thinned paste and the fresh tomatoes to the vegetables. Cook, stirring occasionally, 5 to 10 minutes. Stir in the chard, kale, cabbage, potatoes, puréed and whole beans, the chile, garlic, thyme, and salt and pepper to taste. Add the remaining bean cooking or canned liquid and enough of the cold water to cover the vegetables. Heat to a boil. Reduce the heat to low and simmer covered about 2 hours.

Just before serving, grill or toast 2 slices of bread for every serving. You can sauté the bread in the remaining ¼ cup oil, or brush one side of each slice with oil and bake on a baking sheet at 400° F until golden, or brush the bread with oil and grill under a broiler or over an open fire. Place the bread in the bottom of wide soup bowls and ladle the soup over the bread. Drizzle a fine thread or two of good Tuscan olive oil over each serving. Most Tuscans do not serve Parmesan cheese with this bean soup.

Carabaccia

Florentine Onion and Pea Soup

This fabulous Florentine soup tastes so delicate and fresh with its infusion of puréed peas that it always amazes me that Italians think of it as an onion soup. It actually began life as *carabazada* in the Renaissance when, according to the great cookbook writer Cristoforo Messiburgo, it numbered almonds, cinnamon, and sugar among its ingredients. Needless to say, those sweet tastes have been banished from the modern version, which I have modified further by adding chicken broth to make it a true soup instead of the thicker original *minestra* that is served under a blanket of poached eggs. I have found in serving this *carabaccia* to Italians that it evokes the most remarkable memories in my guests of springtime lunches in the Tuscan countryside or wonderful meals in tiny little hill towns with several generations of Italian family, baskets of bread on the table, and a pervasive sense of well-being.

Makes 4 servings

⅓ cup olive oil
3 large yellow onions, cut into small dice
4 ribs celery, cut into small dice
2 carrots, peeled and cut into small dice
Salt
Freshly ground pepper
12 ounces (340 grams) fresh peas, shelled, or 1 package (10 ounces, 285 grams) frozen peas, thawed
2 cups chicken broth
4 slices stale country bread
Olive oil for the bread (optional)
Freshly grated Parmesan cheese

Heat ⅓ cup oil in a heavy large pan or Dutch oven over low heat; add the onions, celery, carrots, and salt and pepper to taste. Cook uncovered over very low heat, stirring occasionally, for at least 1 hour but preferably 1½ hours. Don't add any water, for the vegetables will render enough liquid to keep them sufficiently moist.

Meanwhile, cook the fresh peas in ½ cup of the broth; drain them, reserving the broth. Purée half the cooked or thawed frozen peas in a food processor fitted with the steel blade or in a blender.

Toast the bread or sauté in oil until golden and place 1 slice in the bottom of each soup bowl. Stir the broth into the vegetable mixture and heat to a boil. Reduce the heat, add the whole and puréed peas and heat until warmed through, about 5 minutes. Ladle the soup over the bread in the bowls. Pass the Parmesan cheese.

Soupe Paysanne Val d'Aosta

Peasant Soup with Fontina Cheese from the Val d'Aosta

The hearty soups of the Val d'Aosta in the mountains of Piedmont are meals in themselves. All of them start with rustic country bread—sometimes it is black and sometimes a rough chewy wheat—and they are usually layered with the Fontina cheese for which the valley is so famous. This particular soup is so rich that it is very filling, perfect after a day of skiing or hiking. It is best if you use a good homemade beef stock. The local residents start with a bouillon left from boiling meat (if you make *bollito misto*, this soup would be a perfect use for the stock), then flavor it with any number of herbs and seasonings, and cook it very slowly to concentrate the flavors. Don't be bewildered by the name; French is the language of the valley and the bread-and-cheese–thickened soup is absolutely indigenous to the area.

Makes 6 servings

6 to 9 thick slices stale rustic country bread
8 ounces (225 grams) Italian Fontina cheese, thinly sliced
8 ounces (225 grams) Toma Valdostana or Taleggio, thinly sliced (if you can't find these, use 8 ounces more Fontina)
4 ounces (115 grams) freshly grated Parmesan cheese
6¼ cups beef broth, preferably homemade
Freshly ground pepper

Place a third of the bread in a single layer in the bottom of a deep casserole or baking dish; cut the slices to fit. Top with a third of the sliced cheeses and sprinkle with a third of the Parmesan. Repeat the layers two more times. Heat the broth to boiling and pour over the bread and cheeses.

Baking. Heat the oven to 400° F. Bake uncovered 20 to 30 minutes. Grind pepper over the top and serve immediately.

Zuppa di Verdure all'Agliata

Garlicky Vegetable Soup

Liguria lies on the shores of the Mediterranean, stretching in a thin band from the French border at Provence to Tuscany. It is famous for its fabulous vegetables, the garlic that seems to suffuse the whole region, its basil, as well as the pesto that it becomes, and the olive oil from the trees of its hillsides. This soup is quintessentially Ligurian. It is more delicate in taste than its ingredients might suggest. Don't try to reheat it as the peas won't stand up to a second appearance. In winter the Ligurians use turnips instead of the peas.

Makes 4 servings

¼ cup olive oil
1 large yellow onion, very finely sliced
About ½ pound (225 grams) kale, stems removed, leaves finely chopped or shredded
2 zucchini, finely chopped
2 ribs celery, finely chopped
2 large carrots, peeled and finely chopped
1 large potato, peeled and finely diced
2 tomatoes, peeled, seeded, and chopped
Salt and freshly ground pepper
4½ cups chicken broth or a combination of chicken and beef
12 ounces (340 grams) fresh peas, shelled, or 1 package (10 ounces, 285 grams) frozen peas, thawed
2 or 3 large cloves garlic, finely minced
2 to 3 tablespoons finely chopped fresh parsley
4 to 6 slices country bread
Olive oil for the bread (optional)
Freshly grated Parmesan cheese

Heat the oil in a heavy large pan or Dutch oven over medium heat. Add the onion and sauté until pale golden. Stir in the kale, zucchini, celery, carrots, potato, tomatoes, and salt and pepper to taste. Sauté until lightly browned. Pour the broth over the vegetables and cook uncovered over medium heat 20 to 30 minutes. If you are using fresh peas, add them with the garlic and parsley after 15 minutes of cooking and cook 15 minutes longer. If you are using thawed frozen peas, add them with the garlic and parsley after 25 minutes of cooking and cook briefly, no more than 3 to 4 minutes.

Lightly toast the bread in the oven or sauté in oil and place 1 slice in the bottom of each soup bowl. Ladle the hot soup over the bread and serve immediately. Pass the Parmesan cheese.

Minestra Mariconda

Beef Broth with Eggs, Cheese, and Cheese Bread

Minestra mariconda is a special soup of the town of Brescia, which sits in the lovely countryside of Lombardy north of Milan. It dates as far back as the Renaissance and belongs to the fine old tradition of cooking bread with eggs and cheeses in fine homemade broth. Many cooks chop up leftover chicken or meat and add it with the leftover bread. In Mantua, families add minced cooked chicken livers to the mixture. *Squisito*, as the Italians say.

Although it is in no way traditional, I like making this soup with a cheese bread because it has such a rich and wonderful taste. You could also try using *pan giallo*—a typical Lombard cornbread—or any rustic country loaf, white or mixed-grain.

Makes 6 to 8 servings

8 ounces (225 grams) stale bread, crusts trimmed
1¼ cups milk
1 stick (115 grams) unsalted butter
4 eggs, beaten
1 cup (100 grams) freshly grated Parmesan cheese
Freshly grated nutmeg
Salt
Freshly ground pepper
6½ cups homemade beef broth

Crumble the bread into a bowl and pour the milk over it. Let stand 30 minutes. Squeeze the bread dry with your hands and tear it into small pieces. Melt the butter in a small skillet over low heat. Add the bread and sauté gently until dry but still soft.

Beat the eggs, ¼ cup of the Parmesan, and nutmeg, salt, and pepper to taste together in a mixing bowl. Add the bread and stir until thoroughly blended. Let stand covered 1 hour.

About 10 minutes before serving, heat the broth in a large saucepan to a rolling boil. Shape the bread mixture between your hands into even balls, using ½ to 1 tablespoon of the mixture for each ball. Slide the balls into the broth and cook uncovered over medium heat about 5 minutes.

Serve the soup steaming hot. Pass the remaining Parmesan cheese.

Panada di Milano
Rich Easter Soup

Every region has its *pancotto*, which simply means cooked bread and is a soup made with crumbs of leftover loaves, but this *panada* is particularly rich and filling, having been traditionally served for Easter lunch in Milan. Because the eggs and cheese are beaten in the tureen before the hot broth and bread crumbs are added, it looks quite a lot like *stracciatella*, with its lovely little ribbons of egg. Your guests will be surprised when their spoons bring up the lightly crunchy bread crumbs floating in their bowls.

Makes 6 servings

½ cup plus 2 tablespoons fine stale bread crumbs
6½ cups homemade beef broth
½ stick (55 grams) unsalted butter
3 eggs
3 tablespoons freshly grated Parmesan cheese

Place ½ cup bread crumbs in a small bowl and pour ¼ cup of the broth over the bread. Heat the remaining broth in a large saucepan to a rolling boil.

About 10 minutes before serving, heat the butter in a small skillet over low heat. Add the moistened bread crumbs and sauté until golden, about 5 minutes.

Place the 2 tablespoons dry bread crumbs in a soup tureen and break the eggs into the bottom of the tureen. Add the cheese and beat with a fork or whisk until well blended. Pour the boiling broth into the tureen and add the sautéed bread crumbs. Beat vigorously for 1 to 2 minutes. Serve immediately.

Canederli
Bread Dumplings

Canederli are wonderfully flavored bread dumplings made in the mountainous Italian-speaking part of the Trentino region, north of Venice. Because they originate from the Austro-Hungarian culinary tradition and because the word is really a translation of *Knodel,* you might think of them as northern gnocchi. I like to serve them floating in a good homemade chicken or turkey broth, but there are many other genuine possibilities. They often turn up at Italian tables with a ragout sauce, gravy, or, at their most Teutonic, a big helping of sauerkraut.

Makes 6 servings

About 10 ounces (300 grams) stale white bread, crusts trimmed (or use stale rye bread as they do in the Alto Adige)
About 1 cup milk
2 to 3 tablespoons olive oil
3½ ounces (100 grams) *pancetta*, diced
2 ounces (60 grams) salami, diced
1 small yellow onion, minced
1 garlic clove, minced
1 egg
1 egg, separated
1 tablespoon chopped fresh parsley
Grated zest of 1 lemon
Freshly grated nutmeg
Salt and freshly ground pepper
½ cup (65 grams) unbleached all-purpose flour
6 to 7 cups homemade chicken broth

Cut the bread into rough 1-inch cubes and place in a large mixing bowl. Pour the milk over the bread. There should be enough milk to moisten the bread but not enough to make it really wet. Let stand for about 1 hour.

Heat 2 tablespoons of the oil in a small skillet over medium-high heat. Add the *pancetta* and salami and sauté 3 to 4 minutes. Remove with a slotted spoon to a mixing bowl. Add 1 tablespoon oil, if you need it, to the skillet and heat. Add the onion and garlic and sauté just until translucent. Add to the *pancetta*. Squeeze the bread dry with your hands and tear it into small pieces. Add the bread, egg, egg yolk, parsley, lemon zest, nutmeg, and salt and pepper to taste to the *pancetta* mixture and stir thoroughly. Add enough of the flour so that the mixture will hold its shape. If it is too dry, you may need to add a little of the egg white from the separated egg. Before you make all the dumplings, shape a small amount of the mixture into a ball the size of a walnut and slide it into a small pan of boiling water. If it holds its shape and doesn't disintegrate, shape the remaining mixture; if it does fall apart, add a little more flour and test again. The mixture should be slightly moist and sticky.

Heat the broth in a large saucepan to a slow boil. Slide the dumplings into the broth and simmer uncovered for about 15 minutes. Serve immediately with the broth.

Passatelli

Passatelli are special fat little noodles of bread, eggs, and cheese that got their name from the kitchen tool, called a *passatello,* that gives them their shape. Don't worry about the utensil. You can use a ricer or the coarsest disk of a food mill to make the delicate little strands that float in hot broth. They are a specialty of Romagna and the cities of the Marche on the Adriatic coast.

Makes 6 servings

6 cups homemade beef broth
¾ cup bread crumbs, preferably from stale *Pasta Dura* (page 247)
About ¾ cup (75 grams) freshly grated Parmesan cheese
1 or 2 eggs, beaten
Grated zest of ½ lemon
¼ to ½ teaspoon freshly grated nutmeg
½ teaspoon salt

Heat the broth in a large saucepan to a gentle boil.

Mix the bread crumbs, Parmesan, 1 egg, lemon zest, nutmeg, and salt in a mixing bowl. The mixture should be firm enough to put through a ricer but not too stiff. If necessary, mix in the second egg, a little at a time, until the mixture is the desired consistency.

Spoon the bread mixture into a ricer, a food mill fitted with the coarsest disk, or a coarse sieve. Press the mixture through your utensil into the slowly boiling stock. Little strands of the bread mixture should float in the stock like tiny wiggly bits of pasta. Remove from the heat and let stand for a minute or two before serving.

Bread-based Desserts

Torta Nicolotta
Bread Pudding

This old and very popular cake gets its name from the inhabitants of the poorest neighborhood of Venice, who are called *I Nicolotti* and live by begging. They make this very simple dessert with leftover bread, milk, and a few sweeteners.

Makes 8 to 10 servings

12 to 14 ounces (350 to 400 grams) stale white bread or raisin bread
4¼ cups milk
5 tablespoons (70 grams) unsalted butter
¾ cup (150 grams) sugar
1¼ cups (175 grams) raisins
2 tablespoons rum
5 eggs, beaten
Grated zest of 1 lemon
¾ cup (100 grams) chopped candied citron (optional)
¼ teaspoon ground cinnamon
1 teaspoon vanilla extract
Unsalted butter and fine bread crumbs for the baking dish

If you are using a rough rustic bread, trim the crusts. Cut the bread into rough cubes and place in a large mixing bowl. Heat the milk, butter, and sugar in a medium-size saucepan just to a low boil and pour over the bread cubes. Let stand 2 hours.

Place the raisins and rum in a small bowl; add warm water to cover. Let stand at least 15 minutes to plump the raisins. Drain and pat dry.

Squeeze the bread dry and break it up with your hands to a soft, crumbly mass. Stir the raisins, eggs, lemon zest, and citron, if using, into the bread. Add the cinnamon and vanilla and stir thoroughly.

Butter a 2-quart baking dish and lightly coat with fine bread crumbs. Pour the bread mixture into the dish.

Baking. Heat the oven to 375° F. Bake until the top is the golden color of a hazelnut, about 45 minutes.

Torta di Mele
Apple Cake

Apples grow in the north of Italy, especially in Trentino, where the orchards extend for miles along roads that wind toward the border and the Alps. This apple cake is an adaptation of an old recipe from the Brianza, the region above Milan, and it is rather like an apple charlotte in the way it combines leftover stale bread with cooked apples.

Makes 6 to 8 servings

2 pounds (900 grams) apples, preferably Granny Smiths or Pippins, peeled and sliced
½ cup Riesling, Gewürtztraminer, or other slightly sweet white wine
½ cup water
½ cup plus 4 tablespoons (160 grams) sugar
Grated zest of 1 lemon
½ stick (55 grams) unsalted butter, or as needed
About 4 ounces (100 to 125 grams) sliced leftover homemade bread, crusts trimmed
1 egg
¾ cup milk
½ teaspoon vanilla extract
¾ teaspoon ground cinnamon
⅔ cup (100 grams) raisins
2 tablespoons apricot jam

Place the apples, wine, water, ½ cup plus 2 tablespoons sugar, and the lemon zest in a medium-size heavy saucepan. Cook covered, stirring occasionally, until roughly the texture of applesauce, about 25 to 30 minutes.

Butter the bread on both sides and bake on a baking sheet at 350° F until lightly toasted. Mix the egg, milk, vanilla, 2 tablespoons sugar, and ¼ teaspoon of the cinnamon and pour over the bread in a large bowl. Let stand about 30 minutes.

Place the raisins in a small bowl and add warm water to cover; let stand 15 minutes. Drain the raisins and pat dry. Add the raisins, apricot jam, and remaining ½ teaspoon cinnamon to the applesauce and stir thoroughly.

Butter a 2-quart soufflé dish and line the bottom and side with the soaked bread. Pour the apple mixture into the dish and smooth the top. Trim bread even with the apple mixture.

Baking. Heat oven to 350° F. Bake until set and lightly golden on top, about 45 minutes. If you want, unmold the *torta* onto a serving platter. Serve hot or warm.

Torta di Pere e Pan Giallo
Rustic Pear and Cornbread Dessert

Sometimes rustic food made with leftovers is irresistible. Bake a little leftover corn bread with pears poached in wine with lemon peel, cinnamon, cloves, and sugar for a perfect family dessert.

Makes 6 servings

4 to 6 ounces (120 to 170 grams) leftover *Pan Giallo* (Corn Bread from Lombardy, page 130), crusts trimmed
2 tablespoons (30 grams) unsalted butter, room temperature
½ cup dry white wine
⅓ to ½ cup (70 to 100 grams) granulated sugar, depending on how sweet the pears are
Grated zest of 1 lemon
¼ teaspoon ground cinnamon
2 whole cloves
½ cup water, if needed
2 pounds (900 grams) ripe pears, peeled and sliced
¼ cup (50 grams) turbinado or granulated sugar

Heat the oven to 350° F. Cut the bread into 3-inch pieces and butter each piece. Bake on a baking sheet until lightly toasted. Place the bread in a buttered 4-cup baking dish and spread evenly.

Heat the wine, ⅓ to ½ cup sugar, the lemon, cinnamon, and cloves in a 2-quart saucepan over medium heat and simmer for 10 minutes; add the pears and enough of the water to just cover the pears. Poach uncovered over medium heat for about 15 minutes until just tender. Spoon the pears with whatever liquid is left over the corn bread in the baking dish and sprinkle the top with the turbinado sugar.

Baking. Heat the oven to 350° F. Bake 40 to 45 minutes. Let cool to room temperature.

PANI FESTIVI
Celebration Breads

Fruit and nut breads are among the oldest country loaves, invented by poor Italians who used raw and dried fruits and nuts to give sweetness to their doughs in the days when there was no such thing as sugar. I like the thought of medieval peasants, whose lives were difficult at best, adding a bit of sweetness to their days with special breads bursting with fat raisins or figs or studded with walnuts. It was common in those times and much later as well to make regular doughs during the week and then enrich them on Sunday with a splash of milk, an egg or two, and a few handfuls of candied fruit and nuts. Of course, such exotic ingredients as chocolate did not make an appearance until the seventeenth century.

Many of these rich, eggy doughs are very similar. The *colomba* has more butter and is sprinkled with almonds, the *civitavecchia* is flavored with port and anise, and the panettone is studded with raisins, citron, and candied orange peel, but all are essentially variations on a theme of flour, eggs, butter, and yeast. In Italy every bakery has bottles of powerful essences labelled *aroma di panettone, aroma di colomba, aroma di limone,* and *aroma di arancia dolce,* which give the breads their memorable tastes, but some of the finest bakers I met prefer using freshly grated lemon and orange zests or a splash of vanilla extract for flavoring, which is the approach I have used to replicate the mysterious essence of these Italian holiday breads.

The doughs are delicate and complex, and almost all need fairly long rises to create the high, airy loaves. But that does not mean that they cannot be made in a day. I like to start baking right after breakfast and work out a schedule for the first and second rises that fits into the rest of my day. The dough can go in the refrigerator if you have other things to do; the action of the yeast will be slowed down, but the dough will develop more flavor.

Actually, it isn't putting the ingredients together that is time-consuming, but rather the time required for the yeast to do its magical work, which is true for all breads but especially for these loaves which are heavy with eggs and butter as well as fruits and nuts. I have found several ways to encourage the process, however. Covering the bowl tightly with plastic wrap for the dough's first rise traps the heat given off as the yeast begins to work. I never place the dough directly over the pilot of my gas stove, but it can certainly be set near the source of heat. I also have taken note of the warm, moist proofers in bakeries and approximated the method by turning the oven on at 150° F for three minutes and then immediately placing the shaped loaves in the oven along with a pan of steaming water. The warm moisture is a wonderful incentive for the expansion of the dough.

The holiday bread doughs (pages 220–245) must be made by hand or by mixer, for the food processor simply will not create the right airy texture. Don't be daunted by their seeming complexity. After you've tried one recipe, you'll find that the process is not as complicated as it reads. And, when you take a bite of the finished bread, close your eyes and you'll find you're tasting the true flavor of Italy.

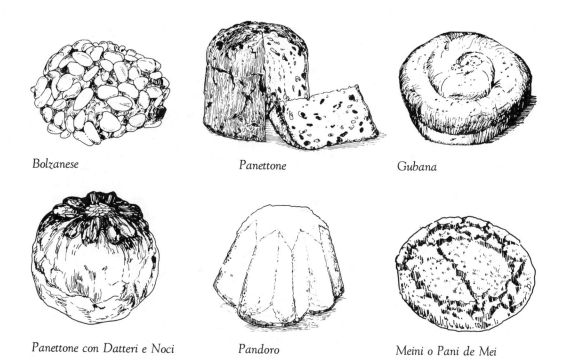

Bolzanese   Panettone   Gubana

Panettone con Datteri e Noci   Pandoro   Meini o Pani de Mei

Fruit and Nut Breads

Pane di Noci
Walnut Bread

The first time I tasted this bread, I was certain that its rich, almost mahogany-colored interior came from freshly milled whole wheat, which shows how much I knew. The lovely dark color comes entirely from the walnuts that saturate the bread with their irresistibly delicate and nutty flavor. Be sure to toast your walnuts lightly to bring out the flavor before you chop and knead them into the dough. Baking the bread in a little ring mold with a few whole walnuts on the bottom makes an appealing loaf when it is unmolded. The Italians like eating this bread particularly with soft, fresh cheeses.

Makes 1 ring or round loaf

2 cups (200 grams) walnut pieces, plus 4 to 6 perfect halves for the ring loaf
2½ teaspoons (1 package) active dry yeast or 1 small cake (18 grams) fresh yeast
¼ cup honey
1⅓ cups warm water
2 tablespoons olive oil
3¾ cups (500 grams) unbleached all-purpose flour
1½ teaspoons (8 grams) salt

Toast the walnuts on a baking sheet in a 400° F oven for 10 minutes. Chop the walnuts to coarse crumbs with a sharp knife or in a food processor fitted with the steel blade. Reserve the perfect halves for the ring mold, if using.

BY HAND

Stir the yeast and honey into the water in a large mixing bowl; let stand until foamy, about 10 minutes. Stir in the oil. Combine the flour, salt, and walnuts and stir 1 cup at a time into the yeast mixture. Mix until the dough looks like whole wheat. Using a dough scraper, knead on a floured surface 8 to 10 minutes, sprinkling with up to ⅓ cup additional flour to keep the dough from sticking. The dough should be soft, moist, and fairly dense but easy to work, although it is not particularly elastic.

BY MIXER

Stir the yeast and honey into the water in a mixer bowl; let stand until foamy, about 10 minutes. Stir in the oil with the paddle. Add the flour, salt, and walnuts and mix until the dough comes together. Change to the dough hook and knead until soft, moist, and fairly dense, 4 to 5 minutes. Knead briefly by hand on a lightly floured surface.

BY PROCESSOR

Stir the yeast and honey into ⅓ cup warm water in a small bowl; let stand until foamy, about 10 minutes. Coarsely chop the nuts in a food processor fitted with the steel blade. Add the flour and salt and process with 2 or 3 pulses to sift. Stir the oil into the dissolved yeast. With the machine running, pour the yeast mixture and 1 cup cold water through the feed tube as quickly as the flour can absorb it and process until the dough comes together. Process 45 seconds longer to knead. If you want, finish kneading briefly by hand on a lightly floured surface.

First Rise. Place the dough in an oiled bowl, cover tightly with plastic wrap, and let rise until doubled, about 1¼ hours.

Shaping and Second Rise. Turn the dough out onto a lightly floured surface. Without punching it down or kneading it, shape it into a log and join the ends to make a ring. You may place the ring in an oiled ring mold with 4 to 6 walnut halves set in the bottom, so that when the bread is baked and turned out of the mold the nuts are on the top. The dough can also be baked in a free-form ring or round loaf. Place the free-form loaf on a floured peel or oiled baking sheet. Cover the dough with plastic wrap and let rise until doubled, about 1 hour.

Baking. Heat the oven to 400° F. If you are using a baking stone, turn the oven on 30 minutes before baking and sprinkle the stone with cornmeal just before sliding the loaf onto it. Bake for 10 minutes. Reduce the heat to 350° F and bake 40 minutes longer. If you are baking the bread in a ring mold, bake the loaf out of the pan on a baking sheet or stone for the last 10 minutes to brown the bottom and sides. Cool completely on a rack.

Pane di Fichi
Fig Bread

The first thing to be said about this bread is that it is succulent and delicious as well as very easy to make. The second thing to be noted is that a bread like this has a lot of history behind it. This bread undoubtedly dates back at least to the early Middle Ages, a time when cities like Perugia, Florence, and Siena were dotted with tower houses that gave warring families and factions a good view of their neighbors and enemies. Even though bakers were busy making the daily bread, they made a point of transforming the dough for Sundays and special celebrations by sweetening it with honey and enriching it with nuts or dried fruits, such as figs.

Makes 1 round loaf

2½ teaspoons (1 package) active dry yeast or 1 small cake (18 grams) fresh yeast
1 cup warm water
1½ tablespoons olive oil
About 3 cups (375 grams) unbleached all-purpose flour, plus 2 tablespoons for the figs
1 teaspoon (5 grams) salt
1 cup (200 grams) figs, preferably Calimyrna or Greek string figs, cut into about 12 pieces each

BY HAND

Stir the yeast into the water in a large mixing bowl; let stand until creamy, about 10 minutes. Stir in the oil. Mix 3 cups flour and the salt and stir into the yeast mixture. Stir until the dough comes together. Knead on a floured surface, sprinkling with additional flour, until velvety and moist, 7 to 10 minutes.

BY MIXER

Stir the yeast into the water in a mixer bowl; let stand until creamy, about 10 minutes. Stir in the oil with the paddle and then 3 cups flour and the salt. Mix until the dough comes together. Change to the dough hook and knead until velvety and moist, 3 to 4 minutes.

BY PROCESSOR

Stir the yeast into ¼ cup warm water in a small bowl; let stand until creamy, about 10 minutes. Place 3 cups flour and the salt in a food processor fitted with the steel blade and process with several pulses to sift. Stir ¾ cup cold water and the oil into the dissolved yeast. With the machine running, pour the yeast mixture through the feed tube as quickly as the flour can absorb it. Process 40 to 45 seconds longer to knead. Finish kneading briefly by hand on a floured surface.

First Rise. Place the dough in a lightly oiled bowl, cover tightly with plastic wrap, and let rise until doubled, about 1 hour.

Filling. Toss the figs in 2 tablespoons flour to coat the surfaces. Turn the dough out onto a floured surface. Without punching it down, pat the dough into an oval and spread half the figs evenly over the surface; roll up the dough. Pat the dough into an oval again and sprinkle evenly with the remaining figs; roll it up again. Shape into a round loaf, being gentle but, at the same time, pulling the skin taut over the figs. Place the loaf, rough side down, on a lightly floured peel or oiled baking sheet, cover with a towel, and let rise until doubled, 1¼ to 1½ hours.

Baking. Thirty minutes before baking, heat the oven with a baking stone in it to 450° F. Sprinkle the stone with cornmeal just before sliding the loaf onto it. Bake 15 minutes. Reduce the heat to 375° F and bake 15 minutes longer. Cool completely on a rack.

Pan Tramvai o Pane all'Uva
Raisin Bread

This outrageously delicious bread is so crammed with raisins that it actually has equal amounts of raisins and flour. A look at its knobby, slightly gnarled form gives no hint of the sweetness inside, but, once you've eaten it, you'll understand why the Milanese gave it such importance in their lives. It was originally made in the nineteenth century by a bread baker at the tramway station in Monza, where commuters caught the horse-drawn tram for Milan, hence its name, *tramvai*, or go by tram. Over time the loaf became as fat, crusty, and long as a French bread loaf, and the old-fashioned trams were replaced by sleek modern trains, but the Milanese continued to eat it as their special breakfast bread, and schoolchildren or anyone forced to eat away from home at midday depended on it as a lunchtime snack.

This raisin bread makes delicious *focaccia* (page 288) and is wonderful for making apple charlottes (page 196). It keeps extremely well, although most people love the bread so much they never find that out.

Pan Tramvai (continued)

Makes 1 large or 2 smaller loaves

About 3 cups (500 grams) golden or dark raisins
3¾ teaspoons active dry yeast or 1½ small cakes (27 grams) fresh
  yeast
1 teaspoon malted grain syrup or liquid malt extract (not with hops)
1 tablespoon sugar
2 teaspoons unsalted butter, room temperature
3¾ cups (500 grams) unbleached all-purpose flour, plus 2 to 3
  tablespoons for the raisins
1½ teaspoons (8 grams) salt

Soak the raisins in water to cover (cool water for the golden raisins, warm water for the dark) at room temperature for 1½ hours. Drain the raisins; warm 1⅓ cups of the raisin water for the yeast (for the processor warm ¼ cup and refrigerate 1 cup plus 3 tablespoons until cold).

BY HAND

Stir the yeast, malt, and sugar into the raisin water in a large mixing bowl; let stand until foamy, about 10 minutes. Stir in the butter. Mix 3¾ cups flour and the salt. Stir the flour mixture, 2 cups at a time, into the yeast mixture. Knead on a lightly floured surface until firm, elastic, and silky, 4 to 5 minutes. You will find that the dough comes together quickly.

BY MIXER

Stir the yeast, malt, and sugar into the raisin water in a mixer bowl; let stand until foamy, about 10 minutes. Stir in the butter with the paddle. Add 3¾ cups flour and the salt and mix until the dough comes together. Change to the dough hook and knead until firm, elastic, and silky, 2 to 3 minutes.

BY PROCESSOR

Dissolve the yeast, malt, and sugar in ¼ cup warm raisin water in a small bowl; let stand until foamy, about 10 minutes. Place 3¾ cups flour and the salt in a food processor fitted with the dough blade and process with several pulses to sift. Stir the butter and 1 cup plus 2 tablespoons of the cold water into the dissolved yeast mixture. With the machine running, pour the yeast mixture through the feed tube as quickly as the flour can absorb it and process until the dough gathers into a ball, adding the remaining 1 tablespoon of water, if necessary. Process 30 to 40 seconds longer to knead. If you want, finish kneading briefly by hand on a lightly floured surface.

First Rise. Place the dough in a lightly oiled bowl, cover tightly with plastic wrap, and let rise until doubled, 1½ to 2 hours.

Filling. Turn the dough out onto a lightly floured surface. Without punching the dough down or kneading it, pat it gently with your palms or roll with a rolling pin into a circle about 14 inches in diameter. The dough will be slightly sticky and tacky. Pat the raisins dry and toss with 2 to 3 tablespoons flour. Work the raisins into the dough in 3 additions: Sprinkle a third of the raisins over the dough, turn in the sides, and roll it up. Flatten the dough with your palms and sprinkle with half the remaining raisins. Roll up and let the dough rest under a towel until relaxed and easy to work again, about 15 minutes. Pat the dough as flat as you can and sprinkle with the remaining raisins. Try to get as many in as you can but don't worry if you can't incorporate them all—this is an extraordinary amount of raisins.

Shaping and Second Rise. Roll up the dough into a long, slightly tapered loaf. You may either bake it as 1 long loaf or cut in half for 2 shorter loaves. Tuck the ends of the loaf under and try to keep the raisins under the taut surface of the skin. Place the loaf on a lightly floured peel, a lightly oiled baking sheet, or a baking sheet lined with parchment paper. Cover with a towel and let rise until well puffed and almost, but not quite, doubled, about 1 hour. Roll the loaf gently back and forth to set the shape before baking and check that the ends are tucked under.

Baking. Heat the oven to 450° F. If you are using a baking stone, turn the oven on 30 minutes before baking and sprinkle the stone with cornmeal just before sliding the loaf onto it. Bake 5 minutes. Reduce the heat to 400° F and bake 40 minutes longer. Cool completely on a rack.

Variation. Transform raisin bread into focaccia by following the basic focaccia recipe (page 289) and sprinkling the top with turbinado sugar.

Rolling up the dough

Dolce Milanese
Milan Sweet Bread

A buttery, sweet fantasy dreamed up by a Venetian baker, this bread is based on the *pan tramvai*, the famous raisin bread of Milan that is essentially half bread and half raisins, but this version is fragrant with rum and orange as well.

Makes 1 large or 2 smaller loaves

FILLING
About 3 cups (500 grams) golden or dark raisins
4 cups cool water

Soak the raisins in the water for 1 to 2 hours. Drain the raisins; warm 1¼ cups of the water for the sponge.

SPONGE
3¾ teaspoons active dry yeast or 1½ small cakes (27 grams) fresh yeast
2½ teaspoons sugar
1 cup plus 1 tablespoon (150 grams) unbleached all-purpose flour

Stir the yeast and sugar into the warm raisin water in a large mixing or mixer bowl; let stand until foamy, about 10 minutes. Add the flour and stir until smooth. Cover with plastic wrap and let rise until doubled, about 45 minutes to 1 hour.

DOUGH
2 tablespoons dark rum
1 tablespoon grated orange zest
About 2½ cups (350 grams) unbleached all-purpose flour, plus 3 to 4 tablespoons for the raisins
2 sticks (225 grams) unsalted butter, room temperature
1 egg white, beaten

BY HAND

Stir the rum, orange zest, and about 2½ cups flour into the sponge. Stir until well blended. Stir in the butter, 2 tablespoons at a time. Knead on a lightly floured surface until velvety and very soft but not sticky, 8 to 10 minutes. The surface will be quite smooth, although you will notice a number of blisters. It smells wonderful.

BY MIXER

Mix the rum, orange zest, and about 2½ cups flour into the sponge with the paddle. Mix in the butter, 2 tablespoons at a time. Change to the dough hook and knead at medium speed until velvety and very soft but not sticky, about 4 minutes. The surface will be quite smooth, although you will notice some blisters under the skin.

First Rise. Place the dough in an oiled bowl, cover with plastic wrap, and let rise until doubled, about 1 hour.

Filling. Pat the raisins dry and toss with 3 to 4 tablespoons flour. Work the raisins into the dough in 4 additions: Spread the dough out on a lightly floured surface, cover with a quarter of the raisins, tuck the sides in, and roll it up. Flatten the dough and repeat. Cover the dough with a towel and let it relax for about 10 minutes. Flatten the dough again and repeat the procedure twice, incorporating the remaining raisins. Let rest 10 minutes.

Shaping and Second Rise. Shape the dough into a large oval or round loaf, a free-form ring, or 2 smaller loaves. To make the 2 small loaves, cut the dough in half and pat each piece into a 9-inch square and roll it up, tucking in the sides so that the raisins don't fall out. It is easiest to pat the dough out with the cut side closest to you. I personally prefer the larger loaf because it has more crumb and less crust, but it is huge. Place the loaf on an oiled baking sheet, cover with a towel, and let rise until not quite doubled, 35 to 45 minutes.

Baking. Heat the oven to 425° F. Brush the top of the loaf with the egg white. Bake the smaller loaves 45 minutes and the large loaf 1 hour. Cool completely on a rack.

Bolzanese
Fruit Bread of Bolzano

These fat buns, stuffed with fruits and nuts and studded with whole almonds, bear more than slight atavistic traces of Bolzano's Austrian origins. They make a robust and tasty breakfast or teatime snack and are big enough to be a meal in themselves if you have a sweet tooth and are on the run.

The baked Bolzanese

Makes 5 fat buns

DOUGH
3¾ teaspoons active dry yeast or 1½ small cakes (27 grams) fresh
   yeast
½ cup plus 2 teaspoons (110 grams) sugar
¾ cup warm water
2 eggs
1 egg yolk
1 stick (115 grams) unsalted butter, room temperature
3¾ cups (500 grams) unbleached all-purpose flour
1½ teaspoons (8 grams) salt

BY HAND

Stir the yeast and 2 tablespoons of the sugar into the water in a large mixing bowl; let stand until foamy, about 10 minutes. Stir in the remaining sugar, the eggs, and egg yolk; stir in the butter until blended. Add the flour and salt and stir until the dough comes together. Knead on a floured surface until soft and elastic, 8 to 10 minutes.

BY MIXER

Stir the yeast and 2 tablespoons of the sugar into the water in a mixer bowl; let stand until foamy, about 10 minutes. Add the remaining sugar, the eggs, and egg yolk and mix with the paddle. Mix in the butter. Add the flour and salt and mix until the dough comes together. Change to the dough hook and knead until soft and elastic, 3 to 4 minutes.

First Rise. Place the dough in a lightly oiled bowl, cover tightly with plastic wrap, and let rise until soft and puffy but not quite doubled, about 2 hours.

FILLING AND TOPPING
⅔ cup (100 grams) halved hazelnuts, toasted and skinned (see page 52)
⅔ cup (100 grams) chopped candied fruit
⅔ cup (100 grams) tightly packed raisins
1 egg, beaten
1 tablespoon water
¾ cup (120 grams) blanched whole almonds

Flatten the dough on a lightly floured surface into a large circle. Mix the hazelnuts, candied fruit, and the raisins and work the mixture into the dough in 3 additions: Sprinkle the dough with a third of the nut mixture, fold the 4 sides of the dough into the center and flatten. Repeat the process 2 more times, flattening the dough as much as you can.

Shaping and Second Rise. Cut the dough into 5 equal pieces (each weighs about 11 ounces or 300 grams) and shape each piece into a ball, rolling the dough between your cupped hands and pulling the skin of the dough taut over the fruits and nuts. Place the buns on an oiled or parchment-lined baking sheet. Mix the egg and water in a small bowl. Brush the buns with the egg wash and cover with the almonds. Let rise until doubled, about 5 hours.

Baking. Heat the oven to 400° F. Bake until golden, about 30 minutes. Cool completely on a rack.

Toasted hazelnuts just before skinning

Schiacciata con l'Uva

Tuscan Sweet Bread with Raisins

There are two ways of making this traditional Tuscan sweet bread: The bread baker adds a little sugar and olive oil to regular bread dough, but the pastry baker makes up an eggy briochelike dough that bakes into a more delicate bread much like coffee cake. Traditionally the *schiacciata* is made at grape harvest time with Sangiovese grapes, which are the basis of Chianti wines; I have tried it with Thompson Red Flame seedless grapes, which made a piquant, tart *schiacciata*. But, because grapes are in season so briefly, I decided to make it with raisins—something that is actually done in the tiny town of Conegliano Veneto—by pressing them between the layers of the dough and then covering the dough with a hailstorm of sugar. It tastes delicious, and you will not have to wait for grape season to make it.

Makes 1 loaf

SPONGE
1¾ teaspoons active dry yeast or ⅔ small cake (12 grams) fresh yeast
3 tablespoons sugar
1 cup warm water
2 eggs
1¾ cups (250 grams) unbleached all-purpose flour

BY HAND

Stir the yeast and sugar into the water in a large mixing bowl; let stand until foamy, about 10 minutes. Beat in the eggs with a wooden spoon. Stir in the flour in 2 or 3 additions and mix thoroughly with a wooden spoon or your hands. Cover tightly with plastic wrap and let stand until bubbly, about 30 minutes.

BY MIXER

Stir the yeast and sugar into the water in a mixer bowl; let stand until foamy, about 10 minutes. Beat in the eggs with the paddle. Add the flour and mix well. Cover tightly with plastic wrap and let stand until bubbly, about 30 minutes.

DOUGH
2 tablespoons lard, room temperature
1¾ cups (250 grams) unbleached all-purpose flour
1 teaspoon (5 grams) salt
½ stick (55 grams) unsalted butter, room temperature

BY HAND

Beat the lard into the sponge. Stir in the flour and salt; then beat in the butter, 1 tablespoon at a time. Knead on a lightly floured surface

6 to 7 minutes. The dough should be stiff enough so that, when you pinch the surface, the little peak you make will hold its shape.

BY MIXER   Beat the lard into the sponge with the paddle. Add the flour and salt and mix until the dough comes together. Mix in the butter. Change to the dough hook and knead about 3 minutes. The dough should be stiff enough so that, when you pinch the surface, the little peak you make will hold its shape.

First Rise. Place the dough in an oiled bowl, cover tightly with plastic wrap, and let rise until doubled, about 1½ hours.

FILLING
3 cups (500 grams) raisins
¾ cup (165 grams) sugar

While the dough is rising, soak half the raisins in cool water to cover 1 hour; drain.

Turn the dough out onto a lightly floured surface and cut in half, without punching the dough down. The dough will be soft and stretchy. Stretch 1 piece on the work surface to a rectangle to fit the bottom of a 16 × 11-inch buttered or oiled baking pan. Place the dough in the pan and sprinkle first with the raisins that haven't been soaked in water and then with half the sugar. Stretch the remaining dough to fit the pan and place over the raisins and sugar. Pat the dough flat and poke holes in it with the tip of a small knife or a skewer to let the trapped air escape. Pat dry the raisins that have been soaked, and sprinkle over the dough. Sprinkle with the remaining sugar.

Second Rise. Cover the baking pan tightly with plastic wrap and let rise until puffy and doubled, about 1 hour.

Baking. Heat the oven to 400° F. Bake 40 minutes. Cool a few minutes in the pan; then remove from the pan and cool completely on a rack.

Note. Should you try making this with wine or table grapes, tilt the pan after 20 minutes of baking and pour the sweet sugar syrup into a small bowl; brush the syrup over the top of the dough and finish baking.

Lightly Sweetened Breads

Pane alla
Cioccolata
_____
Chocolate Bread

The secret of this chocolate bread is that it isn't too sweet. It is wonderful eaten with a mild fresh cheese, such as Mascarpone, with a glass of red wine, or a cup of coffee. You can make it in big loaves to be sliced, in individual fat rolls, or you can layer or braid it with sweet milk dough (recipe follows).

Makes 2 round or oval loaves

2½ teaspoons (1 package) active dry yeast or 1 small cake (18 grams) fresh yeast
½ teaspoon sugar
⅓ cup plus 1 tablespoon warm water
4½ cups (600 grams) unbleached all-purpose flour
½ cup plus 2 tablespoons (125 grams) sugar
⅓ cup unsweetened cocoa powder, preferably Dutch process
2 teaspoons (10 grams) salt
1¼ cups warm water
1 egg yolk
1 tablespoon butter, room temperature
1 cup semisweet chocolate chips

BY HAND

Stir the yeast and ½ teaspoon sugar into ⅓ cup plus 1 tablespoon water in a large mixing bowl; let stand until foamy, about 10 minutes. Mix the flour, ½ cup plus 2 tablespoons sugar, the cocoa, and salt. Stir 1¼ cups water, the egg yolk, and butter into the dissolved yeast; then stir in the flour mixture, 1 cup at a time. Stir in the chocolate chips last. Knead on a lightly floured surface until velvety, elastic, and moist, 8 to 10 minutes.

BY MIXER

Stir the yeast and ½ teaspoon sugar into ⅓ cup plus 1 tablespoon water in a small bowl; let stand until foamy, about 10 minutes. Mix the flour, ½ cup plus 2 tablespoons sugar, the cocoa, salt, and chocolate chips in a mixer bowl. Stir 1¼ cups water, the egg yolk, and butter into the dissolved yeast. Pour the yeast mixture into the flour mixture and mix with the paddle until well blended. Change to the dough hook and knead 2 minutes at low speed, then 2 minutes at medium speed. The dough should be velvety, moist, and elastic.

BY PROCESSOR

Stir the yeast and ½ teaspoon sugar into ⅓ cup plus 1 tablespoon water in a small bowl; let stand until foamy, about 10 minutes. Place the flour, ½ cup plus 2 tablespoons sugar, the cocoa, and salt in a food processor fitted with the dough blade and process with several pulses to mix. Stir 1¼ cups cold water and the egg yolk into the dissolved yeast. Cut the cold butter into 4 pieces and place on top of the dry ingredients. With the machine running, pour the yeast mixture through the feed tube as quickly as the flour can absorb it and process until the dough gathers into a ball. Process 40 to 45 seconds longer to knead, pouring the chocolate chips through the feed tube in the last 10 seconds.

First Rise. Place the dough in an oiled bowl, cover tightly with plastic wrap, and let rise until doubled, about 2 hours.

Shaping and Second Rise. Punch the dough down and cut in half on a lightly floured surface. Shape each piece into a round or oval loaf and place on oiled baking sheets. Cover with a towel and let rise until doubled, about 1 hour.

Baking. Heat the oven to 450° F. Bake 15 minutes. Reduce the heat to 375° F and bake 30 minutes longer. Cool completely on a rack.

Pane al Latte
Milk Bread

Pane al latte is a lightly sweetened bread that is perfect for breakfast with butter or jam, and perfect for a snack. The addition of rum is the fantasy of one Italian baker, who also gave it this charming shape, but it is often made into a fat golden roll with a touch of honey in the dough. This bread has a light, eggy interior with a very slightly sweet taste and a glazed surface.

Makes 3 loaves

SPONGE
1¾ teaspoons dry yeast or ⅔ small cake (12 grams) fresh yeast
1 tablespoon sugar
¼ cup warm milk
1 cup less 1 tablespoon (130–135 grams) unbleached all-purpose flour

Stir the yeast and sugar into the milk in a large mixing or mixer bowl; let stand until foamy, about 10 minutes. Add the flour and

Pane al Latte (continued)

whisk vigorously to make a thick batter. Cover and let stand until doubled, less than 1 hour.

DOUGH
2 eggs
1 tablespoon rum
1 cup milk, room temperature (cold if using a food processor)
½ stick (55 grams) unsalted butter, room temperature (cold if using a food processor)
2¾ cups (375 grams) unbleached all-purpose flour
1 teaspoon (5 grams) salt

BY HAND

Stir 1 of the eggs, the rum, and milk into the sponge and then stir in the butter. Mix the flour and salt and stir into the sponge mixture in 2 additions. Stir for about 3 minutes. Knead on a floured work surface, sprinkling with additional flour as needed, until soft, silky, and elastic, 8 to 10 minutes.

BY MIXER

Add 1 of the eggs, the rum, milk, and butter to the sponge and mix with the paddle for about 1 minute. Add the flour and salt and mix on low speed. Change to the dough hook and knead until soft, silky, and elastic, 3 to 4 minutes. Finish kneading briefly by hand on a lightly floured surface.

BY PROCESSOR

Place the flour and salt in the food processor fitted with the dough blade and process with 2 or 3 pulses to sift. Place the sponge and the butter on top of the flour mixture. Mix 1 of the eggs, the rum, and 1 cup cold milk. With the machine running, pour the milk mixture through the feed tube and process until the dough gathers into a ball. Process 30 to 45 seconds longer to knead. The dough should be elastic and moist. Knead briefly by hand on a lightly floured surface, if you want.

First Rise. Place the dough in a lightly oiled bowl, cover tightly with plastic wrap, and let rise until doubled, 1 to 2 hours. The dough should be very soft but slightly tacky, and if you pinch the surface, the little peaks of dough should hold their shape.

Pinching ends together

Shaping and Second Rise. Cut the dough into 15 pieces the size of a small lemon (2 ounces or 50 grams each) and shape into balls. Roll 5 of the balls with your palms into five 6-inch-long cigars, plumper in the center and tapered at the ends. Keep the remaining dough covered while you are working. Place the 5 cigars next to each other on an oiled baking sheet and pinch the ends together; you will have to stretch the first and fifth cigars so that they will meet at the ends. Repeat twice with the remaining 10 balls. Cover with a towel and let rise until doubled, about 45 minutes.

Baking. Heat the oven to 400° F. Beat the remaining egg and brush over the loaves. Bake 25 minutes. Cool on racks.

Pane al Latte e Cioccolata
Milk and Chocolate Bread

You'd never know it from a quick glance, but this is a bread with something for everyone. Hidden inside its fat chocolate exterior is a secret vein of lightly sweetened milk bread.

Makes 1 large or 2 smaller loaves

Pane alla Cioccolata (page 212), prepared through the first rise
14 ounces *Pane al Latte* (⅓ recipe, page 213), prepared through the first rise
1 egg white, beaten

Shaping and Second Rise. Punch down the chocolate dough and shape into a big ball on a lightly floured surface. Let rest 10 to 15 minutes. Cut the dough in half, and flatten each half into a 12 × 6-inch rectangle. Punch down the milk dough and shape into the same size rectangle. Sandwich the milk dough between the chocolate dough and roll up, starting from one long edge, like a jelly roll. Tuck the edges under so that the bread looks like a long log and roll it back and forth to set the shape. To make 2 smaller loaves, cut the sandwiched layers crosswise in half so that you have two 6-inch squares and shape as directed for the larger loaf. Place the loaf on an oiled baking sheet, cover with a towel, and let rise until doubled, about 1 hour.

Baking. Heat the oven to 425° F. Brush the loaf with the egg white. Bake 1 hour. Reduce the heat to 350° F and bake 35 minutes longer. Bake the smaller loaves 1 hour to 1 hour 10 minutes in all.

Pane del Marinaio

Sailor's Bread

A dome-shaped sweet bread full of raisins, spices, and nuts is popular in Genoa, the seaport town on the Italian Riviera. No wonder the sailors liked it so much—it keeps for weeks.

Makes 2 round loaves

1½ sticks (170 grams) unsalted butter, room temperature
⅓ cup (70 grams) sugar
2 eggs, beaten
1 cup (165 grams) raisins
⅓ cup (50 grams) chopped candied citron
⅓ cup (50 grams) chopped candied orange peel
2 tablespoons pine nuts
1½ tablespoons fennel seeds
2¼ cups (300 grams) unbleached all-purpose flour
1½ teaspoons baking powder
1 tablespoon milk
2 tablespoons Marsala

BY HAND

Using a whisk, cream the butter and sugar together in a large mixing bowl. Beat in the eggs, a little bit at a time or the batter will curdle; reserve a quarter of the eggs for egg wash. Combine the raisins, candied citron and orange peel, 1 tablespoon of the pine nuts, and the fennel seeds and stir into the flour and baking powder. Stir half the flour mixture into the butter mixture. Stir in the milk and Marsala, and then the remaining flour mixture. Knead on a floured surface until the dough can hold its shape, about 2 minutes.

BY MIXER

Cream the butter and sugar together in a mixer bowl with the paddle. Increase the speed to high and add the eggs, a little bit at a time; reserve a quarter of the eggs for egg wash. Beat until well blended. Combine the raisins, candied citron and orange, 1 tablespoon of the pine nuts, and the fennel seeds and stir into the flour and baking powder. Add half the flour mixture to the butter mixture and mix thoroughly. Mix in the milk and Marsala, and then the remaining flour mixture. Knead on a floured surface until the dough can hold its shape, about 2 minutes.

Shaping. Cut the dough in half. Flour your hands well and gently shape the dough into 2 thick logs; then pat each log down into a ball, patching over any cracks as you shape. Sprinkle each ball lightly with flour. Place the loaves on an oiled baking sheet. Make a tic-tac-toe pattern in each top with a razor or dough scraper.

Glazing. Brush the tops with the reserved egg, filling in the cracks as you brush. Sprinkle each loaf with half the remaining pine nuts.

Baking. Heat the oven to 360° F. Bake until a toothpick inserted in the center comes out clean, about 40 minutes. Cool on racks.

Meini o Pani de Mei
Sweet Corn Buns

These sweet buns are a very delicate cross between a corn muffin and a scone. They are particularly appealing because the covering on the top cracks into a pattern that looks like the land after a long dry summer. *Meini* are definitely a Lombard specialty, and the Milanese traditionally eat them on April 24 as a celebration of the liberation of their countryside from the assaults of a ferocious highwayman and his brigands during the Middle Ages.

Makes 15 buns

2 sticks plus 2 tablespoons (250 grams) unsalted butter, room temperature
1¼ cups (250 grams) granulated sugar
2 tablespoons plus 2 teaspoons honey
1 egg
1 egg yolk
½ cup plus 2 teaspoons milk
3¼ cups (450 grams) unbleached all-purpose flour
1¾ cups plus 1 tablespoon plus 1 teaspoon (300 grams) fine yellow cornmeal
3½ teaspoons baking powder
2 drops almond oil or ⅛ teaspoon almond extract
About ⅓ cup (70 grams) granulated sugar
½ cup (70 grams) confectioners' sugar

BY MIXER ONLY

Using the whisk if you have one, beat the butter, 1 cup plus 3 tablespoons sugar, and the honey for 1 to 2 minutes at low speed until combined. Increase the speed to medium-high and beat until light and fluffy. Add the egg, egg yolk, and 2 teaspoons milk and continue beating for 1 minute. Mix in the flour, cornmeal, and baking powder. Add ½ cup milk and the almond oil and mix at the lowest speed until blended. The dough should be stiff but not heavy. Knead briefly by hand or mixer, sprinkling with additional flour as needed, until buttery, soft, pliable, and slightly sticky.

Meini o Pani de Mei (continued)

Shaping. Line baking sheets with parchment paper or buttered brown paper. Cut the dough into 15 equal pieces (3 ounces or 90 grams each). Flour your hands and roll each piece into a ball. Flatten each ball into a ½-inch-thick patty, the size of a hamburger and the width of a woman's hand. Place on the paper-lined baking sheets.

Glazing. Brush the tops with water and then sprinkle with granulated sugar, making sure a thin layer of sugar covers each bun. You can shake off the excess sugar by holding on to the paper and shaking the sugar up and over the edge of the pan. Place the confectioners' sugar in a sifter or sieve and sift the sugar heavily over the buns so that they look as if they're lost in a blizzard of sugar. The excess powdered sugar can stay on the paper, because it will not caramelize.

Baking. Heat the oven to 375° F. Bake until the sugar on top has cracked into an irregular design, 15 to 20 minutes. Cool on racks.

Pan de Mej o Pan Mein Dolce

Sweet Corn Bread

Pan de mej was originally a coarse millet bread of the poor people of Milan, made by mixing wheat and millet (*mej* in the Milanese dialect). The nobles had first choice of the grains the peasants and farmers harvested, leaving the lesser grains for the peasant loaves. In time, the millet in this bread was replaced with corn, which became the grain of the common people, and sugar was added along with the delicate flavor of the *sambuco* flower, an herb of the elder plant. The bread was regularly made on April 24, the feast day of San Giorgio, the patron saint of dairymen. Until a short time ago, the day was celebrated by milk workers whose contracts ran from April 24 to April 24, or from San Giorgio to San Giorgio, as they say. On that day they used to eat this rough bread with rich double cream. The bread is usually shaped into individual English-muffin-size buns, but, because I have included a similar sweet corn bread, *Meini o Pani Dei Mei*, in this chapter (page 217), I have written this recipe for a single large loaf. The herb *sambuco* is next to impossible to find in America, but sambuca liqueur is a good substitute; so use some as a glaze for the top of the bread and put a little in the dough as well.

Makes 1 large loaf

SPONGE

2¼ teaspoons active dry yeast or 1 scant small cake (17 grams) fresh yeast

¼ **cup warm water**
2 **tablespoons milk**
¾ **cup (100 grams) unbleached all-purpose flour**

Stir the yeast into the water and milk in a mixing or mixer bowl; let stand until creamy, about 10 minutes. Stir in the flour until smooth. Cover with plastic wrap and let rise 2 hours.

DOUGH
¾ **cup (100 grams) corn flour or yellow cornmeal finely ground in the blender**
½ **cup plus 2½ tablespoons (100 grams) coarsely ground yellow cornmeal**
1 **cup (200 grams) granulated sugar**
3 **eggs**
2½ **tablespoons sambuca liqueur**
Pinch salt
7 **tablespoons (100 grams) unsalted butter, room temperature**
Turbinado sugar

BY HAND

Stir both fine and coarse cornmeals, granulated sugar, eggs, 1½ tablespoons of the liqueur, and the salt into the sponge. Stir in the butter. Knead on a lightly floured surface until soft and tender but slightly springy, 8 to 10 minutes.

BY MIXER

Mix both fine and coarse cornmeals, granulated sugar, eggs, 1½ tablespoons of the liqueur, and the salt into the sponge with the paddle. Add the butter and mix until the dough comes together. Change to the dough hook and knead until soft and tender but slightly springy.

Rising. Place the dough in a buttered 6-cup baking dish. You may want to line the dish with parchment paper, so that it will be easier to unmold the baked loaf. Cover with a heavy towel and let rise until doubled, about 4 hours.

Baking. Heat the oven to 375° F. Brush the top of the loaf with the remaining 1 tablespoon liqueur and sprinkle with a handful of turbinado sugar, which will give the crust a nice crunch. Bake 50 to 55 minutes. The loaf need not be totally dry inside, because the cornmeal will dry more when it is out of the oven. Cool completely on a rack and turn out of the baking dish.

Sweet and Holiday Breads

Panettone

Panettone is a delicate and porous rich egg bread studded with raisins and bits of candied citron and orange that is traditionally eaten by the Milanese on Christmas. These days it can be found all over Italy and America as well and not only during the holidays. Many panettones from Italy are made with a special natural yeast, and they seem to last almost forever. I received one once that had been two months in transit and still tasted fresh and delicious. Panettones made at home probably will not keep for such a long time, but I have never had panettone around long enough to see.

No bread has more stories of its origins. The most reasonable explanation of the name is that the Milanese passion for terms of affection led them to call regular bread *panett*, so that when a larger or richer bread was made, it was inevitable that it be called *panettone*. Some point instead to the Middle Ages when bakers were divided into two groups: those who baked for the poor with millet and other inexpensive grains and those who baked for the rich with wheat flour. Only at Christmas could bakers for the poor make an enriched bread with butter, eggs, sugar, raisins, and candied fruit, which became known as a *pan di tono*, or rich and fancy bread.

The most famous story of the origins of panettone involves a wealthy young Milanese noble in the fifteenth century who fell in love with the daughter of a poor baker named Tony. He wanted to marry the girl and so put at her father's disposal the means to buy the best flour, eggs, and butter, as well as candied orange and citron and fat sultana raisins. The bread he created, known as *pan di Tonio*, was a great success. It made Tony's reputation as well as his fortune and, as a dividend, Tony's backer got the baker's daughter.

If the beginnings of panettone are clouded with mystery, it is well known that panettone was politicized after the uprisings of 1821 when red candied cherries were substituted for raisins and green citron was added so that the bread symbolized the tricolored Italian flag and liberty itself.

In fact, panettone was a much shorter and less dramatic bread until Angelo Motta founded his industrial company in 1921 and used natural yeast and his own tall cylindrical form to make the dazzlingly tall, domed panettone. The soft and delicate bread was such an immediate success that the following year Motta's friend Giacchino Allemagna set up a rival company making equally light and airy panettones. Today those two firms together turn out more than fifty-five million pounds of panettone a year and have made porous, delicately sweetened breads synonymous with Italy and Christmas. There is nothing better with coffee or cappuccino for breakfast or with tea at midday, but the Milanese insist that it is best at Christmas with cream or, even better, fresh Mascarpone. And they traditionally put aside a piece to eat on February 3rd, the feast day of Saint Biagio, the protector of the throat.

Makes 2 panettone

SPONGE

2½ teaspoons (1 package) active dry yeast or 1 small cake (18 grams) fresh yeast

⅓ cup warm water

½ cup (70 grams) unbleached all-purpose flour

Stir the yeast into the water in a small bowl; let stand until creamy, about 10 minutes. Stir in the flour. Cover tightly with plastic wrap and let rise until doubled, 20 to 30 minutes.

FIRST DOUGH

2½ teaspoons (1 package) active dry yeast or 1 small cake (18 grams) fresh yeast

3 tablespoons warm water

2 eggs, room temperature

1¼ cups (180 grams) unbleached all-purpose flour

¼ cup (50 grams) sugar

½ stick (115 grams) unsalted butter, room temperature

BY HAND

Stir the yeast into the water in a mixing bowl; let stand until creamy, about 10 minutes. Add the sponge and beat thoroughly together. Add the eggs, flour, and sugar and mix well. Stir in the butter thoroughly. The entire process will take 5 to 6 minutes. Cover with plastic wrap and let rise until doubled, 1 to 1¼ hours.

BY MIXER

Stir the yeast into the water in a mixer bowl; let stand until creamy, about 10 minutes. Add the sponge, eggs, flour, and sugar and mix with the paddle. Add the butter and mix until the dough is smooth and consistent, about 3 minutes. Cover with plastic wrap and let rise until doubled, 1 to 1¼ hours.

Panettone (continued)
SECOND DOUGH
2 eggs
3 egg yolks
¾ cup (150 grams) sugar
2 tablespoons honey
1½ teaspoons vanilla extract
1 teaspoon (5 grams) salt
2 sticks (225 grams) unsalted butter, room temperature
About 3 cups (420 grams) unbleached all-purpose flour, plus ¾ cup
   for kneading

BY HAND

Place the first dough in a large mixing bowl, if it isn't already. Add the eggs, egg yolks, sugar, honey, vanilla, and salt and mix well. Add the butter and stir until blended. Stir in the flour and keep stirring until smooth. The dough will be soft, a bit like cookie dough. Knead gently on a well-floured surface with well-floured hands until it is smooth and holds its shape. You may need as much as ¾ cup additional flour during the kneading.

BY MIXER

Add the eggs, egg yolks, sugar, honey, vanilla, and salt to the first dough and mix thoroughly with the paddle. Add the butter and mix until smooth. Add the flour and mix again until smooth. The dough will be soft, a bit like cookie dough. Change to the dough hook and knead until smooth and soft, about 2 minutes. Finish by kneading on a lightly floured work surface, using a little additional flour as necessary.

First Rise. Place the dough in a lightly oiled bowl, cover with plastic wrap, and let rise until tripled, 2½ to 4 hours. The dough can also rise overnight at a cool room temperature (65° to 68° F).

FILLING
1½ cups (250 grams) golden raisins
½ cup (75 grams) chopped candied citron
½ cup (75 grams) chopped candied orange peel
Grated zest of 1 orange
Grated zest of 1 lemon
2 to 3 tablespoons unbleached all-purpose flour

At least 30 minutes before the end of the first rise, soak the raisins in cool water to cover. Drain and pat dry. Cut the dough in half on a floured surface. Combine the raisins, candied citron and orange, and orange and lemon zests and dust with 2 to 3 tablespoons flour. Pat each piece of dough into an oval and sprinkle each with a quarter of the fruit mixture. Roll up into a log. Gently flatten the dough again to create as much surface as possible, sprinkle with the remaining fruit mixture, and roll up again.

Shaping and Second Rise. Shape each piece into a ball and slip into 2 well-buttered panettone molds or 2-pound coffee cans lined with a parchment-paper circle on the bottom. For this panettone, which is as light and airy as the traditional bakery panettone, the pan is very important—if you use a charlotte mold, springform pan, or soufflé dish, you will not get the same spectacular height or delicate porous texture.

Cut an **X** in the top of each loaf with a razor. Cover with a towel and let rise until doubled, about 2 hours. If your kitchen is cold, warm the oven at the lowest possible setting for 3 minutes, place a large pan of hot water on the lowest rack, and let the dough rise in the warm, slightly moist atmosphere. With a gas oven, the heat of the pilot light may be enough.

Baking. Heat the oven to 400° F. Just before baking, cut the **X** in each loaf again. Some bakers insert a nut of butter into the cut. Bake 10 minutes. Reduce the heat to 375° F and bake 10 minutes. Reduce the heat to 350° F and bake until a tester inserted in the center comes out clean, 30 minutes. Cool on racks for 30 minutes; then carefully remove from the molds and place the loaves on their sides on pillows to cool. If you place the warm panettone on a rack to cool, it will collapse.

Mataloc

You won't find a *mataloc* anywhere but at Lake Como. It is made much the same as panettone; sometimes, in fact, the figs, raisins, walnuts, and hazelnuts are simply added to panettone dough before its last rise. The name seems to come from the Arab through the Spanish for whom *matalauga* means anise. The Spanish evidently brought their *matalauga* with them to Como where it met with such an enthusiastic reception that its name was domesticated and its shape transformed into a panettonelike sweet bread. It most truly resembles a panettone from Genoa with its fennel seeds, nuts, raisins, and candied fruits, but, even so, how this exotic sweet with Oriental beginnings came to Como during Spanish rule is still a mystery, although it continues to be made and eaten there today.

Makes 1 tall round loaf

SPONGE
1¾ teaspoons active dry yeast or ⅔ cake (12 grams) fresh yeast
½ cup warm water
½ cup plus 1 tablespoon (75 grams) unbleached all-purpose flour

Stir the yeast into the water in a small bowl; let stand until creamy, about 10 minutes. Stir in the flour. The dough will be rough and shaggy. Cover with plastic wrap and let rise until doubled, about 30 minutes to 1 hour.

DOUGH
½ teaspoon active dry yeast or ⅕ small cake (3 to 5 grams) fresh yeast
1 tablespoon honey
¼ cup warm water
1 cup (200 grams) sugar
3 eggs
2½ cups (350 grams) unbleached all-purpose flour
¼ teaspoon salt
⅛ teaspoon crushed fennel seeds
Grated zest of 2 oranges
Grated zest of 2 lemons
1 stick plus 3 tablespoons (155 grams) unsalted butter, room temperature

BY HAND

Stir the yeast and honey into the water in a large mixing bowl; let stand until foamy, about 10 minutes. Stir in the sugar and eggs. Beat in the sponge; then beat in the flour, salt, fennel seeds, and orange and lemon zests. Work in the butter. Knead on a floured surface until soft, sticky, and delicately elastic, about 8 to 10 minutes.

BY MIXER   Stir the yeast and honey into the water in a mixer bowl; let stand until foamy, about 10 minutes. Add the sugar, eggs, and sponge and mix thoroughly with the paddle. Mix in the flour and salt. Change to the dough hook and add the butter, fennel seeds, orange and lemon zests. Knead at high speed for 4 minutes. Finish kneading briefly by hand on a floured surface, adding up to 3 tablespoons more flour as needed, until the dough is sticky, soft, buttery, and delicately elastic.

First Rise. Place the dough in an oiled or buttered bowl, cover with plastic wrap, and let rise overnight at a cool room temperature, 65° to 68° F. The dough will more than double; it might even triple.

FILLING
1⅓ cups (150 grams) hazelnuts
1⅓ cups (150 grams) walnut pieces
4 dried figs, chopped
1 cup (160 grams) raisins
1 tablespoon unbleached all-purpose flour

The next morning, toast the nuts on a baking sheet at 375° F for 15 minutes. Rub the skins from the hazelnuts in a kitchen towel and chop both nuts. Coat the figs and raisins with the flour and combine with the nuts. Flatten the dough on a lightly floured surface. Spread a quarter of the fruits and nuts over the top, and roll up; flatten again and repeat the process 3 more times, letting the dough rest for 10 to 15 minutes after rolling up the dough the second time.

Shaping and Second Rise. Shape the dough into a ball and place in a well-buttered 2-quart charlotte mold, soufflé dish, or 8-inch springform pan whose sides you have built up with aluminum foil. Cover with a towel and let rise until the dough doubles and fills the mold, about 3 hours.

Baking. Heat the oven to 400° F. Bake 10 minutes. Reduce the heat to 350° F and bake 40 to 45 minutes longer. Unmold very carefully and cool on a rack. Cut into wedges to serve.

Panettone con Datteri e Noci

Panettone with Dates and Walnuts

The baked Panettone con Datteri e Noci

Before I was taken to the bakery where this phenomenal panettone was made, I had to promise not to divulge anything about our intended destination. Carlo Veggetti, who has more than 500 bakeries of his own under his protective wing, did not blindfold me, but he did take a roundabout route through Milan so I would not be able to find it again. If he'd thought of it, he would probably have inked out the shop's name from the front of its bakery boxes. I don't blame him for trying to keep it a secret, although two Milanese who really care about such things had already slipped me its name and whispered superlatives about everything in that bakery. My informants were absolutely right, but the great baker, Don Carlo Oldani, has since retired, so there's no knowing where he is currently producing his miracles. His panettone is made exactly like *pasta sfogliata* (puff pastry); I've adapted his method to the dough on page 220. The dough is then cut into three pieces, and one is covered with dates, one with walnuts, and one left empty. The doughs are then stacked in layers, rolled into a ball, and baked just like a regular panettone.

Makes 1 panettone

Panettone (page 220), made without butter or filling through the first rise and refrigerated 2 to 3 hours
2½ sticks (280 grams) unsalted butter, cold
⅓ cup (50 grams) unbleached all-purpose flour
1 cup (150 grams) chopped dates
1⅓ cups (150 grams) chopped toasted walnuts

BY HAND

Place the butter between 2 sheets of waxed paper and beat with a rolling pin to soften slightly. Sprinkle the flour on top of the butter and work it into the butter with a dough scraper. The flour shouldn't be thoroughly worked in, and the butter should be cold but malleable, so that it forms a dry but firm butter packet.

BY MIXER

Beat the butter and flour in a mixer bowl with the paddle until smooth. The flour shouldn't be thoroughly worked in and the butter should still be cold.

The dough is turned 4 times as for *Cornetti Dolci* (Italian Croissants, page 304).
Lightly flour the work surface. Roll the cold dough into an 18 × 12-inch rectangle, ½ inch thick, so that one short side is nearest you. Break the butter into small (½ inch) pieces and dot over two-thirds of the dough rectangle nearest you, leaving a 1½-inch border around the edges. Fold as if you were folding a business letter: fold the

unbuttered third over the middle and fold the remaining third over the top. Pinch the edges together so that the butter does not fall out. Tap the surface of the dough with a rolling pin to evenly distribute the butter.

First Set of Two Turns. Keep the work surface clean and lightly dusted with flour at all times. Place the dough on the surface so that the top flap faces your right (like a book). Roll the dough into a 24 × 8-inch rectangle, ½ inch thick. Fold the two short ends to meet in the middle. Then fold in half, as if closing a book, and turn the dough so that the open folded edge is facing away from you toward the top of the table. Tap the dough with the rolling pin from one end to the other to consolidate it, and brush off all the excess flour. Roll the dough out once again to approximately the same size rectangle and fold into thirds, like a business letter. Lightly tap the dough to consolidate it, brush off the excess flour, and place the dough in a plastic bag. Refrigerate 30 to 45 minutes. If the dough is refrigerated too long, the butter will break or crack instead of rolling out smoothly.

Second Set of Two Turns. Place the dough on a lightly floured surface so that the top flap faces your right. Roll the dough into the same size rectangle and fold once again into thirds. The surface should be blistered and the dough springy, elastic, and very smooth. Refrigerate the dough 30 to 45 minutes to let it relax. Roll the dough out a final time and fold again. Let it relax at room temperature for about 15 minutes.

The three layers of dough

Filling and Shaping. Roll the dough out ½ inch thick. Cut the dough into 3 equal rectangles. On one rectangle, sprinkle the dates; on the second, the walnuts. Leave the third one empty. Place the walnut dough on top of the date dough and cover both of them with the plain dough. Pinch the edges to seal and gently shape into a ball, by pulling the dough taut and pinching it together at the bottom. Place in a buttered panettone mold, 2-pound coffee can lined with a round of parchment paper, or 2-quart springform mold with sides built up with aluminum foil. Cover with a towel and let rise until doubled, 3 to 4 hours.

Baking. Heat the oven to 400° F. Bake 10 minutes. Reduce the heat to 375° F and bake 40 to 50 minutes. If the top starts to get too brown, cover it with aluminum foil. Cool completely in the mold and then unmold onto a rack.

Veneziana
Venetian Holiday Bread

This sweet bread from Venice, made for Christmas and especially for New Year's Eve, is very much like panettone, but it has no citron or candied fruits. The top is dusted with confectioners' sugar and studded with whole almonds.

Makes 2 round loaves

SPONGE
3½ teaspoons active dry yeast or 1⅓ small cakes (24 grams) fresh yeast
¼ cup (50 grams) sugar
¾ cup warm water
3 egg yolks
Scant 2 cups (250 grams) unbleached all-purpose flour
½ stick (55 grams) unsalted butter, room temperature

Stir the yeast and sugar into the water in a medium-size mixing bowl; let stand until foamy, about 10 minutes. Stir in the egg yolks, and then mix in the flour to form a soft dough. Beat in the butter thoroughly. Cover with plastic wrap and let rise until tripled, about 2 hours.

DOUGH
1 teaspoon active dry yeast or ⅓ small cake (6 grams) fresh yeast
1 tablespoon honey
3 tablespoons warm water
½ cup (100 grams) sugar
3 egg yolks
1 cup plus 2 tablespoons (140 grams) cake flour
1 cup (140 grams) unbleached all-purpose flour
1 stick (115 grams) unsalted butter, room temperature
2 teaspoons vanilla extract
Grated zest of 2 oranges
Grated zest of 1 lemon
1 teaspoon (5 grams) salt

BY HAND

Stir the yeast and honey into the water in a large mixing bowl; let stand until foamy, about 10 minutes. Stir in the sugar and egg yolks; add the sponge and mix until smooth. Stir in the flours, 1 cup at a time. The dough should be soft. Stir in the butter, vanilla, and orange and lemon zests, and then the salt. Knead on a lightly floured surface until smooth but still soft and slightly sticky, 8 to 10 minutes.

BY MIXER

Stir the yeast and honey into the water in a large mixer bowl; let stand until foamy, about 10 minutes. Add the sugar, egg yolks, and sponge and mix with the paddle until smooth. Add the flours and mix until the dough comes together. Mix in the butter, vanilla, orange and lemon zests, and salt. Change to the dough hook and knead until smooth but still soft and slightly sticky, about 3 minutes.

First Rise. Place the dough in a lightly buttered bowl, cover tightly with plastic wrap, and let rise until doubled, about 2 hours. The dough should be full of air bubbles.

Shaping and Second Rise. Pour the dough out onto a floured surface, punch it down, and knead lightly. Cut the dough in half and shape each piece into a ball. Because the dough is very sticky, shape the ball in your hands, holding it in the air and stretching the skin taut as you turn it and pinch the dough together on the bottom. Place each ball in a buttered 2-quart charlotte mold or soufflé dish. Cover with plastic wrap and let rise until doubled, about 2½ hours.

TOPPING
¼ **cup (40 grams) blanched almonds, plus 10 to 12 whole unpeeled for the top**
1½ **teaspoons bitter almonds**
¾ **cup (150 grams) granulated sugar**
1 **to 2 egg whites**
1½ **tablespoons turbinado sugar**
Confectioners' sugar

Process ¼ cup almonds, the bitter almonds, and sugar in a food processor fitted with the steel blade or grind the nuts in a nut grinder, then add the sugar. Remove to a small bowl and stir in enough of the egg whites to make the mixture easily spreadable but not runny. When the loaves have fully risen, delicately brush the topping all over the surfaces. Dot each loaf with whole almonds and then sprinkle with the turbinado sugar. Finish with a heavy dusting of confectioners' sugar.

Baking. Heat the oven to 400° F. Bake 10 minutes. Reduce the heat to 350° F and bake 35 to 40 minutes longer. Let cool 10 minutes and unmold very carefully onto racks to cool completely.

Focaccia Veneziana Laced with Zabaglione Cream

One morning I walked through the streets of Venice at 2 A.M. to join the bread bakers of Il Fornaio at San Luca at their work. The bakery itself was huge, but it took only three men to turn out a prodigious selection of regional breads, rolls in any number of forms, and big *pani in cassette* for sandwich loaves. As they worked, they joked, told stories, tossed the dough at the worktables with abandon before shaping it. Around 5 A.M., the pastry bakers started to arrive along with a second crew to tend the ovens. By eight o'clock, as I was wondering how anyone could keep up the unremitting pace, there suddenly appeared a tray of espressos and cappuccinos and the most extravagant dome of sweet bread that was laced with hidden veins of zabaglione cream. It was every bit as wonderful as it sounds. Although the recipe looks complicated because of the three initial steps in putting the dough together, if you can plan to do it on a day when you will be home and have other things to do, it shouldn't be a problem. I suggest baking the *focaccia* on one day and making the filling and injecting it the next day.

Makes 1 round loaf

SPONGE
1¼ teaspoons active dry yeast or ½ small cake (9 grams) fresh yeast
½ teaspoon sugar
¼ cup warm water
2 eggs
1 cup plus 1 tablespoon (150 grams) unbleached all-purpose flour

Stir the yeast and sugar into the warm water in a large mixing or mixer bowl; let stand until foamy, about 10 minutes. Stir in the eggs and then the flour to make a soft dough. Cover with plastic wrap and let rise until bubbly and doubled, about 45 minutes.

FIRST DOUGH
½ teaspoon active dry yeast or ⅙ small cake (3 grams) fresh yeast
1 tablespoon warm water
2 tablespoons nonfat dry milk
¼ cup (50 grams) sugar
2 tablespoons unsalted butter, room temperature
1 egg
3 egg yolks
1 cup plus 1 tablespoon (150 grams) unbleached all-purpose flour
1 teaspoon (5 grams) salt

Stir the yeast into the water in a medium-size bowl; let stand until creamy, about 10 minutes. Stir in the milk. Beat the sugar, butter, egg, and egg yolks together until blended, stir into the yeast mixture, and then stir into the sponge. Add the flour and salt and stir just until the dough comes together. Cover with plastic wrap and let rise until doubled, 1½ to 2½ hours.

SECOND DOUGH
1 tablespoon honey
Scant ½ cup (90 grams) sugar
4½ teaspoons rum
1½ teaspoons vanilla extract
Grated zest of 1 orange or ½ teaspoon best-quality orange oil
4 egg yolks, beaten
2¼ cups (300 grams) unbleached all-purpose flour
⅓ cup (75 grams) unsalted butter, room temperature

BY HAND

Add the honey, sugar, rum, vanilla, and orange zest to the first dough and beat until blended. Add the egg yolks and stir vigorously. The dough will look stringy and lumpy, but it will smooth out later. Stir in the flour, 1 cup at a time, and beat vigorously until the dough is stretchy and smooth. Beat in the butter, 1 tablespoon at a time, and continue stirring until the dough comes together. Knead vigorously on a floured surface until smooth and elastic, 10 to 12 minutes.

BY MIXER

Add the honey, sugar, rum, vanilla, and orange zest to the first dough and beat with the paddle until blended. Beat in the egg yolks. The dough will look stringy and lumpy, but it will smooth out later. Beat in the flour, 1 cup at a time; then beat in the butter, 1 tablespoon at a time, at medium speed. Beat until the dough comes together, although it will never pull entirely away from the bottom of the bowl. Change to the dough hook and knead at medium speed until smooth and elastic, about 4 minutes.

Shaping. Shape the dough into a round ball and place in a buttered 2-quart charlotte mold or soufflé dish. Cut a **Y** in the top of the loaf with a razor. Cover with a towel and let rise until doubled, about 2½ to 3 hours.

GLAZE
2 to 3 tablespoons amaretto liqueur
¼ cup (50 grams) turbinado sugar
2 to 3 tablespoons confectioners' sugar

Focaccia Veneziana (continued)
Brush the top of the loaf with the liqueur, sprinkle with the turbinado sugar, and then sift the confectioners' sugar over the top. Recut the Y to be sure it is open.

Baking. Heat the oven to 350° F. Bake 1 hour 10 minutes. It will puff up dramatically in the oven, rising over the top of the form almost to twice its height. Let cool completely in the mold.

Filling. Make the zabaglione cream (recipe follows).
Use the special long-nosed (Bismarck) pastry tip for injecting the zabaglione cream into the *focaccia*. First, spoon the cream into a pastry bag fitted with the tip. Make 8 to 10 small indentations in the *focaccia* with the tip and then squirt little rivulets of filling into the interior and into the Y-shaped opening. If you don't have the special tip, use a sharp bread knife to cut the *focaccia* into three horizontal layers and fill with the cream as you would a layer cake.

Zabaglione Cream

I think this Marsala-flavored cream is so good that I would happily dip my fingers into it and eat it unaccompanied. No wonder it is named for San Giovanni di Vaylon, the protective saint of pastry cooks.

2 tablespoons unbleached all-purpose flour
6 tablespoons sugar
1⅓ cups milk
1 whole egg
3 egg yolks
1 tablespoon unsalted butter
Grated zest of ½ lemon
3 tablespoons Marsala

Mix the flour and sugar in a small heavy saucepan. Stir in the milk. Heat to a simmer and simmer, stirring constantly, until as thick as hot cereal, about 5 minutes. Beat the egg and egg yolks in a mixing bowl. Pour half of the milk mixture into the eggs and beat until smooth; add the rest of the milk and beat again. Return to the saucepan and heat just until it comes to a boil. Return to the bowl and dot the butter over the top. Stir in the lemon zest. Cool to lukewarm. Add the Marsala and beat until smooth.

Colomba Pasquale
Easter Bread

Everyone agrees that the *colomba pasquale* is a sweet bread made at Easter from a dough almost identical to panettone; it is shaped like a dove and veiled with crystallized sugar and studded with toasted unpeeled almonds. There are, however, two very different stories about its origins. One traces the *colomba* of Milan to the victory of Legnano in 1176 when the cities of the Lombard League finally defeated Frederick Barbarossa, who was intent on capturing Italy for the Holy Roman Empire. It is said that two doves, symbolizing the Holy Ghost, appeared during the battle on the altar of the chariot carrying the battle standards and that the *colomba* memorializes that event and victory. Others say that, while the panettone comes from Milano, the *colomba* clearly derives from nearby Pavia during the time when Alboin conquered the city. As tribute, they say, he exacted an enormous number of precious jewels as well as twelve girls to do with as he pleased. All except one girl wept and sobbed at her fate, but the one who used her head took some eggs, yeast, sugar, flour, candied fruits, and spices and made a sweet cake in the shape of a dove. When the king called her to his bed, the story goes, she brought him her *colomba*, which he ate with pleasure and then allowed her to go free. Yet another story says that she baked him a sweet cake shaped like a dove, the symbol of peace, and Alboin made Pavia his capital and spared it from destruction.

Makes 1 shaped loaf

SPONGE

3½ teaspoons active dry yeast or 1⅓ small cakes (24 grams) fresh
   yeast
1 tablespoon sugar
½ cup warm water
3 egg yolks
½ cup (70 grams) unbleached all-purpose flour

Stir the yeast and sugar into the water in a large mixing or mixer bowl; let stand until foamy, about 10 minutes. Vigorously stir in the egg yolks and flour and continue stirring until smooth. Cover tightly with plastic wrap and let rise until doubled, about 30 minutes.

continued

Colomba Pasquale (continued)

FIRST DOUGH
1 teaspoon yeast or ⅓ small cake (6 grams) fresh yeast
5 tablespoons warm water
3 tablespoons (45 grams) unsalted butter, room temperature
1½ cups (210 grams) unbleached all-purpose flour

Stir the yeast into the water in a small bowl; let stand until creamy, about 10 minutes. Stir the dissolved yeast into the sponge. Stir in the butter and then the flour. The dough should be stiff but sticky. Cover tightly with plastic wrap and let rise until doubled, 1 to 2 hours.

SECOND DOUGH
½ cup plus 3 tablespoons (145 grams) sugar
1 tablespoon honey
3 egg yolks
1½ teaspoons vanilla extract
Grated zest of 2 oranges
1 stick (115 grams) unsalted butter, room temperature
Scant 2 cups (250 grams) unbleached all-purpose flour
1 teaspoon (5 grams) salt
1 cup (150 grams) chopped candied orange peel

BY HAND   Add the sugar, honey, and egg yolks to the first dough and stir thoroughly. Stir in the vanilla, orange zest, and butter. Mix the flour and salt and stir into the dough, 1 cup at a time. Continue stirring until a soft dough is formed. Knead on a floured surface until soft but elastic, 7 to 10 minutes.

BY MIXER   Add the sugar, honey, egg yolks, vanilla, orange zest, and butter to the first dough in the mixer bowl. Mix with the paddle until smooth. Add the flour and salt and beat until a soft dough is formed. Change to the dough hook and knead briefly. Knead gently by hand on a floured surface until elastic.

First Rise. Place the dough in an oiled bowl, cover tightly with plastic wrap, and let rise until tripled, about 3½ hours. The dough will have lots of air bubbles beneath the surface when it is fully risen.

Shaping and Second Rise. Cut the dough in half on a lightly floured surface. Pat each piece flat and sprinkle the candied orange peel over the surface. Roll up each piece into a log. Pat the dough flat again and roll up one piece into a 10-inch log with slightly tapered ends, the other into a fatter 7-inch log also with slightly tapered ends. Place the shorter log across the other, shaping them into a stylized dove, on a lightly oiled or buttered baking sheet. Make a slight indentation in the bottom log where the top log crosses it. Cover with a towel and let rise until doubled, 2 to 3 hours. If your kitchen is very cold or dry, let rise in a slightly warm oven (85° to 90° F) over a pan of steaming water.

TOPPING
5 tablespoons (50 grams) blanched almonds
2 to 2½ tablespoons (25 grams) bitter almonds or apricot kernels
½ cup plus 2 tablespoons (130 grams) granulated sugar
1 or 2 egg whites
¼ cup (40 grams) whole unpeeled almonds
1 to 2 tablespoons turbinado sugar
Confectioners' sugar

Process the blanched almonds, bitter almonds or apricot kernels, and sugar in a food processor fitted with the steel blade. Alternatively, grind the almonds and apricot kernels in a nut grinder until fine; remove to a small bowl and add sugar. Stir in enough of the egg whites to make the mixture easily spreadable but not runny. Delicately brush the topping over the fully risen dough. Dot with the whole almonds and then sprinkle with the turbinado sugar. Sift the confectioners' sugar lightly over the top.

Baking. Heat the oven to 400° F. Bake 10 minutes. Reduce the heat to 350° F and bake 40 minutes longer. Cool completely on a rack.

Other Shapes. The dough can also be shaped into a round loaf and baked in a buttered 2-quart mold or soufflé dish. Bake 15 minutes longer at 350° F.

Pandoro
Christmas Bread of Verona

This buttery golden bread is the Christmas specialty of Verona and is always baked in a star-shaped mold beneath a hail of confectioners' sugar. Although the name suggests *pan d'oro* (golden bread), *pandoro* is actually a dialect word for a Veronese dessert made more than two centuries ago. The bread is not complicated to make, but it needs plenty of time for each one of the rises, which are the secret of its delicate, buttery texture. If you start around breakfast time, you can easily have the *pandoro* out of the oven by supper, and you will not have spent much time with the dough itself. This dough is difficult, but not impossible, to make by hand. Serve *pandoro* with fresh Mascarpone whipped with sugar and egg yolks, flavored with good rum, and sprinkled with chopped toasted almonds.

Makes 2 tall round loaves

SPONGE
4¼ teaspoons active dry yeast or 1⅔ small cakes (30 grams) fresh yeast
½ cup warm water
1 egg
2 tablespoons sugar
¾ cup (100 grams) unbleached all-purpose flour

Stir the yeast into the water in a large mixing or mixer bowl; let stand until creamy, about 10 minutes. Add the egg, sugar, and flour and beat until smooth. Cover tightly with plastic wrap and let rise until doubled, about 30 minutes.

FIRST DOUGH
3 cups plus 3 tablespoons (380 grams) pastry flour
3¼ cups (435 grams) unbleached all-purpose flour
1 teaspoon active dry yeast or ⅓ small cake (6 grams) fresh yeast
1 tablespoon warm water
¼ cup (50 grams) sugar
2 eggs
½ stick (55 grams) unsalted butter, room temperature

Mix the pastry and all-purpose flours; measure 2½ cups for this dough and reserve the remaining flour for the second dough. Stir the yeast into the water in a small bowl; let stand until creamy, about 10 minutes. Add the dissolved yeast, sugar, 2½ cups mixed flour, and the eggs to the sponge and stir vigorously. Add the butter and beat until blended. Cover with plastic wrap and let rise until doubled, about 45 minutes.

SECOND DOUGH

4 eggs
2 egg yolks
1 cup (200 grams) sugar
Reserved mixed pastry and all-purpose flours from the first dough
1 teaspoon (5 grams) salt
2 teaspoons vanilla extract
1 teaspoon best-quality lemon extract or grated zest of 1 lemon
2½ sticks (285 grams) unsalted butter, room temperature
½ cup (75 grams) chopped candied citron
4 tablespoons unbleached all-purpose flour, plus ½ cup (70 grams) for kneading, as necessary

BY HAND

(By all means, use the mixer, if you have one, for this dough.) Add the eggs, egg yolks, sugar, reserved flour, salt, and vanilla and lemon extracts to the first dough and stir until blended. Stir in the butter gradually. Toss the citron and 1 tablespoon of the all-purpose flour together and stir into the dough. Knead on a floured surface, sprinkling with additional flour (a generous ½ cup), until soft, light and delicately elastic, 10 to 12 minutes.

BY MIXER

Add the eggs, egg yolks, sugar, and vanilla and lemon extracts to the first dough and beat thoroughly with the paddle. Toss the citron and 1 tablespoon of the all-purpose flour together and mix into the dough. Mix in the butter gradually and then the reserved flour and the salt. Change to the dough hook and knead at low speed for 4 to 6 minutes, adding the additional ½ cup flour as necessary and stopping occasionally to scrape the dough down from the hook. The dough should be soft, buttery, and delicate.

First Rise. Place the dough in a buttered bowl, cover tightly with plastic wrap, and let rise at warm room temperature (75° to 80° F) until doubled, 2 to 3 hours. The rise may take as long as 4 hours in a cold kitchen; you may place the bowl in a warm water bath (about 90° F) and cover it with a towel to encourage the rising.

Shaping and Second Rise. Sprinkle the top of the dough with the remaining 3 tablespoons flour. Pour the very buttery and sticky dough onto a well-floured surface. Flour your hands as well. Cut the

Pandoro (continued)

dough in half with a dough scraper and gently shape each piece into a ball. Place in buttered pandoro molds, 2-quart springform pans, or 2-pound coffee cans that have been lined with parchment paper. Cover with a towel and let rise until doubled, about 2½ to 4 hours, depending on the size of the mold and the warmth of the room.

Baking. Heat the oven to 350° F. Bake 30 minutes. Reduce the heat to 300° F and bake 20 to 30 minutes longer. Let cool completely before removing them from the molds.

Pizza Civitavecchia

Easter Sweet Bread from Civitavecchia

The sweet Easter bread of the port of Rome is always distinguished not only by its slanting domed top but also by its unusual taste derived from the port, ricotta, and anise seeds that flavor it. This makes extraordinary French toast.

Makes 2 tall domed loaves

SPONGE

3½ teaspoons active dry yeast or 1⅓ small cakes (24 grams) fresh yeast
½ cup warm water
¾ cup (100 grams) bread flour

Stir the yeast into the water in a small bowl; let stand until creamy, about 10 minutes. Add the flour and stir vigorously to make a thick batter. Cover tightly with plastic wrap and let rise until doubled, about 1 hour.

DOUGH

3¼ cups (420 grams) unbleached all-purpose flour
¼ cup (50 grams) sugar
1 teaspoon (5 grams) salt
4 eggs
9 egg yolks
⅓ cup (75 grams) ricotta, pressed through a fine-mesh sieve
½ cup port or rum
2 tablespoons plus 2 teaspoons crushed aniseeds
Grated zest of 1 lemon
½ teaspoon ground cinnamon
2 sticks (225 grams) unsalted butter, room temperature
1 egg white, beaten

BY MIXER ONLY   Beat the flour, salt, sugar, eggs, and egg yolks in a mixer bowl with the paddle until blended. Add the sponge and beat 6 to 7 minutes, half at medium speed and half at high. The dough should be golden, springy, and stretchy. Mix the ricotta, port, aniseeds, lemon zest, and cinnamon and beat into the dough. Cut the butter into 7 or 8 pieces and place on top of the dough.

First Rise. Cover the dough, leaving the butter on top, with plastic wrap, and let rise until doubled, 1 to 1½ hours. The risen dough should be soft and very elastic. Beat in the butter by hand or with the dough hook until the dough is quite smooth and no longer ropy, 3 to 4 minutes for the mixer.

Shaping and Second Rise. This sticky dough seems more like pound-cake batter than bread dough. You can simply pour it into 2 well-buttered 2-quart charlotte molds or soufflé dishes, or, if you want to shape it before you place it in the molds, flour the work surface and your hands well, place a small mound of flour nearby, and shape the dough into 2 round loaves. Cover with a towel and let rise to the tops of the molds, 1 to 1½ hours.

Baking. Heat the oven to 400° F. Brush the tops of the loaves with the egg white. Bake 15 minutes. Reduce the heat to 350° F and bake 1 hour longer. The loaves will rise high above the baking dish like a panettone, and the dome will always be tilted.

Note. To double the recipe, double all the ingredients, but use 20 egg yolks and 7 eggs in the dough.

Pizza di Pasqua

Easter Pizza

This sweet bread made only for Easter comes from an old Roman recipe. Even though it is rich with eggs and butter, it is airy, light, and flavored delicately with orange and lemon. Because it is made with bread flour, it must be beaten at a high speed for a long time. Unless you have phenomenal muscles and remarkable stamina, and are willing to beat by hand for 25 to 30 minutes, you will have to use an electric mixer.

Makes 2 tall domed loaves

SPONGE

3½ teaspoons active dry yeast or 1⅓ small cakes (24 grams) fresh yeast
½ cup warm water
½ cup (70 grams) bread flour

Stir the yeast into the water in a large mixer bowl; let stand until creamy, about 10 minutes. Add the flour and stir until smooth. Cover tightly with plastic wrap and let rise until the sponge has enormous bubbles, is very soupy, and has doubled, about 1 hour.

DOUGH

3⅓ cups (450 grams) bread flour
10 egg yolks
½ cup plus 2 tablespoons (125 grams) granulated sugar
½ cup milk
3 oranges
2 lemons
1½ teaspoons vanilla extract
1 stick plus 1 tablespoon (130 grams) unsalted butter, room temperature

1 egg white, beaten
2 to 3 tablespoons turbinado sugar

BY MIXER ONLY

Add the flour to the sponge and beat with the paddle until smooth. Beat in the egg yolks, one at a time. Mix in the granulated sugar. Add the milk and mix until well blended. Grate the zests of the oranges and lemons directly into the bowl, so that none of the oils are lost. Add the vanilla and mix until blended. Beat in the butter, 2 tablespoons at a time. Beat at medium and medium-high speeds for at least 10 minutes. You may want to turn the mixer off once or twice to be sure that it doesn't overheat. The dough should be very, very soft and extremely elastic.

First Rise. Cover the bowl tightly with plastic wrap and let rise until doubled, about 3 hours.

Shaping and Second Rise. Flour your work surface generously before you pour the dough out. Depending on the wetness of the dough and your ease in handling it, you may need to have a mound of flour nearby to sprinkle on top as you work the dough. Cut the dough in half and shape into 2 round loaves. Place in 2 well-buttered 2-quart soufflé dishes or charlotte molds. Cover with a towel and let rise until doubled, 2½ to 3 hours. The dough should fill the entire baking dish.

Baking. Heat the oven to 400° F. Just before baking, brush the top of each loaf with the egg white and then sprinkle with the turbinado sugar. Bake 35 to 40 minutes. The top will puff into a big dome like a panettone. Because the dough is very eggy and porous, it will need the entire baking time. Cover the top with aluminum foil when it is baked to a golden brown. Let cool 15 minutes and unmold very carefully onto a rack to cool completely. If it seems very delicate to you, you may let it cool completely in the dish.

Gubana

Almost everyone has heard of panettones and *colombe*, but even many Italians are unaware of the *gubana*, the Easter bread of Friuli, the region east of Venice that sits tightly against the Yugoslav and Austrian borders. As soon as I tasted this dense, complicated, nut and raisin bread, I was a convert, ready to convince the world of the allure of its bittersweet tastes. I've even tried to import *gubane*, which keep very well even for a journey by sea if they are made with natural yeast. *Gubana* actually exists in two versions, one wrapped in puff pastry and this one from Cividale, made according to a genuine recipe given to me by Dottore Angelo Albini, the fourth generation baker in his family. It is essentially equal amounts of dough and filling, which is raisins, walnuts, hazelnuts, pine nuts, and almonds moistened with the robust flavors of five different wines and liqueurs. The sweet briochelike dough is rolled up like a strudel, twisted around itself like a snail, and generously showered with crunchy sugar. Some say the *gubana* dates back to the sixth to eighth centuries when the Lombards settled on Cividale as the capital of their duchy. The first documentary evidence dates it to 1700, but that hardly makes it an upstart.

Its name presumably comes from the Slavic *guba*, which describes the snail shape, although there are those who say the name is derived from *bubane*, Friulian dialect for abundance. You can certainly taste the Slavic influence in the dense, chewy, nut-and-fruit-filled interior and in the bittersweet bite of its liqueurs. In Italy, *gubana* is made with the local grappa, a rustic kind of brandy, but, because grappa is difficult to find even in large cities, you may substitute plum brandy, aquavit, slivovitz, or marc. Because it is laced with liqueurs, *gubana* is usually eaten for dessert and is especially good with sweet white wines, such as the Verduzzo of Friuli.

Makes 2 round loaves

SPONGE

2 tablespoons plus 2 teaspoons active dry yeast or 3 small cakes (48 grams) fresh yeast

¾ cup milk, warmed to 110° F and then cooled to 75° to 80° F

1 cup plus 1 tablespoon (140 to 150 grams) unbleached all-purpose flour

Stir the yeast into the milk in a large mixing or mixer bowl; let stand until creamy, about 10 minutes. Stir in the flour with a wooden spoon until smooth. Cover with plastic wrap and let rise 30 minutes to 1 hour.

DOUGH

2 eggs

2 egg yolks

½ cup plus 2 tablespoons (130 grams) sugar

3 to 4 tablespoons milk

3¾ cups (500 grams) unbleached all-purpose flour

1¼ teaspoons (7 grams) salt

Grated zest of 2 lemons

2½ teaspoons vanilla extract

1 stick (115 grams) unsalted butter, room temperature

BY HAND

Add the eggs, egg yolks, sugar, and 3 tablespoons milk to the sponge and stir until smooth. Stir in the flour, 1 cup at a time, and the salt and keep stirring until smooth. Stir in the lemon zest, vanilla, and 1 tablespoon milk if needed. Finally stir in the butter (the butter can also be cut into 8 pieces and set on top of the kneaded dough for the first rise). Flour your work surface generously, flour your hands, and have a dough scraper ready to help knead the dough, which will be sticky at first. Knead until velvety, supple, and blistered, 8 to 10 minutes.

BY MIXER

Add the eggs, egg yolks, sugar, and 3 tablespoons milk to the sponge and mix with the paddle until smooth. Mix in the flour and salt until smooth. Mix in the lemon zest, vanilla, and 1 tablespoon milk if needed. Change to the dough hook and knead until velvety, supple, and blistered, 3 to 4 minutes. Cut the butter into 8 pieces and set on top of the dough for the first rise.

Gubana (continued)

First Rise. Place the dough in a lightly buttered bowl, cover with plastic wrap, and let rise at warm room temperature until doubled, 2 to 3 hours. You can speed up the rising a bit by placing the bowl in a warm water bath (90° F).

FILLING

2¾ cups (300 grams) hazelnuts, toasted, skinned, and chopped
Generous ¾ cup (90 grams) walnuts, toasted and chopped
⅓ cup (35 grams) pine nuts, lightly toasted
2 tablespoons (20 grams) blanched almonds, chopped
1½ cups (160 grams) crumbs from leftover sweet breads, cookies, and/or homemade breads
Generous 1 cup (180 grams) raisins
½ cup plus 1 tablespoon apricot jam
½ cup (70 to 80 grams) candied orange peel, chopped
Grated zest of 1 lemon
1½ tablespoons unsweetened cocoa powder
1 teaspoon ground cinnamon
3 tablespoons Marsala
2 tablespoons plus 1 teaspoon grappa
2 tablespoons rum
1 tablespoon amaretto liqueur
1 teaspoon maraschino liqueur

1 egg
2 teaspoons water

1 egg white, beaten

1. *Rolling filling into dough*

2. *Rolling dough into snail shape*

Combine the nuts, bread crumbs, raisins, jam, orange peel, lemon zest, cocoa, cinnamon, Marsala, grappa, rum, and liqueurs. Work the butter into the dough, if necessary. Cut the dough in half on a lightly floured surface. Roll out each piece into an 18 × 12-inch rectangle. Spread the filling over the dough rectangles, leaving a 2-inch border on all sides. Mix the egg and water in a small bowl and brush the edges of the dough with the egg wash.

Shaping and Second Rise. Starting at one long edge, roll up each dough rectangle and pinch the ends. Shape each log into a spiral so that it looks like a big snail. Place each dough spiral in a well-buttered 2- to 3-quart baking or soufflé dish. The *gubana* can also be baked free form on a buttered baking sheet, but the dish will help keep its shape. Cover with plastic wrap or a towel and let rise until well puffed but not doubled, 2 to 2½ hours.

Baking. Heat the oven to 375° F. Just before baking, brush the tops of the loaves with the egg white and poke several holes in the tops with a skewer to let air escape from any air pockets. Bake 25 minutes. Reduce the heat to 325° F and bake until deep golden, about 25 minutes longer. Unmold very carefully and cool completely on racks.

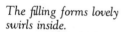

The filling forms lovely swirls inside.

PANINI E GRISSINI
Rolls and Breadsticks

Panini

*I*f anything indicates the changing pace of Italian life, it's the explosion of *panini*, the little bread rolls that appear in numerous shapes and sizes all over Italy. Walk into any *caffe* bar in Milan, Rome, or another good-size city after 10:30 A.M. and you will find the glass cases full of rolls, sliced and bursting with the most extraordinarily inventive and tasty combinations. Here's lunch between two slices of bread, eaten standing at a counter elbow-to-elbow with masses of other Italians, who can no longer spend several hours in a restaurant or at home for the midday meal.

The possibilities seem endless, limited only by the variety of rolls, the ingredients at hand, and the imagination of the person behind the counter. In addition to soft *panini* or crisp, crunchy rolls filled with the obvious prosciutto and cheese are rolls thickly studded with olives and filled with tuna and artichoke hearts; sesame-seed-topped golden bread with spicy local salami and sweet red and yellow peppers; spinach rolls with Gorgonzola cheese melted on top; braids of *pasta dura* moistened with tomatoes and fresh mozzarella; fat *panini* stuffed with mozzarella, anchovies, and parsley.

Panini are every bit as regional as breads, and Italians develop fierce loyalties to the *panini* they grew up with. Plump, soft *biove* come from Piedmont; small cleft *spaccatini* are made at Lugano and Como; extravagant *coppiette*, shaped like starfish, artichokelike *carciofi*, and scroll-like *montasu* come from Emilia; and crunchy *ciriole*, with their soft interiors, are the classic Roman roll. There's absolutely no question that the *michetta* is the quintessential bread of Milan. With its five-sided central button and a design that looks like a flower opening, the *michetta* has a crisp crunchy crust and an interior that is almost entirely hollow, which makes it the perfect vehicle for a sandwich. These big, empty rolls appear on breakfast, lunch, and dinner tables all over Lombardy. Some Americans confronting their first *michetta* let it be known that they feel certain they've been cheated. The *rosetta* of Florence, Rome, and points south and the *michetta* are almost identical, although sometimes the central shape of the *rosetta* has only three sides and it can be somewhat puffier and sometimes not quite as hollow. Moot points, perhaps, to outsiders, but sources of controversy and regional pride to dedicated Italians. These two particular rolls cannot be made at home, because they must be cut with special machines and baked in very hot ovens. These facts are evidently not known to all bakers, for a baker in Rimini assured a knowledgeable Italian cook that they are made by inserting a syringe inside the rolls as they expand in the oven to draw out the air and create the cavity.

There are numerous breads in this book that can be made into excellent rolls. Try particularly the olive bread, *pane di chiavari,* spinach bread, *pan bigio, pane siciliano,* and any of the vegetable, herb, and cheese breads. The *pane all'olio* and the *integrale alle erbe* are simply a number of rolls set in a ring; the olive breads and some of the vegetable and herb breads can be shaped the same way. A particularly delicious treat is to spread a cooled spinach roll with a tablespoon or two of Gorgonzola that has been beaten to a buttery consistency and heat it in the oven just long enough for the cheese to melt and brown slightly.

Pasta Dura
Various Rolls from Emilia Romagna

If you have ever been to Bologna or Modena or Ferrara and were served a roll that had a hard, matte crust and a dense, stark white, slightly cottony interior, you've eaten *pasta dura.* You may have had it as a *coppietta,* whose characteristic form was already known in the sixteenth century when it was served at banquets at the Este court. Its double croissant shape with the connecting ends knotted in the center can look rather like a starfish. Or you may have had it shaped like an open hand, a scroll (*montasu*), or an artichoke or open flower (*carciofo*). *Baulette* from Mantua are thick cylinders of the dough slashed open at the top, while *banane* from Lombardy look more than slightly phallic and may seem at first glance to be croissants made of flat dough.

Pasta dura is one of the oldest breads in the world. Long before there were machines to mix and knead the dough, the Egyptians and Romans made it with their feet or by pounding it with a wooden bar. Bakeries, of course, have machines to mix the dough and form the cylinders that are the basis of many traditional *pasta dura* shapes;

Pasta Dura (continued)

you'll have to use an electric mixer to put the dough together, because it has so little water that it is extremely difficult to make by hand. You'll also need a rolling pin or pasta machine to give the dough its correct density.

Pasta dura is a rather controversial bread; there are as many who praise it as the tastiest and most typical bread of Italy as those who are mystified by the appeal of its dense interior. It is traditionally eaten with sliced and smoked meats, veal roasts, sausages, and stews. Make sandwiches of it with salami or mozzarella and tomatoes and put slightly stale slices into vegetable soups.

Makes 7 coppietta, montasu, mustafa, bauletta *or 15* carciofo *rolls*

1¼ teaspoons active dry yeast or ½ small cake (9 grams) fresh yeast
¼ cup warm water
1¾ cups plus 2 tablespoons very cold water
¼ cup (60 grams) lard (at room temperature) or olive oil
7½ cups (1000 grams) enriched bleached all-purpose flour or 2 cups pastry flour (250 grams) and 5½ cups (750 grams) enriched bleached all-purpose flour
2 teaspoons (10 grams) salt

BY HAND

Stir the yeast into the warm water in a large mixing bowl; let stand until creamy, about 10 minutes. Stir in the cold water and lard. Add 3 cups of the flour and the salt and beat vigorously with a wooden spoon, whisk, or rubber spatula until smooth. Stir in the remaining flour, 1 to 2 cups at a time. When the dough is too stiff to stir, plunge in with your hands and mix until the dough is no longer sticky. Knead firmly on a floured surface until stiff, resistant, and satiny, 6 to 8 minutes. (If it is too hard to knead, let it rest covered for about 5 minutes and try again.) To get the characteristic dense, smooth crumb, beat the dough with a rolling pin without stopping, folding and turning the dough from time to time, until smooth, compact, and dense, about 5 minutes.

BY MIXER

Stir the yeast into the warm water in a large mixer bowl; let stand until creamy, about 10 minutes. Stir in the cold water and lard with the paddle. Add the flour and salt and mix at low speed for 2 to 3 minutes, then briefly at a slightly faster speed. Change to the dough hook and knead at medium speed for 4 to 5 minutes. Knead by hand on a lightly floured surface until stiff, resistant, and satiny. (If it is too hard to knead, let it rest covered for about 5 minutes.) To get the characteristic dense, smooth crumb, beat the dough with a rolling pin without stopping, folding and turning the dough from time to time, until smooth, compact, and dense, about 5 minutes.

Resting. Let the dough rest under a towel until it softens slightly, about 30 minutes. The dough should feel cold and clammy like modeling clay.

Shaping. To keep this dough elastic, cover any pieces you aren't working under plastic wrap. Shape the dough into any of the following shapes. First cut the dough into the appropriate size, either 7 pieces (7 ounces, 200 grams each) or 15 pieces (3½ ounces, 100 grams each). Roll each piece into a tight ball. With a rolling pin, roll each ball into a thick ribbon. Grasping the end nearest you in your left hand, use your right hand to roll up the ribbon at a slight angle into a tightly graduated cylinder that looks like a fat cigar. With the rolling pin, roll each cylinder into a long, thin strip of dough, about 9 to 10 inches long and 1½ to 2 inches wide.

Coppietta. Place one strip of dough, short end facing you, on a work surface. Turn over a small edge of dough at the top. Holding the bottom edge with your left hand, stretch the dough as you roll it toward you from the opposite end. The way to get the dough properly stretched and thin is to push the dough down and away as you roll it up. Push down hard and roll fast so the dough spreads out into long thin rolls. When the roll is about 5 inches wide, lessen the pressure so that it will narrow as you continue to stretch and roll it into a shape fatter in the center and narrower at the edges. Roll to about 1 inch from the center. Turn the strip around and repeat on the other end, leaving a 2-inch bridge. Twist one roll completely around the other in two 360° turns to make a double twist in the center. Place the roll on a lightly oiled baking sheet with the twisted bridge piece on top. Pinch the two pieces together from the middle beneath the bridge.

Rolling dough into cylinder

Forming the double twist

The baked Coppietta

Pasta Dura (continued)

Montasu (Scroll Shape). Place 1 strip of dough, short end facing you, on a work surface. Fold over a small edge of dough at each end; then roll up the two short ends toward the middle, leaving a 2-inch gap in the middle. Use less tension in pressing and rolling the dough than in the coppietta, as these rolls should be short and fat. Press down firmly as you roll and, at the same time, stretch the dough away from the center. When both ends are rolled up, hold the dough up and, with your finger under the stretched center, twist one roll at a 90° angle and place it on top of the other. With your thumb press hard at the center where they meet so that the roll holds its shape. Place on lightly oiled baking sheets.

1. Rolling up dough   *2. Pressing to hold final shape*

Mustafa. Place 1 strip of dough, long side facing you, on a work surface. Fold over a small triangle of dough at each end (the right end goes up, the left down), so that the strip looks like a parallelogram. Roll up from each end, stretching the dough at the same time and keeping the top edge straight even though the ends roll up a bit on the diagonal, until you have a 2-inch space in the center. Pull up the center with a finger and twist one roll completely around the other in a 360° turn to make a double twist in the center. Set one roll at a 90° angle to the other and with your two thumbs on either side of the knot, press the two rolls firmly together. Place on lightly oiled baking sheets.

Bauletta (Little Trunk from Mantua). Roll up each strip from the short end into a tightly graduated cylinder, as you did in the coppietta initial shaping. Use your left hand to create tension, and with your right push down hard on the dough to spread it out as quickly as possible to be 5 inches wide. At that point, decrease pressure so that the strip narrows as you continue to stretch and roll it into a tapered form that is narrow at the tips and fatter in the middle. Place on lightly oiled baking sheets.

Rising. To capture the heat generated by the fermentation, prop up plastic wrap above the dough with juice glasses or herb jars. Cover with a towel and place the dough in a 90° F gas oven or an electric oven that you have heated at 150° F for 3 minutes only. Let the rolls stand 1 to 1½ hours or until they puff about ¼ inch. They will never double, but the small rise is important. Let the thicker *baolette* stand about 2½ hours. Just before baking the *baolette*, slash each one with a razor in a long, narrow cut that is deeper at the center than at the ends.

Baking. Heat the oven to 425° F. Five minutes before baking, place 1½ cups boiling water in a pan on the bottom rack of the oven. Bake the rolls for 20 minutes, spraying 3 times with hot water in the first 10 minutes. Cool on racks.

Variation. To make *streghe*, a wonderful crunchy, crackly snack or hors d'oeuvre, roll out the dough very, very thin and cut it into diamond shapes. Place on oiled baking sheets, brush the diamonds with oil, and sprinkle with salt. Bake at 425° F until lightly golden, about 10 minutes.

Carciofo (Artichoke Shape). Roll each strip a bit wider to 3 inches. Using a razor or dough scraper, make 1-inch-deep cuts into one long edge every ½ inch. Starting at the short end, roll the dough up and pinch the seam closed. Stand each roll on end on an oiled baking sheet and carefully pull open the "petals" so that it looks like a flower or the leaves of an artichoke. Place on lightly oiled baking sheets.

Rolling the dough up   *Opening the "petals"*

Semelle
Little Rolls from Florence

The names of rolls in Italy are even more confusing than the names of breads. Bakers in Florence use this dough to make *rosette*, the flower-shaped *panini* that are similar to the *michette* of Milan. Both the *rosetta* and *michetta* get their height and almost empty interior from the combination of a special cutter and very high oven temperatures. When made by hand, these rolls become *semelle* and are shaped in this simple form. Of course, they don't have the empty interior, but they are crunchy and have a lovely fragrance. I think they are perfect dinner rolls.

Makes 10 rolls

2½ teaspoons (1 package) active dry yeast or 1 small cake (18 grams) fresh yeast
1¼ cups warm water
3¾ cups (500 grams) unbleached all-purpose flour
2 teaspoons (10 grams) salt
Olive oil for brushing the dough

BY HAND

Stir the yeast into the water in a mixing bowl; let stand until creamy, about 10 minutes. Stir in the flour, 1 cup at a time, and the salt. When the dough is too stiff to stir, plunge in with your hands. Knead on a lightly floured work surface until solid and elastic, 8 to 10 minutes.

BY MIXER

Stir the yeast into the water in a mixer bowl; let stand until creamy, about 10 minutes. Add the flour and salt and mix with the paddle until the dough pulls away from the side of the bowl. Change to the dough hook and knead until solid and elastic, 3 to 4 minutes.

First Rise. Place the dough in a lightly oiled bowl, cover tightly with plastic wrap, and let rise until doubled, about 1 hour.

Shaping and Second Rise. Cut the dough into 10 equal pieces and shape each piece into a ball. Brush a little oil over each and let rest 10 minutes under a towel. With the edge of your hand, make a deep indentation down the center of each ball; be sure to press down firmly. Place the rolls, cleft side down, on floured parchment or brown paper. Cover with a towel and let rise until doubled, about 1 hour.

Baking. Heat the oven to 425° F. Just before baking, turn each roll over and reemphasize the cleft. Place the rolls, cleft side up, on an oiled baking sheet. Bake 15 to 18 minutes, spraying 3 times with water in the first 10 minutes. Cool on a rack.

Rosette Veneziane
Rosettes of Venice

Rosette are extremely popular in Venice, perhaps because the tender rolls are shaped delicately to look like a flower with all its petals neatly tucked into the center. When *rosette* are made by hand, they look a lot like *kaiser semel* rolls. This recipe is my variation of the Venetian roll.

Makes 12 to 14 rolls

1 teaspoon active dry yeast or ⅓ small cake (6 grams) fresh yeast
2 tablespoons warm water
¼ cup (50 grams) lard
¼ cup olive oil
3 tablespoons sugar
2 cups (500 grams) *Biga* (page 100)
2¼ cups (300 grams) unbleached all-purpose flour
1 teaspoon (5 grams) salt
1 or 2 egg whites, beaten

BY HAND

Stir the yeast into the water in a large mixing bowl; let stand until creamy, about 10 minutes. Stir in the lard, oil, sugar, and starter and mix until the starter is broken up. Add the flour and salt and stir until the dough comes together. Knead on a floured surface until moist, elastic, and slightly blistered, 8 to 10 minutes.

BY MIXER

Stir the yeast into the water in a mixer bowl; let stand until creamy, about 10 minutes. Add the lard, oil, sugar, and starter and mix with the paddle until the starter is broken up. Add the flour and salt and mix until the dough comes together. Change to the dough hook and knead at low speed until moist, elastic and slightly blistered, 3 to 4 minutes.

First Rise. Place the dough in a lightly oiled bowl, cover tightly with plastic wrap, and let rise until doubled, about 2 hours.

Rosette Veneziane (continued)

Shaping and Second Rise. Rosette look like flowers and are somewhat complicated to shape. Turn the soft, springy dough out onto a floured surface and pat or roll it out ¾ inch thick. Using a cookie cutter, cut out 5½-inch circles. Mark the center of each circle lightly. You will shape 5 equidistant points of dough around the circle, using your left thumb as an anchor and guide throughout the process, if you are right-handed. Place your left thumb in the center of the dough from the 9 o'clock position. With your other hand, pick up the dough at 12 noon and roll the edge over (on top of the dough), turning and twisting it to set the point at the center of the dough. (You can cover your thumb, if that's easier, and then pull it out.) Be sure to roll the dough with a good turn to create a 3-dimensional roll. Turn the circle of dough clockwise so that the rolled point is at 12 noon and continue to shape 3 more points, placing your left thumb in the center of the dough from the 9 o'clock position and starting the roll at 12 noon, but ending with the point covering your thumb in the center of the dough. The last point should be tucked into the last pocket. Press the center firmly with your thumb to seal the rosette. If all this sounds complicated and you make mistakes, don't worry, for this dough is very forgiving. Take apart any rosettes you aren't pleased with, let the dough rest briefly, and shape again.

Place on lightly oiled baking sheets, cover with a towel, and let rise until doubled, about 1½ to 1¾ hours.

Baking. Heat the oven to 400° F. Brush the rolls with the egg white. Bake until golden, about 20 minutes. Cool on racks.

Spaccatini
Little Cleft Rolls

These wonderful rolls from Lugano are really something to sink your teeth into. With a light, chewy crust and full-bodied, soft crumb, they add a mellow wheat flavor to a meal. If you are willing to wait slightly longer, you can cut the amount of yeast for these rolls in half, and the flavor will be even mellower.

Makes 16 rolls

¾ teaspoon active dry yeast or ⅓ small cake (6 grams) fresh yeast
½ cup warm water
2 cups (500 grams) *Biga* (page 100)
About 2 cups (250 grams) unbleached all-purpose flour
1 teaspoon (5 grams) salt

BY HAND

Stir the yeast into the water in a large mixing bowl; let stand until creamy, about 10 minutes. Add the starter; stir vigorously with a wooden spoon and squeeze the starter between your fingers to break it up. Add the flour, 1 cup at a time, and salt and stir until the dough comes together. Knead on a well-floured surface, sprinkling with 1 to 2 tablespoons additional flour, until elastic and supple, 4 to 5 minutes.

BY MIXER

Stir the yeast into the water in a mixer bowl; let stand until creamy, about 10 minutes. Add the starter and mix with the paddle until the starter is broken up. Add the flour and salt and mix until the dough comes together. Change to the dough hook and knead at low speed 2 minutes, then at medium speed 1 minute. If you want, finish kneading briefly by hand on a floured surface; you will probably need 1 to 2 tablespoons additional flour.

First Rise. Place the dough in a lightly oiled bowl, cover tightly with plastic wrap, and let rise until doubled, 1½ to 2 hours.

Shaping and Second Rise. Cut the dough into 16 pieces, each about the size of a lemon. Shape each piece into a ball on a floured surface; then, with the edge of your hand, a dowel, or the floured handle of a wooden spoon, make a deep indentation down the center of each ball. Place the rolls, cleft side down, on a well-floured surface. Cover with a towel and let rise until doubled, about 1 hour.

Baking. Heat the oven to 425° F. Just before baking, turn each roll over and reemphasize the cleft. Place the rolls, cleft side up, on lightly oiled or parchment-lined baking sheets. Bake 20 to 25 minutes, spraying 3 times with water in the first 10 minutes. Cool on a rack.

Biovette
Plump Rolls from Piedmont

The golden crust and soft light interior of *biove* are among the happiest memories of many people who grew up eating them in the Piedmont region. They are, however, as difficult to reproduce as they are wonderful, so this recipe is just a fragrant memory of the real thing.

Makes 8 rolls

1¼ teaspoons active dry yeast or ½ small cake (9 grams) fresh yeast
1½ teaspoons malt syrup
1 cup plus 3 tablespoons warm water
2 tablespoons (30 grams) lard
2½ tablespoons olive oil
3¾ cups (500 grams) unbleached all-purpose flour
2 teaspoons (10 to 12 grams) salt

BY HAND

Stir the yeast and malt into the water in a large mixing bowl; let stand until foamy, about 10 minutes. Stir in the lard and oil, and then the flour, 1 cup at a time, and the salt. Stir until a soft dough is formed. Knead on a floured surface, sprinkling with up to ¼ cup additional flour, until velvety, soft and elastic, 8 to 10 minutes.

BY MIXER

Stir the yeast and malt into the water in a mixer bowl; let stand until foamy, about 10 minutes. Mix in the lard and oil with the paddle, and then the flour and salt. Mix until the dough comes together. Change to the dough hook and knead at medium speed until velvety, soft, and elastic, about 4 minutes.

First Rise. Place the dough in a lightly oiled bowl, cover tightly with plastic wrap, and let rise until doubled, 1 to 1¼ hours.

Shaping and Second Rise. Cut the dough into 8 equal pieces (about 4 ounces, 120 grams each). Let the dough rest under a towel for 10 minutes. Flatten each piece into a rectangle, 10 to 12 inches long and 4 inches wide. Roll up from one short side into a fat log or lozenge shape. Place the rolls, seam side down, on a well-floured surface, cover with a towel, and let rise until almost doubled, 1 to 1½ hours.

Final Shaping. Turn the rolls over. In Italy a special knife is used to cut the *biove*, but a wooden dowel or even the edge of a dough scraper will do fine. Cut each roll lengthwise through the center pressing down hard and then pushing with a single snapping motion to open and almost cut through the dough. Place the rolls, cut sides up, on oiled baking sheets.

Baking. Heat the oven to 425° F. Bake about 25 minutes. Cool on racks.

Other Shape. Biove in Italy are characteristically larger than these rolls, which are *biovette* or dinner-roll size. To make true *biove*, shape the dough into 4 rolls and cut them almost in half in the final shaping.

Panini al Pomodoro *Tomato Rolls*	This is my version of the tomato rolls I saw being made by the dozens in Venice. The decoration of tomato paste and rosemary leaves makes the rolls look a bit like jaunty rosy tomatoes. *Makes 12 rolls* 2½ teaspoons (1 package) active dry yeast or 1 small cake (18 grams) fresh yeast 1 teaspoon sugar 1 cup plus 3 tablespoons warm water ¼ cup olive oil ½ cup (125 grams) *Biga* (page 100), optional 3¾ cups (500 grams) unbleached all-purpose flour 2 teaspoons (10 grams) salt ¼ cup finely chopped onion 1½ tablespoons tomato paste slightly thinned with warm water Tomato paste 24 fresh rosemary or oregano leaves
BY HAND	Stir the yeast and sugar into the water in a large mixing bowl; let stand until foamy, about 10 minutes. Add 2 tablespoons of the oil and the starter, if you are using it; stir vigorously and squeeze the starter between your fingers to break it up. Stir in the flour, 1 cup at a time, and the salt and stir until the dough comes together. Knead on a floured surface until silky and elastic, 8 to 10 minutes.
BY MIXER	Stir the yeast and sugar into the water in a mixer bowl; let stand until foamy, about 10 minutes. Add 2 tablespoons of the oil and the starter, if you are using it, and mix with the paddle until the starter is broken up. Add the flour and salt and mix until the dough comes

Panini al Pomodoro (continued)

together. Change to the dough hook and knead at medium speed until silky and elastic, 2 to 3 minutes.

BY PROCESSOR

Refrigerate the starter, if you are using it, until cold. Stir the yeast and sugar into ¼ cup warm water in a small bowl; let stand until foamy, 10 minutes. Place the flour and salt in a food processor fitted with the dough blade and process with several pulses to sift. Place the starter, if you are using it, on top of the flour. With the machine running, pour the dissolved yeast, 2 tablespoons of the oil, and ¾ cup plus 3 tablespoons cold water through the feed tube and process until the dough gathers into a ball. You may need to add up to 2 tablespoons more water. Process 30 seconds longer to knead.

First Rise. Place the dough in a lightly oiled bowl, cover tightly with plastic wrap, and let rise until doubled, about 45 minutes to 1 hour.

Shaping and Second Rise. While the bread is rising, sauté the onion in the remaining oil until softened and set aside to cool. Do not drain. Knead the onion and thinned tomato paste into the dough on a lightly floured surface. Cut the dough into 12 pieces and roll each piece into a round ball. Place on a lightly oiled baking sheet, cover with a towel, and let rise until doubled, about 45 minutes.

Baking. Heat the oven to 400° F. Just before baking, spoon a dab of tomato paste on top of each roll, and place a couple of rosemary leaves on the paste. Bake 20 minutes. Cool on a rack.

Pane in Cassetta
Sandwich Bread

Pane in cassetta is nothing other than *pain carré,* the equivalent of good old American sandwich bread. It is suddenly chic in Italy as part of *il sandwich* boom, for more and more people are eating lunch between two slices of bread at the local *caffè* bar rather than lingering over a long meal at home or in a restaurant. Its fillings and functions sometimes determine its name or where it comes from: *Tartine* are filled with chicken salad, creamy pastes, or pâté, while *tramezzini,* the generic word for sandwich in Rome, often hold even softer fillings, such as *insalata russa.* Toast may have a slice of prosciutto, a slice of cheese, and be topped with artichoke hearts, sliced sweet peppers, or mushrooms preserved in oil. Open-faced sandwiches can turn into canapés (you may notice an international theme to this bread), spread with mayonnaise and topped with a variety of tastes limited only by the imagination of the person putting them together. The bread is also used for *mozzarella in carrozza* and for the base of apple charlottes and fruit tarts. It's named *cassetta* for the boxlike shape of the Pullman pan in which it is baked.

The only trick to making *pane in cassetta* is rolling the dough out with a rolling pin, folding it, and then flattening it firmly with your rolling pin to make it strong and compact. Don't forget to butter the inside of the lid of the pan before you slide it in place. The crust of *pane in cassetta* is very fine, and the bread is best eaten very fresh, preferably the day it is baked.

Makes 1 loaf

4 teaspoons active dry yeast or 1⅔ small cakes (30 grams) fresh yeast
1 tablespoon sugar
¼ cup warm water
1¼ cups plus 3 tablespoons water, room temperature
¼ cup (50 grams) lard
About 5½ cups (750 grams) unbleached all-purpose flour
1⅓ teaspoons (7 grams) salt

BY HAND

Stir the yeast and sugar into the warm water in a large mixing bowl; let stand until foamy, about 10 minutes. Stir in 1¼ cups plus 3 tablespoons water and the lard; then stir in the flour, 2 cups at a time, and the salt. Knead vigorously on a floured surface until silky and very dry with a powdery feel to the surface, 8 to 10 minutes.

BY MIXER

Stir the yeast and sugar into 1½ cups plus 3 tablespoons warm water in a mixer bowl; let stand until foamy, about 10 minutes. Stir in the lard with the paddle. Add the flour and salt and mix until the dough comes together. Change to the dough hook and knead at medium speed until very stiff, silky, and dry, about 4 minutes.

BY PROCESSOR

If the capacity of your food processor is 7 cups or less, process this recipe in 2 batches. Stir the yeast and sugar into the warm water in a small bowl; let stand until foamy, about 10 minutes. Place the flour, salt, and lard in a food processor fitted with the steel blade and process with several pulses to mix. Mix the dissolved yeast and 1¼ cups plus 3 tablespoons cold water. With the machine running, pour the dissolved yeast through the feed tube and process until the

Pane in Cassetta (continued)

dough gathers into a ball. If the dough is too dry, add up to 3 tablespoons additional cold water. Process 30 seconds longer to knead.

First Rise. Place the dough in a lightly oiled bowl, cover tightly with plastic wrap, and let rise until doubled, about 1 to 1¾ hours.

Shaping and Second Rise. Flatten the dough on a lightly floured surface to break up the air bubbles. Roll out the dough with a rolling pin to a 24 × 12-inch rectangle. Either fold in thirds, like a business letter, or fold the top and bottom edges to meet in the center and then fold the top half over the bottom (fourths). Flour the dough and work surface again, roll out the dough and repeat the same folds. Then flatten the dough well to fit into a Pullman pan, 13 inches long, and place in the well-buttered pan. The strong and compact dough should fill the pan about halfway. Butter the lid and slide into the pan. Let rise until 1 inch short of the top of the pan, about 1 to 1½ hours.

Baking. Heat the oven to 400° F. Bake 1 hour. Carefully unmold onto a rack and cool completely.

Panini Dolci

Maritozzi
Roman Sweet Buns

These fat buns, which are bursting with raisins, appear in Rome today as they did in medieval times when they were a traditional Lenten sweet bread made with sugar and spices. Now Romans have them all year long and are as likely to eat them for breakfast or tea as with a glass of white wine.

Makes 16 to 18 buns

SPONGE
1½ cups (225 grams) raisins
Water to cover
3½ teaspoons active dry yeast or 1⅓ small cakes (24 grams) fresh
    yeast
½ cup plus 2 tablespoons milk, warm
½ cup (70 grams) unbleached all-purpose flour

Soak the raisins in cool water to cover at least 30 minutes; drain but reserve ¼ cup of the water. Stir the yeast into the warm milk in a small bowl; let stand until creamy, about 10 minutes. Add the flour and reserved raisin water and stir until smooth. Cover with plastic wrap and let rise until doubled, 20 to 30 minutes.

DOUGH
3¼ cups (430 grams) unbleached all-purpose flour
½ cup (100 grams) sugar
1 teaspoon (5 grams) salt
2 eggs
1 egg yolk
Grated zest of ¼ lemon
Grated zest of ¼ orange
¼ teaspoon vanilla extract
1 stick (115 grams) unsalted butter, room temperature

¼ cup unbleached all-purpose flour for the raisins

BY HAND

Place the flour, sugar, and salt in a large mixing bowl. Stir in the sponge and eggs, egg yolk, grated lemon and orange zests, and vanilla; then stir in the butter. Knead on a lightly floured surface until soft, springy, and very smooth, 8 to 10 minutes.

BY MIXER

Place the flour, sugar, salt, sponge, eggs, egg yolk, grated lemon and orange zests, and vanilla in a mixer bowl and mix with the paddle until blended. Add the butter and mix thoroughly. Change to the dough hook and knead at medium speed until soft, springy, and smooth except for a few blisters, 3 to 4 minutes.

First Rise. Place the dough in a buttered bowl, cover with plastic wrap, and let rise until doubled, about 1 hour.

Shaping and Second Rise. Pat the raisins dry and toss with ¼ cup flour. Add the raisins to the dough in 1 or 2 additions by flattening the dough, patting the raisins over the surface, and rolling up the dough. Cut the dough into 16 to 18 pieces and roll each piece into a ball. Place the rolls on lightly buttered or parchment-lined baking sheets. Cover with a towel and let rise half their original volume, about 30 minutes.

Baking. Heat the oven to 400° F. Bake 18 minutes. The rolls should double in size and puff up into fat buns as they bake. Cool on racks.

Pan di Ramerino

Rosemary and Raisin Buns

Pan di Ramerino resembles a hot cross bun flavored with rosemary. It was traditionally eaten in Tuscany only on Holy Thursday of Easter week, but now you can find it all year long in Florence, where its glossy crosshatched top is instantly recognizable. This recipe comes from Giovanni Galli, an imaginative baker in Florence, who has made the very lightly sweetened bread richer by adding eggs. The combination of raisins, rosemary-scented oil, and a sprig of rosemary sounds strange to Americans, who would never think of putting them together, but there is something intangibly wonderful about the taste. Florentines speak with real nostalgia about these buns, whose crosses on top are reminders that the buns are permeated with religious meaning, as well as the taste of the past.

Makes 12 buns

3½ teaspoons active dry yeast or 1⅓ small cakes (24 grams) fresh yeast
¾ cup warm water
2 large eggs
1 large egg yolk
4 tablespoons olive oil, plus additional for brushing the dough
2½ tablespoons sugar
3¾ cups (500 grams) unbleached all-purpose flour
1 teaspoon (5 grams) salt
3 to 4 sprigs fresh rosemary
⅔ cup (100 grams) golden or Monukka raisins
⅓ cup Apricot Glaze (page 345)

BY HAND

Stir the yeast into the warm water in a large mixing bowl; let stand until creamy, about 10 minutes. Whisk in the eggs, egg yolk, 2 tablespoons of the oil, and the sugar thoroughly. Stir in the flour, 1 cup at a time, and the salt; keep stirring until the dough is no longer sticky. Knead on a lightly floured surface until elastic and supple, 7 to 9 minutes.

BY MIXER

Stir the yeast into the warm water in a large mixer bowl; let stand until creamy, about 10 minutes. Add the eggs, egg yolk, 2 tablespoons of the oil, and the sugar and mix thoroughly with the paddle. Add the flour and salt and mix until the dough pulls away from the side of the bowl. Change to the dough hook and knead at low speed 2 minutes, then at medium speed 2 more minutes. The dough should be elastic and supple.

First Rise. Place the dough in a lightly oiled bowl, cover tightly with plastic wrap, and let rise until doubled, about 1 hour.

Shaping and Second Rise. While the dough is rising, sauté 2 or 3 sprigs fresh rosemary very briefly in the remaining 2 tablespoons oil. Toss the rosemary out after it has flavored the oil. Add the raisins and sauté very briefly in the oil. Remove from the heat and add 1 chopped fresh rosemary sprig to the raisins, if you want. Cool to room temperature. Knead the raisins into the dough; it is much easier to do by mixer than by hand if you have the choice.

Cut the dough into 12 pieces and roll each piece into a ball. Place on lightly oiled baking sheets, cover with a towel, and let rise until doubled, about 1 hour.

Reshape the buns, which will have slumped a bit, into definite balls. Flatten each ball with your hand and brush the tops with oil. Using a razor, slash a deep tic-tac-toe pattern in the top of each bun. Let the buns rest under a towel 10 to 15 minutes.

Baking. Heat the oven to 400° F. Bake 20 minutes. Remove the buns to racks to cool, let cool slightly, and brush with the apricot glaze.

Grissini

Grissini Torinesi

Breadsticks from Turin

Most Americans know *grissini* from the pale breadsticks in the elongated waxen envelopes that appear on the tables of Italian restaurants, but they bear about as much resemblance to authentic *grissini* as packaged industrial white bread does to true country loaves. Real *grissini* are made of yeast, flour, water, and either olive oil, lard, or butter. They are shaped between the hands by gently vibrating and stretching the dough to about the span of the baker's arms, and are then baked directly on the floor of a wood-burning oven. They are as thick and irregular as knobby fingers and look like cordwood when stacked. They have crunch and an earthy taste. Even when made at home with the methods and recipes that follow, they are still redolent of the countryside and the old ways.

Grissini Torinesi (continued)

Although there is some dispute about who came up with the first *grissini*, there is no question that they first appeared in Turin sometime in the seventeenth century. Some say that a baker in Turin invented them in 1668 in response to inquiries from the doctor of the young duke Vittorio Amadeo II, who had stomach disturbances, for a bread that would be good for the duke's digestion. The baker stretched out the traditional local bread dough so long that it became a long, thin, crunchy stick that was essentially all crust. Although there is no word of their effect on the patient's health, it is safe to assume that they met with great success, because *grissini* were well known all over Italy by the next century when Napoleon discovered *"les petits batons de Turin."* Napoleon was so enthusiastic about the breadsticks that he instituted a fast postal service expressly for transporting them to court every day. The most popular rival story to that of the young duke credits a Florentine abbot on a diplomatic mission near Turin in 1643 with the discovery of "a thin bread as long as an arm and very, very fine."

Serve *grissini* with eggs, green salad, prosciutto and smoked beef, and with all imaginable kinds of *antipasti*. Some Italians eat them for breakfast with milk or coffee, an old, once widespread custom.

Makes 20 to 22 breadsticks

1¾ teaspoons active dry yeast or ⅔ small cake (12 grams) fresh yeast
1 tablespoon malt syrup
1¼ cups warm water
2 tablespoons olive oil, plus additional for brushing the dough
3¾ cups (500 grams) unbleached all-purpose flour
1½ teaspoons (8 grams) salt
½ cup semolina flour for sprinkling

BY HAND

Stir the yeast and malt into the warm water in a large mixing bowl; let stand until foamy, about 10 minutes. Stir in 2 tablespoons oil. Add the flour and salt and stir until the dough comes together. Knead on a lightly floured surface until smooth, soft, velvety, and elastic, 8 to 10 minutes.

BY MIXER

Stir the yeast and malt into the water in a mixer bowl; let stand until foamy, about 10 minutes. Mix in the 2 tablespoons oil with the paddle. Add the flour and salt and mix until the dough comes together. Change to the dough hook and knead at low speed about 3 minutes. Finish kneading briefly by hand on a lightly floured surface.

BY PROCESSOR

Stir the yeast and malt into ¼ cup warm water in a small bowl; let stand until foamy, about 10 minutes. Place the flour and salt in a standard food processor fitted with the dough blade or a large (over 7 cups capacity) processor fitted with the steel blade and process with several pulses to sift. Mix 1 cup cold water and 2 tablespoons oil. With the machine running, pour the water mixed with oil and the dissolved yeast through the feed tube and process until the dough comes together. Process 45 seconds longer to knead. Finish kneading by hand on a lightly floured surface.

First Rise. Pat the dough with your hands into a 14 × 4-inch rectangle on a well-floured surface. Lightly brush the top with oil. Cover with plastic wrap and let rise until doubled, about 1 hour.

Shaping. Sprinkle the dough with semolina flour before cutting and stretching. The baker's method of shaping breadsticks is ingenious, simple, and quick, for he certainly doesn't have time to roll out individual *grissini*. Cut the dough crosswise into 4 equal sections and then cut each section crosswise again into 5 strips, each about the width of a fat finger. The dough is so elastic that you can simply pick up each piece, hold each end with your fingers, and pull and stretch to fit the width (or length) of a baking sheet. Place the breadsticks several inches apart on lightly oiled baking sheets (unless they are rimless, I find it easier to use the backs of the baking sheets). There is no need to let them rise.

Grissini dough stretched on baking sheet

Baking. Heat the oven to 450° F. If you are using a baking stone, turn the oven on 30 minutes before baking. Bake the breadsticks for 20 minutes. If you like crunchy breadsticks, bake directly on the baking stone, which has been sprinkled with cornmeal or semolina flour, for the last 5 minutes. Cool on racks.

Variations. For *Grissini Siciliani,* sprinkle the dough with ½ cup sesame seeds instead of semolina flour before cutting and shaping.
For *Grissini al Papavero,* sprinkle the dough with ½ cup poppy seeds instead of semolina flour before cutting and shaping.

Grissini Integrali
Whole-Wheat Breadsticks

Makes 20 to 22 breadsticks

1¾ teaspoons active dry yeast or ⅔ small cake (12 grams) fresh yeast
1¼ cups warm water
1 tablespoon malt syrup
¼ cup olive oil, plus additional for brushing the dough
2¼ teaspoons (10 grams) lard
1 cup less 2 tablespoons (125 grams) unbleached all-purpose flour
2⅔ cups (375 grams) whole-wheat flour
1½ teaspoons (8 grams) salt

Follow the directions for *Grissini Torinesi* (recipe precedes), adding the lard with the oil. Omit sprinkling the dough with semolina flour.

Grissini alle Cipolle
Onion Breadsticks

Makes 20 to 22 breadsticks

1 large yellow onion
4 tablespoons olive oil, plus additional for brushing the dough
1¾ teaspoons active dry yeast or ⅔ small cake (12 grams) fresh yeast
1¼ cups warm water
1 tablespoon malt syrup
2 tablespoons (25 grams) lard
3¾ cups (500 grams) unbleached all-purpose flour
2 teaspoons (10 grams) salt

Cut the onion into small dice and sauté in 2 tablespoons of the oil over low to medium heat until golden and almost dry roasted, 10 to 15 minutes. Watch that it doesn't burn.

Follow the directions for *Grissini Torinese* (page 263), adding the lard with the remaining 2 tablespoons oil. Work the onion into the dough at the very end of the kneading. Omit sprinkling the dough with semolina flour.

Grissini al Formaggio
Cheese Breadsticks

Makes 20 to 22 breadsticks

1¾ teaspoons active dry yeast or ⅔ small cake (12 grams) fresh yeast
1⅓ cups warm water
2 tablespoons olive oil, plus additional for brushing the dough
3¾ cups (500 grams) unbleached all-purpose flour
1½ teaspoons (8 grams) salt
2 ounces (60 grams) grated Parmesan cheese

Follow the directions for *Grissini Torinesi* (page 263). Work the cheese into the dough at the very end of the kneading. Omit sprinkling the dough with semolina flour. Bake at 450° F for 12 to 15 minutes.

Grissini Cric-Crac alla Salvia
Sage Breadsticks from Como

I suppose you could call this recipe and the variations that follow *grissini nuovi*, for they are imaginative departures from the classical breadstick of Turin. *Cric-crac* is really a musical bit of onomatopoeia.

Makes 20 to 22 breadsticks

1¾ teaspoons active dry yeast or ⅔ small cake (12 grams) fresh yeast
1¼ cups warm water
1 tablespoon malt syrup
¼ cup olive oil, plus additional for brushing the dough
3¾ cups (500 grams) unbleached all-purpose flour
1½ teaspoons (8 grams) salt
¼ cup chopped fresh sage

Follow the directions for *Grissini Torinese* (page 263), adding the malt with the yeast to the water. Work in the sage at the very end of the kneading. Omit sprinkling the dough with semolina flour.

Variations. Cric-Crac alla Pancetta: Substitute 2 ounces (60 grams) diced *pancetta* for the sage.
Cric-Crac al Salame. Substitute 2 ounces (60 grams) diced salami for the sage.
Cric-Crac alla Gorgonzola. Substitute 2 ounces (60 grams) softened Gorgonzola for the sage.
Cric-Crac agli Spinaci. Substitute 2 ounces (60 grams) frozen chopped spinach, thawed and well drained, for the sage.

PIZZE E FOCACCE
Pizza and Focaccia

What are pizzas and *focacce* but primitive rustic food made of the tastiest ingredients harvested from the fields, the vines of the hillsides, and the seas? These crisp or chewy country breads are the food of peasants and wily city dwellers with little money but lots of imagination. Flavored with oils from local olives, cheeses from herds that graze neighboring pastures, tomatoes planted in the nearby countryside, and herbs that grow in wild tangles or are cultivated in gardens and window boxes that punctuate the facades of houses all over the country, pizza and *focaccia* represent a triumph of *fantasia* and strategy over a scarcity of ingredients, the instinct for survival transformed into an infinite variety of tastes. Clever Italians simply take a little dough, sprinkle it with products of the countryside, and turn it into a delicious and edible plate; flat or slightly raised with rims, they are easier to eat out of hand than with knife and fork. In one of those delicious bits of irony, these most basic of rustic breads have become popular and chic, symbols of the relaxed easy pleasures of eating with friends.

Perhaps it has always been so. The thin, chewy bread that Italians call *focaccia* may have been the first national dish of the country. Remains of carbonized *focacce* as old as Neolithic man indicate that, even before recorded time, Italians were grinding grain between stones, mixing it with water, and boiling it into a mush not unlike polenta. This mush was probably left out one night, and an adventurous Neolithic baker must have decided to cook it under the embers or roast it, pancake style, over the stones.

Although we are still in the realm of educated guessing, we know that Egyptians discovered the miracle of fermentation, but we don't know how. It is probable that the flour and water mixed together for a batch of breads was left out and trapped the wild yeasts of the air, which transformed yesterday's ingredients into a puffy mass. Cooks and scholars surmise that someone—an insolent slave or perhaps an angry one—tossed a bit of this risen mass into the fresh dough and, in a single, inspired, off-hand gesture, discovered the process of leavening dough. Which is a long preamble to the fact that pizza and *focaccia* are simply branches of the family of bread, once made without leavening and now parts of the baker's art that are treated a bit differently than the wheels and loaves of the Italian repertoire. Both are flat round breads seasoned with oil and cooked in the oven or over embers and are called pizza in the south and *focaccia* in the north.

Pizza seems to date to the era when the Greeks settled the region in the south of Italy that has become known as Magna Graecia because it was so purely Greek. The Greeks taught the Romans the secrets of their trade, for they were very inventive bakers who made breads with many flavorings and baked them in a variety of forms. At about the time that the Etruscans, who settled initially in the north of Italy, were baking flat *focacce* and *schiacciata*-like breads, the Italians of the south, including the early Neapolitans of that time, were probably eating an ancestor of pizza called *laganum* by the poet Horace. Virgil, who lived in Augustan Rome and went to Naples to visit, wrote a poem celebrating *moretum*, a flat disk of dough that was baked on a griddle and covered with an herb sauce of garlic, parsley, rue, coriander, and a dry cheese, all ground together in a mortar and bound together with olive oil and a few drops of strong vinegar. The topping certainly sounds very much like pesto without the basil. Had the rustic *moretum* been leavened, it would be a direct relative of pizza, even though it was cooked first and sprinkled with the herb mixture just before eating.

The *piadina* of Romagna is yet another ancestral flat bread, which still appears at every country festival and rustic celebration in the area contained between the low hills east of the Apennines and the quiet flat coast of the Adriatic Sea. The thin tortillalike circle of dough that was originally baked not in an oven but on a thick piece of terra-cotta called a *testo* is yet one more flat peasant bread that can claim ancestry. Today you can still find *piadine*, folded over fat slices of country salamis or wrapped around boiled or sautéed greens, in restaurants as well as at local *sagras* all over the countryside. All these unleavened rustic breads are predecessors of the *focacce* and pizzas we eat today and reach far, far back in the history of Italy.

The *focaccia* of today derives its name from *focus*, the Latin word for hearth, for *focaccia*, which began life long before ovens were common, was made by patting the dough into a flat round and cooking it directly on a hot stone or under a mound of hot ashes on the hearth itself. *Schiacciata*, the term still used in Tuscany, simply means flattened or crushed. One look at these low, crisp, crunchy rounds is convincing evidence that the word was well chosen. The word *pizza* may simply mean pie; it can be sweet or savory, flat or risen, although it is most frequently encountered in the plate-shaped circle of dough with a raised edge that has conquered America. The word has several derivations, although the Italian Encyclopedia of Science, Literature, and Art virtually shrugs its shoulders in dismay and says only "uncertain etymology." Pizza comes from the Roman *placenta,* a flat *focaccia*-like dish made, as Cato described it, of wheat flour, cheese, and honey and baked over a low fire, but it also comes from *picea,* a Greek adjective that describes the dark black coating left on the bottom of the dough by the burning ashes of the early ovens. Pizza, according to many sources, is simply the Neapolitan dialect word for Greek *picea,* which denotes both the pie and the black color of the ash that cooked it.

Now that that is clear, perhaps it would be better not to acknowledge the fact that stuffed doughs such as *calzone, pizza rustica,* and fried stuffed turnovers also go by the name of pizza. There is method in the madness, but it helps to know the history to understand, for instance, how the half-moon-shaped turnovers that are today's *calzoni* got their name. *Calzoni,* meaning pant legs, were originally long, narrow tubes of dough enclosing sausages or salamis; they looked very much like the baggy pants Neapolitan men wore in the eighteenth and nineteenth centuries. *Panzarotti,* fat envelopes of pizza dough stuffed with various fillings, are named from the Neapolitan dialect word for stomach, because when they are fried in extremely hot oil they suddenly swell up just like big full bellies.

It wasn't until the mid-1700s that pizza became a common dish in Naples, although pizza as we know it didn't really come into its own until the introduction of the tomato, that strange globe of red fruit brought to Italy from Peru and Mexico in the wake of Columbus's voyage. Initially the Italians were extremely suspicious of this foreign invader, which they called *pomodoro,* or golden apple (the first tomatoes were, in fact, yellow). It took two centuries for them to overcome their reluctance and accept it. Pizzas were still being made in the middle of the eighteenth century with tomatoes as an optional ingredient. It was only when the particular chemistry of the dough and the tomato or tomato sauce clicked that pizza took on its incredible popularity.

"The word *pizza* is not found in the {official Italian} dictionary because it is made with flour and because it is a specialty of the Neapolitans and of the very city of Naples itself. If you want to know what a pizza is, take a piece of dough, roll it out, then pull or spread it a bit with a rolling pin or push it out with the palm of your hand, put whatever comes into your head on it, season it with oil or lard, bake it in the oven, eat it, and you will know what a pizza is. Though more or less the same, the *focaccia* and the *schiacciata* are but embryos of the art." So said Sir Emanuele Rocco in the anthology *Usi e Costumi di Napoli* compiled in 1850 by a Frenchman named De Bourcard, whose chauvinistic convictions reflect his attachment to the pizzas of Naples baked at the little stalls and shops of his day.

A few years previous Alexander Dumas, author of *The Three Musketeers*, wrote in his *Grand Dictionnaire de la Cuisine*, "Pizza is a sort of bun like the ones made at Saint-Denis; it is round in shape and made with the same bread dough. It seems simple enough, but on closer inspection it is really very complicated." He continues, enumerating its ingredients. "Pizza is made with oil, bacon, lard, cheese, tomato, or small fish. It is the yardstick by which the whole food market is measured; prices rise and fall according to the prices of these ingredients and their relative availability." Imagine what a vast public pizza must have had to make such an impact on the price of its flavorings—did hamburgers ever influence the price paid for beef on the hoof in the stockyards of Chicago or fried chicken change the economy of the south? Dumas's appreciation for pizza was great, but, as any number of eminent authorities have pointed out, he was off-base in one of his observations. Dumas thought that *pizza oggi a otto* was made eight days before it was eaten; actually it was (and still is) eaten hot out of the oven but paid for eight days later—easy financial terms provided then, as now, by neighborhood *pizzaioli* to local residents who as likely as not are a bit strapped. Not only is the arrangement light on the wallet, but it also guarantees that your last pizza is free if you die before eight days have elapsed. In another bit of financial strategy, canny Neapolitans frequently use anchovies on pizzas because the little fish can easily be cadged from the sea virtually free. Anchovies not only give the taste of salt for very little money, but they also spare the pizza maker the expensive tax the government levies on salt, the most basic of all seasonings.

The first pizzas as we know them today were probably flavored very simply with oil, garlic, mozzarella, and anchovies or tiny local fish called *cicinielli*. The wit of Neapolitan bakers soon spawned a much greater variety of combinations. The single most famous story of toppings and pizza concerns Queen Margherita, who traveled with King Umberto I to Naples in 1889 when he was on a visit to the lands of his kingdom. The queen, who had heard about pizza, was anxious to sample the dish, but, because she could hardly go off to an open-air pizza stand or pizzeria, the premier pizza maker of the time called upon her. Don Raffaele Esposito, owner of the pizzeria Pietro il Pizzaiuolo, and his wife went to the Capodimonte Palace with several varieties for the queen to taste. She was most enthusiastic about the pizza made with mozzarella, tomatoes, and fresh basil, which was red, white, and green, the colors of the Italian flag. In the flush of success, Don Raffaele christened it pizza Margherita in her honor. It didn't take long for word to spread throughout the kingdom and make pizza Margherita an instant success. Whether the tale is apocryphal or not, pizza Margherita helped put pizza on the national culinary map of Italy.

Today pizza is so various and widespread that *pizza alla napoletana*, *pizza alla romana* (thin, crunchy, and rimless with only salt and oil on top), *pizza pasquale* (sweet and risen), and *pizza rustica* (filled and risen) only hint at its protean forms. From the *sfinciuni* of Sicily— pizza dough covered with tomato sauce, cheeses, onions, oil, and bread crumbs and baked in the oven—to the *sardenaria* of San Remo, named for its topping of local sardines or sardine paste, pizza expresses the extraordinarily diverse tastes of regional traditions. The *focaccia* of Recco, which has put the little town outside Genoa on the gastronomic map, is made with a strudellike dough, while the pizza named for the admiral Andrea Doria is made with durum flour and covered with the inevitable tomatoes, anchovies, garlic, onion, and black olives.

Some of the most basic pizzas and variations from south to north are included in these recipes, but you should use your own imagination and be guided by the desires of your own taste buds to make your own toppings. Formal recipes are much less important than the flavorful ingredients at hand. Neapolitans start with the sun and the fish of the gulf and add strong local tastes without intricate mystery or shadings—let that be your guide. You can add anchovies to one pizza or mozzarella to another; you can use Fontina instead of mozzarella or add prosciutto, mushrooms, clams, pesto, or mussels. Pizza is really only a platter of bread topped with the provender of the countryside and mixed with real passion and imagination.

Pizza

Pizza alla Napoletana
Pizza of Naples

Like the discoverer of fire or the maker of the wheel, the creator of pizza remains unknown. We do know that by the eighteenth century pizza was the food of Naples, an extravagantly delicious dish combining the simplest and cheapest of ingredients with fabulous imagination. The crisp, slightly smoky tang of the pizza, made as it should be, depends on the hands and secrets of the *pizzaioli locali*, heirs of a tradition passed orally from one baker to the next, as well as heirs of the oils of their olives and the lard of their pigs, the waters of their hills, the tomatoes of their vines, the leaves of basil ripened by their sun, the mozzarella of their buffalo, and the wood-burning fires of their brick-lined ovens.

These pizzas are as big as a plate, with rings of dough raised at the outer edges (all the better to grasp them with). Ask a Neapolitan and he'll tell you that pizza is a grace note of life, a subtle piece of magic transmuted by the alchemy of fire into a delicacy for the nose, the mouth, and the eyes.

Numerous pizzerias dot the streets, the narrow curling *vicoli* and mazes of tiny dark lanes that wind through the labyrinthine heart of the city, but once pizza vendors wandered through Naples carrying dozens of pizzas, each folded in half in the shape called a "libretto" because it looked like a pocketbook, and calling out phrases describing their wares in ringing tones, in rhyming couplets, in double entendres, and in simple descriptive phrases. Though few of these troubadours with the slang and song and come-ons are left, the circle of dough, holding within it a world of southern Italian tastes, still dazzles the taste buds and remains the remarkably rustic treat that conquered the world.

A couple of tips: To shape the dough, you may use either a rolling pin (the easiest) or your fists by draping the dough over them and then moving them apart to within an inch of the rim, slowly and gently turning them and stretching the dough ¼ to ⅜ inch thick. The experts get it even thinner. The edge, called the *cornicione* (like a big picture frame), is a favorite of babies and gastronomes, and it should be a bit thicker to keep the sauce and ingredients in their place. Always brush the rim of the pizza with a bit of olive oil when it is still hot from the oven so that the entire dish glistens.

Pizza dough can be frozen at 3 stages (but be sure to label your

Pizza alla Napoletana (continued)

dough, so that you know where to start again): when fully mixed and kneaded, but before the first rise; after the first rise but punch it down before you freeze it; after it is partially cooked, with topping but no cheese. Wrap in aluminum foil and wrap again in plastic wrap or a plastic bag. Thaw the dough in the refrigerator for 24 hours—it should be supple and elastic—and just take up where you left off. If you have any frozen precooked pizza, don't thaw it. Bake at 400° F 30 to 45 minutes, depending on the thickness.

Makes one 15- to 16-inch pizza, 2 medium-size, or 5 or 6 individual pizzas

1¾ teaspoons active dry yeast or ⅔ small cake (12 grams) fresh yeast
Pinch sugar
1⅓ cups warm water
¼ cup olive oil, plus additional for brushing the crust
3¾ cups (500 grams) unbleached all-purpose flour
1½ teaspoons (8 grams) salt (if using anchovies in the topping, reduce the salt to a pinch)

BY HAND

Stir the yeast and sugar into the water in a large mixing bowl; let stand until foamy, about 5 minutes. Stir in the oil. Mix the flour and salt and stir, 1 cup at a time, into the yeast mixture, beating well to get all the lumps out. Knead on a lightly floured surface until soft and satiny but firm, about 8 minutes.

BY MIXER

Stir the yeast and sugar into the water in a mixer bowl; let stand until foamy, about 5 minutes. Stir in the oil with the paddle. Mix the flour and salt and add to the yeast mixture. Mix until the dough comes together. Change to the dough hook and knead at medium speed until soft and satiny but firm, about 3 minutes. Finish kneading briefly by hand on a lightly floured surface.

BY PROCESSOR

Stir the yeast and sugar into ⅓ cup warm water in a small bowl; let stand until foamy, about 5 minutes. Place the flour and salt in a food processor fitted with either the steel or dough blade and process with several pulses to sift. With the machine running, pour the dissolved yeast, oil, and 1 cup cold water through the feed tube as quickly as the flour can absorb it and process until the dough gathers into a ball. Process 20 seconds longer to knead. Finish kneading by hand on a lightly floured surface until soft and satiny.

First Rise. Place the dough in a lightly oiled bowl, cover tightly with plastic wrap, and let rise until not quite fully doubled, 45 minutes to 1 hour.

Shaping and Second Rise. You may shape the dough with a rolling pin or your hands. Knead the dough briefly on a lightly floured surface to expel the air bubbles, 1 to 2 minutes. Divide the dough if you are making more than 1 pizza. Roll each piece into a ball and then flatten into a thick disk. With a rolling pin, roll out the dough ¼ to ⅜ inch thick, leaving a 1-inch rim. Place the dough in an oiled pizza pan or on a peel that has been sprinkled with cornmeal or flour.
To shape by hand, push the dough out from the center on a lightly floured surface, working around the circle and pushing to within an inch of the edge. When the dough is a bit more than ½ inch thick, place it over your fists and start moving them gently away from each other, stretching the dough between them. Move your fists back to center, turn the dough a bit (you might even make it jump a bit in the air to accomplish this), and then move your fists apart again, being careful not to tear the fine dough in the middle. When it is almost the size you want, place it in an oiled pizza pan or on a peel that has been sprinkled with cornmeal or flour. Finish shaping the dough with your fingers.

Cover the dough with a towel and let rise for no longer than 30 minutes. The dough should be puffy and softly risen.

Topping. Select one of the topping recipes that follow, or, if you have gotten into the spirit of Italian baking, use whatever combinations of mushrooms, cheeses, greens, onions, anchovies, and herbs that strike your imagination.

Baking. Heat the oven to 400° F. Use a baking stone if you have one (turn the oven on 30 minutes before baking) and sprinkle the stone with cornmeal just before sliding the pizza onto it. You can bake the pizza in a pan or on the back of a baking sheet, but you won't get the true crisp crust of a Neapolitan pizza without the stone. Bake large pizzas 25 to 30 minutes and smaller ones 15 to 25 minutes. The pizza is done when the crust is golden brown and crisp with little burst blisters visible and the cheese, if you used it, is melted and bubbling. Immediately brush the crust with oil.

Pizza Aglio e Olio Topping

The simplest and most traditional topping of all.

Makes enough to top Pizza alla Napoletana dough

¼ cup fruity olive oil
3 to 6 cloves fresh garlic, very thinly sliced
1 tablespoon chopped fresh oregano or 1½ teaspoons dried
1½ teaspoons (8 grams) salt
Freshly ground pepper

Drizzle a little of the oil over the dough and sprinkle with the garlic, oregano, salt, and pepper to taste.

Bake at 450° F.

Pizza alla Napoletana Topping

Makes enough to top Pizza alla Napoletana dough

2 to 3 tablespoons olive oil
1½ pounds (675 grams) fresh medium-size tomatoes, peeled, seeded, and roughly chopped, or one can (14 ounces, 400 grams) San Marzano plum tomatoes, drained and roughly chopped
2 large cloves garlic, very thinly sliced
1½ teaspoons dried oregano or 7 or 8 fresh basil leaves
1 teaspoon (5 grams) salt
1 teaspoon freshly ground pepper (optional)

Drizzle a little of the oil over the dough and spread the tomatoes over the top. Sprinkle with the garlic, oregano or basil, salt, and pepper, if desired; then drizzle with more oil.

Pizza Margherita Topping

Makes enough to top Pizza alla Napoletana dough

2 to 4 tablespoons olive oil
1 to 1½ pounds (450 to 650 grams) fresh medium-size tomatoes, peeled, seeded, and cut into strips, or 1 can (14 ounces, 400 grams) San Marzano plum tomatoes, drained and cut into strips
8 ounces (225 grams) sliced fresh mozzarella or Italian Fontina
¼ cup (25 grams) freshly grated Parmesan or *pecorino* (optional but tasty)
7 to 10 fresh basil leaves
1 teaspoon (5 grams) salt

Lightly moisten the dough with a bit of the oil. Spread the dough with the tomatoes, cheeses, and basil (in order) and sprinkle with the salt. Drizzle the remaining oil over the top. If you are making 1 large pizza, top it with all the ingredients but the mozzarella. Bake 10 to 15 minutes, top with the cheese, and bake until done. Because mozzarella is high in butter fat, it tends to burn before the crust is done, but this baker's secret solves the problem. Save a few basil leaves to dapple the cheese with.

Bake at 450° F for 15 to 30 minutes, depending on the size of the pizza.

Pizza alla Marinara Topping

Makes enough to top Pizza alla Napoletana dough

¼ cup olive oil
1 to 1½ pounds (450 to 650 grams) fresh medium-size tomatoes, peeled, seeded, and cut into strips, or 1 can (14 ounces, 400 grams), San Marzano plum tomatoes, drained and cut into strips
2 cloves garlic, very thinly sliced
4 to 6 anchovy fillets or to taste

Brush a little of the oil onto the dough. Spread the tomatoes and garlic on top; then sprinkle with small pieces of anchovy or use the whole fillets or cut them in half to make a sunburst pattern of them on top. Drizzle with the remaining oil.

Pizza alla Romana

Pizza by the Meter

The invariable image of pizza to an American is of a thick- or thin-crusted round of dough that is covered with topping, cut into wedges, and eaten out of hand. Italians, who go to bakeries to buy pizza by the meter, know another way. This extraordinary recipe comes from Gianfranco Anelli in Rome. He allows the soft, supple dough a very long rest—up to seven and a half hours, the longer the better—and then places it on a baker's peel two and a half feet long, and rhythmically pounds it with such vigor that it literally dances beneath his fingers. He paints the dough with oil and then sets the peel in the oven where the totally unforeseen occurs: the baker slowly, slowly withdraws the peel, stretching the remarkably elastic dough to a thin, incredibly light dough of an astonishing six-foot length.

Romans eat *pizza bianca,* white pizza sprinkled with only oil and salt, in the morning the way Florentines eat *schiacciate* and other northern Italians snack on *focacce.* You'll know just what I mean if you have ever been in a Roman bakery in the middle of the morning when a flood of schoolchildren at recess tumbled through the doors, queued up at the counter for individual lengths of *pizza bianca* still steaming from the oven, and then washed out again, snacks wrapped in waxed paper clutched in their hands. The rest of the day there is always a crowd of people at the counter just at the moment the pizza is about to emerge from the oven; they seem to have a sense of just when the next long plank of pizza will arrive hot, its fragrance scenting the warm air.

Because six-foot-long wood-burning ovens are hardly standard equipment, I've adapted the recipe for traditional round pizza shapes. Each round of dough can be set in a fourteen- or fifteen-inch pan, and you can dimple and pummel and stretch it until it becomes very fine. Give it time to recover and then go back with those fingers and work it some more. If you keep oil on your hands and on the top of the dough, it will not develop a skin. You can try to make long strips of pizza, Roman style, which can then be cut with scissors into any length you want, but be sure to put lots of flour on parchment paper on your peels or baking sheets for once the dough is shaped and topped, it is virtually impossible to move it.

A final secret from Rome: The pizza is washed with oil and sauce, if there is one, and, halfway through the baking, it is pulled out of the oven, dappled with shreds of mozzarella, and baked a few more minutes in the extreme heat of the fire. When it reappears, it is quickly brushed with oil and rushed to the front counter where the inevitable press of hungry Romans is waiting impatiently for its arrival.

Because this dough uses so little yeast and wants a long rising, you can work it into a busy American schedule by making the dough at night with cool water and refrigerating it immediately after it is mixed. Next morning, place it in a cool spot to rise slowly at room temperature (65° to 70° F is optimal) all day. Then shape and bake it for dinner.

Makes three 14- or 15-inch pizzas

2½ teaspoons (1 package) active dry yeast or 1 small cake (18 grams) fresh yeast
¼ cup warm water
About 5½ cups (750 grams) unbleached all-purpose flour
1 teaspoon (5 grams) salt
1¾ cups plus 1 tablespoon water, room temperature
1 tablespoon olive oil, plus additional for shaping the dough
1 tablespoon plus 1 teaspoon (20 grams) lard or olive oil

BY HAND

Stir the yeast into the warm water in a small bowl; let stand until creamy, about 10 minutes. Mix the flour and salt in a large wide-mouthed bowl. Make a well in the center of the flour; then pour the dissolved yeast, 1¾ cups plus 1 tablespoon water, 1 tablespoon oil, and the lard into the well. Gradually stir the flour into the liquid and work to a soft dough that can be gathered into a ball. Knead on a floured surface or in the bowl if it is large enough until soft, smooth, and elastic, 10 to 15 minutes, sprinkling with additional flour as needed. Slam the dough down hard from time to time to help develop the gluten.

continued

Pizza alla Romana (continued)

BY MIXER

Stir the yeast into the warm water in a mixer bowl; let stand until creamy, about 10 minutes. Add 1¾ cups plus 1 tablespoon water, 1 tablespoon oil, and the lard, and mix with the paddle. Add the flour and salt and mix until the dough comes thoroughly together (it can take as long as 5 minutes). Change to the dough hook and knead until soft and sticky but smooth, 5 to 6 minutes. Finish kneading by hand on a floured surface, sprinkling with additional flour as needed. Slam the dough down hard from time to time to help develop the gluten.

BY PROCESSOR

If the workbowl of your processor holds less than 8 cups, make the dough in 2 batches. Stir the yeast into the warm water in a medium-size bowl; let stand until creamy, about 10 minutes. Stir in 1¾ cups plus 1 tablespoon cold water, 1 tablespoon oil, and the lard. Place the flour and salt in a food processor fitted with the steel or dough blade and process with several pulses to sift. With the machine running, pour the liquid mixture through the feed tube and process until the dough is smooth and moist. Process the soft dough 10 to 15 seconds longer to knead. Don't allow the dough to gather into a ball. Finish kneading with well-floured hands on a floured surface, sprinkling with up to 4 tablespoons additional flour as needed, until delicate, velvety, and somewhat elastic, 2 to 3 minutes. Slam the dough down hard from time to time to help develop the gluten.

First Rise. Place the dough in a lightly oiled bowl, cover tightly with plastic wrap, and let rise at a cool room temperature until doubled, at least 4 hours but preferably 8 hours. If the dough looks as if it is rising too fast, simply punch it down.

Shaping. The trick in dealing with this delicate dough is to keep oil on your hands and on the top of the dough at all times. Turn the elastic, bubbly dough out onto a floured surface and cut into 3 equal pieces. Shape each piece into a rough ball. Oil the tops and let rest under a kitchen towel 30 minutes.

Oil three 14- or 15-inch pizza pans or flour 3 pieces of parchment paper that have been set on baker's peels or the backs of baking sheets. Place the balls of dough on the peels or pizza pans and dimple them vigorously, stretching each to a 14- or 15-inch circle, ⅛ inch thick, and leaving a thick edge.

If you want, you can place the dough over your oiled fists and gradually pull them apart, while at the same time turning and stretching the dough. Keep moving your hands to the outside to avoid tearing the center. For both methods, you will need to let the dough rest several times when it becomes unmanageable. The process may be slow, but it makes an outstanding crust; the first time through simply demands a bit of patience. When you have finished the shaping, carefully place each dough circle on floured parchment paper or the prepared pizza pan.

The dough can stand covered for 30 minutes to 1 hour before being spread with topping. The Italian baker insists that the internal temperature of the dough must be 78° F for 12 minutes before it can go into the oven.

Topping. Select one of the topping recipes that follow, use one of the Neapolitan toppings (double or triple the recipe for 3 pizzas) or, if you have gotten into the spirit of Italian baking, use whatever combinations of mushrooms, cheeses, greens, onions, anchovies, and herbs that strike your imagination. Remember to add any fresh cheese halfway through the baking, so that it doesn't burn.

Baking. Heat the oven to 525° to 550° F (as hot as you can get it). Use baking stones if you have them (turn the oven on 30 minutes before baking). Place the pans directly on the preheated stones, or bake the pizzas on the parchment paper on the stones or the backs of heavy baking sheets. Bake until the edge of the dough is golden and bubbly, 20 to 30 minutes. Immediately brush the crust with oil and drizzle a bit more oil over the pizzas. Serve very hot.

Pizza Bianca Topping

Makes enough to top Pizza alla Romana dough

About ½ cup best-quality olive oil
10 to 12 cloves fresh garlic, very, very thinly sliced
2 to 3 tablespoons chopped fresh rosemary (optional)
Salt
Freshly ground pepper

Brush the dough with some of the oil and sprinkle with garlic and rosemary, then salt and pepper to taste. Brush the top liberally with the remaining olive oil.

Pizza Rossa Topping

Makes enough to top Pizza alla Romana dough

About 4 pounds (1¾ kg) fresh ripe medium-size plum tomatoes, peeled, seeded, and roughly chopped, or 3 cans (14 ounces, 400 grams, each) San Marzano plum tomatoes, drained and chopped
¼ cup olive oil
2 teaspoons salt
Freshly ground pepper
About 1 pound (450 grams) best-quality whole-milk mozzarella, grated or sliced

Sauté the tomatoes in the oil over medium heat for 7 to 8 minutes. Drain in a sieve or colander and then force through the coarsest blade of a food mill. Brush the dough with the tomatoes and sprinkle lightly with the salt and pepper to taste. About halfway through baking, distribute the cheese evenly over the dough.

Pizza Pugliese Topping

Makes enough to top 1 large pizza

2 medium-size eggplants, peeled and sliced crosswise
¾ to 1 teaspoon salt
Vegetable oil for frying
6 ounces Provolone cheese, sliced
1 or 2 anchovies, boned and cut crosswise into slices
⅓ to ½ cup chopped fresh basil
3 fresh medium-size tomatoes, peeled, seeded, and diced
2 to 3 ounces pitted black olives
1 tablespoon olive oil
Freshly ground pepper

Place the eggplant slices in a colander, sprinkle liberally with salt, and toss to distribute the salt. Let stand 1 hour and pat the eggplant dry. Heat ½ inch vegetable oil in a heavy skillet over high heat. Fry the eggplant in a single layer in the oil until creamy but not golden. Drain on paper towels. Arrange a single layer of the eggplant over the dough; top with the cheese, then the anchovy pieces. Arrange another layer of eggplant over the cheese and anchovies and make a fine layer of the basil on top. Cover with the tomatoes and black olives. Drizzle olive oil over the top and sprinkle with salt and pepper to taste. Bake at 450° F for 15 to 20 minutes, following the baking directions in the dough recipe.

Pizza alla Siciliana

Sicilian Pizza

If you come to Palermo and explore the long curving streets of its fascinating market, the Vucciria, you'll see all the ingredients that give this fat pizza its typically Sicilian flavor. Sharp, tangy anchovies and a tomato sauce that is rich, sweet and full of flavor play against the herbs and cheeses in this juicy, light pizza.

Makes one 15- to 16-inch round pizza or one 12 × 17-inch pizza

DOUGH

2½ teaspoons (1 package) active dry yeast or 1 small cake (18 grams) fresh yeast
1½ teaspoons sugar
1½ cups plus 1 tablespoon lukewarm water
2 tablespoons (25 grams) lard or olive oil
1½ teaspoons (8 grams) salt
4¼ cups (550 grams) unbleached all-purpose flour

BY HAND

Stir the yeast and sugar into the water in a large mixing bowl; let stand until foamy, about 10 minutes. Stir in the lard. Whisk in the salt and 2 cups of the flour, 1 cup at a time; add the remaining flour and stir until the dough comes together. Knead on a lightly floured surface until soft and velvety, 10 to 12 minutes.

BY MIXER

Stir the yeast and sugar into the water in a mixer bowl; let stand until creamy, about 10 minutes. Mix in the lard with the paddle. Add the salt and flour and mix 1 to 2 minutes. Change to the dough hook and knead at medium speed until soft and velvety, 3 to 4 minutes.

BY PROCESSOR

Stir the yeast and sugar into ½ cup warm water in a small bowl; let stand until creamy, about 10 minutes. Place the flour and salt in a food processor fitted with the dough blade and process with several pulses to sift. With the machine running, pour the dissolved yeast, 1 cup plus 1 tablespoon cold water, and the lard through the feed tube and process until the dough gathers into a ball. Process no longer than 20 seconds to knead. Finish kneading by hand on a lightly floured surface until smooth, soft, and velvety.

Rising. Place the dough in a lightly oiled bowl, cover tightly with plastic wrap, and let rise until almost doubled, about 1 hour. Punch it down, cover again, and let rise just 20 minutes.

Shaping. Turn the dough out onto a lightly floured surface and shape into a thick disk. Roll it out with a rolling pin to a 12-inch circle,

Pizza alla Siciliana (continued)

about ¼ inch thick, leaving a thick edge. Turn the dough over several times as you roll it, so that it won't shrink back later. Place on an oiled baking sheet, a peel sprinkled with cornmeal, or a 12-inch oiled pizza pan.

TOPPING
3 large anchovies, boned and cut into small pieces
3 to 4 tablespoons grated fresh Caciocavallo or mild Provolone
    cheese
1 jar (4 ounces, 120 grams) artichoke hearts (packed in oil), drained
    and roughly chopped
Sfinciuni Tomato Sauce (opposite)
2 to 2½ teaspoons dried oregano
½ teaspoon salt
Freshly ground pepper
About 1 tablespoon olive oil, plus additional for brushing the crust
2 ounces (60 grams) prosciutto, sliced and roughly chopped
3 to 3½ ounces (85 to 100 grams) shredded mozzarella

Sprinkle the anchovies, half of the Caciocavallo, and three-quarters of the artichokes over the dough. Spread with half the tomato sauce and then sprinkle with 1½ teaspoons of the oregano, the salt, and pepper to taste. Drizzle with about 1 tablespoon olive oil, and spread with the remaining tomato sauce.

Baking. Heat the oven to 425° F. Use a baking stone if you have one (turn the oven on 30 minutes before baking). Sprinkle the stone with cornmeal just before sliding the pizza onto it or place the baking pan directly on the stone. Bake until the crust is crisp and crunchy, 20 to 25 minutes. Remove the pizza and sprinkle the prosciutto, remaining artichoke hearts, the mozzarella, the remaining oregano, and remaining Caciocavallo on top. Bake until the cheese is completely melted, 5 to 10 minutes. Immediately brush the crust with oil.

Sfinciuni alla Palermitana

Sfinciuni from Palermo

Sfinciuni is the quintessential pizza of Palermo. Some versions, like this one that uses Sicilian pizza dough, are rustic and countrified, while others, such as the one made famous by the nuns of the monastery of San Vito, which encloses a meat filling between two very fine layers of dough, are much more elegant. People pick up a slice or two at bakeries or fast-food shops to eat as they walk around the city, and sometimes there are even vendors in side squares selling *sfinciuni* right off their carts. They are usually baked in big rectangular pans and cut into whatever size matches the buyer's appetite.

Makes one 15-inch round pizza or one 12 × 17-inch pizza

TOMATO SAUCE
2 medium-size yellow onions (about 1 pound, 450 grams), chopped
4 cups water
2 tablespoons tomato paste
2 tablespoons olive oil
1 anchovy, chopped

Simmer the onions in the water in a covered heavy saucepan at least 30 minutes but preferably 1 hour. Stir in the tomato paste, oil, and anchovy and simmer covered at least 1 more hour; the longer you cook the sauce, the lighter and sweeter its taste will be. Cool to room temperature.

SFINCIUNI
Pizza alla Siciliana dough (recipe precedes), made through the first rising
3 to 4 tablespoons grated fresh Caciocavallo or mild Provolone cheese
3 ounces (85 grams) artichoke hearts (packed in oil), drained and chopped
¼ cup plain fresh bread crumbs, lightly toasted
1 to 2 tablespoons olive oil, plus additional for brushing the crust

Shaping. Knead the dough briefly on a lightly floured surface and shape it into a thick disk. Roll it out to fit a 15-inch round pizza pan, leaving a thick edge. Lightly oil the pan and place the dough in the pan. Cover with a towel and let rise for 30 minutes.

Sprinkle the cheese and artichoke hearts over the dough; then spoon on the tomato sauce and sprinkle with the bread crumbs. Drizzle the oil over the surface.

continued

Baking. Heat the oven to 400° F. Use a baking stone if you have one (turn the oven on 30 minutes before baking) and place the pan directly on the preheated stone. Bake until the dough is golden, 20 to 25 minutes. Immediately brush the crust with oil. Serve hot.

Calzoni Pugliesi

Half-Moon-Shaped Filled Pizza from Puglia

Makes 6 to 7 calzoni

DOUGH

2½ teaspoons (1 package) active dry yeast or 1 small cake (18 grams) fresh yeast
4 teaspoons (20 grams) sugar
3 to 4 tablespoons warm water
1 cup plus 1 tablespoon milk
1 egg
3¾ cups (500 grams) unbleached all-purpose flour
1½ teaspoons (8 grams) salt

BY HAND

Stir the yeast and sugar into 3 tablespoons warm water in a small bowl; let stand until foamy, 5 to 10 minutes. Whisk the milk and egg together. Mix the flour and salt, make a mound of it in a large bowl or on a well-floured work surface, and then make a large well in the center. Gradually pour the dissolved yeast and milk mixture into the well, working the flour from the inside of the well into the liquid with your fingers. Continue until the flour is absorbed, adding 1 tablespoon water, if needed. Knead until soft, velvety, strong, and elastic, 10 to 15 minutes.

BY MIXER

Stir the yeast and sugar into 3 tablespoons warm water in a mixer bowl; let stand until foamy, 5 to 10 minutes. Mix in the milk and egg with the paddle. Add the flour and salt and mix until the dough comes together, adding 1 tablespoon water, if needed. Change to the dough hook and knead at medium speed until soft, velvety, strong, and elastic, 3 to 4 minutes.

BY PROCESSOR

Stir the yeast and sugar into the water in a small bowl; let stand until foamy, 5 to 10 minutes. Place the flour and salt in a food processor fitted with the dough blade and process with several pulses to sift. With the machine running, pour the dissolved yeast, the milk, which must be cold, and egg through the feed tube and process until the dough comes together in 1 or 2 balls on top of the blade. You may need to add a bit more water. Finish kneading by hand on a lightly floured surface 4 to 5 minutes.

Rising. Place the dough in a lightly oiled bowl, cover with plastic wrap, and let rise until doubled, about 2 hours.

Shaping. Knead the dough briefly on a lightly floured surface. Cut into 6 or 7 pieces (about 4 ounces, 110 grams each). Shape each piece into a ball, flatten each hard with your hand, and roll it with a rolling pin into a ¼-inch-thick oval.

TOPPING
1 teaspoon minced garlic
¼ cup olive oil
12 ounces (340 grams) fresh mozzarella, shredded
2 cups chopped seeded peeled fresh tomatoes or drained canned Italian plum tomatoes
2 to 3 tablespoons freshly grated Parmesan
¼ cup chopped fresh basil leaves
Salt
1 egg, beaten
1 tablespoon water

Warm the garlic in the oil in a small heavy skillet over low heat 4 to 5 minutes. Place 1½ to 2 ounces (⅓ cup) of the mozzarella and about ⅓ cup chopped tomato in the center of each dough oval. Sprinkle with a little Parmesan, basil, and salt to taste. Mix the egg and water in a small bowl. Brush the egg wash on the edge of each oval and let rest 10 minutes covered by a towel. Fold each oval in half and press the edges together with your fingertips. Brush the tops with the garlic-scented olive oil. Place the calzoni on an oiled baking sheet if you don't have a baking stone.

Baking. Heat the oven to 450° F. If you are using a baking stone, turn the oven on 30 minutes before baking and sprinkle with cornmeal just before sliding the calzoni onto it. Bake 20 to 25 minutes. Brush again with the garlic-scented olive oil and serve hot.

Focaccia

Focaccia alla Genovese

Focaccia from Genoa

Focaccia has become a national dish. This disk or large rectangle of leavened dough is found from the tiny towns of the Italian Riviera to Naples on the Mediterranean and Ostuni on the Adriatic, but its true home is Genoa, which is to *focaccia* what Naples is to pizza. It is called *focaccia* in Genoa and much of Liguria, but it changes names elsewhere. It is known as *sardenaira* in Provence and as *sardenara* or *sardinaira* in the most western parts of Liguria, which feel a magnetic attraction to the French tradition just over the border, *schiacciata* in Florence and pockets of Puglia, and *pinze* in the south. The *fougasse* of France and hearth cakes of England share the same ancestry, for as the Romans extended their empire, they brought with them not only their carefully reasoned city plans, their temples and amphitheaters, but their *focacce* and flat disks of bread as well.

Focacce are simplicity itself; herbs of the countryside and the golden oils of Liguria flavor the interior, while a little local garlic or tiny savory olives stud its surface. In Puglia a variety called *puddica* is enriched with the ingredients of a pastoral people—tomatoes, garlic, oregano, capers, and oil, and variations on that theme. Anchovies and cheeses from herds tended by local shepherds flavor other southern specialties. The bakers of Italy, never willing to rest on their laurels, are always using their fertile imaginations to create other possibilities; you, too, should combine appealing ingredients—*pancetta*, grated cheeses, shreds of basil, or sweet onions sweated in oil—according to your own desires. *Focacce* are usually savory, seasoned with oil or other fats, but there are sweet ones as well, such as the *focaccia* from Bologna made from simple briochelike dough that becomes the envelope for ice cream sandwiches, Italian style. Try making *Pan Tramvai* (raisin bread) as a *focaccia* with a hail of crystallized or turbinado sugar on top; this innovative departure makes a sensational breakfast bread.

Focacce can be soft or crisp, thick or thin, light and almost plain or topped with any number of condiments, but they are always rustic, a convivial treat eaten as a snack. When I bake them at home, the entire house is lightly perfumed by their cooking, bringing the flavors of the countryside dancing in the air, tickling the nose, and encouraging the taste buds to prepare for a treat.

Bakers sometimes tuck flavoring right into the dough and sometimes they only dapple the top. The dough is always stretched in a well-oiled pan, then dimpled with the fingertips, leaving little indentations to collect the oil and salt on top. Sprinkle water, oil, and salt over the surface just before baking so that the *focaccia* emerges golden, moist, and perfectly cooked from the oven. When this rustic dish is ready for eating, you'll undoubtedly be inspired to take it on country outings and picnics, to slip it to children for lunch and snacks, and to keep it for eating with salads, cheeses, roast chickens and meat, along with a glass of good earthy wine.

Makes enough dough for three 9- or 10-inch round focacce or two 10½ × 15½-inch thinner rectangular focacce

2½ teaspoons (1 package) active dry yeast or 1 small cake (18 grams) fresh yeast
¼ cup warm water
2¼ cups plus 1 to 2 tablespoons water, room temperature
2 tablespoons olive oil
About 7½ cups (1000 grams) unbleached all-purpose flour or half all-purpose flour and half bread flour
1 tablespoon (15 grams) fine sea salt or table salt

BY HAND

Stir the yeast into the warm water in a large mixing bowl; let stand until creamy, about 10 minutes. Stir in 2¼ cups plus 1 tablespoon water and the oil. Add 2 cups of the flour and the salt and whisk or stir until smooth. Stir in the remaining flour, 1 cup at a time, until the dough comes together. Knead on a floured surface until velvety and soft, about 8 to 10 minutes.

BY MIXER

Stir the yeast into the warm water in a mixer bowl; let stand until creamy, about 10 minutes. Stir in 2¼ cups plus 1 tablespoon water and the oil with the paddle. Add the flour and salt and mix until the dough comes together, 1 to 2 minutes, adding 1 tablespoon water if needed. Change to the dough hook and knead at low speed for 1 to 2 minutes, then at medium speed for another 3 minutes, stopping to push the dough down from the collar. The dough should be velvety and elastic.

BY PROCESSOR

Process this dough in 2 batches. Stir the yeast into the warm water in a small bowl; let stand until creamy, about 10 minutes. Place the flour and salt in a food processor fitted with the steel blade and process with 2 or 3 pulses to sift. With the machine running, pour 2¼ cups plus 1 tablespoon cold water, the dissolved yeast, and oil

Focaccia alla Genovese (continued)

through the feed tube and process until the dough gathers into a rough mass. Process 20 seconds longer to knead. Finish kneading by hand on a floured surface until the dough is velvety and elastic, 2 to 3 minutes.

First Rise. Place the dough in a lightly oiled bowl, cover tightly with plastic wrap, and let rise until doubled, about 1½ hours.

Shaping and Second Rise. For round *focacce,* cut the dough into 3 equal pieces on a lightly floured surface. Shape each piece into a thick disk; roll out each disk to a 9- or 10-inch circle and place in the bottom of an oiled 9- or 10-inch pie plate. For rectangular focacce, cut the dough in half and shape to fit 2 oiled 10½ × 15½-inch pans. Cover the dough with towels and let rise for 30 minutes.

Dimpling the dough

Dimpling and Third Rise. Dimple the dough vigorously with your fingertips, leaving indentations that are as deep as ½ inch. The bakers of Genoa do this to trap the little pools of oil and salt that flavor the surface. Cover the tops with moist towels and let rise until doubled, about 2 hours.

Topping. Select one of the topping recipes that follow. One baker of Genoa told me that the great secret of keeping these doughs so moist and yet cooking them thoroughly is to cover the tops with equal amounts of olive oil and water mixed with salt; the water evaporates slowly during the cooking, allowing the interiors to cook fully without drying out. Alas, home ovens don't get hot enough to make use of this wonderful piece of advice; but you can paint the tops with oil and sprinkle with salt, and, when you place the *focacce* in the oven, spray them with water.

Baking. Heat the oven to 400° F. Use baking stones if you have them (turn the oven on 30 minutes before baking) and place the pans directly on the preheated stones. Bake 20 to 25 minutes, spraying with water 3 times in the first 10 minutes; immediately invert the *focacce* onto racks to cool so that the bottom crusts don't get soggy. Bakers in Genoa set them on bamboo racks to cool because they leave no taste. Eat *focacce* warm or at room temperature the same day you bake them. No matter what, don't refrigerate; they simply won't taste right.

Focaccia col Sale
Focaccia with Sea Salt

Makes three 9- or 10-inch round focacce or two 10½ × 15-inch rectangular focacce

**Focaccia alla Genovese dough (recipe precedes), made through the
  third rise**
2 to 3 tablespoons olive oil
1½ to 2 teaspoons (8 to 10 grams) coarse sea salt

Brush the doughs with the oil and sprinkle with the salt. Bake as directed for *Focaccia alla Genovese.*

Focaccia alla Salvia
Focaccia with Sage

Makes three 9- or 10-inch round focacce or two 10½ × 15-inch rectangular focacce

Focaccia alla Genovese **dough (page 288)**
**24 to 30 chopped fresh sage leaves or 1½ tablespoons dried sage
  leaves, crumbled (not powdered, which is much too pungent)**
2 tablespoons olive oil
1½ tablespoons (25 grams) salt
Whole fresh sage leaves (optional)

Work the chopped sage leaves into the dough in the first kneading. Follow the directions for *Focaccia alla Genovese* through the third rise. Just before baking, brush the dimpled dough with oil and sprinkle with the salt. Decorate the tops with the whole sage leaves. Bake as directed for *Focaccia alla Genovese.*

Variation. To make *Focaccia al Rosmarino,* substitute 1½ tablespoons chopped fresh rosemary or 2 teaspoons dried rosemary for the chopped sage. Decorate each *focaccia* with several sprigs of fresh rosemary, if you want.

Focaccia alle Olive

Focaccia with Olives

Makes three 9- or 10-inch round focacce or two 10½ × 15½-inch rectangular focacce

Focaccia alla Genovese dough (page 288), made through the third rise
8 ounces (225 grams) black Ligurian olives or combination of black and green olives, preferably Ponentine, Ardoino, or Niçoise
2 tablespoons olive oil

Pit the olives and push the olives into the dimpled doughs just before baking. Brush the doughs with olive oil. Bake as directed for *Focaccia alla Genovese.*

Focaccia al Gorgonzola

Gorgonzola Focaccia

This *focaccia* is very appealing to look at as well as to eat. It is about 1½ to 2 inches high and the Gorgonzola covering settles slightly unevenly on the surface, creating irregular valleys with deep golden cheese patches and higher raised sections lightly brushed with the topping.

Makes two 9- or 10-inch round focacce or one 12 × 17-inch focaccia

DOUGH
3½ teaspoons active dry yeast or 1⅓ small cakes (24 grams) fresh yeast
1½ cups warm water
¼ cup olive oil
3¾ cups (500 grams) unbleached all-purpose flour
2½ teaspoons (12½ grams) salt

BY HAND

Stir the yeast into the warm water in a large mixing bowl; let stand until creamy, about 10 minutes. Stir in the oil, then the flour and salt. Knead on a lightly floured surface until smooth and elastic, 8 to 10 minutes.

BY MIXER

Stir the yeast into the water in a mixer bowl; let stand until creamy, about 10 minutes. Stir in the oil with the paddle, then the flour and salt. Change to the dough hook and knead until smooth and elastic, about 3 minutes.

BY PROCESSOR

Stir the yeast into ¼ cup warm water in a small bowl; let stand until creamy, about 10 minutes. Place the flour and salt in a food processor fitted with the dough blade and process briefly to sift. With the machine running, slowly pour the dissolved yeast, oil, and 1¼ cups cold water through the feed tube and process until the dough gathers into a ball. Process 40 seconds longer to knead. Finish kneading by hand on a lightly floured surface for 2 to 3 minutes.

First Rise. Place the dough in an oiled bowl, cover tightly with plastic wrap, and let rise until doubled, 1 to 1½ hours.

Shaping. Cut the dough in half and place each piece in a lightly oiled 9- or 10-inch pie plate. Flatten and stretch the dough to cover as much of the bottom as possible; then dimple the tops quite vigorously with your fingertips to stretch it some more. Cover with a towel and let it relax 10 minutes. Dimple and stretch the dough more, so that it really covers the bottom. Let rest under a towel another 20 to 25 minutes.

TOPPING
¼ cup whipping or heavy cream
8 ounces (225 grams) Gorgonzola cheese
½ teaspoon dried thyme
Olive oil for brushing the tops

Mix the cream, cheese, and thyme in a food processor fitted with the steel blade, with the paddle of an electric mixer, or mash the cheese in a mixing bowl with a wooden spoon and beat in the cream and thyme. Spread the cheese mixture equally over the doughs with a rubber spatula or wooden spoon.

Second Rise. Brush the tops lightly with oil, cover with a towel, and let rise until well puffed, 50 minutes to 1 hour.

Baking. Heat the oven to 425° F. Bake 10 minutes. Reduce the heat to 375° F and bake until the topping is golden brown and just starting to bubble, about 10 minutes. Unmold immediately onto a rack. This *focaccia* is best hot but can also be served warm or at room temperature. Do not refrigerate.

continued

Focaccia al Gorgonzola (continued)

Variations. To make *Focaccia al Sale,* omit the Gorgonzola topping. Sprinkle the top of the dough with coarse salt and brush with olive oil. Brush again with oil after baking.

To make *Focaccia alle Cipolle,* substitute 2 finely sliced and sautéed yellow onions for the topping. Sprinkle with salt and brush with olive oil. Brush again with oil after baking.

To make *Focaccia ai Peperoni,* sauté 2 to 3 finely sliced red and yellow bell peppers in 3 tablespoons olive oil and 1½ tablespoons butter over medium-low heat until soft, about 15 minutes. Substitute the sautéed pepper mixture for the Gorgonzola topping. Brush the *focacce* with oil after baking.

To make *Focaccia alla Ricotta,* mix 8 ounces (225 grams) ricotta, ½ cup (about 85 grams) diced prosciutto, ⅓ cup (35 grams) grated *pecorino* or Parmesan cheese, 5 tablespoons milk, and ⅛ teaspoon freshly grated nutmeg as directed for the Gorgonzola topping.

Schiacciata alla Fiorentina
Flatbread from Florence

Schiacciata, which simply means squashed or crushed, is the word Florentines use for the flatbreads that other Italians call *focaccia* or pizza. At the Il Fornaio bakery on Via Matteo Palmieri in Florence, I watched as the bakers shaped *schiacciate* as big as a small pizza and as small as an hors d'oeuvre, but to me they were at their most appealing as 6-inch disks topped with brilliant strips of red and yellow peppers, ribbons of zucchini, or almost translucent slices of ripe tomatoes dusted with tiny basil leaves, and all glossy from a wash of local olive oil. They are wonderful eaten cold for lunch with a salad; take them on picnics, too, or serve them with a platter of cold meats.

Makes six 6-inch schiacciate; *two 10-inch and one 8-inch* schiacciate;

DOUGH
2½ teaspoons (1 package) active dry yeast or 1 small cake (18 grams) fresh yeast
Dash malt syrup (optional)
1½ cups warm water
2 tablespoons olive oil

2½ tablespoons (30 grams) lard, at room temperature
2½ tablespoons nonfat dry milk
3¾ cups (500 grams) unbleached all-purpose flour
1½ teaspoons (8 grams) salt
Olive oil for brushing the tops
Salt for sprinkling the tops

BY HAND

Stir the yeast and malt, if using, into the water in a medium-size bowl; let stand until creamy, about 10 minutes. Stir in the oil, lard, and dry milk. Mix the flour and salt in a widemouthed bowl and make a well in the center. Pour the yeast mixture into the well and gradually stir the flour into the liquid. Stir until well combined. Knead on a floured surface or in the big bowl until velvety and smooth, 8 to 10 minutes. The dough should be soft, so add any extra flour sparingly.

BY MIXER

Stir the yeast and malt, if using, into a mixer bowl; let stand until creamy, 10 minutes. Stir in the oil, lard, and dry milk with the paddle. Add the flour and mix at low speed about 2 minutes. Change to the dough hook and knead 4 to 5 minutes. Add the salt and knead another 1 to 2 minutes. The dough will climb up the collar of the hook, and you will have to stop several times to push it down. The dough should be smooth, velvety, and softer than bread dough but firmer than croissant dough.

BY PROCESSOR

Unless you have a food processor with an enormous capacity, process this recipe in 2 batches. Stir the yeast and malt, if using, into ¼ cup warm water in a small bowl; let stand until creamy, about 10 minutes. Place the flour and dry milk in a food processor fitted with the steel blade and process with several pulses to mix. Place the lard on top of the flour. With the machine running, pour 1¾ cups cold water, the dissolved yeast, and oil through the feed tube and process until the dough comes together. Add the salt and process briefly to incorporate it. Finish kneading by hand on a lightly floured surface 3 to 5 minutes.

First Rise. Place the dough in a lightly oiled bowl, cover tightly with plastic wrap, and let rise until doubled, 1 to 2 hours.

Shaping Large Schiacciate. Flatten the dough firmly on a lightly floured work surface and divide into two 8-ounce (225 grams) and one 10½-ounce (300 grams) pieces. Roll each piece into a ball and let rest

Schiacciata alla Fiorentina (continued)

under a towel for 15 minutes. Dimple and spread the balls with your fingers to cover the bottoms of two oiled 8-inch pie plates and one oiled 10-inch pie plate, or shape free form on floured peels. Brush the tops with oil and sprinkle with salt.

Shaping 6-inch Schiacciate. Cut the dough into 6 pieces (5 ounces, 140 grams each) on a lightly floured surface and shape into balls. Let rest under a towel for 15 minutes. Dimple the doughs, spreading each into a circle, and let rest under a towel another 15 minutes. Dimple the dough again, stretching each piece to a 6-inch circle. Brush the tops with oil and sprinkle lightly with salt. Place the dough circles on parchment-lined or oiled baking sheets or baker's peels sprinkled with cornmeal.

Second Rise. Cover with a towel and let rise until doubled, about 1 hour.

Topping. Dimple the dough again with your fingertips, stretching it as you go. Sprinkle with salt and brush with oil. Mist water very lightly over the top to cover and trap the oil and then cover with one of the following toppings.

2 finely sliced red onions sautéed in 2 tablespoons oil and 1 tablespoon unsalted butter over low heat for 15 to 20 minutes; sprinkle with 1 tablespoon torn fresh basil leaves

or 3 to 4 thinly sliced fresh medium-size tomatoes; sprinkle with chopped fresh basil leaves and ¾ teaspoon salt

or 2 finely sliced yellow and/or red sweet peppers lightly sautéed with a large garlic clove in 2 to 3 tablespoons olive oil for 15 minutes; discard the garlic

or 1 to 2 very thinly sliced peeled eggplants, salted, drained, and lightly sautéed with 1 or 2 whole cloves garlic in ¼ cup olive oil until creamy, 10 to 15 minutes; drain on paper towels and layer with 2 fresh medium-size ripe tomatoes, thinly sliced, or 1 can (14 ounces, 400 grams) San Marzano plum tomatoes, drained and chopped

or about 3 cups shredded stracchino or Taleggio cheese

or 4 to 6 small zucchini, cut lengthwise into thin slices and lightly sautéed with 2 whole cloves garlic in 3 to 4 tablespoons olive oil; discard the garlic; sprinkle with 2 tablespoons chopped fresh basil

Brush the tops with oil, sprinkle with salt, and brush or mist lightly with water.

Baking. Heat the oven to 425° F. Use baking stones if you have them (turn the oven on 30 minutes before baking) and place the baking pans directly on the preheated stones. Bake the 10-inch *schiacciata* 25 to 30 minutes, the 8-inch 22 to 25 minutes, and the 6-inch 18 to 20 minutes. Immediately brush the surfaces with oil. You may bake the larger *schiacciate* out of their pans directly on the stones for the last 10 minutes. Serve hot, or cool on racks to room temperature.

Pizzette Fiorentine

Little Pizzas of Florence

Pizzette are much thinner than pizzas and are wonderful little rounds for snacks.

Makes eight 5-inch pizzette

Schiacciata alla Fiorentina dough (page 294), made through the first rising
2 to 2½ tablespoons olive oil
¾ to 1 teaspoon salt
Choice of toppings for Schiacciata alla Fiorentina

Shaping and Second Rise. Cut the dough into 8 pieces (4 ounces, 110 grams each) on a lightly floured surface; flatten each piece with your palms (not fingertips) and brush with oil. Let rest on a floured surface under a towel for 15 minutes. Spread the pieces with your fingertips into very, very thin 5-inch circles. Brush with oil, set on cornmeal-sprinkled peels or oiled baking sheets, cover with a towel, and let rise half their original volume, about 30 minutes.

Topping. Sprinkle salt over the tops and brush with oil. Top with your choice of lightly sautéed, finely sliced vegetables, as for *schiacciate*. Drizzle oil over the topping and mist or brush lightly with water.

Baking. Heat the oven to 425° F. Use baking stones if you have them (turn the oven on 30 minutes before baking) and place the baking pans directly on the preheated stones. Bake 15 minutes. Immediately brush the pizzette thoroughly with oil to give them a luscious finish. Serve hot or at room temperature. Do not refrigerate.

Schiacciate Integrali
Whole-Wheat Flatbreads

These Florentine *schiacciate* are simply tasty flatbreads made of whole-wheat flour; top them with sweet red onions flavored with thyme or wash the tops with garlic-scented olive oil. If you bake them without toppings, these make wonderful buns for sandwiches; just cut them in half, stuff with slices of prosciutto and cheese, and warm them briefly. Whether you make them as big as pizzas or as small as hors d'oeuvres, you can be sure you're making the Tuscan equivalent of *focacce* in the stylish whole-wheat variation.

Makes 5 to 6 pizzette; *two 10-inch* schiacciate; *or about 60* focaccette

2½ teaspoons (1 package) active dry yeast or 1 small cake (18 grams) fresh yeast
1½ cups warm water
1 tablespoon plus 1 teaspoon (20 grams) lard
About 2¾ cups (375 grams) unbleached all-purpose flour
1 cup less 2 tablespoons (125 grams) whole-wheat flour
1½ teaspoons (8 grams) salt
Olive oil for brushing the tops

BY HAND

Stir the yeast into the water in a large mixing bowl; let stand until creamy, about 10 minutes. Stir in the lard. Mix the flours and salt and whisk the first 2 cups, 1 cup at a time, into the yeast mixture; stir in the remaining flour mixture thoroughly with a wooden spoon. Knead on a lightly floured surface until velvety and elastic, 8 to 10 minutes.

BY MIXER

Stir the yeast into the water in a mixer bowl; let stand until creamy, about 10 minutes. Stir in the lard with the paddle. Mix in the flours thoroughly; add the salt and mix until incorporated. Change to the dough hook and knead until velvety and elastic, 2 to 3 minutes. If you want, finish kneading briefly by hand on a floured surface.

BY PROCESSOR

Stir the yeast into ¼ cup warm water in a small bowl; let stand until creamy, about 10 minutes. Place the flours and salt in a food processor fitted with the dough blade. Process with several pulses to sift. Place the lard on top of the flour. With the machine running, pour 1¼ cups cold water and the dissolved yeast through the feed tube and process until the dough gathers into a rough mass. Add the salt. Process 25 seconds longer to knead. Finish kneading by hand 2 to 3 minutes.

First Rise. Place the dough in a lightly oiled bowl, cover tightly with plastic wrap, and let rise until puffy but not doubled, 1 to 1¼ hours.

Shaping. Knead the dough briefly on a lightly floured surface. Cut the dough in half for two 10-inch *schiacciate* or into 5 or 6 pieces for *pizzette*. Shape each piece into a ball. Roll out each ball on a lightly floured surface or stretch the dough over your fists to a 10-inch circle for *schiacciate* or a 5-inch circle for pizzette, leaving a thick edge. Place on floured baker's peels or lightly oiled pizza pans, pie plates, or baking sheets. You may need to stretch the dough, let it relax for a few minutes under a towel, then stretch it again. Brush the tops with oil.

To Make Focaccette. Roll the dough out thin on a floured surface and cut out circles with a 1¼- to 1½-inch cookie cutter. Place on lightly oiled baking sheets. Do not oil the tops. Cover with towels and let rise without any topping.

Topping for Schiacciate or Pizzette. Sauté 2 thinly sliced large red onions in 2 tablespoons olive oil and 1 tablespoon unsalted butter over very low heat 15 to 20 minutes; spread the onions over the dough and sprinkle with a fat pinch dried thyme. Or sauté 2 whole large cloves garlic in 2 to 2½ tablespoons olive oil over medium heat for 4 to 5 minutes; brush the dough with the oil and sprinkle with 2 tablespoons chopped fresh sage or rosemary or 1 tablespoon sea salt.

Second Rise. Cover the dough with towels and let rise until puffy but not doubled, about 45 minutes. Dimple and stretch the dough again with your fingers. Before baking and after the second rise, dimple the *focaccette* with your index fingers; then oil the tops and sprinkle with a bit of fine sea salt.

Baking. Heat the oven to 400° F. Use baking stones if you have them (turn the oven on 30 minutes before baking) and place the baking pans directly on the preheated stones. Bake the *schiacciate* 22 to 25 minutes, the *pizzette* 15 to 18 minutes, and the *focaccette* 12 to 15 minutes. Serve hot, or cool on racks to room temperature.

Focaccia alla Pugliese
Potato Flatbread from Puglia

I discovered this unusual kind of *focaccia* in Puglia, the region right on the heel of the boot in southern Italy, where huge well-kept farms with great green and golden fields of grain are interrupted only by stands of olive trees, stone walls, and *trulli*, charming whitewashed round houses with conical roofs. Of course we stopped to enter the *trulli* which were actually open in the countryside and in the town of Alberobello, and then set out for Mia Casa, a restaurant patronized by local people who know good regional food when they taste it. We began a large lunch with an antipasto of wonderful homemade sausages, salamis, olives, and this special version of *focaccia* made with the potatoes that grow throughout the entire region. About 1¼ inches high with what looks like a dense breadlike texture, it is actually as light as cake when you eat it. The tomato-scented oil painted across the top leaves a veil of red sprinkled with a dusting of oregano.

Makes two 9-inch focacce

DOUGH
1¾ teaspoons active dry yeast or ⅔ small cake (12 grams) fresh yeast
1 cup plus 3 tablespoons warm water
3¾ cups (500 grams) unbleached all-purpose flour
1⅓ cups (275 grams) lightly packed riced, peeled, boiled potatoes
2 teaspoons (10 grams) salt

BY HAND

Stir the yeast into ⅓ cup of the water in a small bowl; let stand until creamy, about 10 minutes. Mix the flour, potatoes, and salt in a large bowl; mound the mixture in the bowl and make a well in the center. Pour the dissolved yeast into the well and gradually add ⅔ cup plus 3 tablespoons water, stirring the dry ingredients from the side of the well into the liquid. Stir until the dough comes together. Knead on a floured surface until soft and elastic, 8 to 10 minutes.

BY MIXER

Stir the yeast into all the warm water in a mixer bowl; let stand until creamy, about 10 minutes. Add the flour, potatoes, and salt, and mix with the paddle until the mixture comes together. Change to the dough hook and knead at medium speed until soft and elastic, about 3 minutes.

First Rise. Place the dough in a lightly oiled bowl, cover tightly with plastic wrap, and let rise until doubled, about 1½ hours.

Shaping and Second Rise. Cut the dough in half on a lightly floured surface and shape each piece into a ball. Place in 2 lightly oiled 9-inch pie plates; stretch the dough out toward the edges.

Cover with a damp towel and let rise until the dough has doubled and completely filled the pans, about 45 minutes.

TOPPING

2 to 3 tablespoons oil from a jar of sun-dried tomatoes; or 2 to 3 tablespoons olive oil mixed with 1 tablespoon mashed plum tomatoes or ½ teaspoon tomato paste

2 teaspoons dried oregano

Dimple the tops of the doughs, letting your fingertips dance across the surface and leave little indentations in the dough. Using a pastry brush, lightly wash the tops of the *focacce* with the oil and sprinkle with the oregano.

Baking. Heat the oven to 400° F. Use baking stones if you have them (turn the oven on 30 minutes before baking) and place the pie plates directly on the preheated stones. Bake until the edges are golden, 25 to 30 minutes; if you want, bake the *focacce* out of the pans directly on the stones for the last 10 minutes. Cool to room temperature.

Focaccia di Patate e Cipolle
Potato and Onion Focaccia

There is nothing ordinary about this focaccia, for it is made not only without yeast but also without flour. The secret is in the potatoes, which make a wonderful foil for the intriguing onion, olive, and caper filling. I happened upon it in Lecce, the city in Puglia that is sometimes called the Florence of Baroque Art. No wonder—the facade of almost every cathedral, *palazzo*, and building is awash in voluptuous cupids, elegant virgins, grinning monkeys, fat little cupids, gargoyles, and demons clearly up to no good. Lecce had its centuries of privilege and influence under the Normans and Spanish, but this *focaccia* reflects a much humbler tradition. The potato is part of a rustic style of cooking and eating and enjoys a popularity in Puglia that isn't matched anywhere else in Italy.

Makes 1 focaccia

SAUCE
¼ cup olive oil
2 pounds (900 grams) medium-size yellow onions, roughly chopped
1 crumbled bay leaf
¼ cup dry white wine
1½ teaspoons (8 grams) salt
Freshly ground pepper
3 cups water
4 chopped pitted black olives, preferably Gaeta or Kalamata
Scant 1 tablespoon capers, drained

Pour the oil into a Dutch oven or heavy saucepan; it should cover the bottom of the pan. Add the onions, bay leaf, wine, salt, and pepper to taste and pour in the water. Cook uncovered over medium heat, stirring occasionally, until all the water is evaporated. The mixture must be really dry or the interior of the *focaccia* will be gummy. Remove from the heat and stir in the olives and capers.

DOUGH
This really isn't a dough at all but a mixture based on boiled potatoes.

1¼ pounds (560 grams) baking potatoes (about 2 large) peeled, boiled, and riced or mashed
2 tablespoons freshly grated Parmesan cheese
1½ teaspoons (8 grams) salt
Freshly ground pepper

3 to 4 tablespoons dry white wine
5 to 7 tablespoons coarsely ground fresh bread crumbs
Olive oil for the top

Place the hot potatoes in a mixing bowl; beat in the Parmesan, salt, pepper to taste, and enough of the wine to make a consistent dough.

Oil a 9-inch pie plate and coat with 2 to 3 tablespoons of the bread crumbs, enough for a thin layer to keep the potatoes from sticking. Spread slightly more than half the potato mixture in a layer about ¾ inch thick in the pie plate. Spread with the onion sauce and cover with a second layer of the remaining potatoes. Spread a little olive oil on your hand and rub it over the top. Sprinkle with the remaining bread crumbs, so that the top is completely covered.

Baking. Heat the oven to 350° F. Bake until the top is golden and the crumbs are crisp, about 45 minutes. Serve warm or at room temperature.

PANI RAFFINATI
Elegant Breads

It may be stretching the term just a bit to think of croissants and puff pastries, those two supreme accomplishments of the baker's art, as *pani raffinati*, refined breads, although, of course, that is exactly what they are. A bit of flour, a bit of water, a little yeast, and salt layered with butter and suddenly—or slowly—you have incredibly flaky and tender doughs that can be sweet or savory, for breakfast or dinner, for appetizers or dessert. These *pani raffinati* are very versatile, as well as more than a little tricky. Even in Italy they are considered the most rarified expression of the cook's art, so it's no wonder that many cookbooks simply suggest that their readers buy *pasta sfogliata* already prepared.

A few tastes of these Italian treats will immediately convince you to make them yourself. These fragrant, delicate doughs flavored with any number of ingredients are turned into *mignon* hors d'oeuvres and sweets, tiny little mouthfuls permeated with a flash of cheese, a crunch of caraway, a bit of anchovy, or a whiff of sweet apple and nut. Their delicacy and elegance simply have no rival; so, while these wonderful discoveries for every course of every meal may take a bit of work, you can make dozens at a time, freeze them with ease, and pull them out any time to dazzle your guests.

Sweet Croissants

Cornetti Dolci
Italian Croissants

In big cities, such as Milan and Rome, hot *cornetti* are all the rage. Kids flock to the back doors of bakeries at one and two o'clock in the morning to buy them still steamy from the ovens. It's slightly tricky, because it's against the law to sell bread until it is cool, but that probably only makes these delicate, flaky pastries all the more appealing. *Cornetti* come plain or filled with apricot jam, almond

The baked croissant

paste, or pastry cream, which is a particular favorite all over the south.

What makes Italian *cornetti* different from French croissants? Certainly not their heritage, for both are descendants of a pastry devised by a Viennese baker to celebrate the city's liberation from the Turkish siege of 1793. The shape is the same—it comes from the crescent on the Turkish flag—but the sweet yeast dough of *cornetti* is enriched with egg and sometimes even has a bit of butter tucked into it. This particular recipe makes *cornetti* that are delicate, tender, and amazingly light and airy. It is inspired by the Venetian baker's *cornetti*, which are sugary and full of butter, and uses high-gluten bread flour to produce the spectacularly light and delicious effect.

Makes enough for 20 cornetti

DOUGH
5 teaspoons (2 packages) active dry yeast or 2 small cakes (36 grams) fresh yeast
1½ cups warm water
1 stick (115 grams) unsalted butter, room temperature
5 tablespoons (75 grams) sugar
2 eggs
2⅓ cups (325 grams) unbleached all-purpose flour
2⅓ cups (325 grams) bread flour
2½ teaspoons (12 grams) salt

BY HAND

Stir the yeast into the water in a large mixing bowl; let stand until creamy, about 10 minutes. Beat in the butter, sugar, and eggs until blended. Mix the flours and the salt and stir, 1 cup at a time, into the yeast mixture until the soft dough comes together. Turn out onto a lightly floured surface. Knead lightly until smooth, about 1 minute (18 to 20 times). Do not overknead or the dough will be too elastic.

BY MIXER

Stir the yeast into the water in a mixer bowl; let stand until creamy, about 10 minutes. Beat in the butter, sugar, and eggs with the paddle until blended. Mix the flours and salt into the yeast mixture just until the dough comes together, about 30 seconds. Mix at medium speed for 1 minute. Knead on a lightly floured surface, lightly dusting the top with additional flour, until smooth, about 1 minute. Do not overknead or the dough will be too elastic.

First Rise. Place the dough in a lightly oiled bowl, cover tightly with plastic wrap, and let rise until doubled, 1 to 1½ hours.

Cornetti Dolci (continued)

Chilling. Turn the dough out onto a lightly floured surface and sprinkle the top of the dough lightly with flour. Knead 5 or 6 times or just enough to expel some of the air without developing the gluten. Flatten the dough with your hand, sprinkle the top with flour, wrap in plastic wrap, and refrigerate until the dough is cold throughout, 4 to 6 hours or overnight.

BUTTER BLOCK
4 sticks (450 grams) unsalted butter, cold
1 cup less 2 tablespoons (125 grams) unbleached all-purpose flour

BY HAND

Place the butter on a work surface. Holding a rolling pin by one handle, beat the butter until malleable and creamy. Sprinkle ½ cup of the flour on the work surface. Scrape the softened butter from the work surface with a dough scraper, and using the scraper, cut the butter into the flour. Sprinkle the remaining flour over the mixture. Working quickly, smear the butter and flour together with the dough scraper and the heel of your hand until smooth. Scrape the mixture together into a smooth block about ½ inch thick. Wrap in plastic wrap; refrigerate until cold but not hard, 15 to 20 minutes.

BY MIXER

Cut the butter into ¼-inch pieces and place the butter and flour in a mixer bowl. Beat at low speed with the paddle about 1 minute; beat at high speed until smooth, 30 seconds. Wrap in plastic wrap; refrigerate until cold, 15 to 20 minutes.

Enclosing the Butter Block. Remove the dough from the refrigerator and place on a lightly floured surface. Sprinkle the dough lightly with flour and roll into a 20 × 12-inch rectangle, ¼ inch thick, so that one short side is nearest you. Remove the butter block from the refrigerator; break off small (½ inch) pieces. Dot the butter pieces over two-thirds of the dough rectangle nearest you, leaving a 1½-inch border around the edges. Fold as if you were folding a business letter: fold the unbuttered third over the middle and fold the remaining third over the top. Pinch the edges together so that the butter does not fall out. Tap the surface of the dough with the rolling pin to evenly distribute the butter.

First Set of Turns. Turn the dough 90° so that the top flap faces your right (like a book). Sprinkle the dough and work surface lightly with flour. Roll the dough into a 20 × 12-inch rectangle, ¼ inch thick.

Fold into thirds as described above, pinch edges to seal, and tap the dough with the rolling pin to evenly distribute the butter. Rotate the dough 90° and lightly sprinkle the dough and work surface with flour. Roll out as before to a 20 × 12-inch rectangle, ¼ inch thick. You may notice that rolling is slightly harder this time. Fold into thirds as described above, pinch the edges to seal, and tap the dough with the rolling pin to distribute the butter evenly. Brush off excess flour, and straighten the sides of the dough. Wrap the dough in plastic wrap and refrigerate 45 minutes to 1 hour.

Second Set of Turns. Lightly flour the work surface and the dough. Lightly tap the surface of the dough with the rolling pin. Roll into a 20 × 12-inch rectangle, ¼ inch thick, so that one short side is nearest you. Fold again as if you were folding a business letter: the top third is folded down and the bottom third is then folded up. Pinch the edges together. Turn the dough 90° so that the top flap faces your right (like a book). Sprinkle the dough and work surface lightly with flour. If at any time the dough resists rolling or the butter is noticeably soft, refrigerate it to relax the dough or harden the butter. Roll the dough into a 20 × 12-inch rectangle, ¼ inch thick. Fold dough into thirds as described above, pinch edges to seal, and tap the dough with the rolling pin. Wrap the dough in plastic wrap and refrigerate 4 hours or overnight. Weight the dough with a brick or 5-pound bag of sugar or flour if it begins to rise.

Dough rolled to parallelogram

Croissant shapes cut from dough

Cutting. Cut the block of cold dough in two and place half on a lightly floured surface and dust the top with flour. Tap the dough with a rolling pin to flatten and expel some of the air. Roll to a 26 × 8-inch rectangle, frequently lifting the dough and sprinkling the work surface and dough lightly with flour to prevent sticking. Try to keep the edges of the dough as straight as possible. Trim the edges with a sharp knife, if necessary. Brush off any excess flour. To make equal size triangles for the *cornetti,* turn the dough so that one long edge is facing you. Make a parallelogram of the rectangle by first rolling on the diagonal from the middle of the dough to the upper left edge and then to the lower right edge. Trim the edges with a sharp knife and measure and mark the dough at 5-inch intervals on the top and bottom of the dough. Beginning at the bottom left-hand point, cut across at a diagonal to the first mark on the top edge. Cut diagonally back to the first mark on the bottom. Keep cutting triangles diagonally from top to bottom connecting at the marks. Repeat with the second piece of dough.

Cornetti Dolci (continued)

Shaping. Position a triangle so that the base is nearest to you. Pull gently on the two nearest corners, stretching them slightly. Tug dough from the center of the base towards the two nearest corners so that the base of the triangle is stretched to 6–7 inches. Gently pull the height to 10 inches. Do not pull from the tips, because the dough will break off. With one hand, hold the tip of the triangle opposite the elongated base and with the other hand roll up the triangle from the base, stretching the dough thinner as you roll. Put pressure on the sides, not the center, of the roll. Finish with the point of the triangle facing you. Repeat with the remaining triangles.

Final Rise. Place the *cornetti* on oiled or parchment-lined baking sheets. Shape each *cornetto* into a crescent by gently pulling the tips toward each other to make a half-moon shape. Cover loosely with plastic wrap and let rise until doubled, about 2 hours. To encourage the rising, you can place the sheet of *cornetti* over a bowl of warm water or place it in a turned-off oven with a pan of warm water under it. Do not let rise over direct heat, such as a pilot light or hot radiator.

GLAZE
1 egg, beaten

Brush the risen *cornetti* lightly with the beaten egg.

Baking. Heat the oven to 425° F. Bake 6 minutes. Reduce the heat to 375° F and bake until golden, about 15 minutes. Cool completely on racks.

Freezing. The dough may be frozen for up to 10 days after the final turn or after shaping. Wrap the dough airtight in aluminum foil or tightly cover the shaped dough on baking sheets with foil. Thaw in the refrigerator 24 hours before shaping or the final rise and baking.

Laying in filling

Variation. To make filled *cornetti*, use 1 teaspoon raspberry or strawberry jam, 1 teaspoon almond paste (just before baking sprinkle the tops with slivered almonds), or 1 teaspoon Pastry Cream (page 343) for each *cornetto*. Spoon the filling onto the stretched triangle about 1 inch from the base. Flatten the mound slightly and then roll up. Proceed as directed but allow 2 to 3 hours for the final rise. Bake the filled *cornetti* 3 to 5 minutes longer than the plain.

Girelle

These raisin-studded breakfast pastries are made from the *cornetti* dough. The cinnamon is definitely an American addition.

Makes 12 pastries

¾ recipe *Cornetti Dolci* dough (page 304), made through the second set of turns and refrigerated
1 egg, beaten
3½ tablespoons turbinado sugar
1½ cups (250 grams) raisins, soaked in water, drained, and patted dry
1 teaspoon ground cinnamon (optional)
3 tablespoons apricot jam
1½ teaspoons water

Place the cold dough on a lightly floured surface; sprinkle the top lightly with flour. Roll the dough into a 15 × 12-inch rectangle, lifting the dough frequently with a dough scraper and sprinkling with flour to prevent the dough from sticking. Brush the entire surface of the dough with the beaten egg. Sprinkle the sugar evenly over the egg and distribute the raisins evenly over the sugar. Sprinkle with cinnamon, if using.

Shaping. Starting with the shortest side, roll up the dough tightly, without pulling or stretching, into a log. Press the seam with your fingertips to seal it. Transfer to a sheet of aluminum foil and wrap securely. Refrigerate until cold, about 20 minutes. Cut the cold dough into 1-inch slices, using a very sharp thin-bladed knife. Place the slices, cut sides up, 2 inches apart on a parchment-lined or buttered baking sheet. Press down on each slice lightly with the palm of your hand to even it and then reshape into a circle. If the spirals are stuck together, gently separate with the tip of a knife.

Cutting dough into slices

Rising. Cover loosely with plastic wrap and let rise until doubled, 1½ to 3 hours. See rising directions for *Cornetti Dolci*, page 304.

Baking. Heat the oven to 375° F. Bake until lightly browned, 25 to 30 minutes. Remove to a rack to cool.

Glazing. Glaze *girelle* while still warm from the oven. To form a glaze, stir the apricot jam and water together over medium heat. Strain to remove any remaining chunks of fruit and lightly brush over the tops of the *girelle* with a pastry brush.

Savory Croissants

Croissant Salato Dough

Savory Croissant Dough

Although the Italians are famous for their collective sweet tooth, it isn't just sweet croissants or *cornetti* that they eat. Walk into any *caffè* bar in the morning to pick out a pastry to go with espresso or cappucino, and you will always see both sweet and savory croissants. Croissant salato dough is used for all kinds of appetizers and hors d'oeuvres, turnovers, and one baker's special recreation of the famous, delicate *focaccia di Recco,* the cheese-filled specialty of a tiny town near Genoa. If you've never made croissants before, start with the larger savory pastries, such as *Focaccia di Recco* (page 317). The smaller turnovers and *mignon* pastries require more dexterity and familiarity with croissant dough.

Makes 3 pounds (1350 grams) dough

3¾ teaspoons active dry yeast or 1½ small cakes (27 grams) fresh yeast
1 teaspoon malt syrup
1⅓ cups warm water
2 tablespoons (30 grams) unsalted butter, room temperature
2 tablespoons (30 grams) lard or unsalted butter, room temperature
2¾ cups (375 grams) unbleached all-purpose flour
1 cup less 2 tablespoons (125 grams) bread flour
2½ teaspoons (12½ grams) salt

BY HAND

Stir the yeast and malt into the water in a large mixing bowl; let stand until foamy, about 10 minutes. Beat in the butter and lard. Mix the flours and salt and stir into the yeast mixture, 1 cup at a time, until the dough comes together. Knead on a lightly floured surface until smooth, firm, and velvety, 2 to 3 minutes. Do not overknead or the dough will be too elastic.

BY MIXER

Stir the yeast and malt into the water in a large mixer bowl; let stand until foamy, about 10 minutes. Beat in the butter and lard with the paddle until blended. Mix the flours and salt and mix into the yeast mixture at the lowest speed just until the flour is absorbed. Mix at medium speed for 1 minute, no longer. Knead by hand on a lightly floured surface only 16 to 18 times. The dough should be smooth, firm, velvety, and slightly springy.

First Rise. Place the dough in a lightly oiled bowl, cover tightly with plastic wrap, and let rise until doubled, 1 to 1½ hours.

Chilling. Punch the dough down hard on a lightly floured surface; flatten to a 1-inch-thick circle without kneading it. Wrap in plastic wrap and refrigerate until the dough is absolutely cold throughout, at least 3 hours or overnight.

BUTTER BLOCK
4 sticks (450 grams) unsalted butter, or 3 sticks plus 1 tablespoon (355 grams) unsalted butter and ½ cup (115 grams) lard, cold
½ cup (70 grams) unbleached all-purpose flour

BY HAND

Place the butter on a work surface. Holding a rolling pin by one handle, beat the butter until malleable and creamy. Sprinkle the flour on the work surface. Scrap the softened butter from the work surface with a dough scraper, and, using the scraper, cut the butter into the flour. Working quickly, smear the butter and flour together with the dough scraper and the heel of your hand until smooth. Scrape the mixture together into a smooth block about ½ inch thick. It should still be cold, but if it isn't, refrigerate, wrapped in plastic wrap, 15 to 20 minutes.

BY MIXER

Cut the butter into ½-inch pieces and place the butter and flour in a mixer bowl. Beat at low speed with the paddle 1 to 2 minutes; beat at medium speed until smooth, about 2 minutes. The mixture should still be stiff and still cold, but if it isn't, refrigerate, wrapped in plastic wrap, 15 to 20 minutes.

BY PROCESSOR

Cut the butter into ½-inch pieces and place the butter and flour in a food processor fitted with the steel blade. Process until smooth.

Enclosing the Butter Block. Remove the dough from the refrigerator and place on a lightly floured surface. Sprinkle the dough lightly with flour and roll into a 20 × 12-inch rectangle, so that one short side is nearest you. Break off small (½ inch) pieces from the butter block and dot them over two-thirds of the dough rectangle nearest you, leaving a 1-inch border around the edges. Fold as if you were folding a business letter: fold the unbuttered third over the middle and fold the remaining third over the top. Pinch the edges together so the butter doesn't fall out. Shape the folded dough with your fingers to even the edges and keep the rectangular shape. Tap the surface of the dough lightly with the rolling pin to evenly distribute the butter.

Croissant Salato Dough (continued)

First Set of Turns. Turn the dough 90° so that the top flap faces your right (like a book). Lightly flour the work surface and the dough. Roll the dough into a 20 × 12-inch rectangle, lifting the dough and lightly dusting the work surface with the flour to prevent it from sticking. The dough should slide freely on the table and you can brush off any excess flour later. Fold again as if you were folding a business letter; pinch edges to seal, and tap the surface evenly with the rolling pin. Turn the dough 90° so that the top flap faces your right (like a book). Sprinkle the dough and surface lightly with flour. Roll the dough into a 20 × 12-inch rectangle. Fold the dough again into thirds and brush off the excess flour. Pinch the edges to seal and tap the entire surface lightly with the rolling pin. Wrap the dough in plastic wrap and refrigerate for 45 minutes to 1 hour.

Second Set of Turns. Lightly flour the work surface and the dough. Place the dough on the surface with the top flap facing your right. Lightly tap the surface of the dough evenly with the rolling pin. Roll into a 20 × 12-inch rectangle, rolling first for length, then width. You may need to pull the dough gently with your fingers to get the right width. Adjust the corners carefully to keep the dough even. Fold the short edges to meet in the middle and then fold in half, flipping one piece over the other (as if closing a book). Brush off the excess flour and turn the dough 90° so that the top flap faces your right. Lightly tap the surface of the dough evenly with the rolling pin. You may need to refrigerate the dough for 30 minutes before the next turn if the dough is feisty and fights back. Roll again into a 20 × 12-inch rectangle and fold like a business letter (thirds) and brush off the excess flour. Pinch the edges to seal and lightly tap the surface of the dough evenly with the rolling pin. Wrap in plastic wrap and refrigerate at least 3 hours or overnight.

Freezing. The dough may be frozen for up to 10 days after the final turn or after shaping. Wrap the dough airtight in aluminum foil or tightly cover the shaped dough on baking sheets with foil. Thaw in the refrigerator for 24 hours.

Fazzoletti Salati
Savory Turnovers

Makes 20 turnovers

1½ pounds (675 grams, ½ recipe) Croissant Salato Dough (recipe page 310)
Any Savory Filling (page 314)

Cutting. Place the cold dough on a lightly floured surface and dust the top with flour. Roll the dough into a 18½ × 15-inch rectangle, keeping the edges as straight as possible. Trim the edges, as necessary, with a sharp knife. Cut the dough into twenty 3½-inch squares.

Filling and Shaping. Stretch the center of each square slightly to make a pocket for the filling. Spoon ¾ to 1 teaspoon of the filling on each square. Lightly moisten a soft pastry brush with water and brush the circumference of 1 square; immediately fold the dough in half to make a triangle. Press the edges firmly to seal in the filling, without pressing directly on the cut edges. Repeat with the remaining squares. Place 2 inches apart on buttered or parchment-lined baking sheets.

Rising. Cover with plastic wrap and let rise until doubled, 1½ to 2½ hours.

Baking. Heat the oven to 450° F. Bake on a rack in the upper third of the oven 6 minutes. Reduce the heat to 375° F and bake until golden brown, 12 to 14 minutes longer. Cool completely on racks.

Variation. To make smaller turnovers, which are the perfect size for hors d'oeuvres, roll 1 pound (450 grams, ⅓ recipe) dough into a 20 × 10-inch rectangle and cut into 3-inch squares. Proceed as directed, spooning ¾ teaspoon of the filling on each square. They will need to bake about 2 minutes less than the slightly larger turnovers.

Canoe Salate

Savory Canoes

Makes 16 pastries

1 pound (450 grams, ⅓ recipe) Croissant Salato Dough (page 310)
Any Savory Filling (recipes follow)

Cutting. Place the cold dough on a lightly floured surface and dust the top with flour. Roll the dough into a rectangle slightly larger than 24½ × 8 inches, keeping the edges as straight as possible. Trim the edges, if necessary, to 24 × 7 inches with a sharp knife. Cut the dough into 16 rectangles, 3½ × 3 inches.

Filling and Shaping. Spoon 1 teaspoon of the filling on the center of each rectangle. Lightly moisten a soft pastry brush with water and brush the long edges of each rectangle. Fold the short edges over to meet; they will barely meet at the center because of the filling but will overlap at the sides by ¾ inch. Open up the center so that the filling peeks out. Press the edges firmly to seal, without pressing directly on the cut edges. Repeat with the remaining rectangles. Place 1 to 1½ inches apart on oiled or parchment-lined baking sheets.

Rising. Cover with plastic wrap and let rise until doubled, 1½ to 2½ hours.

Baking. Heat the oven to 425° F. Bake on a rack in the upper third of the oven 6 minutes. Reduce the heat to 375° F and bake until golden brown, 12 to 14 minutes longer. Cool completely on racks.

Savory Fillings for Croissant Salato Dough

I was so inspired by the buttery, flaky quality of savory croissant dough that I dreamed up these fillings. Most use just a few ingredients, and you can certainly create your own variations.

Makes enough for 16 to 20 turnovers or canoes

Ricotta, Prosciutto and Cheese Filling

⅔ cup ricotta
1½ tablespoons diced prosciutto
2 tablespoons grated *pecorino* or freshly grated Parmesan cheese
⅛ teaspoon freshly grated nutmeg
1 egg

Press the ricotta through a wire-mesh sieve into a mixing bowl; stir in the prosciutto, cheese, nutmeg, and egg with a wooden spoon or rubber spatula until well blended. Or place the ricotta in a food processor fitted with the steel blade and process with several pulses; add the prosciutto, cheese, nutmeg, and egg and process until blended.

Tomato Filling

4 to 6 tablespoons chopped sun-dried tomatoes (packed in oil)
⅔ cup fresh bread crumbs
⅔ cup water or half water and half olive oil, preferably from the jar of tomatoes
2 tablespoons freshly grated Parmesan cheese

Process all ingredients in a blender or a food processor fitted with the steel blade until blended.

Olive Paste Filling

½ cup fresh bread crumbs
⅔ cup olive paste
½ teaspoon minced garlic
2 tablespoons freshly grated Parmesan cheese
2 tablespoons milk

Process all ingredients in a blender or a food processor fitted with the steel blade until blended.

Anchovy Filling

2 small cans (3½ ounces, 100 grams, each) flat anchovy fillets (packed in oil), drained
1 cup fresh bread crumbs
½ cup milk
2 tablespoons (30 grams) unsalted butter, room temperature

Process all ingredients in a blender or a food processor fitted with the steel blade until blended.

Croissants Mignons Salati con Cumino e Sale

Tiny Savory Croissants with Caraway Seeds and Salt

Serve with smoked turkey, prosciutto, or ham. These make perfect hors d'oeuvres.

Makes 26 pastries

1 pound (450 grams, ⅓ recipe) Croissant Salato Dough (page 310)
1 egg, beaten
1 tablespoon water
Salt
Caraway seeds

Cutting. Place the cold dough on a lightly floured surface and dust the top with flour. Roll the dough into a 28 × 11-inch rectangle. Trim to a 28 × 10-inch rectangle with a sharp knife; then cut the rectangle lengthwise in half. The croissants will be formed from triangles cut from the 2 pastry strips, now each 28 × 5 inches. Cover the strip of dough that you are not working with. Place 1 strip on the work surface so that one long edge is facing you. Measure each strip into 14 triangles by marking off every 4 inches at the top and base. Beginning at the lower left-hand corner, cut across diagonally to the first mark on the top. Cut straight back to the first mark on the bottom. Keep cutting triangles by cutting diagonally from bottom to top and straight down from top to bottom, connecting at the marks. Repeat with the second strip of dough.

Shaping. Position a triangle so that the base is nearest you. Stretch the base to 5 inches and gently stretch the height to 9 inches. Holding the top with one hand, tightly roll up the triangle from the base with the other hand. Put firm but gentle pressure on the sides, not the center, of the roll. Mix the egg and water in a small bowl and brush the tops with the egg wash. Sprinkle with a pinch of salt and a dash of caraway seeds. Repeat with the remaining triangles. Place 1½ inches apart on buttered or parchment-lined baking sheets. Don't shape the ends into a crescent, like *cornetti*, but leave them straight.

Rising. Cover loosely with a towel and let rise until doubled, 1 to 2 hours.

Baking. Heat the oven to 425° F. Bake on a rack in the upper third of the oven 6 minutes. Reduce the heat to 375° F and bake until dark golden, 12 to 14 minutes longer. Cool completely on racks.

Focaccia di Recco

Cheese Focaccia from Recco

Signs on every restaurant and bakery in the seaside of Recco boast of Focaccia di Formaggio, which is essentially two veils of strudel-like dough enclosing delicate *straccinella* (a local cheese). This elegant fantasy with its melting cheese interior was inspired by the famous version from the restaurant Manuellina but, as baked by Giancarlo Grignani in Milan, it uses flaky croissant dough, stracchino cheese and a bit of salt. It is as elegant a dish as Italy offers.

Makes one 9- to 11-inch focaccia

1 pound (450 grams, ⅓ recipe) Croissant Salato Dough (page 310)
6 to 8 ounces (180 to 225 grams) Crescenza, Stracchino, or Taleggio cheese, thinly sliced
1 to 1½ teaspoons oil
Generous pinch of salt

Shaping and Filling. Place the cold dough on a lightly floured surface and dust the top with flour. Roll the dough into a 20 × 10-inch rectangle and cut crosswise in half. Pull out the sides of each square and shape each into a rough circle; trim off the square corner edges. The dough circles can be 9 to 10 inches in diameter, but they should be the same size. Place 1 dough circle on a baking sheet lined with parchment or brown paper. Arrange the cheese over the circle on the baking sheet, leaving a 1½-inch border. Brush the edge with water. Place the second dough circle over the cheese. Trim and seal the edges. Brush the surface lightly with water.

Rising. Cover with plastic wrap and let rise in a spot warm enough to aid the rising but not so warm that the butter will melt in the dough. The dough should be puffy and risen, although not truly doubled, about 2 hours for the 9-inch and 2½ to 3 hours for the 11-inch pastry.

Baking. Heat the oven to 450° F. Just before baking, brush the top with 1 to 1½ teaspoons oil and sprinkle with a generous pinch of salt. Bake on a rack in the upper third of the oven 8 to 10 minutes. Reduce the heat to 350° F. and bake the smaller *focaccia* 20 minutes longer and the larger *focaccia* 22 to 25 minutes longer. Serve warm or reheat before eating.

Puff Pastry

Pasta Sfogliata

Pasta sfogliata (puff pastry) is just what its name implies: sheets and sheets of fine dough, each separated by an exquisitely thin layer of butter, that rise magically from a flat rectangle, about ½ inch thick, into a phenomenally delicate and flaky pastry dough 4 to 5 inches high. Italian bakers use puff pastry for a dazzling array of hors d'oeuvres and sweets. They sprinkle strips of dough the width of baby's fingers with cheeses, anchovy paste, sesame or poppy seeds, and then twist and bake them into straws to be nibbled upon; they make fine flaky snacks with the ironic name of *rustici;* they construct sweet puff pastry into turnovers, tarts, little horns, and fanciful boats, the vehicles for pastry cream and fruit.

Many Italian cookbooks with recipes for *pasta sfogliata* begin by suggesting that the reader go to the nearest bakery and buy the dough, or, failing that, to the supermarket for one of the frozen varieties that are now available. Unless you have a special arrangement with your baker, you probably won't be able to negotiate such a deal, but, if you have a fine gourmet grocery store in your area, you're in luck. Since there is nothing more dramatic, delicate, and delicious than puff pastry made at home, I encourage you to make your own.

There is no question that *pasta sfogliata* takes a bit of practice and patience. The dough encloses a block of cold butter and is then rolled out and folded six times. The dough must be chilled between turns but, by the end, you'll have layered the dough into a miracle of light flakiness. You will need time—at least six hours, although you can easily refrigerate the dough overnight and work it into your schedule—and you will need practice, because there are a few tricks to making puff pastry. But, once you've mastered it, you'll be able to make such extraordinary dishes that you'll actually be delighted that Italian bakers use puff pastry with abandon.

Because the classical method of making *pasta sfogliata* is so time-consuming, I'd recommend making a big batch and freezing what you can't use in plastic wrap or aluminum foil. The dough keeps wonderfully in the refrigerator for two to three days or in the freezer up to three months. Allow the dough to thaw slowly in the refrigerator over twenty-four hours.

A good rolling pin, 15 to 18 inches long, a good work surface— some people insist on marble, although I love my butcher-block table—and cold ingredients are essential. The minute your dough starts to go limp or your butter block gets soft, refrigerate it until it has chilled enough to proceed, usually about 30 minutes. If the dough snaps back on itself when you are rolling it out, let it rest in the refrigerator so that the gluten relaxes; after anywhere from 30 minutes to 2 hours, it will be more than happy to cooperate. Be sure to keep your work surface and your dough floured enough so that the dough can move freely on the table. You can always brush off the excess flour at the end, and you won't be caught with layers tearing because they stuck to the surface. The most important secret of puff pastry is in the chilling that is necessary after each set of turns to keep it tender and malleable as the process progresses. You'll need patience, time, and a bit of self confidence, but, once you've tackled it and succeeded, you'll be delighted with your accomplishment and can truly feel that yours is a fine Italian hand in the kitchen.

Makes 2 pounds 10½ ounces (1200 grams) dough

DOUGH
2¾ cups (375 grams) unbleached all-purpose flour
1 cup (125 grams) cake or pastry flour
1½ teaspoons (8 grams) salt
1 stick (115 grams) unsalted butter, cool room temperature, cut into
    ½-inch pieces
1 cup cold water, plus 1 to 2 tablespoons if needed
1 tablespoon fresh lemon juice

BY HAND

Mix the all-purpose flour and cake flour in a large bowl. Remove ½ cup of the flour mixture and reserve for use in the butter block. Stir the salt into the remaining flour mixture. Add the butter and work it in with your fingertips or a pastry blender until the mixture resembles coarse meal. Mix 1 cup water and the lemon juice. Gradually add the liquid to the flour mixture, tossing with a fork, until the flour is evenly moistened and the dough begins to clean the side of the bowl. If the dough is dry, add the additional water, 1 tablespoon at a time, as needed. Turn out onto a floured work surface and press (do not knead) the dough together into a round disk, about 1 inch thick. Wrap in plastic wrap and refrigerate until firm and very cold, at least 1 to 2 hours or overnight.

BY MIXER

Place the unbleached flour and cake flour in a large mixer bowl and stir to blend. Remove ½ cup of the flour mixture and reserve for

Pasta Sfogliata (continued)

use in the butter block. Stir the salt into the remaining flour mixture. Add the butter; beat with the paddle on low speed until the mixture resembles coarse meal. Mix 1 cup water and the lemon juice. Pour the liquid in a thin, steady stream into the flour mixture while beating on low speed. Increase the speed slightly and beat until the dough cleans the side of the bowl, 1 to 2 minutes. If the dough is dry, add the additional water, 1 tablespoon at a time, as needed. Beat at medium speed for 20 seconds. Turn out onto a floured work surface and press (do not knead) the dough together into a round disk, about 1 inch thick. Wrap in plastic wrap and refrigerate until firm and very cold, at least 1 to 2 hours or overnight.

BY PROCESSOR

If the capacity of your food processor is 8 cups or less, process this dough in 2 batches. Mix the unbleached flour and cake flour in a large bowl. Remove ½ cup of the flour mixture and reserve for use in the butter block. Stir the salt into the remaining flour mixture. Place the flour mixture in a food processor fitted with the steel blade. Place the *cold* butter pieces on top of the flour and process with 8 to 10 pulses until the mixture resembles coarse meal. With the machine running, pour 1 cup cold water and the lemon juice in a thin, steady stream through the feed tube. Add the additional water, 1 tablespoon at a time, as needed. Do not process until the dough gathers into a ball; it should still be ragged. Turn out onto a lightly floured surface and press (do not knead) into a round disk, about 1 inch thick. Wrap in plastic wrap and refrigerate until firm and very cold, at least 1 to 2 hours or overnight.

BUTTER BLOCK
The dough should be completely chilled before you make the butter block. Once the butter block is the correct consistency, it is best to proceed with the remaining steps.

3 sticks (340 grams) unsalted butter, very cold
½ cup flour mixture reserved from the flour for the dough

Place the butter on a work surface. Holding the rolling pin by one handle, beat the butter until malleable and creamy. Sprinkle the flour on the work surface. Using the dough scraper, scrape the butter from the work surface and cut the butter into the flour. Working quickly, smear the butter and flour together until the mixture is smooth. The mixture should be cool and malleable, not cold and hard or soft and runny. Flatten to a ½-inch-thick block. Refrigerate or let stand at room temperature to harden or soften it if necessary.

Enclosing the Butter Block. Lightly flour the work surface. Remove the dough from the refrigerator and lightly flour both sides. With a floured rolling pin, tap the dough gently across the surface both horizontally and vertically. Roll the dough carefully into an 18-inch circle, ½ inch thick, frequently lifting the dough with a dough scraper and lightly dusting the work surface with flour to prevent sticking. Place the butter block in the center of the dough and fold the dough over the butter to completely enclose it. The edges of the dough should overlap slightly. Lift the package with the dough scraper and sprinkle flour on the work surface and the top of the dough. Tap the dough lightly with the rolling pin both horizontally and vertically. Begin to roll out the dough, pressing very lightly from the center towards you and then from the center away from you. Roll the dough carefully into an 18 × 9-inch rectangle, ¼ inch thick, keeping the edges as straight as possible. If the dough becomes too warm, transfer it to a baking sheet and refrigerate just long enough to chill it, usually about 30 minutes. Dust the surface of the dough and the work surface frequently with flour as you roll, lifting the edges of the dough with the dough scraper. Do not touch the dough with your hands if possible.

Folding in the butter block

First Set of Turns. Fold the top third of the dough down over the middle and then fold the bottom third up over the top. Press the edges to seal. Turn the rectangle 90° so that the top flap faces your right (like a book). Roll again into an 18 × 9-inch rectangle and repeat the folding. Brush off excess flour. Wrap in plastic wrap and refrigerate 1 hour.

Pasta Sfogliata (continued)

Second Set of Turns. Roll the dough again into an 18 × 9-inch rectangle. Fold and turn as described for the first set of turns. Reroll; dust the work surface and dough lightly with flour to prevent sticking. Fold and turn once again. (This is the fourth and last turn if you are making *Ventagli.*) Brush off excess flour. Wrap in plastic wrap and refrigerate 1 hour.

Third Set of Turns. Roll the dough again into an 18 × 9-inch rectangle. Fold and turn as described for the first set of turns. Reroll; dust the work surface and dough lightly with flour to prevent sticking. Fold and turn once again. This is the sixth and final turn. Brush off any excess flour from the surface of the dough. Wrap in plastic wrap and refrigerate 4 to 6 hours before using in any of the following recipes calling for *pasta sfogliata.*

Storing. The dough can be stored in the refrigerator up to 3 to 4 days or frozen up to 2 or 3 months. Puff pastry is best frozen after either the fourth or last turn. Wrap airtight in foil and then wrap again in plastic wrap and freeze. Thaw in the refrigerator for 24 hours. Give it the last 2 turns, if necessary, and refrigerate just for 2 hours before rolling out the dough for shaping.

Binario di Ricotta
Ricotta-Filled Pastry Tart

Inside this long, thin puff pastry case is a creamy ricotta filling. Be sure to give a scalloped edge to the pastry case with the back of a butter knife.

⅔ cup (100 grams) raisins
3 tablespoons Marsala, rum, or maraschino liqueur
¾ cup plus 1 tablespoon (200 grams) ricotta
⅓ cup (70 grams) sugar
2½ tablespoons unbleached all-purpose flour
2 egg yolks, beaten
1½ teaspoons vanilla extract
¼ cup (40 grams) finely chopped candied orange peel or mixed candied fruit, or finely diced zest of ½ orange
10½ ounces (300 grams, ¼ recipe) *Pasta Sfogliata* (page 318)

Combine the raisins and Marsala in a small bowl; let stand until the raisins are plumped, about 30 minutes. Press the ricotta through a wire-mesh sieve or process briefly in a food processor fitted with the steel blade. Beat the ricotta and sugar with a wooden spoon in a large bowl until creamy. Stir in the flour. Add the egg yolks and beat until blended. Stir in the raisins with the Marsala, vanilla, and candied orange peel. Refrigerate covered while preparing the pastry.

Cutting and Shaping. Roll the cold dough on a lightly floured surface into a rectangle slightly larger than 16 × 8½ inches. Pick up the edges of the dough with the dough scraper frequently while rolling to let the dough shrink back into shape before rerolling. Using a ruler and a very sharp knife, trim the dough to exactly 16 × 8½ inches.

1.

2.

1. Cutting strips.

2. Positioning strips on the dough.

Using the straight edge of the ruler, cut a 1-inch-wide strip from each edge of the rectangle. Don't pick the strips up, just scoot them to one side. Very carefully transfer the remaining rectangle of dough to a parchment-lined baking sheet, placing your hands well under the dough, without pulling at the edges or stretching the rectangle. Dampen a soft pastry brush with water and brush a thin border around the rectangle. Gently transfer the long pastry strips to the long sides of the rectangle and the short strips to the short sides of the rectangle. Tap down gently with your fingertips in the center of the strips, without pressing on the cut edges. Dampen the strips where they overlap and trim the excess dough with a sharp knife. Prick the bottom of the tart shell evenly with a fork. Scallop the edges, using the flat side of a table knife and drawing the dough up between two fingers.

Binario di Ricotta (continued)

Chilling. Refrigerate the dough until cold, at least 1 hour or overnight. Cover airtight as soon as dough is cold if storing longer than 1 hour.

Baking. Heat the oven to 425° F. Bake for 10 minutes, pricking the dough every 3 minutes to keep it from rising too much. Don't be timid; really let your fork do a vigorous dance on the bottom of the tart shell. Reduce the heat to 350° F and bake 10 minutes longer. Cool on a rack.

Filling. Spoon the filling into the baked pastry and spread evenly. Bake at 350° F until set, about 15 minutes.

Variation. To make *Binario di Sfoglia* (Puff Pastry Case), you need only line the puff pastry rectangle with strips on the long sides. Proceed as directed but bake until golden, about 20 minutes longer at 350° F, so that the case is fully baked. Cool on a rack. Fill as desired or spread ¼ inch Pastry Cream (page 343) over the pastry and top with rows of fresh whole strawberries.

Strudel di Mele
Apple Strudel

The apple strudel of the northern Alto Adige region is an edible memory of the days before World War I when the whole area was the South Tirol of Austria. The German-speaking Austrians who live there have remained true to their culinary traditions as well as their language—everything is bilingual including street signs and shop names—and apple strudel is as ubiquitous as apple pie is in America. The plains and hillsides stretching as far north as the Alps are extensively planted with orchards of the apple trees that furnish the red and golden Delicious and Granny Smiths of this strudel's succulent interior.

Makes 1 strudel; 8 servings (recipe can easily be doubled to make 2 strudels)

2½ cups peeled and diced (¾ inch) cooking apples
Grated zest of ½ lemon
¾ teaspoon fresh lemon juice
¾ cup (150 grams) turbinado sugar

¾ cup (80 grams) cake crumbs—use the leftovers from a particularly good cake made with nuts, raisins, or dried fruit and grind in a food processor or blender
½ cup (80 grams) raisins
¼ cup pine nuts
2 tablespoons apricot jam
¾ teaspoon ground cinnamon
¼ teaspoon salt
10½ ounces (300 grams, ¼ recipe) *Pasta Sfogliata* (page 318)
1 egg yolk
1 tablespoon water

Toss the apples with the lemon zest and juice. Add the sugar, cake crumbs, raisins, pine nuts, apricot jam, cinnamon, and salt and stir until blended. Set aside until ready to use.

Cutting and Shaping. Roll the cold dough on a lightly floured surface into a 16 × 11-inch rectangle. Using a straight edge and a sharp knife, trim the dough to 15 × 9½-inch rectangle. Carefully transfer, without stretching, to a parchment-lined baking sheet. Using a ruler, make light indentations in the dough 2½ inches in from each long side. This will leave a middle strip of dough about 4½ inches wide. Spoon the apple filling evenly along this middle strip. Make 2½-inch-long cuts, 1¼ inches apart, in both long sides of the rectangle. Carefully separate the dough strips with your fingers. Cut off and discard the first strip on each side from the far end and flip the small flap of dough over the filling. Starting at the far end, overlap opposite strips on a modified diagonal over the filling forming a modified braid. As you work, brush the underside of each strip with a lightly dampened pastry brush. At the near end, cut off the final strip on each side. Finish the braid by folding up the small flap and using the last strip to seal the end. Refrigerate 1 hour.

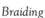

Braiding

Baking. Heat the oven to 450° F. Mix the egg yolk and water and brush the top lightly with the egg wash. Bake on a rack in the upper third of the oven 5 minutes. Reduce the heat to 375° F and bake 55 minutes longer. If after 30 minutes the top is too dark, reduce the heat to 325° F to finish baking. Cool on a rack.

Canoe di Mele
Apple Canoes

A fantasy of puff pastry: canoe-shaped pastry boats layered with rum-spiked pastry cream and topped with sugar-glazed apples.

Makes 9 pastries

1 pound 5 ounces (600 grams, ½ recipe) *Pasta Sfogliata* (page 318)
2 eggs, beaten
9 tablespoons Pastry Cream (page 343)
2 cooking apples, peeled, cored, and cut into ⅛-inch slices
2 tablespoons turbinado sugar
⅓ cup apricot jam
1 teaspoon water
1 teaspoon fresh lemon juice

Positioning apples atop pastry cream

Cutting. Roll the cold dough on a lightly floured surface into a 16 × 10-inch rectangle, ⅛ inch thick. Using a straight edge and a sharp knife, trim to a 15 × 9-inch rectangle. Cut the dough into nine 5 × 3-inch rectangles. Brush the surface with the beaten eggs. Gently stretch each rectangle very slightly from the short ends.

Shaping and Filling. Position 1 rectangle with a long side facing you. Place 1 tablespoon of the pastry cream on the center of the rectangle. Place 4 or 5 apple slices, slightly overlapping, diagonally across the rectangle and on top of the pastry cream. Brush the edges of the dough lightly with the beaten eggs. Fold 1 short side of the dough, from left to right, over the apples to the center. Fold the other short side of the dough, from right to left, over the apples to the center. Press the edges to seal. Don't worry if you can't see the apples inside; the center opens when it is baked. Using a dough scraper or spatula, carefully transfer to a parchment-lined baking sheet. Repeat with the remaining dough, pastry cream, and apples. Space 2 inches apart on the baking sheet.

Refrigerate covered loosely with plastic wrap, at least 1 hour but no longer than overnight.

Folding up the dough

Baking. Heat the oven to 400° F. Lightly brush the tops with the beaten egg and sprinkle with sugar. Bake until lightly browned, about 30 minutes. Remove to a rack to cool.

Glazing. Combine the apricot jam, water, and lemon juice in a small saucepan. Place over low heat, stirring constantly until hot. Brush over the apple canoes while they are still warm. Eat while still slightly warm or at room temperature.

Ventaglini
Little Fans

In France these sugar-glazed and caramelized pastries are known as *palmiers*, or palm leaves, but when you cross the border into Italy, they become *ventagli* or *ventaglini*, little fans of delicate puff pastry that are crunchy with the sugar that covers their folds and shiny surfaces.

Makes 26 pastries

1 cup (200 grams) sugar
1 pound 5 ounces (600 grams, ½ recipe) *Pasta Sfogliata* (page 318), made through two sets of turns

Sprinkle ½ cup of the sugar onto your work surface, place the cold dough on top of it, and give the dough its last two turns. Roll the dough into a 15 × 12-inch rectangle. Fold it in thirds, as for a business letter. Press the edges to seal and tap the dough lightly with the rolling pin both horizontally and vertically. Turn the rectangle 90°, so that the top flap faces your right (like a book). Roll into a 15 × 12-inch rectangle about ¼ inch thick, dusting the surface with the sugar on your work surface to prevent sticking and lifting the dough frequently with the dough scraper. Fold in thirds once again. Lift the dough and sprinkle the sugar that remains on the surface over and under the dough. Work in as much sugar as you can.

Shaping. Position the dough on your work surface so that the short edge is nearest you. Fold 1½ inches from the top toward the center. Fold 1½ inches from the bottom up towards the center. Continue to fold the dough from the top and bottom until they meet at the center, and then fold in half as if you were closing a book. The dough will now be 10 layers thick. Tap the entire surface firmly with your rolling pin. Cut the dough crosswise into ½-inch slices, about

Folding the dough toward the center

Closing the "book"

Ventaglini (continued)

the width of a finger. Place the *ventagli*, cut sides up, 2 to 3 inches apart on parchment-lined baking sheets. Sprinkle about ½ to ¾ teaspoon of the remaining sugar over each pastry and cover with plastic wrap. Reserve any more remaining sugar for the baking.

Refrigerate for about 30 minutes. The dough must be cold but do not refrigerate too long because the sugar will ooze out during the baking and will not caramelize properly.

Baking. Heat the oven to 400° F. Open the top of each piece of dough like a flower by separating the layers, then pinch the bottom together. *Ventagli* look like the little fans for which they are named, but they also resemble tulips or fuchsia blossoms. Sprinkle the remaining sugar over the cookies. Bake until the tops are golden brown and well caramelized, about 10 minutes. Using a spatula, check the bottoms; as each caramelizes, turn it over and bake until equally caramelized on the other side, 5 to 10 minutes. Watch them carefully, because they burn with almost no warning and they bake at surprisingly different speeds. Place the *ventagli* on a rack to cool. Be sure they are completely cooled before you stack them or they'll stick to each other. They keep well for at least a week in an airtight container.

Fazzoletti Dolci
Little Handkerchiefs of Puff Pastry

These little pastries, filled with a delicate ricotta, raisin, and rum-flavored filling, are really turnovers, Italian style.

Makes 12 pastries

7 ounces (200 grams) ricotta
5 tablespoons (80 grams) granulated sugar
2 egg yolks
3 tablespoons rum, Marsala, or maraschino liqueur
1½ tablespoons vanilla extract
2 teaspoons unbleached all-purpose flour
⅔ cup (100 grams) raisins or ⅓ cup (50 grams) finely chopped candied orange peel and ⅓ cup (50 grams) raisins
10½ ounces (300 grams, ¼ recipe) *Pasta Sfogliata* (page 318)
1 to 2 eggs, beaten
Confectioners' sugar (optional)

Press the ricotta through a wire-mesh sieve into a mixing bowl or process with several pulses in a food processor fitted with the steel blade and transfer to a mixing bowl. Add the sugar, egg yolks, rum, vanilla, and flour and stir to blend. Stir in the raisins and orange peel, if using. Refrigerate covered until very cold, about 1½ to 2 hours or overnight.

Cutting. Place the cold dough on a lightly floured surface and dust the top lightly with flour. Roll the dough into a rectangle ⅛ inch thick and slightly larger than 20 × 15 inches. This is very fine thin dough that must have straight edges. Trim the edges with a sharp knife. Cut the dough into twelve 5-inch squares.

Filling and Shaping. Stretch the center of each square gently, taking care not to handle the cut edges, to make a pocket for the filling. Spoon 2 tablespoons of the filling on each square. Brush the circumference of 1 square with the beaten egg; fold the dough in half, enclosing the filling and making a triangle. Press the edges firmly to seal in the filling, without pressing directly on the cut edges. Repeat with the remaining squares. Place 2 inches apart on parchment-lined baking sheets.

Chilling. Refrigerate at least 1 hour. If you don't want to bake them all, freeze the cold unbaked pastries in plastic bags. You can bake the frozen pastries without thawing them first.

Glazing. Brush the tops with the beaten egg and poke 2 or 3 little holes in each to allow steam to escape. Sprinkle the pastries with confectioners' sugar, if you want.

Baking. Heat oven to 400° F. Bake until golden, about 30 minutes. Transfer to racks to cool.

Cannoncini
Little Cannons

These pastries look just like the little cannons they are named for, but, instead of being filled with lethal ammunition, they are rich with pastry cream, which is lethal only for the waistline. These shiny little spirals of puff pastry are found all over Italy from Piedmont and the Veneto to the tip of the boot and are favorites of children who love to bite into one side and feel the cream shoot out the other.

Makes 10 pastries

8 ounces (225 grams, about $\frac{1}{5}$ recipe) *Pasta Sfogliata* (page 318)
1 egg, beaten
$\frac{1}{3}$ cup (70 grams) sugar
$1\frac{1}{4}$ to $1\frac{1}{2}$ cups Pastry Cream (page 343) or $\frac{3}{4}$ cup cold whipping or heavy cream, whipped and flavored with $1\frac{1}{2}$ tablespoons sugar and $\frac{1}{2}$ teaspoon vanilla extract

Rolled dough measured for cutting

Cutting and Shaping. Roll the cold dough on a lightly floured work surface into a 10 × 8-inch rectangle, ¼ to ½ inch thick. Cut the dough crosswise into ten 1-inch-wide strips. Butter cannoli sticks or forms. Wrap 1 strip of the dough around each cannoli stick, moistening it with a brush while rotating the mold; overlap the dough about ¼ inch as you wrap, leaving 1 inch of the stick uncovered at one end. Lightly brush the wrapped dough with the beaten egg and then roll in the sugar. Place the sticks 2 inches apart on a parchment-lined baking sheet.

Refrigerate covered for 30 minutes. The dough can also be stored, wrapped airtight, in the freezer at this point and baked later.

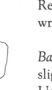

Wrapping the dough around cannoli stick

Baking. Heat the oven to 400° F. Bake until lightly browned and slightly caramelized, about 20 minutes. Let cool completely on a rack. Using the tip of a knife, gently remove the cannoli sticks.

Filling. Just before serving, fill a pastry bag with the pastry cream or flavored whipped cream. Pipe each *cannoncino* full of cream. Some bakers dip the ends in chocolate chips or biscotti crumbs or dust the pastries lightly with confectioners' sugar.

Savory Appetizers

Salatini alle Acciughe

Anchovy-Flavored Straws

In Italy these savory appetizers are also called *stuzzichini*. This piece of Italian slang comes from the word *stuzzicare*, which means to prod or poke, and these lovely buttery puff pastry straws are meant to excite your tastebuds. Like French *amuse-gueules*, they melt in your mouth and then surprise it with the bite of anchovy at the end.

Makes about 24 inch-long straws

10½ ounces (300 grams, ¼ recipe) *Pasta Sfogliata* **(page 318)**
2 tablespoons anchovy paste

Place the cold dough on a lightly floured surface and dust the top lightly with flour. Roll the dough into a 16 × 8½-inch rectangle, about ¼ inch thick. Beat the anchovy paste vigorously with a fork or wooden spoon and then spread it over half the dough. Fold the dough in half so that the short ends meet, enclosing the filling. Lightly roll into a 10 × 8½-inch rectangle, distributing the paste evenly. Straighten the edges with your hands so that the dough looks neat and trim.

Chilling. Cover the dough with plastic wrap and refrigerate until completely cold, at least 30 minutes.

Cutting and Shaping. Place the dough on a lightly floured surface. Cut lengthwise into ½-inch-wide strips, using a sharp knife and a straight edge. Twist each strip 3 or 4 times, so that it looks like an old-fashioned barber's pole, and place 1 inch apart on unoiled aluminum baking sheets. Press the edges down firmly to anchor them in place. If they pop up, simply retwist them and press them firmly back in place. I like to use the backs of 10-inch-wide baking pans so that the edges can be pressed onto the edges of the pans; it seems to help.

Baking. Heat the oven to 400° F. Bake until golden, 15 to 18 minutes. Transfer to racks to cool. You may reheat at 300° F for 5 minutes before serving.

Salatini al Sesamo
Sesame-Seed Straws

Makes about 2 dozen straws

10½ ounces (300 grams, ¼ recipe) *Pasta Sfogliata* **(page 318)**
1 egg, beaten
1 teaspoon water
½ cup (75 grams) sesame seeds

Place the cold dough on a lightly floured surface and dust the top lightly with flour. Roll the dough into a 16 × 8½-inch rectangle, about ¼ inch thick. Beat the egg and water together in a small bowl. Using a pastry brush, brush the entire surface of the dough with the egg wash and sprinkle with half the sesame seeds. Pat the seeds gently into the dough with your hands. Turn the dough over, brush the surface with the egg wash and sprinkle with the remaining sesame seeds. Fold the dough in half so that the short ends meet. Lightly roll the dough into a 10 × 8½-inch rectangle, distributing the seeds evenly.

Chilling. Cover the dough with plastic wrap and refrigerate until completely cold, about 30 minutes. The dough can also be refrigerated up to 24 hours or frozen, wrapped airtight, up to 3 months.

Cut, shape, and bake the straws as directed for Salatini alle Acciughe (recipe precedes).

Variations. To make *Salatini ai Papaveri* (Poppy Seed Straws), substitute ¼ cup poppy seeds for the sesame seeds.
To make *Salatini al Formaggio* (Cheese Straws), roll out the dough in ⅔ cup (65 grams) grated Parmesan or *pecorino* cheese instead of flour. You can also combine the cheese with the sesame seeds for a tender, delicate hors d'oeuvre full of toasted sesame seeds.

Rustici
Little Puff Pastry Treats from Lecce

The people in Lecce eat *rustici* for quick lunches and snacks the way Neapolitans eat pizza. Every bakery and *caffè* bar has its own version, but they all start with flaky puff pastry filled with a creamy cheese-flavored *beschiamella* sauce and a slice of tomato. Some bakers make them as tiny bite-size hors d'oeuvres and others as bigger rounds, but most make them into perfect 3½- or 4-inch ovals, which are as likely to turn up at birthdays and celebrations as at everyday meals. And should you go to Lecce and find people walking around eating something flaky wrapped in a napkin, you'll see *rustici* on the run.

Makes 12 pastries

BESCHIAMELLA SAUCE
6 tablespoons (85 grams) unsalted butter
⅔ cup (95 grams) unbleached all-purpose flour
2⅓ cups milk
5 ounces (140 grams) freshly grated Parmesan or *pecorino* cheese
9 ounces (250 grams) grated or shredded mozzarella cheese
Salt
Freshly ground black pepper

Melt the butter in a medium-size heavy saucepan over low heat and gradually whisk in the flour. Cook, whisking occasionally, 5 to 6 minutes. Gradually whisk in the milk; cook, stirring constantly, until thick and smooth, about 10 minutes. Stir in the cheeses, and salt and pepper to taste.

Base circle with filling

PASTRIES
1 pound 5 ounces (600 grams, ½ recipe) *Pasta Sfogliata* (page 318)
1 egg
2 teaspoons water
6 sun-dried tomatoes (packed in oil), cut in half, or 12 slices fresh ripe plum tomatoes
12 fresh basil leaves (optional)

Adding top circle

Place the cold dough on a lightly floured surface and dust the top lightly with flour. Roll the dough into a 21 × 15-inch rectangle. Using a 3½-inch round or oval cookie cutter, cut out the dough. Mix the egg and water together. Brush the circumference of half the cutouts with the egg wash and spoon about 2 to 2½ teaspoons of the sauce on the middle of the egg-washed circle. Cover with a slice of tomato and a fresh basil leaf (the basil is strictly my addition, but I like how it tastes). Top each filled circle with a plain circle and press the edges firmly to seal in the filling without pressing directly on the cut edges. With the edges of your palms, press gently around the filled center, so that you can see the outline of the filling clearly. Place the pastries 1 inch apart on buttered or parchment-lined baking sheets. Refrigerate, covered with plastic wrap, for at least 4 hours or overnight. Brush the tops with the egg wash.

Top pressed down, ready to bake

Baking. Heat the oven to 400° F. Bake 15 minutes. Reduce the heat to 350° F and bake 15 minutes longer. Serve hot, warm, or at room temperature. Do not refrigerate.

The Italian Baker

DOLCI

CROSTATE E TORTE
Tarts

O f the two traditions of baking sweets in Italy, one is based on the simple and homey desserts that families make year after year for friends and guests. These simple desserts are much cozier than the Italian extravaganzas that look more designed than baked, architectural marvels tucked full of pastry creams and sumptuous frothy interiors. These more domestic sweets have perfumed mountain houses in the Val d'Aosta, simple farmhouses near Bologna, villas in the Tuscan countryside, and apartments in Rome. Emanating from a simple way of life, they almost invariably start with *pasta frolla,* the basic sweet dough of Italy, which dates back to the late Renaissance.

Crostate are made only with *pasta frolla,* and each dessert takes its name from the fruit or jam that fills the tart. The first *crostata* I ate in Italy was made by the woman who came to help when we had just moved into our house in a small Ligurian town. From her string bag, she pulled eggs from her chickens and a jar of homemade strawberry preserves. She went right to work, making a simple sweet dough with a bit of flour and sugar, some butter, and the two eggs that were still warm to the touch. She kneaded them together quickly with a light hand, telling me that I could pat the dough in place immediately by hand but that I would have to refrigerate it if I wanted to roll it for a thinner crust. Then she simply lined the pie plate with the dough, baked it enough to set it, filled it with her strawberry preserves, made a lattice of dough strips on top, and baked it in the oven until it was golden. It was simple and uncomplicated, a bit of a sweet ending to a cozy country dinner. Over the time that we lived there, she repeated that *crostata,* sometimes with berries or peaches (the peaches of Italy must be the Platonic ideal, for there are none so sweet and juicy and full of flavor) and each one was always wonderful.

These *crostate* are, in fact, sold at the *forni,* bakeries where both bread and pastries are made, and the baking tends to be simple and straightforward. Nuts, fruits, and jams are the bases of most of the tarts, although bakers can transform the simplest ingredients into extravagant fare. The *torta del nonno* is essentially chocolate pudding tucked in a soft, buttery crust. Even the *torta dumont* is a simple dessert from the mountains of France that found its way over the border and into the Italian tradition. Of course, you will not be surprised that a few lemons may be transformed into a cool lemon soufflé set in a crust or that hazelnut filling may be glazed with chocolate, for Italian bakers are given to invention and can create tantalizing tastes from the simplest ingredients.

Basic Tart Doughs

Pasta Frolla

Sweet Short Pastry

Pasta frolla, which is named for the tenderness of the dough, is the basic pastry dough of Italian baking. Although there are numerous variations on the basic theme, most recipes are based on ratios of flour to butter and sugar. The most common proportions seem to be 2 parts flour to 1 part butter and 1 part sugar or 3 parts flour to 2 parts butter and 1 part sugar. Which is not to say that a baker's individuality isn't expressed in numerous personal touches. Some bakers use a lot more sugar or a lot less, others use more butter or add a bit of lard; some use potato flour to make a finer dough, while others add baking powder when they are putting the crust together for tarts. Some use only egg yolks instead of whole eggs, and some insist that the only permissible flavoring is vanilla, while others would never use it or would add lemon or orange flavoring, orange-flower water, or a liqueur, depending on the dough's destination.

   Pasta frolla is often made into cookie dough and can be made with corn flour (and is then known as *pasta melgun*) or with whole wheat (*pasta frolla integrale*). Then there is a special *pasta frolla* used only on November 11, the saint's day of Saint Martin, when bakers in Venice sculpt a pastry portrait of Saint Martin on horseback and decorate it with a medallion of quince jam and silver and gold confetti. A chocolate-spiked *pasta frolla* from Piedmont is used mainly for cream-filled *crostate*. The great nineteenth-century cookbook writer Pietro Artusi gave only three variations for *pasta frolla* doughs: he sometimes sieved powdered sugar for his *pasta frolla*, sometimes used part lard and part butter, and in one case insisted on using only egg yolks.

There are three main *pasta frolla* recipes used in this book: a basic all-purpose one, which is the easiest to handle; a more delicate version that uses all pastry flour; and a third, the finest, silkiest version, made with all-purpose flour and potato starch.

Pasta Frolla I

Makes 1½ pounds (680 grams) dough

Enough for three 8-inch tarts; two or three 9- or 10-inch tarts, depending on the thickness; one two-crust or two latticed 9- or 10-inch tarts; one 11 × 8-inch tart, with or without lattice; or ten to fifteen 3½-inch tartlets. In some cases you may have a bit of dough left over, but you can always use the extra to make a few tartlets or cookies (see Sweet Pastry Dough Cookies, page 415–18).

2¼ cups (300 grams) all-purpose flour
½ cup (100 grams) sugar
Pinch salt
1¾ sticks (200 grams) unsalted butter, at cool room temperature and malleable
1 egg
1 egg yolk
1 teaspoon vanilla extract
1 teaspoon fresh lemon juice or ½ teaspoon lemon extract or grated zest of 1 lemon

BY HAND

Place the flour, sugar, and salt in a bowl and stir to mix. Cut the butter into small pieces and cut it into the flour mixture with a pastry blender or 2 knives until the mixture resembles coarse meal. Slowly stir in first the egg and then the egg yolk, mixing thoroughly. Then stir in the vanilla and lemon juice. Gather the dough together and knead it roughly and briefly on a lightly floured surface just until the dough comes together.

BY MIXER

Cream the butter and the sugar in a mixer bowl with the paddle until pale and creamy. Add the egg, egg yolk, vanilla, and lemon juice, one at a time, mixing thoroughly after each addition. Add the flour and salt and mix until the dough comes together and is consistent but still soft. Be careful not to overmix or the pastry will be tough.

Pasta Frolla I (continued)

BY PROCESSOR

Place the flour, sugar, and salt in a food processor fitted with the steel blade. Cut the butter, which must be cold, into small chunks and scatter over the flour. Process with 4 to 6 pulses until the mixture resembles coarse meal. Mix the egg, egg yolk, vanilla, and lemon juice. With the machine running, pour the egg mixture through the feed tube and process just until the dough comes together on top of the blade. Do not process until it gathers into a ball or the pastry will be tough. Knead the dough very briefly on a lightly floured surface just until it is no longer sticky.

At this point you may pat the dough into place in a buttered tart pan and bake it immediately after chilling. Otherwise, divide it into thirds or halves, depending on the size of the tart you are planning, or flatten the whole amount into a 4- to 5-inch disk.

Chilling. Wrap the dough with plastic wrap or aluminum foil, and refrigerate at least 1 hour but no longer than 1 day.

Shaping. Let the dough stand at room temperature for 30 to 45 minutes before rolling it out. Knead the dough briefly on a lightly floured surface to loosen it and make it supple enough for shaping. Roll the dough out ¼ to ⅜ inch thick with a rolling pin and ease the dough into a lightly buttered pan. Trim the edge by running the rolling pin or a dough scraper over the edge of the pan to cut the dough neatly and then tidy the edge with your fingers.

Laying dough into baking pan

For one 11 × 8-inch tart shell, use 1 pound (450 grams, ⅔ recipe) dough and roll into a rectangle. Line a buttered 11 × 8-inch tart pan with the dough.

For one 9- or 10-inch tart shell, use 9 to 10 ounces (250 to 300 grams) dough and roll into a circle. Line a buttered 9- or 10-inch tart pan with the dough.

For one 8-inch tart shell, use 8 ounces (225 grams, ⅓ recipe).

For ten to twelve 3½-inch tartlet shells, roll out 12 to 16 ounces (340 to 450 grams, ½ to ⅔ recipe) dough ¼ to ⅜ inch thick. Cut into 4½-inch circles and line 3½-inch tartlet pans with the dough.

For one deep 8- or 9-inch tart shell, use 12 ounces (340 grams, ½ recipe) dough. Proceed as directed for other tart shells. If you find it difficult to keep the dough from sliding down the side of the pan while baking, press the dough firmly against the springform sides with the back of a fork after 7 minutes; bake until lightly golden, 5 to 8 minutes longer, pressing the dough against the side of the pan two more times or as needed.

For latticed tarts, use two-thirds of the dough specified for each shell to line the pan. Roll a ½-inch-thick rope of dough between your hands and smooth it onto the upper edge of the bottom crust, so that the edge is substantial enough for the lattice to be attached later. Partially bake the shell, if necessary, and fill. Roll out the remaining dough ⅜ inch thick and cut into ½-inch-wide strips with a straight edge and a sharp knife or ravioli cutter. Arrange the strips in a diagonal lattice over the filling, trim, and press onto the edges, pinching the strips lightly onto the tart shell. Bake as directed in the tart recipe.

Storage. Store the remaining unrolled dough, including all scraps which may be used again, in the refrigerator for 1 to 3 days or the freezer up to 1 month. Let frozen dough thaw in the refrigerator for 24 hours before rolling it out.

Resting. Refrigerate the dough-lined pan for 20 to 30 minutes to reduce shrinking when the pastry is baked.

Baking. Heat the oven to 350° F.

For partially baked shells: Line each shell with aluminum foil and fill with dried beans or pie weights. Bake until set, 12 to 15 minutes for large shells or 10 to 12 minutes for tartlet shells. Remove the foil and weights and let cool 5 to 10 minutes. Place the tart pan on top of a smaller can, such as a coffee can for large tart shells, and gently release the side of the pan from the baked tart crust. Let cool completely on a rack.

For an 11 × 8-inch partially baked shell, bake with the weights for 8 to 10 minutes; remove the foil and weights and bake 5 minutes longer; then reduce the heat to 325° F and bake until golden, 5 to 7 minutes longer.

For fully baked shells: Line each shell with aluminum foil and fill with dried beans or pie weights. Bake until the dough is no longer

Pasta Frolla I (continued)

shiny, about 12 to 15 minutes; remove the foil and weights, prick the bottom of the dough, and bake until fully set and golden, about 10 to 13 minutes longer. Let cool 5 to 10 minutes. Place the tart pan on top of a smaller can, such as a coffee can for large tart shells, and gently release the side of the pan from the baked tart crust. Let cool completely on a rack before filling.

Other Proportion. You can cut the recipe in half by dividing all the ingredients except the eggs in half. Use 2 egg yolks if you are making the dough by hand or by mixer, but use 1 whole egg if you are using a food processor.

Pasta Frolla II

2½ cups (300 grams) pastry flour or a combination of all-purpose flour and cake flour, sifted after measuring
½ cup (100 grams) sugar
Pinch salt
1¾ sticks (200 grams) unsalted butter, at cool room temperature and malleable
1 egg
1 egg yolk
1 teaspoon vanilla extract
1 teaspoon fresh lemon juice or ½ teaspoon lemon extract or grated zest of 1 lemon

Follow the directions for *Pasta Frolla I*. Roll out ⅛ inch thick or slightly thicker.

Pasta Frolla III

1½ cups (200 grams) all-purpose flour, sifted after measuring
¾ cup plus 1 tablespoon (100 grams) potato starch
½ cup (100 grams) sugar
Pinch salt
1¾ sticks (200 grams) unsalted butter, at cool room temperature and malleable
1 teaspoon vanilla extract
Grated zest of 1 lemon
Grated zest of ½ orange

Follow the directions for *Pasta Frolla I*. Roll out ⅛ to ¼ inch thick.

Pasta Frolla Integrale

Whole-Wheat Pastry Dough

Makes 14 ounces (400 grams); enough for one latticed 10-inch tart or two 8-inch tarts

1½ cups plus 2 tablespoons (200 grams) whole-wheat pastry flour
¾ cup (100 grams) firmly packed brown sugar
½ teaspoon salt
7 tablespoons (100 grams) unsalted butter, at cool room temperature and malleable
1 egg
1 teaspoon vanilla extract

Follow the directions for *Pasta Frolla I*. The food processor works especially well with this dough.

Basic Pastry Creams

Crema Pasticceria

Pastry Cream

Makes 4¼ cups

3¼ cups milk
½ cup plus 2 teaspoons (110 grams) sugar
3 fine strips lemon zest
7 egg yolks
1 egg
¼ teaspoon salt
½ cup (70 grams) unbleached all-purpose flour
1 to 2 tablespoons vanilla extract or 1½ teaspoons vanilla and 3 to 4 tablespoons rum
3 tablespoons (45 grams) unsalted butter

Slowly heat the milk, 2 teaspoons of the sugar, and the lemon zest in the top of a double boiler over simmering water or in a small heavy saucepan over low heat. Meanwhile, whisk the remaining sugar, the egg yolks, egg, and salt in a small bowl until thick but still golden, 2 to 3 minutes. Sift in the flour, a little at a time, whisking briskly to mix thoroughly. Whisk ½ cup of the boiling milk mixture, 2 tablespoons at a time, into the egg mixture; then pour the egg mixture into the remaining milk mixture. Cook over medium-high

Crema Pasticceria (continued)

heat, whisking constantly, until thickened, 2 to 3 minutes. As it begins to reach a boil and look lumpy, whisk it vigorously to smooth it. When the cream is as thick as mayonnaise, reduce the heat and whisk or stir for another minute. Remove from the heat and discard the lemon zest. Beat in the vanilla and then the butter, 1 tablespoon at a time. Cool the cream quickly by placing the pan in a bowl of cold water or by spreading the cream out on 2 baking sheets. Smear a little butter on top and cover tightly with plastic wrap so that the cream doesn't develop a skin. Cool completely in the refrigerator. You may want to thin it with 1 to 2 tablespoons milk before using. This pastry cream will keep 4 to 5 days in the refrigerator or in the freezer up to 2 months.

Other Proportion. You can cut the recipe in half by dividing all the ingredients except the eggs in half and reducing the egg yolks and whole egg to 4 egg yolks.

Crema al Limone

Lemon Cream

This lemon curd-like cream comes from Gianfranco Anelli in Rome. It makes a wonderful lemon tart in a simple *pasta frolla* shell.

Makes 2 cups

3 eggs, lightly beaten
1 cup plus 1 tablespoon (150 grams) confectioners' sugar
¾ cup (150 grams) granulated sugar
Scant ½ cup fresh lemon juice (4 lemons)
Grated zest of 3 lemons
7 tablespoons (100 grams) unsalted butter

Beat the eggs and sugars lightly in the top of a double boiler until mixed. Stir in the lemon juice, grated zest, and butter. Heat water in the bottom of the double boiler to a boil; then reduce the heat to maintain a steady simmer. Place the top of the double boiler over the bottom and cook the custard, whisking constantly, until as thick as cooked cereal, 10 to 12 minutes. Cool the cream quickly by placing the pan in a bowl of cold water. Refrigerate the cream, covered tightly with plastic wrap, until set.

Pasta di Mandorle

Almond Paste

Makes about 2 pounds (900 grams), or 3¼ cups

1 pound 2 ounces (500 grams) blanched almonds, very lightly toasted
¾ cup (100 grams) confectioners' sugar, plus additional for kneading
2 cups (400 grams) granulated sugar
½ cup water
¼ cup light corn syrup
½ teaspoon almond extract

Grind the almonds to a coarse powder in a nut grinder, blender, or food processor fitted with the steel blade. (If you use the processor, process with 2 tablespoons of the confectioners' sugar.) Then add the confectioners' sugar and grind to a fine powder. Remove to a mixer bowl.

Heat the sugar, water, and corn syrup in a small heavy saucepan over low heat and stir to dissolve the sugar. Heat to a boil over high heat and cook until the syrup registers 234° to 236° F on a candy thermometer (a drop of the syrup should form a soft ball when dropped into a glass of cold water). Pour the sugar syrup over the almond mixture and mix by hand or with the paddle at the lowest speed until blended. Cool to room temperature. Mix in the almond extract. Knead well on a surface sprinkled with confectioners' sugar until soft and elastic, about 2 to 3 minutes. Shape into a thick disk and wrap securely in plastic wrap. It will keep for months in the refrigerator.

Apricot Glaze

Makes about ¼ cup glaze

⅓ cup best-quality apricot jam or preserves
1–2 teaspoons water or fresh lemon juice

Heat the preserves and water in a small heavy saucepan over moderate heat until the mixture comes to a boil and strain through a sieve. Use the glaze while it is still warm. Any leftover glaze will keep indefinitely in a covered jar; heat again before using. This recipe is easily doubled.

Fruit and Jam Tarts

Crostata di Marmellata
Jam Tart

The famous Italian sweet tooth is indulged by the baker's art, but desserts made and served at home are usually extremely simple—a bowl of fresh fruit, a platter of cookies, or this simple jam tart, an unpretentious sweet pastry shell filled with homemade preserves. The quality of the jam is very important, because the fruit is not complicated with other flavorings. In Rome this *crostata* is made with *visciole*, a sour dark cherry that resembles *amarena*; in Emilia Romagna, Liguria, and Tuscany, you will most likely find the tart filled with fruit or berry preserves.

Makes one 11 × 8-inch tart; 12 servings

3 cups best-quality raspberry or apricot jam
**11 × 8-inch partially baked tart shell with dough reserved for lattice
 (*Pasta Frolla I or II or Pasta Frolla Integrale*, pages 339–43)**
½ cup Apricot Glaze (page 345)

Spread the jam ½ inch thick over the tart shell. Make the lattice as directed on page 341.

Baking. Heat the oven to 400° F. Bake until the lattice is golden brown, 15 to 20 minutes. Immediately brush the top with the glaze. Cool to room temperature on a rack.

Variations. To make *Torta di Marmellata* or *Tartine alla Marmellata*, partially bake a 9- or 10-inch tart shell or 3½-inch tartlet shells made with *Pasta Frolla I* or *II* flavored with rum instead of vanilla. You will need about 2 cups jam for the 9- or 10-inch tart and 1½ to 2 cups jam for 10 to 12 tartlets. Make the lattice as directed on page 341. Bake as directed above; the tart will be done in 20 to 25 minutes and the tartlets in about 15 to 20 minutes. Glaze and cool as directed.

Crostata di Frutta
Baked Fruit Tart

Use any of the fruits of summer to make this tart: golden pink peaches, brilliant strawberries or raspberries, blackberries, blueberries, or cherries.

Makes one 11 × 8-inch tart; 12 servings

1¼ to 1½ cups apricot jam
11 × 8-inch partially baked tart shell with dough reserved for lattice
    (*Pasta Frolla I* or *II*, pages 339–42)
3½ to 4 cups fresh fruit, such as sliced peaches; halved strawberries;
    whole raspberries, blackberries, or blueberries; or sliced pitted
    cherries
1 egg, beaten
½ cup Apricot Glaze (page 345)

Spread the jam ¼ inch thick in the bottom of the tart shell. Arrange the fruit in an attractive pattern over the jam. Make the lattice as directed on page 341. Brush the lattice with the beaten egg.

Baking. Heat the oven to 425° F. Bake until the lattice is medium brown, 20 to 25 minutes. Immediately brush the top with the glaze. Cool to room temperature on a rack.

Variations. For a 9-inch tart, use about ¾ cup jam and 3 cups fruit. For 10 to 12 tartlets, use 1 to 1¼ cups jam and 8 ounces to 1 pound fruit.

Torta di Frutta Fresca
Fresh Fruit Tart

A fresh fruit tart is a fresh fruit tart in any language you care to name, but this one comes from Italy, the land of Botticelli and Bellini, so make it as glorious to look at as it is to eat. Set curved slices of golden peaches and scarlet plums within an enclosure of pastry dough, weave pointillist fantasies of dark blueberries and red raspberries, or fan slices of strawberries in radiating circles and shine them all with apricot glaze.

Makes one 9- or 10-inch tart; 6 to 8 servings

¾ to 1 cup Pastry Cream (page 343)
9- or 10-inch fully baked tart shell (*Pasta Frolla I, II or III or Pasta Frolla Integrale*, pages 339–43)
2 to 3 cups fresh fruit, such as sliced strawberries, peaches, or plums; or whole raspberries, blueberries, or blackberries
¼ cup Apricot Glaze (page 345)

Spread the pastry cream ¼ inch thick in the bottom of the tart shell. Arrange the fruit in concentric circles over the cream. Brush the fruit with the glaze.

Variations. For an 11 × 8-inch tart, use about 1 to 1⅓ cups pastry cream and 3 to 4 cups fresh fruit. For 10 to 12 tartlets, use about 2 cups pastry cream and 1⅓ to 2 cups fresh fruit. If you are using strawberries for the tartlets, arrange the slices in concentric circles to make a pyramid shape.

Crostata al Limone
Souffléed Lemon Tart

This delicate lemony tart is as light as a soufflé baked in crust, but it has the wonderful advantage of not having to be made at the very last minute. It could be the perfect finish to almost any meal but seems especially right at the end of a rich or complex dinner.

Makes one 9-inch tart; 6 to 8 servings

4 large eggs, separated, room temperature
½ cup plus 2 tablespoons (125 grams) sugar
3 tablespoons (25 grams) all-purpose flour
⅓ cup fresh lemon juice
Grated zest of 2 lemons
Deep 9-inch partially baked tart shell (*Pasta Frolla I, II, or III*, pages 339–42)

With an electric mixer, beat the egg yolks, gradually adding ¼ cup of the sugar, until thick and foamy; add the flour, lemon juice, and zest and beat 2 to 3 minutes longer. Transfer to the top of a double boiler. Cook, stirring constantly, over simmering water until the mixture is thick and coats the back of a spoon. Remove the pan from the water and cool completely. Beat the egg whites until soft peaks are formed; gradually beat in the remaining ¼ cup plus 2 tablespoons sugar and continue beating until stiff and glossy. Fold a quarter of the egg whites into the lemon mixture to lighten and then gently fold in the remaining with a rubber spatula. Gently pour the filling into the tart shell and smooth the top.

Baking. Heat the oven to 350° F. Bake until the crust is deep golden, 20 to 25 minutes. Cool on a rack and then remove the sides of the pan.

Torta di Limone
Lemon Tart

The first time I tasted this lemon tart I loved its tart lemon flavor and smooth, buttery texture. The secret? In Italy it is made with a dry Pinot Grigio, but I prefer to use a Chardonnay or Pomino Bianco to give it a slightly fruitier rich taste.

Makes one 9-inch tart; 6 to 8 servings

FILLING
This lemon custard is best if made and refrigerated for 24 hours so that the tart lemon flavor can mellow.

4 egg yolks, room temperature
⅔ cup plus 3 tablespoons (180 grams) sugar
¼ cup (35 to 40 grams) all-purpose flour
¾ cup Pinot Grigio, Pomino Bianco, or Chardonnay wine
4 to 5 tablespoons fresh lemon juice
Grated zest of 1 lemon

Whisk the egg yolks, ⅔ cup sugar, and the flour until smooth in a mixing bowl. Heat the wine and 3 tablespoons sugar in a 2-quart noncorrodible saucepan to a boil; stir in the lemon juice and zest. Whisk 3 tablespoons of the hot wine mixture, 1 tablespoon at a time,

Torta di Limone (continued)

into the egg yolk mixture. Then gradually stir the egg yolk mixture into the remaining wine mixture with a wooden spoon. Heat over low heat, stirring constantly, until bubbly. If the mixture looks lumpy, whisk it vigorously to smooth it. Cook until it is as thick as cooked cereal, about 2 minutes. Let cool to room temperature. Refrigerate covered for 24 hours before using, if possible.

MERINGUE
1 egg white, room temperature
¼ cup (50 grams) sugar

9-inch partially baked tart shell (*Pasta Frolla, I, II, or III*, pages 339–42)

Beat the egg white in a mixer bowl until soft peaks are formed. Beat, gradually adding ¼ cup sugar, until the peaks are stiff and shiny.

Spoon the lemon filling into the tart shell and smooth the top. Spoon the meringue into a pastry bag fitted with a large star tip and pipe a ring of rosettes around the edge.

Baking. Heat the oven to 350° F. Bake until the meringue colors slightly, 15 to 20 minutes. Cool to room temperature on a rack.

Torta Primavera
Springtime Cake

This is a cake for all hours and occasions from breakfast to teatime to dessert. A rich pastry crust wraps around layers of apricot jam, raisins, and a pound-cake-like filling that is topped with fanned slices of apple and crunchy baker's sugar.

Makes 1 deep 8-, 9-, or 9½-inch cake; 8 to 10 servings

1¼ cups apricot jam
2 teaspoons water
7 tablespoons (100 grams) unsalted butter, room temperature
½ cup (100 grams) granulated sugar
2 eggs, room temperature
2 egg yolks, room temperature
Grated zest of ½ orange
½ teaspoon vanilla extract
1 cup (140 to 150 grams) all-purpose flour or 1⅓ cups pastry flour

1½ teaspoons baking powder
Deep 8-, 9-, or 9½-inch unbaked tart shell with a thick rim (*Pasta
Frolla I or II*, pages 339–42)
¾ cup plus 2 tablespoons (140 grams) golden raisins
2 cooking apples, peeled and cut into 8 to 12 slices each
1½ tablespoons turbinado sugar

Heat the jam and water in a small heavy saucepan until they boil,
and then press through a sieve. Cream the butter and granulated
sugar by hand with a wooden spoon or paddle or by electric mixer
(use the whisk if you have one) at high speed for 4 to 5 minutes
until fluffy and almost creamy white. Add the eggs and egg yolks,
one at a time, beating thoroughly at high speed after each addition.
Add the orange zest and vanilla and beat 5 minutes by hand or 1 to
2 minutes by mixer. Sift the flour and baking powder over the butter
mixture and fold in gently with a rubber spatula until well blended.

Spread some of the warm sieved jam ¼ inch thick on the bottom of
the tart shell. Don't be tempted to add more jam, even though it
seems like a good idea, because the cake will be too sweet and the
jam will overwhelm the other flavors. Sprinkle the raisins over the
jam; they should completely cover the jam. Pour the cake batter over
the raisins and smooth the top. Arrange the apples without overlapping
the slices in 2 concentric circles. Sprinkle with the turbinado sugar.

Baking. Heat the oven to 350° F. Bake until a skewer inserted into
the center comes out clean, 1¼ to 1½ hours. Let cool on a rack.
While the cake is still somewhat warm, brush with the remaining
sieved jam. Serve at room temperature.

Crostata di Quattro Stagioni

Four Seasons Tart from Lake Como

Raspberries for summer, wild *amarena* for fall, apricot preserves for winter, and pastry cream for the spring: four seasons in four quadrants of a simple sweet-pastry tart. But don't feel confined by the ingredients listed above; you should use whatever appeals to you and arrange it with your own *fantasia*. Try poached apples or pears, fat blueberries or fresh currants, sliced peaches or even blood oranges, if you are in the mood for something as beautiful to look at as it is to eat.

Makes one 9-inch tart; 6 to 8 servings

2 ounces (60 grams) *Pasta Frolla* dough
9-inch partially baked tart shell (*Pasta Frolla I, II, or III*, pages 339–42)
½ cup raspberry preserves or jam
½ cup apricot preserves or jam
1 cup Pastry Cream (page 343)
30 to 35 preserved *amarena* cherries
1 egg, beaten
⅓ cup Apricot Glaze (page 345)

Cut the 2 ounces dough in half, shape each half into a 9- to 10-inch rope with your palms, and flatten the ropes slightly. Place the ropes in the tart shell, one across the other at right angles, so that the shell is divided into 4 equal quadrants. Spoon the raspberry and apricot preserves, pastry cream, and cherries each separately into 1 quadrant. Brush the dough with the egg.

Baking. Heat the oven to 350° F. Bake until light golden, 20 to 25 minutes. Immediately brush the fruit with the glaze. Let cool to room temperature on a rack.

Variations. You can substitute the slices of 1 Newtown Pippin or cooking apple that have been poached briefly in sugar and white wine for the cherries. Other possible fillings are blackberry or blueberry preserves, sliced lightly blanched peaches or apricots, and pear slices that have been very lightly poached in white wine, sugar, and a few drops lemon juice.

Crostata di Zucca

Pumpkin Tart

I have to admit that this particular pumpkin dessert is truly my *fantasia*. Giorgio, the baker in Venice, was busy one day and told me to take a look at his recipes, which were really just a list of ingredients and the most rudimentary instructions. After so much time spent being beguiled by the imaginations of Italian bakers and the phenomenal desserts they made with a few simple ingredients, I went to work when I got home to my kitchen on a tart I imagined would be a close cousin to Giorgio's. When I returned to Italy, I told him what I had done. He paused for a very long time, with a look of some confusion on his face, and then described his *crostata di zucca*. It was an extravaganza of 2 days' work, complicated processes, and fondant coverings; so, although this *crostata di zucca* is made with the ingredients listed in Giorgio's little book, it is absolutely my invention. Delicate and delicious, this tart has been the finale for our Thanksgiving dinners for the past two years.

Makes one 10-inch tart plus several tartlets or individual budini *(custards); tart makes 8 servings*

½ stick (55 grams) unsalted butter, room temperature
¼ cup (50 grams) sugar
3 eggs, separated, room temperature
2 cups homemade or canned pumpkin purée
Scant ½ cup milk
1 tablespoon potato starch or all-purpose flour
Grated zest of 1 lemon
¼ cup rum or Cognac
10-inch partially baked tart shell (*Pasta Frolla I, II, or III*, pages 339–42)
3 partially baked tartlet shells (optional)

Cream the butter and sugar by hand with a wooden paddle or spoon or by electric mixer until light and fluffy. Add the egg yolks, one at a time, beating thoroughly after each addition. Stir in the pumpkin, milk, flour, lemon zest, and rum. Beat the egg whites until the peaks are stiff. Fold a quarter of the egg whites into the pumpkin mixture, and then gently fold in the remaining. Pour the filling into the tart shell to within ½ inch of the top. Pour the remaining filling either into the tartlet shells or into buttered ramekins.

Baking. Heat the oven to 375° F. Bake until the filling is set, about 50 minutes for the tart, about 30 to 35 minutes for the tartlets, and about 35 to 45 minutes for the custards. Cool completely on a rack.

Torta di Pere
Pear Tart

The top crust of this wonderfully rustic pear tart from Piedmont shifts and settles and even cracks over the pears beneath it like dry land after an earthquake. The slightly gritty texture of the cornmeal pastry makes a wonderful contrast to the smooth pears underneath. There is something elementally soothing and satisfying about this down-to-earth dessert.

Makes one 8½-inch tart; 8 servings

DOUGH
1 stick plus 2½ tablespoons (150 grams) unsalted butter, room temperature
¾ cup (150 grams) sugar
3 egg yolks
About 1½ cups (200 grams) all-purpose flour
½ cup plus 1 tablespoon (100 grams) yellow cornmeal
1 teaspoon (5 grams) salt

BY HAND

Cream the butter and sugar in a mixing bowl with a wooden spoon until well blended. Add the egg yolks, one at a time, mixing thoroughly after each addition. Sift the flour, cornmeal, and salt over the mixture and stir just until the dough comes together. Knead lightly on a floured surface until the dough is no longer sticky.

BY MIXER

Cream the butter and sugar with the paddle until well blended, 1 to 2 minutes. Add the egg yolks, one at a time, beating thoroughly after each addition. Sift in the flour, cornmeal, and salt, and mix at low speed; continue mixing just until the dough comes together. Knead lightly on a floured surface until the dough is no longer sticky.

BY PROCESSOR

Place the flour, cornmeal, salt, and sugar in a food processor fitted with the steel blade. Cut the butter into small pieces and scatter over the flour. Process with 3 or 4 pulses just until the mixture resembles coarse meal. Beat the egg yolks lightly. With the machine running, pour the egg yolks in a steady stream through the feed tube and process just until the dough comes together. You may need to add a little ice-cold water. Stop the machine as soon as the dough masses on top of the blade. Overprocessing will make a tough dough.

Chilling. Gather the dough into a ball, wrap it with plastic wrap, and refrigerate for 20 minutes to 1 hour.

FILLING

2 cups full-bodied red wine; a Barolo or Cabernet Sauvignon would be perfect

¼ cup (50 grams) sugar

3 whole cloves

3 long strips lemon zest

¾ to 1 teaspoon ground cinnamon

2 pounds (900 grams) peeled cooking pears (weighed after peeling), cut into fat slices and then cut crosswise in half

1 egg, beaten

Heat the wine, sugar, cloves, lemon zest, and cinnamon to a boil in a medium-size enameled saucepan. Gently boil until reduced to 1½ cups, about 15 minutes. Stir in the pears and cook over medium heat until tender, 15 to 20 minutes. Strain the pears; discard the cloves, lemon peel, and cooking liquid. Cool to room temperature.

Shaping. Cut the dough in half and return half to the refrigerator. Roll the remaining dough on a lightly floured surface into a ¼-inch-thick circle. Butter an 8½-inch tart pan. Ease the dough into the prepared pan and trim the edge. Build up the edge of the bottom pastry with the trimmings rolled into 1 or 2 coils and flattened onto the edge, so that the edge is substantial enough for the top pastry to be attached.

Filling and Top Crust. I sometimes sprinkle a very little cornmeal or finely ground cookie or cake crumbs on the bottom of the tart shell to soak up the juices from the pears. Spoon the drained pears into the tart shell. Roll out the remaining dough into a ¼-inch-thick circle and place over the pan. Trim the overhanging dough, press the two edges together, and crimp decoratively. Lightly brush the pastry with the beaten egg.

Baking. Heat the oven to 375° F. Bake until golden, 40 minutes. Cool on a rack. Serve warm or at room temperature.

Torta di Mele e Ciliege

Apple and Wild Cherry Tart

Set a layer of maraschino-soaked cake inside a rich pastry crust, spread it with pastry cream, and fan finely sliced apples inside a circle of wild *amarena* cherries.

Makes one 9-inch tart; 8 servings

About ⅓ baked Maddalena (page 384), cut into ¼-inch-thick slices or enough slices of pound cake or Génoise or even ground cake crumbs to line the 9-inch tart shell
9-inch partially baked tart shell (*Pasta Frolla I, II, or III*, pages 339–42)
2 to 3 tablespoons maraschino liqueur
1 to 1¼ cups Pastry Cream (page 343)
1 Newtown Pippin or cooking apple, peeled, cut into about twenty-four ¼-inch slices
45 to 50 preserved *amarena* cherries (about ⅓ of a 21-ounce jar)
2 to 3 tablespoons turbinado or granulated sugar
⅓ cup Apricot Glaze (page 345)
3 tablespoons coarsely chopped toasted walnuts

Arrange the cake slices in a single layer in the tart shell, cutting and trimming as needed. Brush the liqueur over the cake slices and then spread with a ¼-inch layer of pastry cream. Fan the apple slices in a circle in the center of the tart. Arrange the cherries in a border around the apples and place 10 to 15 cherries in the center of the apples. Sprinkle with the sugar.

Baking. Heat the oven to 375° F. Turn over a rimmed baking sheet and place the tart pan on it. This strange arrangement will keep the bottom from overbrowning. Bake until the apple slices are slightly browned and the cherries are plump and slightly glazed, about 25 minutes.

I have also baked this without the cherries when I discovered that I was totally without at the last moment. I rushed to the store while the tart was cooling and added the cherries when I got home. The unbaked cherries were fine, but they must be pressed into the pastry cream to keep them from sliding all over when you cut into the tart.

Brush the hot tart with the glaze and sprinkle the walnuts over the apple slices. Cool to room temperature on a rack.

Nut Tarts

**Torta di
Nocciole con
Cioccolata**

*Hazelnut Cake
with Chocolate
Glaze*

This cake is rich, densely nutty, and flavored with just a touch of orange. It is wonderful unadorned or sprinkled with a fine shower of confectioners' sugar, although it would be hard to imagine anyone objecting to the smooth dark chocolate glaze, which gives it an entirely different elegant life.

Makes one 9-inch cake; 8 servings

1 cup (125 grams) hazelnuts, plus additional for garnish
½ cup plus 2 tablespoons (125 grams) sugar
⅓ cup (50 grams) chopped candied orange peel
1 stick plus 2 tablespoons (140 grams) unsalted butter, room temperature
1 large egg, room temperature
2 large egg yolks, room temperature
9-inch partially baked tart shell (*Pasta Frolla I, II, or III*, pages 339–42)

Heat the oven to 350° F. Toast all the hazelnuts on a baking sheet until the skins blister, 10 to 15 minutes. Rub the skins off the nuts in a kitchen towel, or place the nuts in a food processor fitted with the plastic blade and process with 1 or 2 pulses until the skins come off. Set aside 10 to 12 perfect nuts for garnishing the cake.

Process the nuts and 2 tablespoons of the sugar in a food processor fitted with the steel blade to a coarse powder. Add the remaining sugar and the orange peel and process until finely ground. Remove to a mixer bowl, add 1 stick plus 2 tablespoons butter and cream with the paddle until very light and fluffy, about 5 minutes. Change to the whisk if your mixer has one. Add the egg and egg yolks, one at a time, beating thoroughly after each addition. Beat at medium-high speed 3 to 4 minutes. Pour the cake batter into the tart shell and smooth the top.

Baking. Heat the oven to 350° F. Bake until a skewer inserted in the center comes out clean, 35 to 40 minutes. Cool completely on a rack.

continued

Torta di Nocciole con Cioccolata (continued)

GLAZE
5 ounces (140 grams) dark bittersweet chocolate
6½ tablespoons (90 grams) unsalted butter, room temperature
1½ teaspoons corn syrup or clear glucose

Melt the chocolate in the top of a double boiler over simmering water. When the chocolate is completely melted, stir in the butter, 1 tablespoon at a time, waiting until each tablespoon of butter melts before adding the next, and then add the corn syrup. The glaze should be stiff and shiny. Pour the hot glaze over the cake; you may refrigerate the cake to set the glaze quickly. Garnish with the perfect whole hazelnuts.

Variations. This cake can also be baked with a top crust of pastry. Roll out 10 ounces pastry dough ¼ inch thick. Place over the batter before baking, trim the edges, and press onto the tart shell. Cut out small shapes from the leftover dough with a ravioli cutter or small knife and arrange on the pastry. Make a hole in the center to allow steam to escape. Brush the top with 1 egg yolk mixed with 1 tablespoon water and, if you want, decorate the edge with skinned whole hazelnuts. Bake as directed.

Torta Piana con Mandorle
Almond Tart

There seem to be endless numbers of almond tarts in Italy, all slightly different depending on the region and its traditions. This particular one is a delicate almond cake flavored with a hint of orange set on a fine layer of apricot jam and baked in a rich, buttery pastry shell. It is hauntingly delicious, but the *piana* in its name has nothing to do with rhapsodies, rapture, or music. Italian for "level" or "even," *piana* indicates that the top is as flat as a ribbon, although bakers always toss a couple of handfuls of sliced almonds over the top to accentuate the almond flavor and give it a lovely crunch.

Makes one 9-inch tart; 8 servings

½ cup (50 grams) blanched almonds
3½ ounces (100 grams) prepared almond paste
7 tablespoons (100 grams) unsalted butter, room temperature
¼ cup (50 grams) sugar
2 large eggs, room temperature

¼ teaspoon almond extract
Grated zest of 1 orange or 1 ounce chopped candied orange peel
¾ cup (100 grams) all-purpose or pastry flour
½ teaspoon baking powder
⅔ cup apricot jam, melted and sieved
9-inch partially baked tart shell (*Pasta Frolla I, II, or III,* pages 339–42)
1 egg, beaten
⅓ cup (35 grams) sliced unpeeled almonds

You can substitute 7 ounces Almond Paste (page 345) for the whole almonds, sugar, and prepared almond paste and proceed to the next step. Otherwise, grind the whole almonds to a coarse powder using a nut grinder, a mortar and pestle, or a food processor fitted with the steel blade. If you are using the processor, add 2 tablespoons of the sugar to keep the almonds from becoming oily.

Mix the almond powder, almond paste and butter in a mixer bowl with the paddle at low speed. Add the sugar slowly but steadily and beat until smooth. If you have made the 7 ounces of Almond Paste (page 345) start here and beat it in the mixer bowl at low speed. Increase the speed to high and beat until light and fluffy, 2 to 3 minutes. Change to the whisk if your mixer has one and beat at high speed for 5 minutes. Add the eggs, one at a time, beating thoroughly after each addition. Add the almond extract and orange zest and beat at high speed for another 5 minutes. Sift the flour and baking powder over the batter and gently fold with a rubber spatula until blended.

Spread the jam ¼ inch thick on the bottom of the tart shell. Spoon heaping tablespoons of the filling evenly over the jam, sealing in the jam at the edge. It's difficult to cover the slippery jam with the filling, which is why bakers use a pastry bag to pipe the filling in a continuous spiral over the jam, but I have discovered that a little overflow of jam at the edges does no harm. Smooth the top of the filling. Very carefully, brush the beaten egg over the filling and then sprinkle with the sliced almonds.

Baking. Heat the oven to 375° F. Bake until deep golden brown, 25 to 35 minutes. Cool completely on a rack.

Variation. You can substitute raspberry jam for the apricot and hazelnuts for the almonds.

Torta di Mandorle
Almond Tart

A rich, dense, moist almond tart made without flour. The top can be covered with handfuls of any toasted nut—hazelnut, almond, or walnut—or with a composed design of unpeeled almonds and skinned toasted hazelnuts.

Makes one 9-inch tart; 8 servings

⅔ cup (75 grams) unpeeled almonds
8 bitter almonds or apricot kernels or ¼ teaspoon almond extract
½ cup plus 2 tablespoons (125 grams) sugar
2 sticks plus 1 tablespoon (240 grams) unsalted butter, room temperature
1 egg
1 egg yolk
1 teaspoon vanilla extract
9-inch unbaked tart shell (*Pasta Frolla I, II,* or *III,* pages 339–42)
1 cup (110 grams) halved skinned toasted hazelnuts, halved toasted blanched almonds, or toasted pine nuts, or a combination of halved hazelnuts and halved almonds (see page 52)

Grind the sweet and bitter almonds, if using, and the sugar to a coarse powder in a food processor fitted with the steel blade. Remove to a mixer bowl. If you prefer to use a nut grinder or mortar and pestle, grind the nuts, then transfer to the mixer bowl, add the sugar, and mix well. A heavy-duty mixer is best for preparing the tart filling. Add the butter, and beat with the paddle at medium speed until light and fluffy, about 5 minutes. Change to the whisk. Add the egg and egg yolk, one at a time, as quickly as possible but whisking thoroughly at medium speed after each addition. Add the vanilla extract and almond extract, if using, and whisk at medium speed 3 to 4 minutes.

Spread the nut batter in the tart shell and smooth the top. Shower the top with the nuts and shake off the excess, or alternate rows of hazelnuts and almonds.

Baking. Heat the oven to 350° F. Bake until the pastry shell is golden and the interior is set, 35 to 40 minutes. Cool completely on a rack.

Chocolate Tarts

Torta del Nonno

Grandfather's Tart

A homey, old-fashioned tart with a filling that definitely brings chocolate pudding to mind. Warm and reminiscent of childhood memories and pleasures, it is as comforting to eat as it is well named.

Makes one 8-inch tart; 6 to 8 servings

12 ounces (340 grams, ½ recipe) *Pasta Frolla I, II,* or *III* dough (pages 339–42), made through chilling
1 cup plus 2 teaspoons Pastry Cream (¼ recipe, page 343), room temperature
¼ cup (25 grams) unsweetened cocoa powder, preferably Dutch process
1 egg white
1 teaspoon water
1 teaspoon milk
¼ cup pine nuts

Cut the pastry in half and return half to the refrigerator. Roll out the remaining half to an 8½-inch circle, turning and flipping the dough frequently to keep it even. Using the bottom of an 8-inch tart or springform pan, trim the dough to an 8-inch circle. Place the dough circle on a buttered baking sheet and refrigerate for 1 hour.

Heat the oven to 375° F. Prick the bottom of the pastry all over with a fork, and bake until the edge is pale golden, about 12 minutes. Cool completely on a rack.

Mix the pastry cream and cocoa; set aside 2 teaspoons of the chocolate cream. Place the tart shell on a buttered baking sheet and spoon the remaining cream onto the center of the pastry. Spread the cream to within 2 inches of the edge. Beat the egg white and water together and brush over the 2-inch border. Roll out the remaining dough on a lightly floured surface to a 9-inch circle. Gently place the dough over the cream-covered pastry, centering the circle carefully. Press the edges lightly together and trim the edge of the dough even with the bottom pastry. Mold the dough to the shape of the pastry cream with the edges of your hands. The tart should look somewhat like the flat-brimmed hats worn by Italian priests.

continued

Torta del Nonno (continued)

Mix the reserved chocolate cream and the milk and carefully spread it over the dome of the tart. Lightly brush the 2-inch rim with the remaining egg white. Sprinkle the pine nuts over the painted dome.

Decorate the side of the pastry with a continuous double half-moon pattern using the top half of the bowl of a teaspoon or a small cookie cutter.

Baking. Heat the oven to 375° F. Bake until the edge is golden, about 30 minutes. Slide onto a rack and cool completely.

Torta Dumont
Chocolate-Nut Latticed Tart from Venice

"But where did this wonderful chocolate nut tart get its name?" I asked the Venetian baker, for Dumont scarcely sounds Italian. As it turns out, it is French, or the Venetian fantasy of a country dessert from the mountains of France. I suspect that it acquired a little city sophistication once it came to Venice, where a bit of enchantment is to be expected.

Makes one 8-inch tart; 6 to 8 servings

2 sticks plus 1 tablespoon (240 grams) unsalted butter, room temperature
½ cup plus 2 tablespoons (125 grams) sugar
3 large eggs
⅔ cup (75 grams) blanched almonds
¼ cup (25 grams) unsweetened cocoa powder, preferably Dutch process
Grated zest of 1 lemon
¾ cup less 1 tablespoon (90 grams) all-purpose or pastry flour
1 teaspoon baking powder
8-inch unbaked tart shell with 2 ounces dough reserved for lattice (*Pasta Frolla I, II, or III*, pages 339–42)

Using the whisk if you have one, cream the butter and sugar in a mixer bowl until light and fluffy. Add the eggs, one at a time, beating thoroughly after each addition. Grind the almonds and cocoa to a fine powder in a food processor fitted with the steel blade. Stir the almond mixture and the lemon zest into the butter mixture by hand.

Sift the flour and baking powder over the batter and fold in with a rubber spatula until well blended.

Spread the filling in the tart shell. Make a lattice of 6 strips of dough as directed on page 341. If you want, you can roll the strips with your fingers and flatten each one slightly before setting it on top. The dough is so rich that it is easy to work by hand. Join the strips firmly to the edge of the tart shell.

Baking. Heat the oven to 375° F. Bake until the pastry is golden, 30 to 35 minutes. Let cool 10 to 15 minutes and remove the side of the pan. Cool completely on a rack.

The baked Torta Dumont

TORTE
Cakes

Stroll down any street in an Italian town and you'll see unmistakable evidence of the famous Italian sweet tooth. Bakeries and *pasticcerie* on almost every block boast windows and shelves full of rustic tarts and richer creamier *dolci*, examples of the satisfying simple desserts and the more ornate category of sweets that includes confections dreamed up to celebrate holidays, saint's days, festivals, and feast days. Who could be surprised? Even the Romans had a bakers' guild and loved their layer cakes, flat cheesecakes, little tarts filled with custard or cheese, and baked pastries sweetened with honey or grape must.

The craze for sweets has been with the Italians for a very long time. The entire tradition of cooking with sugar began particularly early in Italy as a result of the Crusades and the voyages of Venetian traders. Sugar came to Sicily with the Arabs, who brought their elaborate pastries, as well as sugarcane and almond paste, and transformed Palermo into a city of sumptuous pastries made of lemons and sweet oranges, almonds, dates, and figs. Venice was the great center of the medieval spice trade, and its cooks were apt pupils who quickly learned the secrets of Arab pastry baking. When sugar first arrived, it was called *il sale dolce*, sweet salt, and the Italians used it as a flavoring in all food, not just desserts, which were not set aside until the end of a meal, as they are now, but interspersed with other courses. Both sugar and spices were first sold in pharmacies, because they were considered medicinal wonders with benefits for health, although they were also destined for luxurious preparations on the tables of the rich. By 1300 Florence allowed only 100 special bakers to work with sugar and spices and make marzipan, the base of almost all medieval and modern baking. Marzipan was called *frutta di martorana* from the convent in Palermo famous for its extraordinary trompe l'oeil fruits, vegetables, and animals.

Pastry baking became an art separate from bread baking in the late fifteenth century—the pastry cooks' guild was formed in 1492— but *torte* then were both sweet and savory—*pasta frolla* wrapped around meats and poultry, mushrooms, and dried fruits seasoned with spices. Four and twenty blackbirds really were baked into a pie; the recipe was published in the first European cookbook, *De Honesta Voluptate e Valetudine* in 1474 (in Italy, of course). The monks of early medieval Siena may have been enjoying their *panforte,* in which spices and pepper joined forces with sweet fruits and nuts, but it wasn't until the Renaissance that most true sweets came into their own. Bartolomeo Scappi, the chef of Pope Pius IV, wrote an enormous treatise that contained the first in-depth look at pastry baking; it even had a recipe for dough layered with lard and rolled and folded like the puff pastry we make today. Pastry cooks appeared in the kitchens of great houses and courts and created radical innovations in the art of desserts.

Soon the secrets of the pastry baker spread to the West. As a young bride, Maria de'Medici took her cooks to France where they taught the French cooks so well that a century later, when La Varenne wrote his first careful cookbook with its meticulous measurements and instructions, the French had become the acknowledged masters of the art. Now we tend to forget the importance of Italy's contributions. What, after all, is a Génoise but the pastry of Genoa given a Gallic name? It is much easier to see the culinary stamp of other countries. *Pan di spagna,* Spanish bread, is sponge cake brought by the Spaniards when they conquered Sicily in the fifteenth century, and plum cake came from England with the Duke of Wellington who didn't want to leave his cake behind. These sweets mingling with the indigenous specialties and the tastes of individual regions came to life as the Genoese made sweet *focaccia* with raisins, the Venetians invented the *zaletti* they still eat today, and the Sicilians made the *cannoli* and *cassata* that bear the culinary stamp of the earlier Normans and Arabs. The monasteries and nunneries of Sicily played such a crucial role in the making of sweets that they had a virtual monopoly on the most important recipes of the region. Until the unification of Italy in 1860, cookies, cakes, and numerous pastries were made only in these religious retreats, and it was only as the nuns began to move out of the convents that the tradition began to change.

The Italian passion for sweets has had centuries to develop, so it is no surprise that every celebration comes with dessert. Easter couldn't arrive in Naples without *pastiera* or in Palermo without *cassata.* *Panforte* is the quintessential sweet of Christmas in Siena. For birthdays, marriages, confirmations, and baptisms, the art of the pastry baker is always at the table.

Ricotta Cheesecakes and Creamy Rice Tarts

Pastiera

Neapolitan Easter Ricotta Cake

The two ingredients that give the *pastiera* its special flavor are somewhat difficult to find, but look in Middle Eastern shops for orange-flower water and try health-food stores for the soft white winter wheat berries. The berries must be the soft ones (the hard, red winter wheat berries will never cook to the right consistency—I know because I have tried); the white berries are often used in Naples as ornaments of the tomb of Christ in the days leading up to Easter. One Neapolitan cookbook suggests that the grain be soaked for fifteen days in a frequently refreshed water bath, but that seems excessive to me. Even three to four days require planning beyond what most of us care to undertake, but these grains need that long to soften. The berries are the lightly chewy center of the filling and are reminders of the rebirth that comes with every spring; the exotic flavors are evidence of the Phoenicians, Romans, Crusaders, and Arabs who arrived over the centuries at the port of Naples with their own spices, flavorings, and ingredients.

Makes one 9½-inch cake; 8 servings

WHEAT BERRIES
3½ ounces (100 grams) soft white wheat berries
1 tablespoon lard
2½ cups milk
1 teaspoon sugar
¼ teaspoon ground cinnamon
2 thin strips lemon zest

Three or four days before you plan to bake the *pastiera*, soak the wheat berries in 2½ cups cold water, changing the water daily, until softened. Pour the berries and the final soaking water into a medium-size saucepan and add the lard. Boil uncovered for 15 minutes. Drain the berries and return them to the clean saucepan. Add the milk, sugar, cinnamon, and lemon zest and cook uncovered over medium-low heat, stirring occasionally, until the berries are plump, split open, and look creamy from having absorbed the milk, about 2 hours. Drain the berries and place in a bowl; add just enough water to cover and let stand at least 3 hours or overnight.

DOUGH
2¼ cups (300 grams) unbleached all-purpose or 2½ cups pastry flour
¾ cup (150 grams) sugar
Pinch salt
1 stick (115 grams) unsalted butter, room temperature
¼ cup (50 grams) lard, room temperature
1 egg
2 egg yolks

BY HAND   Place the flour, sugar, and salt in a bowl and stir to mix. Cut the butter and lard into small pieces and cut it into the flour mixture with a pastry blender or 2 knives until the mixture resembles coarse meal. Slowly stir in first the egg and then the egg yolks, mixing thoroughly. Gather the dough together and knead it roughly and briefly on a lightly floured surface just until the dough comes together.

Refer to *Pasta Frolla I* (page 339) instructions for electric mixer and food processor methods.

Dough Preparation. Roll out two thirds of the dough (refrigerate the remaining third) on a lightly floured surface to ¼ to ⅜ inch thick and ease the dough into a well-buttered and lightly floured 9½-inch springform pan. Trim the edge with a sharp knife and neaten with your fingers. Build up the top edge with the dough trimmings so that the latticework will have something to grip on to. Refrigerate ½ hour. Remove from the refrigerator and partially bake the dough in a 350° F oven. If you find it difficult to keep the dough from sliding down the side of the pan while baking, press the dough firmly against the springform side with the back of a fork after 7 minutes. Bake until lightly golden, 8 to 10 minutes longer, pressing the dough against the side of the pan two more times or as needed.

FILLING
12 ounces (340 grams) fresh ricotta
1½ cups (300 grams) sugar
3 eggs, separated, room temperature
1 tablespoon orange-flower water
1 teaspoon vanilla extract
1 cup (150 grams) chopped candied orange peel

Press the ricotta through a wire-mesh sieve into a mixing bowl, or process with several pulses in a food processor fitted with the steel blade until smooth. You may transfer the ricotta to a mixing bowl

Pastiera (continued)

or continue in the processor. Add the sugar and beat until creamy. Add the egg yolks, orange-flower water, and vanilla and stir or process with repeated pulses until thoroughly blended. If you haven't before, transfer to a mixing bowl. Drain the wheat berries and add to the ricotta mixture. Add the orange peel and stir by hand until blended. Beat the egg whites until soft peaks are formed and fold into the ricotta mixture. Pour the filling into the tart shell and smooth the top.

Roll out the remaining dough ¼ to ⅜ inch thick on a lightly floured surface. Using a straight edge and a sharp knife or ravioli cutter, cut the dough into ¾-inch-wide strips. Arrange the strips over the filling in a lattice. Trim the strips and press onto the tart shell.

Baking. Heat the oven to 375° F. Bake until the filling is set and the crust golden brown, 65 to 75 minutes. Cool on a rack.

Crostata di Ricotta
Italian Cheesecake or Ricotta Tart

Although it seems unlikely that such an elegant cake could come from humble beginnings, this cheesecake, from the mountainous Garfagnana region of Tuscany, is based on the highly prized ricotta of that rustic area. Its popularity survives in various forms in Italy today, although this recipe comes from Joyce Goldstein, who lived in Italy before becoming chef first at the Café at Chez Panisse and now at Square One, her restaurant in San Francisco, where the Italian cheesecake appears on the menu from time to time.

Makes one 9½-inch cheesecake; 8 to 10 servings

½ cup (80 grams) golden raisins
3 to 4 tablespoons Marsala
1 pound (450 grams) ricotta, perferably whole milk
½ cup (100 grams) sugar
1 tablespoon unbleached all-purpose flour
4 eggs, separated, room temperature
¼ cup heavy or whipping cream
¼ cup sour cream
1 teaspoon vanilla extract
¼ teaspoon salt
Deep 9½-inch unbaked pastry shell (*Pasta Frolla II or III*, pages 339–42, made with 2 tablespoons Marsala and 1 teaspoon grated lemon zest instead of the vanilla)

Soak the raisins in the Marsala at least 15 minutes. Drain but reserve the Marsala.

Press the ricotta through a wire-mesh sieve into a mixing bowl, or process with several pulses in a food processor fitted with the steel blade until smooth and transfer to a mixing bowl. Add the sugar and flour and beat with a wooden spoon until creamy. Add the egg yolks, heavy and sour creams, reserved Marsala, and the vanilla; stir until thoroughly blended. Stir in the raisins. Beat the egg whites and salt until the peaks are stiff and fold into the ricotta mixture. Pour the filling into the tart shell and smooth the top.

Baking. Heat the oven to 350° F. Bake until the filling is set and the pastry golden brown, 50 to 60 minutes. Turn off the oven and let the cake cool with the oven door open for 30 minutes. This cake is so much better served warm that I urge you to bake it 2 to 3 hours before serving or at least the same day you plan to eat it. If you must refrigerate it, warm it at 350° F for 20 to 30 minutes before serving.

Binario di Frolla alla Ricotta

This is essentially an Italian ricotta cheesecake in a flat strip of pastry that looks like the railroad track for which it is named. Follow the ricotta filling ingredients and instructions for the previous recipe but use 12 ounces (340 grams) *Pasta Frolla* dough instead of the unbaked pastry shell.

Roll the chilled dough into a 17 × 7-inch rectangle on a lightly floured surface. Trim to about 16 × 6 inches and transfer to a buttered or parchment-lined baking sheet. Refrigerate while you prepare the filling.

Remove the rolled-out dough from the refrigerator and place on a work surface. Using a ruler and very sharp knife, cut 2 long strips, each ½ inch wide, from one long side, and 2 short strips, each ½ inch wide, from one short side. Return the large dough rectangle to the baking sheet. Lightly brush a ½-inch border on the large rectangle with water and place the long strips on each long side of the rectangle; then fit the short strips neatly on the short sides of the rectangle, trimming the strips as needed. Press the strips onto the rectangle lightly with your fingertips.

Spread the ricotta filling, adding 4 tablespoons chopped candied fruit (optional), inside the pastry strips. Sprinkle 2 to 3 tablespoons pine nuts over the filling. You may have enough filling left to make small *budini* in individual buttered baking dishes.

Heat the oven to 350° F. Bake the Binario until the top is set and lightly golden, 35 to 40 minutes; bake the *budini* about 20 minutes. Cool about 10 minutes on the baking sheet and transfer to a rack to cool completely.

Torta di Riso
Rice Tart

Rice tarts are a very ancient tradition in Italian desserts, but no one knows whether they actually date back to Marco Polo's voyage to the East when Venetian traders, merchants, and sailors began bringing rice back from the Orient in ever-increasing amounts. By the sixteenth century there was an explosion of rice planting in the countryside around Venice, and housewives gave free rein to their imaginations and dreamed up elaborate rice dishes to satisfy their culinary fantasies. Perhaps that explains the origins of a venerable Venetian dessert exotically named *torta alla turchesca*, a Turkish tart, that combined rice cooked in milk with butter, sugar, raisins, almonds, a few dates, and pine nuts and then bound with eggs and egg yolks. It sounds remarkably similar to this *torta di riso*, which is but one of many variations on the theme available in Italy today. Almonds are often de rigueur in this particular dessert and can certainly be added to this tart as well.

Makes one deep 8-inch tart; 8 servings

3 cups milk
1¼ cups water
½ cup plus 2 tablespoons (125 grams) sugar
2 strips lemon zest
Pinch salt
1 cup plus 1½ tablespoons (200 grams) Originario or long-grain rice
1 heaping cup (165 grams) raisins
¼ cup Marsala or rum, plus 1 to 2 tablespoons for brushing the top
2 large eggs, separated, room temperature
1 teaspoon vanilla extract
5 tablespoons (65 grams) unsalted butter, room temperature
Deep 8-inch tart shell (*Pasta Frolla I, II,* or *III,* pages 339–42), baked 20 to 25 minutes

Heat the milk, water, sugar, lemon zest, and salt to a boil in a medium-size heavy saucepan. Stir in the rice and reduce the heat to very low. Simmer covered, stirring occasionally, until all the liquid is absorbed, 35 to 40 minutes. Spread the rice on a dinner plate to cool and discard the lemon zest.

While the rice is cooking, soak the raisins in ¼ cup Marsala for at least 30 minutes.

When the rice has cooled to room temperature, whisk the egg yolks and vanilla in a mixing bowl until blended. Stir in the rice. Add the butter and raisins with the Marsala and mix thoroughly. Beat the egg whites until the peaks are stiff but not dry and fold into the rice mixture. Pour the filling into the tart shell.

Baking. Heat the oven to 400° F. Bake just until lightly creamy inside (a skewer inserted in the center should not come out completely clean), about 30 minutes. If the top is too pale, you can brown it briefly under the broiler. Cool on a rack, and brush the surface with 1 to 2 tablespoons Marsala, making a few holes with a toothpick to allow the liquor to penetrate the interior. Serve at room temperature.

Variations. To make *Budini di Riso,* bake the rice pudding in 6 fully baked tartlet shells at 400° F for 20 minutes.

Cassata

Easter Cake of Sicily

For centuries all the *cassate* of Sicily were made by nuns in their convents, and there are stories that those nuns worked so hard before Easter that some even forgot their regular devotions. They were busy making the quintessential Sicilian dessert that combines tastes brought by the Arabs with the *pan di spagna* that came with the Spanish. Some think that the word *cassata* comes from the Arab *qas'at*, big deep bowl; others convincingly argue that it comes from the old Sicilian word *caseata*, from the Latin *caseus* for cheese. Either way, it is a delicious dessert of *pan di spagna* layered with ricotta flavored with candied fruit and bits of chocolate. In Italy the top is decorated with pale green candied strips of a squash related to the pumpkin family (I've seen it in the market as tall as a ten-year-old child), but citron makes a fine substitute.

Makes one 8- or 9-inch filled cake

1 pound 2 ounces (500 grams) ricotta
¾ cup (150 grams) granulated sugar
4 to 5½ tablespoons rum
5 ounces (140 grams) chopped semisweet chocolate or about ¾ cup semisweet chocolate chips
5 ounces (140 grams) chopped candied orange peel or candied fruit
8-inch Pan di Spagna (page 383) or 8½-inch Pasta Maddelena (page 384)
7 ounces (200 grams) marzipan or almond paste
About ¼ cup confectioners' sugar

Press the ricotta through a wire-mesh sieve into a mixing bowl, or process with several pulses in a food processor fitted with the steel blade until smooth and transfer to a mixing bowl. Add the granulated sugar and beat with a wooden spoon until creamy. Stir in 2 to 3 tablespoons of the rum. Add the chocolate and orange peel and stir to combine.

Cut the cake horizontally with a long thin-bladed knife into 3 equal layers. Place the top layer of cake, cut side up, in an unbuttered 8- or 9-inch springform pan (use an 8-inch pan for the 8-inch cake or a 9-inch pan for the 8½-inch cake). Brush the cake with 1 tablespoon rum. Knead the almond paste or marzipan on a work surface sprinkled with the confectioners' sugar until stiff enough to hold its shape when rolled out and cut. Roll into a 10 × 3-inch rectangle. Line the side of the pan with parchment paper. Cut the second cake layer and the almond paste into 3-inch squares and line the side of the pan with alternating cake and almond paste squares. Trim the top edges so that the squares are even with the top of the pan.

Spoon the ricotta filling over the bottom cake layer and smooth the top. Lightly press the last cake layer, cut side down, onto the filling and fold the tops of the cake and almond paste squares over the cake. Brush the top with the remaining 1 to 1½ tablespoons rum. Refrigerate covered with waxed paper until cold, several hours or overnight.

ROYAL ICING
2 cups plus 2 tablespoons (300 grams) confectioners' sugar, sifted after measuring
3 large egg whites
2 teaspoons lemon juice

Beat the sugar, egg whites, and lemon juice in a deep mixer bowl until well blended. Beat at medium-high speed until smooth, thick, creamy, and white, about 5 minutes. Use immediately or remove to a bowl and place plastic wrap over the surface to prevent a crust from forming. It will keep a week in the refrigerator. Invert the cake onto a serving platter and spread the top and sides with the icing. Let dry at room temperature for several hours. Refrigerate at least 3 hours before serving.

If you want, garnish the cake by setting a candied orange half in the center and arranging four to ten ¼-inch-thick citron strips in loops around it.

Spice Cakes and Fruitcakes

Plum Cake

Every baker in Italy has his own recipe for plum cake, an English classic that is now found all over Italy and is a favorite at teatime. It is essentially a pound cake made with the same weight of raisins as flour, sugar, and butter. It was first introduced after Waterloo when the Duke of Wellington, unmoved by French cuisine, brought his own pastry chefs with him to Paris and thus spread the recipe for plum cake. The Italians took to it with the same fervor that the English have taken to Italy, and it appears everywhere, in small towns as well as large. You might even encounter industrialized versions sealed hermetically in small packages of plastic wrap. It is slightly dry and is permeated with the lovely fragrance of rum.

Makes one 9 × 5-inch cake

2 sticks (225 grams) unsalted butter, room temperature
1 cup plus 2 tablespoons (225 grams) sugar
4 eggs, room temperature, lightly beaten
1 egg yolk, room temperature, lightly beaten
¼ cup plus 3 tablespoons rum
1 teaspoon vanilla extract
1⅓ cups (200 grams) currants (soaked in rum overnight, if you want, and drained but rum reserved)
2¼ cups (225 grams) sifted cake or pastry flour
1 teaspoon baking powder
⅓ cup (35 grams) sliced blanched almonds

Cream the butter and sugar with a wooden paddle or electric mixer until light and fluffy, about 5 minutes by hand or 3 to 4 minutes by mixer at high speed. Add the eggs and egg yolk, one at a time, beating thoroughly after each addition. Add the rum and vanilla and beat until light and fluffy, 5 minutes longer by hand or 2 to 3 minutes longer by mixer at high speed. Toss the currants in a bit of the flour to coat them. Sift the flour and the baking powder over the batter and fold in with a rubber spatula just until blended. Gently fold the currants into the batter.

Butter and flour an 8½ × 4½-inch or 9 × 5-inch loaf pan. Pour the batter into the pan but don't smooth the top; instead, mound the batter a bit in the center so that it rises like a pound cake. Sprinkle the almonds over the top.

Baking. Heat the oven to 350° F. Bake until a skewer inserted in the center comes out clean, 1 hour 10 minutes to 1 hour 15 minutes. The cake will begin to shrink away from the side of the pan. Don't be surprised if the cake breaks open on top like many pound cakes. Cool for 10 minutes, and then unmold by inverting onto a rack, removing the pan, and inverting onto a second rack so it can cool right side up.

Variation. To make Plum Cake *Integrale* (whole wheat), substitute 1¼ cups (115 grams) whole-wheat flour and a scant ⅔ cup (65 grams) sifted unbleached cake flour for the 2¼ cups flour. Make as directed.

Torta Rustica di Noci e Caffè
A Rustic Country Cake of Espresso and Walnuts

This simple, moist cake of walnuts and espresso was once commonly made at home on the Tuscan coast north of Viareggio; it has since become almost a memory and today only the old people still eat and remember it.

Makes one 8-inch cake or small cake ring; 6 to 8 servings

About 1⅔ cups (200 grams) walnut pieces
7 tablespoons (100 grams) unsalted butter, room temperature
½ cup plus 2 tablespoons (125 grams) sugar
2 large eggs
1¾ cups less 1 tablespoon (225 grams) all-purpose flour
½ teaspoon baking powder
½ teaspoon salt
½ cup warm strong brewed espresso or 3 tablespoons instant espresso powder dissolved in ½ cup warm water
1 teaspoon vanilla extract

Finely grind about 10 of the walnut pieces and set aside for the top; chop (but not finely) the remaining walnuts.

Cream the butter and sugar with a wooden paddle or electric mixer until light and fluffy. Add the eggs, one at a time, beating thoroughly after each addition. Sift the flour, baking powder, and salt together.

Torta Rustica di Noci e Caffè (continued)

Beat in the flour mixture alternately with the coffee and vanilla in 3 additions, beginning and ending with the flour. Stir the chopped walnuts into the cake batter.

Butter and lightly flour an 8-inch cake pan or 6-cup ring mold. Pour the cake batter into the prepared pan and sprinkle with the ground walnuts.

Baking. Heat the oven to 350° F. Bake the cake until a skewer inserted in the center comes out clean, 50 to 60 minutes for the 8-inch cake or 40 to 50 minutes for the ring mold. Cool completely on a rack.

Torta Speziata
Spice Cake

Spice cake, Italian style, is very moist and tender and is delicious with rum-flavored whipped cream.

Makes one 8-inch cake

⅔ cup (100 grams) raisins
7 tablespoons (100 grams) unsalted butter, room temperature
½ cup (100 grams) granulated sugar
1 large egg
1¾ cups less 1 tablespoon (230 grams) all-purpose flour
½ cup plus 1 tablespoon (60 grams) best-quality Dutch-process cocoa
2 teaspoons baking powder
1 heaping teaspoon ground cinnamon
1 teaspoon ground nutmeg
¼ teaspoon ground cloves
¾ teaspoon salt
¾ cup plus 1 teaspoon warm strong brewed espresso or 3 tablespoons
    instant espresso powder dissolved in ¾ cup plus 1 scant tablespoon
    plus 1 teaspoon hot water
Confectioners' sugar

Soak the raisins in warm water to cover 15 to 30 minutes; drain. Cream the butter and granulated sugar with a wooden paddle or electric mixer until light and fluffy. Add the egg and beat thoroughly. Sift 1¾ cups flour, the cocoa, baking powder, cinnamon, nutmeg, cloves, and salt together. Beat in the flour mixture alternately with the espresso in 3 additions, beginning and ending with the flour. Toss the raisins with 1 tablespoon flour and fold into the batter.

Butter and flour an 8-inch cake pan; pour the batter into the pan and smooth the top.

Baking. Heat the oven to 350° F. Bake until the cake shrinks slightly from the side of the pan; it should still be slightly moist inside, 40 minutes. Cool on a rack. Invert the cake onto a serving plate and sieve confectioners' sugar over the top.

Torta Contadina
A Country Cake

A rich, moist chocolate filled with nuts and fruits that is neither a spice cake nor a true chocolate cake, but is, instead, the best of both worlds.

Makes one 8- or 8½-inch cake

Scant ½ cup (75 grams) raisins
1¾ cups (225 grams) candied orange peel or half candied orange peel and half candied fruit
3 cups (375 grams) leftover cake crumbs, from pound or sponge cake or ladyfingers; bakeries use whatever they have on hand and, within reason, so may you
¾ cup plus 3 tablespoons milk
1 egg
1 egg yolk
½ cup (50 grams) unsweetened cocoa powder, preferably Dutch process
¼ cup (50 grams) sugar
2 teaspoons baking powder
1 teaspoon ground cinnamon
¾ teaspoon freshly grated nutmeg
¾ teaspoon ground cloves
5 tablespoons (70 grams) unsalted butter, room temperature
About ½ cup (50 grams) pine nuts

Coarsely chop the raisins with an oiled knife and place in a mixing bowl. Grind the orange peel and half the cake crumbs in a blender or food processor fitted with the steel blade to a coarse mixture; add to the raisins. Transfer to a mixing bowl and add half the milk and the egg and mix well. Coarsely grind the remaining cake crumbs in the food processor. Stir the cake crumbs, the remaining milk, the egg

Torta Contadina (continued)

yolk, cocoa, sugar, baking powder, cinnamon, nutmeg, and cloves into the raisin mixture. Add the butter and stir until thoroughly blended.

Grease and flour an 8- or 8½-inch cake pan and pour the batter into the pan. Sprinkle enough of the pine nuts over the batter to cover the top.

Baking. Heat the oven to 350° F. Bake until a skewer inserted in the center comes out clean, about 50 minutes. Cool in the pan 10 to 15 minutes and then unmold onto a rack to cool completely.

Panforte
Traditional Fruitcake of Siena

Panforte means "strong bread" in Italian, and this phenomenal dessert is the best fruitcake you could ever imagine, denser than sweet bread and only slightly less rich than candy. The monks of Siena may have been among the first to find pleasure in its rich nutty flavors, and Crusaders may have taken it as a long-lasting food to give them quick bursts of energy on their rigorous pilgrimages. No one is quite sure when *panforte* was first prepared, although there are stories that it dates back to the year 1000 when Siena was one of the first cities in Italy to use sugar and rare spices, including the white pepper that gives *panforte* its authentic medieval taste.

These days *panforte* remains the true Christmas treat of Siena. I remember reading an article once by Sean O'Faolain in which he expressed amazement that some people went to Siena only for this remarkable chewy sweet. It's true that Siena has numerous other enchantments—its extraordinary *Campo*, which may be the most beautiful piazza in all the world, its sinuous curving streets of pink and gray stone buildings, its almond-eyed madonnas, and its moment of collective madness in a horse race called the *Palio*—but surely there is also fascination in finding your way to Siena in a quest for *panforte*, one of the best *dolci* Italy has to offer.

Makes one 9-inch cake

1 cup (115 grams) whole hazelnuts, coarsely chopped
1 cup (115 grams) blanched almonds
1 cup (130 grams) coarsely chopped candied orange peel

1 cup (130 grams) finely chopped citron
1 teaspoon grated lemon zest
½ cup (70 grams) unbleached all-purpose flour
1 teaspoon ground cinnamon
¼ teaspoon ground coriander
¼ teaspoon ground cloves
¼ teaspoon freshly ground nutmeg
Pinch ground white pepper
¾ cup (150 grams) granulated sugar
¾ cup honey
2 tablespoons (30 grams) unsalted butter
Confectioners' sugar

Heat the oven to 350° F. Toast the hazelnuts on a baking sheet until the skins pop and blister, 10 to 15 minutes. Rub the skins from the hazelnuts in a kitchen towel. Toast the almonds on a baking sheet until very pale golden, about 10 to 15 minutes. Chop the almonds and hazelnuts very coarsely. Mix the nuts, orange peel, citron, lemon zest, flour, cinnamon, coriander, cloves, nutmeg, and pepper together thoroughly in a large mixing bowl.

Butter a 9-inch springform pan; line the bottom and sides with parchment paper and then butter the paper. Heat the granulated sugar, honey, and butter in a large heavy saucepan over low heat, stirring constantly, until the syrup registers 242° to 248° F on a candy thermometer (a little of the mixture will form a ball when dropped into cold water). Immediately pour the syrup into the nut mixture and stir quickly until thoroughly blended. Pour immediately into the prepared pan and smooth the top with a spatula. The batter will become stiff and sticky very quickly, so you must work fast.

Baking. Heat the oven to 300° F. Bake about 30 to 40 minutes. The *panforte* won't color or seem very firm even when ready, but it will harden as it cools. Cool on a rack until the cake is firm to the touch. Remove the side of the pan and invert the cake onto a sheet of waxed paper. Peel off the parchment paper. Dust heavily with the confectioners' sugar.

Variation. To make *Panforte Scuro* (dark), add 2 ounces (60 grams) coarsely chopped dried figs and 1 to 2 tablespoons unsweetened cocoa powder.

Sponge Cakes

Amor Polenta
Cornmeal Cake

This lightly sweetened cornmeal cake from Varese, in the upper Brianza region around Como and Bergamo, is a relative of pound cake, although it has more character, which comes from the distinctive flavor and texture of the corn and the splashes of maraschino liqueur. The delicacy of this cake belies most people's idea of cornmeal; Americans are likely to eat it at teatime, while Italians pour cream over the sliced cake for dessert.

Makes two 10 × 4-inch cakes made in rehrücken, or saddle of venison, pans

¾ cup plus 3 tablespoons unsalted butter, room temperature
Scant 1 cup (200 grams) sugar
3 eggs, room temperature
6 egg yolks, room temperature
2 to 4 tablespoons maraschino liqueur or ½ teaspoon almond extract
¾ cup plus 1 tablespoon (100 grams) sifted all-purpose flour
½ cup plus 1 tablespoon (100 grams) yellow cornmeal, plus additional for the pans
2½ teaspoons baking powder
½ teaspoon (3 grams) salt
Confectioners' sugar (optional)

This dough can be made by hand, but it requires lots of vigorous beating and whisking to achieve the characteristic lightness. Given the choice, I'd definitely use an electric mixer.

Cream the butter and 1 cup sugar with the whisk, if you have one, of an electric mixer until very light and fluffy, about 5 minutes at medium speed. Add the eggs and egg yolks, one at a time, beating thoroughly after each addition. The batter should be lemony yellow. Stir in the liqueur. Sift the flour, cornmeal, baking powder, and salt together and fold into the batter, smoothing out any lumps but taking care not to deflate the batter.

Butter 2 rehrücken (saddle of venison) pans and coat with cornmeal. Pour the batter into the 2 prepared pans.

Baking. Heat the oven to 375° F. Bake until a skewer inserted in the center comes out clean, about 30 minutes. Cool on a rack and unmold while the cake is still very slightly warm. If you like, you may follow the example of some bakeries and sift confectioners' sugar over the tops so lightly that you can still see the ridges of the cakes.

Tiramisù
"Pick Me Up"

Tiramisù means "pick me up," and this version of the traditional Venetian dessert is a dream, because it is as easy to make as it is delicious to eat. Pan di Spagna is given an infusion of rum and then layered with whipped cream and fresh mascarpone, the sweet buttery cheese from Lombardy, dusted with cocoa, and finished with shavings of chocolate. If you don't find mascarpone in your market, use the freshest finest cream cheese instead, and, if you'd prefer to dust a bit of espresso powder in with the cocoa, don't let caution inhibit you.

Makes one 2-layer rectangular cake (14 × 8 inches); 10 to 12 servings

1 pound 2 ounces (500 grams) fresh mascarpone or best-quality cream cheese
3 cups heavy or whipping cream
1½ cups plus 2 tablespoons (225 grams) confectioners' sugar
7 to 8 tablespoons rum
1 teaspoon vanilla extract
Pan di Spagna alla Cioccolata (see Variation for Pan di Spagna, page 384) baked in half-sheet pan and cooled completely
2 tablespoons unsweetened cocoa powder, preferably Dutch process
½ ounce (15 grams) semisweet chocolate (optional)

Press the mascarpone through a wire-mesh sieve into a mixing bowl, or process with several pulses in a food processor fitted with the steel blade until smooth. Add the cream, 1½ cups sugar, 3 to 4 tablespoons of the rum, and the vanilla and beat with a wooden spoon or process until smooth and creamy.

Cut the cake in half horizontally; you will have two equal layers. Brush each layer with 2 tablespoons rum. Spread half the cheese mixture on top of 1 cake layer and top with the second cake layer. Spread the remaining cheese filling over the top layer.

Mix the cocoa and remaining 2 tablespoons sugar and sieve over the cake. If you want, grate the chocolate over the cocoa.

Torta Savoia
Savoy Cake

This delicious lemony chocolate cake is essentially a marble pound cake with a lovely silky texture.

Makes one 9 × 5-inch cake

2 sticks (225 grams) unsalted butter, room temperature
1 cup plus 2 tablespoons (225 grams) sugar
4 eggs, room temperature
1 egg yolk, room temperature
Grated zest of 1½ lemons
2 tablespoons plus 1 teaspoon fresh lemon juice
2 cups (200 grams) sifted cake or 1½ cups (200 grams) sifted all-purpose flour
1 teaspoon baking powder
3 ounces (85 grams) best-quality bittersweet chocolate

Cream the butter and sugar with a wooden paddle or an electric mixer until light and fluffy, about 5 minutes by hand or 3 to 5 minutes by mixer at high speed. Add the eggs and egg yolk, one at a time, beating thoroughly after each addition. Beat in the lemon zest and juice and continue beating until light and fluffy again, about 5 minutes by hand or 2 to 3 minutes by mixer at high speed. Sift in the flour and baking powder, a bit at a time, over the batter and gently fold with a rubber spatula into the batter just until smooth.

Pour half the batter into another mixing bowl. Carefully melt the chocolate in a small heavy saucepan over low heat. Quickly stir a little batter from one bowl into the melted chocolate so that the warm chocolate won't harden and then fold into the remaining batter in that same bowl.

Butter and flour a 9 × 5-inch loaf pan. Pour half the chocolate batter into the pan and then pour half the lemon batter. Repeat with the remaining batters. The pan should be about two-thirds full. Don't smooth the top; let the batter mound in the center so that it bakes like a pound cake. To marble the cake, draw a table knife lengthwise back and forth through the cake batter several times.

Baking. Heat the oven to 325° F. Bake until a skewer inserted in the center comes out clean, about 1 hour 20 minutes. Cool on a rack for about 10 minutes. Invert the cake onto a rack, gently remove the pan, and invert the cake onto a second rack so that it can cool right side up. Let cool to room temperature.

Pan di Spagna
Sponge Cake

Pan di Spagna, literally "bread from Spain," actually did come to Italy with the Spanish who conquered Sicily and ruled it from 1412 to 1713. Now this delicate sponge cake is the basis for numerous sweets in Sicily, the island of extravagant desserts, including the famous *cassata*. You can certainly use it instead of Génoise or *biscotti savoiardi* in any number of other desserts as well.

Makes one 17 × 14-inch or 18 × 13-inch sheet sponge cake, two 9 × 5-inch cakes, or one 8-inch round cake baked in a springform

5 eggs, separated, room temperature
¾ cup (150 grams) sugar
2 tablespoons honey
2 tablespoons rum
1 teaspoon vanilla extract
Pinch salt
1¼ cups (175 grams) pastry flour, unsifted
½ teaspoon baking powder

Beat the egg yolks, half the sugar, the honey, rum, and vanilla in a mixer bowl until light, creamy, and lemon colored, about 5 minutes by hand-held electric mixer or 3 minutes by standing electric mixer. Warm the egg whites in a bowl set in warm water for a few minutes; add the salt and beat until soft peaks are formed. Gradually beat in the remaining sugar and continue beating until the peaks are stiff. Sift the flour and baking powder together and return to the sifter. Fold a quarter of the egg whites into the egg yolk mixture with a rubber spatula. Sift a quarter of the flour mixture over the top and fold in. Continue folding in the egg whites and flour mixture alternately until all is incorporated.

Line the bottom and long sides of a jelly-roll or half-sheet pan (18 × 13 inches or 17 × 14 inches) with parchment paper, or flour and butter two 9 × 5-inch loaf pans, or flour and butter an 8-inch springform pan. Pour the batter into the prepared pan/s and smooth the top/s.

Baking. Heat the oven to 350° F. Bake until the cake springs back when touched lightly near the center, 20 to 25 minutes for the sheet pan, 30 to 35 minutes for the loaf pans, or 40 to 45 minutes for the springform pan. Cool on a rack for 5 to 10 minutes. Use a knife to release any part of the cake that is sticking to the pan. Invert the

Pan di Spagna (continued)

cake/s onto a rack or baking sheet and very gently remove the pan. Peel off the parchment paper if using. Invert onto a second rack so that it can cool right side up. Let cool to room temperature.

Variations. To make *Pane all'Anice*, a Sardinian specialty, add 1 tablespoon lightly crushed anise seeds to the batter with the flour. Bake in the loaf pans as directed.

To make *Anicini*, cut the baked and still hot *Pane all'Anice* into 1-inch-thick slices and then cut again into 4½ × 1-inch strips. Bake on their sides on baking sheets at 350° F until crisp, crunchy, and a bit dry, 5 to 10 minutes. Sardinians dip these into a sweet dessert wine.

To make *Pan di Spagna alla Cioccolata* (chocolate), substitute 1 tablespoon Kahlúa for 1 tablespoon of the rum, 1 tablespoon water for the honey, and ⅓ cup unsweetened Dutch-process cocoa and ⅔ cup pastry flour sifted together 3 times for the 1¼ cups pastry flour. Omit the baking powder. Prepare as directed for *Pan di Spagna*. Bake in a half-sheet pan.

Pasta Maddalena
Génoise-like Cake

The virtues of *pasta maddalena* are many: It can be the base for numerous delicious desserts, such as the extravaganza known as *torta delizia* (page 386), and it can be layered with the simplest or the most elaborately flavored creams. But bakers will tell you more: If you find your tart crusts are soggy or if you make a tart one day and expect to serve it the next, you can bake the tart with a very fine layer of *maddalena* next to the bottom crust. The cake will soak up any fruit juices and leave the crust firm and dry. You can also make several cakes and freeze what you don't need with very good results.

Makes two 8½-inch cakes

1 cup (200 grams) sugar
3 eggs
4 egg yolks, room temperature
2 tablespoons water
1 tablespoon honey
1⅓ cups plus 1 tablespoon (160 grams) pastry or cake flour, unsifted

⅛ teaspoon salt
⅔ cup (80 grams) cornstarch or potato starch
1½ teaspoons baking powder
1 teaspoon vanilla extract
Grated zest of 1 lemon

Whisk the sugar, eggs, egg yolks, water, and honey in the top of a double boiler over simmering, not boiling, water until the mixture feels lukewarm. Remove to a mixer bowl or widemouthed mixing bowl. Beat at high speed until thick, pale lemon, creamy, and about tripled in volume, 3 to 4 minutes. Do not overmix or the batter will fall.

Sift the flour, salt, cornstarch, and baking powder together twice. Sift the flour mixture and fold into the egg mixture in 3 additions. Fold in the vanilla and lemon zest. The batter should be soft, airy, and very light and must be handled very carefully so that the air bubbles aren't inadvertently deflated.

Butter and flour two 8½-inch cake pans. Gently pour the batter into them.

Baking. Heat the oven to 375° F. Bake until the cake springs back when lightly touched, 25 to 30 minutes. Cool the cakes in the pans 5 to 10 minutes; then invert onto cake racks and cool completely.

This cake batter is very much like that for ladyfingers (*savoiardi*) and can be used as the base for numerous filled desserts, like the *Torta di Mele e Ciliege* (page 356), *zuppa inglese,* and other recipes calling for ladyfingers. You can brush each cake with rum and spread with pastry cream or zabaglione cream. You can also layer with whipped cream and fruits or jam or just serve it as is dusted with confectioners' sugar.

Torta Delizia

This extraordinary cake is composed of layers of sponge cake or *pasta maddalena* brushed with maraschino liqueur, spread with apricot jam, and covered with a lattice of almond paste. The classic basket weave covering is complicated. If you are trying it for the first time, practice first on waxed paper.

Makes one 2-layered cake

1 cup water
¼ cup (50 grams) sugar
⅓ cup maraschino liqueur
1 *Pasta Maddalena* cake (½ recipe, page 384), cooled
⅔ cup Apricot Glaze (page 345)
1 pound 2 ounces (500 grams) almond paste
2 egg yolks
3 to 4 egg whites

Whisk the water and sugar together in a bowl until the sugar dissolves; then whisk in the liqueur. Cut the cake horizontally into 2 layers. Place the bottom layer on parchment paper and brush the top with half the liqueur mixture; spread a fine layer of the apricot glaze over the top. Cover with the second layer, making certain to put the cut side down so that no crumbs can flake into the almond paste topping that will cover it. Brush it with the remaining liqueur mixture.

Beat the almond paste at high speed in a mixer bowl until it is well broken up and creamy. Add the egg yolks, one at a time, beating thoroughly after each addition; then beat at high speed 2 minutes longer. The almond paste should be very thick, smooth, sticky, and able to hold its shape. Add 3 of the egg whites and beat thoroughly. Beat in the last egg white, a small amount at a time, until the mixture is the consistency of buttercream; it should be soft enough to be piped through a pastry bag but stiff enough to hold its shape. Have extra almond paste on hand in case you beat in too much egg.

Spoon the almond paste mixture into a pastry bag fitted with a #48 pastry tip (flat ⅜-inch-wide tip with one serrated edge). The almond paste is traditionally piped in a basket-weave pattern. Before you start on the cake you can practice on a piece of waxed paper. When you feel confident with the pattern, you can then peel off the strips and return them to the remaining almond paste in the bag. Because fantasy is such a basic part of the Italian baker's vocabulary, you may also simplify the pattern by piping straight lines in a simple lattice pattern.

To make the basket weave, pipe 1 straight line very near the top of the cake. Pipe a second straight line parallel to the first with a space the width of the piping tip (⅜ inch) between the two lines. To create the illusion that the lines actually go over and under each other, you will pipe short lines that alternately go over or stop at the horizontal lines. Pipe the first vertical line starting at the top center of the cake but stop at the first line. Pipe a line next to it that goes over the first line and stops at the second. Pipe a line on the other side of your first vertical line that goes over the first line and stops at the second. Continue these short alternating lines on both sides of the top center line. Next pipe a third horizontal line ⅜ inch below the second line. All the weaving lines that stopped at the first line can now be piped from the other side of the first line, over the second, and brought to the third line. Continue until the cake is completely covered in basket weave. End your weaving lines precisely at the edge of the horizontal lines so that the piping lines look actually woven. Be sure to clean your tip frequently and to pipe your lines completely to the edge of the cake.

Piping the almond paste basketweave

Finish the cake by piping the almond paste mixture in deep swirls or waves all around the side of the cake. Let the cake dry at a cool room temperature overnight.

GLAZES
1 egg, beaten
⅓ cup Apricot Glaze (page 345)

Brush the top of the cake very gently and carefully with the egg, following the direction of the pattern.

Baking. Heat the oven to 360° F. Bake on the parchment paper on a baking sheet until golden brown, about 30 minutes. Let cool completely on a rack. Brush the top and sides with the apricot glaze.

BISCOTTI
Cookies

The first time I was served cookies for breakfast in an Italian house, I assumed the family had run out of bread and the cookies were the best substitute they could come up with in a hurry. The second time, I realized that Italians actually ate cookies for breakfast. In fact, Italians like cookies so much that they eat them for a mid-morning snack with cappuccino or *caffe latte,* as a little treat with cheese at the end of the midday meal, with abandon at teatime, and at the end of a meal dunked into wine or the local *Vin Santo.*

Italians have given their cookies wonderful names that sound as if they're straight out of fairy tales or nursery rhymes: *brutti ma buoni* (ugly but good), *baci di dama* (lady's kisses), *bocche di lupo* (wolves' mouths). Often the same cookie has an entirely different name in a different city or region. *Brutti ma buoni* in Tuscany unaccountably becomes *bocconcini del nonno* (little bite-size sweets for grandfather), in Rome.

Cookies have been part of the Italian way of eating for a long time. The source of the almond paste cookies that are now favorites from one end of Italy to the other is probably the marzipan of Sicily that came with the Arabs, who also introduced cane sugar, almonds, and spices at about the same time that Crusaders were bringing oranges, lemons, dates, and figs to the island. Normans were refining sugar in Sicily before the twelfth century, and the Arabs brought a tradition of elaborate pastries that transformed Palermo into a city of sumptuous eating. We know that in 1308 at a banquet in honor of Clement V there were at table two trees full of all kinds of fruit—apples, figs, pears, and peaches—that seemed absolutely real but were actually made of *pasta reale,* or marzipan, made at the nearby monastery of Martorana. It was, in fact, the busy fingers and nimble hands of nuns that kept the tradition of marzipan alive as they made ever more extravagant fantasies: little lambs turned up for Easter, and perfect replicas of prickly pears, salamis, and fine slices of prosciutto proved their finesse with a paste made only of almonds, sugar, and egg whites. The nuns kept their recipes secret as they perfected them, and made all kinds of elegant decorations on little cookies. Their sweets were covered with angels and fruits that resembled bas-reliefs on local churches, and some even had geometric fondant frostings and glazes inspired by local cathedral ceilings.

Today the tradition is dying out, but every region still has its own special almond paste cookies. The amaretti of Saronno are famous everywhere, but there are amaretti from Piedmont as well, *ricciarelli* from Siena, *brutti ma buoni* from Florence, *marasche* from Bologna, and *pignolate* from Sicily. Glass cases in bakeries are full of all kinds of cookies; every little *paesi* and town has its own local cookie that is every bit as much a part of the regional tradition as its breads and pastas.

Nut Paste Cookies

Brutti ma Buoni alla Milanese

Hazelnut Paste Cookies

The translation of *brutti ma buoni* is "ugly but good"—and there's no question that these cookies are aptly named. Nothing about their appearance is one bit tempting, but pop one of these chewy, crunchy little hazelnut lumps into your mouth and they're irresistible.

Makes 2½ dozen cookies

8 or 9 egg whites, room temperature
1 cup plus 3 tablespoons (240 grams) sugar
¾ teaspoon vanilla extract
1¾ cups (200 grams) hazelnuts, toasted, skinned (page 52), and chopped to the size of fat rice kernels

Beat 8 egg whites in a mixer bowl until soft peaks are formed. Beat, gradually adding the sugar, and continue beating until the peaks are stiff and shiny. Stir in the vanilla until blended. Fold in the nuts. Transfer the mixture to a saucepan and cook over low heat for 10 minutes. Initially the mixture will soften and then, as it cooks, it should come together in a single, although not well defined, lump. It is done when it is light brown and pulls away from the side of the pan. If the mixture is dry and crumbly, add the last egg white, a bit at a time, to moisten it. Remove the mixture from the heat. Drop the dough by teaspoons 1½ inches apart onto well-buttered or parchment-lined baking sheets.

Brutti ma Buoni alla Milanese (continued)

Baking. Heat the oven to 300° F. Bake until lightly colored, 25 to 30 minutes. If the cookies seem too soft, you can turn off the oven and leave them there for 10 minutes. Cool on racks. These keep well stored in an air-tight container.

Variations. Tuscans use half almonds and half hazelnuts in addition to adding about 1½ teaspoons ground coriander to their dough. In Venice, the cookies are sometimes made with the addition of ½ cup unsweetened cocoa powder to the dough.

Brutti ma Buoni

Almond Paste Cookies

Brutti ma Buoni, Tuscan style.

Makes 2½ dozen cookies

1 pound 5 ounces (600 grams) almond paste
2 or 3 egg whites
⅓ cup (50 grams) chopped candied citron
⅓ cup (50 grams) chopped candied orange peel
⅓ cup (50 grams) chopped candied lemon peel
Scant ½ cup (50 grams) sliced raw almonds
Confectioners' sugar

Beat the almond paste and 2 egg whites together with an electric mixer or in a food processor fitted with the steel blade until blended. Add the citron and orange and lemon peels and mix just until blended. The dough should be sticky but stiff enough to hold its shape. If the mixture is too stiff, mix in the last egg white a bit at a time.

Shaping. Place a small bowl of cold water nearby in which to dip your fingers. Drop the dough by rounded teaspoons 1½ inches apart on buttered or parchment-lined baking sheets. Pinch each cookie between your thumb and first two fingers to form an irregular pyramid. The dough should hold its shape so that the baked cookie is a one-bite experience.

Baking. Heat the oven to 300° F. Bake until very light golden, about 25 minutes. Dust with confectioners' sugar and remove to racks to cool. Store in an airtight container.

Marasche

Dome-shaped cookies wrapped around a cherry and covered with sliced almonds, *marasche* are named for the wild sour cherries from Bologna that are hidden in the center of their almond paste coverings.

Makes about 40 cookies

14 ounces (400 grams) almond paste
1 or 2 egg whites
About 40 (190 to 200 grams) preserved *amarena* cherries
¾ cup (80 grams) sliced raw almonds

Mix the almond paste and 1 egg white at low speed in an electric mixer or in a food processor fitted with the steel blade until smooth. If the almond paste is too dry, mix in the last egg white, a bit at a time.

Shaping. Place a small bowl of cold water nearby in which to dip your fingers. Pinch off a piece of almond paste about the size of a walnut and roll into a ball. Flatten the ball in one hand, place a cherry in the center, and wrap the paste around the cherry. Smooth it by rolling it in your hand. The ball should be about ¾ to 1 inch. Pick up a handful of sliced almonds in your other hand and roll the ball in the almonds until it is generously and thoroughly covered. Repeat with the remaining almond paste, cherries, and almonds. Place about 1½ inches apart on buttered or parchment-lined baking sheets.

Baking. Heat the oven to 350° F. Bake 20 to 25 minutes. Cool on racks.

Variation. To make *Bocche di Lupo* (Wolves' Mouths), spoon the almond paste into a pastry bag fitted with a ⅜-inch star-shaped tip. Pipe a 2-inch-long strip of the mixture on buttered or parchment-lined baking sheets, place 1 cherry at the beginning of each strip and double back to meet the cherry. Repeat with the remaining almond paste and cherries. Omit the almonds. Bake until lightly golden, about 18 minutes.

Amaretti I
Macaroons

Amaretti Lombard-style are crisp little almond-flavored cookies that crunch before they dissolve on the tongue.

Makes 30 cookies

1 cup plus 2 tablespoons (125 grams) blanched almonds
2½ tablespoons (20 grams) bitter apricot kernels or ¾ teaspoon almond extract
¾ cup plus 3 tablespoons (125 grams) confectioners' sugar
1 teaspoon all-purpose flour
2 egg whites
⅓ cup (75 grams) granulated sugar

Grind the almonds and apricot kernels to a fine powder in a nut grinder or food processor fitted with the steel blade. (If using the processor, add ¼ cup of the confectioners' sugar, a bit at a time, to keep the almonds from becoming too oily.) Mix the nuts with the confectioner's sugar and the flour. Beat the egg whites in a bowl until soft peaks are formed. Beat, gradually adding the granulated sugar, until stiff and shiny. Fold in the nut mixture and the almond extract, if you are using it, until blended.

Shaping. Spoon the meringue into a pastry bag fitted with a ½-inch plain tip. Pipe 1½-inch-wide mounds 1½ inches apart on parchment-lined or buttered baking sheets. Smooth the top of each cookie with a damp finger.

Baking. Heat the oven to 300° F. Bake 40 to 45 minutes, until very lightly brown. Turn off the oven and let the amaretti dry in the oven an additional 20 to 30 minutes. Cool on racks. Store in airtight containers.

Amaretti II

Macaroons from Piedmont

Unlike the classic amaretti from Saronno, these Piedmontese maca-roons are soft and slightly chewy and taste intensely of almonds.

Makes 20 macaroons

1¾ cups (200 grams) blanched almonds
5 tablespoons (50 grams) bitter apricot kernels or 1 teaspoon almond
  extract
1 cup (200 grams) superfine sugar
3 to 4 tablespoons egg whites
Confectioners' sugar

Grind the almonds and apricot kernels to a fine powder with a mortar and pestle or in a nut grinder or food processor fitted with a steel blade. (If using a food processor, add 2 tablespoons of the sugar.) Mix the ground nuts and superfine sugar in a mixing bowl. Add 3 tablespoons egg whites and the almond extract, if you are using it, and mix until the dough is soft enough to be piped from a pastry bag but stiff enough to hold its shape. Mix in the last tablespoon egg white, a bit at a time, if needed.

Shaping. Spoon the batter into a pastry bag fitted with a ½-inch plain tip. Pipe 2½-inch-wide rounds 1½ inches apart on buttered or parchment-lined baking sheets and flatten them a bit. Sift a little confectioners' sugar over the tops and let stand at room temperature 1 to 2 hours.

Baking. Heat the oven to 300° F. Bake until very light tan, 25 to 30 minutes. Cool on racks. Store in airtight containers.

Pinolate

Chewy Nut Cookies Covered with Pine Nuts

Why *pinolate?* Because these fat balls of chewy hazelnut cookies are studded with *pignoli,* the famous pine nuts of Italy, which make the cookie look a bit like a porcupine at rest.

Makes about 50 cookies

FIRST PASTE
1 cup minus 2 tablespoons (100 grams) blanched almonds
1½ cups (300 grams) sugar
3 or 4 egg whites

Grind the almonds to a fine powder in a nut grinder or food processor fitted with the steel blade. (If using the processor, add 2 tablespoons of the sugar.) Mix the nuts and the sugar in a mixing bowl. Add 3 egg whites and mix until the dough comes together in a sticky ball, adding the last egg white, a bit at a time, if needed. If using the food processor, add the remaining sugar and process to mix. Add the egg whites to the nut mixture and process to mix.

SECOND PASTE
1 cup minus 2 tablespoons (100 grams) skinned toasted hazelnuts (page 52)
1 cup minus 2 tablespoons (100 grams) raw almonds
About 1¾ cups (350 grams) sugar
3 tablespoons unsalted butter (45 grams), room temperature
1 teaspoon honey
3 or 4 egg whites

Grind the hazelnuts and almonds to a fine powder in a mortar and pestle, a nut grinder or food processor fitted with the steel blade. (If using a food processor, add 2 tablespoons of the sugar.) Mix the nuts and sugar in a mixing bowl, or add the remaining sugar to the food processor and process to mix. Add the butter, honey, and 3 egg whites and mix until the dough comes together in a paste, adding the last egg white, a bit at a time, if needed. If using the processor, add the butter, honey, and egg whites and process until the dough comes together in a paste.

Stir both pastes together with a wooden spoon until well blended. The dough should be stiff.

COATING
6½ ounces (195 grams) pine nuts
Confectioners' sugar

Spread the pine nuts on a large flat platter. Roll a bit of the dough between the palms of your hands to form a ball the size of a walnut and then roll in the pine nuts until completely covered. Repeat with the remaining dough and pine nuts. Place the balls 1½ inches apart on buttered or parchment-lined baking sheets and flatten slightly. Let stand, uncovered, overnight at room temperature.

Baking. Heat the oven to 400° F. Sift confectioners' sugar over the dough balls. Bake until the pine nuts are light golden, 15 to 20 minutes. Cool on racks.

Bolle di Neve
"Snowballs" from the Italian Alps

The snow that lasts all year round in some parts of the Italian Alps inspired these "snowballs" made from freshly ground almond paste and dusted with a shower of confectioners' sugar.

Makes about 4 dozen cookies

1 cup plus 2 tablespoons (125 grams) peeled almonds
½ cup plus 2 tablespoons (125 grams) granulated sugar
½ cup plus 2 tablespoons (80 grams) candied orange peel
Scant 1 cup (125 grams) confectioners' sugar, plus additional for the shaped dough
2 to 3 teaspoons egg white

Process the almonds and granulated sugar in a food processor fitted with the steel blade to coarse crumbs (or you can use 9 ounces almond paste and eliminate this step). Add the orange peel to the almond mixture or almond paste in a food processor and process to a coarse powder. Transfer to a mixing bowl and add the scant 1 cup confectioners' sugar. Beat with an electric mixer until blended. If you are strong, you can beat the dough with a wooden spoon. Add 2 teaspoons egg white and mix well. The dough should be firm enough to be shaped but not dry. Add the last teaspoon egg white, a bit at a time, if needed.

continued

Shaping. Dust a work surface with confectioners' sugar and place more sugar in a mound off to one side. Transfer the dough to the surface and roll into a log the diameter of a nickel; slice the log at 1-inch intervals. Roll each piece into a ball between the palms of your hands and then roll in confectioners' sugar so that it is completely covered. Place 1½ inches apart on buttered or parchment-lined baking sheets.

Baking. Heat the oven to 325° F. Bake until golden brown on the outside but still soft inside, 18 to 20 minutes. Cool on racks.

Ricciarelli

Soft Almond Paste Cookies from Siena

These delicate and soft cookies, shaped like the almond eyes of early Sienese painters' madonnas, are descendants of marzipan and are as ancient a Christmas sweet as *panforte*. Fragrant little cookies scented with vanilla, *ricciarelli* are best when made at home fresh for the eating, although they have become so famous that many industrial firms now package them and sell them for the holidays.

Makes 20 cookies

1 cup (100 grams) blanched almonds
14 ounces (400 grams) almond paste
2 tablespoons egg white
¼ teaspoon ammonium carbonate or ½ teaspoon baking powder
1 teaspoon vanilla
Confectioners' sugar

Grind the almonds to a fine powder in a nut grinder or food processor fitted with the steel blade. Transfer to a mixer bowl and mix in the almond paste with an electric mixer. Add the egg white and mix at the lowest speed until thoroughly blended. The dough should be firm. Crush the ammonium carbonate with the flat side of a cleaver to a powder and add to the almond paste. Add the vanilla and mix until well blended.

Shaping. Transfer the dough to a floured surface and roll into a long log about ¾ inch in diameter. Slice the log at 2-inch intervals and shape each piece into a lozenge or diamond. Sift confectioners' sugar lightly over the shaped dough and flatten each piece slightly with a sugar-coated hand. Place the *ricciarelli* 1 inch apart on parchment-lined baking sheets and let stand uncovered at room temperature at least 1 hour or overnight.

Baking. Heat the oven to 300° F. Bake until very light tan, 20 to 30 minutes. Cool on racks. Take care not to bake until brown or crisp; it is the softness that makes *ricciarelli* so delicious.

Pastine da Thé
Italian Tea Cookies

The Italian sweet tooth gets its full due every afternoon at teatime when plates full of little cookies appear on tables in homes and restaurants all over the country to be consumed with a cool drink in the summer or a cup of cappuccino or espresso later in the year. Tea itself hasn't made much impact in Italy in the face of all those espresso beans, but these sweet morsels are perfect mid-afternoon snacks.

Makes about 3 dozen cookies

1⅔ cups (200 grams) raw almonds
1 cup (200 grams) sugar
½ cup egg whites
¼ cup (50 grams) diced candied orange peel or about 18 candied cherries, halved

Grind the almonds to a powder in a nut grinder or a mortar and pestle, or process them with 2 tablespoons of the sugar to a coarse powder in a food processor fitted with the steel blade; add the remaining sugar and process to a fine powder. Press through a wire-mesh sieve so that the powder is nearly as fine as flour. Place the almond powder and the egg whites in the food processor or in the bowl of an electric mixer and process or mix until well blended. The mixture should have enough body to be piped.

Pastine da Thé (continued)

You can substitute 14 ounces almond paste for the almonds and sugar. Place the almond paste in a food processor fitted with the steel blade or in the bowl of an electric mixer. Process or mix until the paste is broken up. Add the egg whites and process or mix to a smooth paste.

Shaping. Spoon the batter into a pastry bag fitted with a ⅜-inch star-shaped tip. Pipe 1-inch-wide stars 1½ inches apart onto buttered or parchment-lined baking sheets. Top each mound with a piece of candied orange peel or a cherry half. Let stand uncovered at room temperature overnight.

Baking. Heat the oven to 375° F. Bake until lightly browned, 8 to 10 minutes. Cool on racks.

Butter Cookies

Baci di Dama
Lady's Kisses

Big button-shaped buttery cookies fused with a spot of chocolate from Tortona in Piedmont, where sweets with somewhat frivolous, evocative names were served in the mid-nineteenth century to men seriously at work creating a unified Italy.

Makes 4 dozen cookies

1 cup plus 2 tablespoons (125 grams) blanched almonds
1 cup plus 2 tablespoons (125 grams) sugar
1 stick plus 1 tablespoon (130 grams) unsalted butter, room temperature
1¼ teaspoons vanilla extract
¾ teaspoon grated lemon zest
Pinch salt
Scant 1 cup (125 grams) all-purpose flour
4 ounces (115 grams) semisweet chocolate

Grind the almonds to a very fine powder in a nut grinder or food processor fitted with the steel blade. (If using a food processor, add 2 tablespoons of the sugar so that the nuts don't become too oily.) Mix the almonds and the remaining sugar in a mixer bowl or in the

Baci di Dama (continued)

food processor. Add the butter, vanilla, lemon zest, and salt and beat or process until very, very light and creamy, about 4 to 5 minutes with the mixer. If necessary, transfer the dough in the processor to a mixing bowl. Sift the flour over the top and fold in. You can refrigerate the dough overnight at this point or proceed.

Shaping. Break off pieces of the dough the size of fat cherries and roll into balls. Place 1½ inches apart on buttered baking sheets and flatten slightly to about ⅜ inch thick.

Baking. Heat the oven to 350° F. Bake until delicate golden brown, 15 minutes. Cool on racks.

Assembling. Melt the chocolate in the top of a double boiler over simmering water. When the cookies are cool, make sandwiches by joining them in pairs with the melted chocolate, so that they do in fact look just a bit like the lady's lips for which they are named.

Ciambelline all'Uva

Raisin-dotted Cookie Wreaths

These raisin-dotted cookie wreaths are really butter cookies in disguise.

Makes about 4½ dozen

1 stick plus 3 tablespoons (160 grams) unsalted butter, room temperature
1¼ cups (250 grams) sugar
2 eggs, room temperature
6½ tablespoons milk
1 teaspoon vanilla extract
½ teaspoon lemon extract or grated zest of 1 lemon
½ teaspoon orange extract or grated zest of ½ orange
4 cups and 2 tablespoons (500 grams) pastry flour or 1 cup (125 grams) cake flour and 2¾ cups (370 grams) all-purpose flour
2 teaspoons baking powder
Pinch salt
⅔ cup golden raisins
1 egg, beaten

Cream the butter and sugar in a mixer bowl until light and fluffy. Add the eggs, one at a time, beating thoroughly after each addition.

Ciambelline all'Uva (continued)

Mix in the milk and vanilla, lemon, and orange extracts. Sift the flour, baking powder, and salt over the batter and mix until thoroughly blended. Stir in the raisins.

Shaping. Turn the soft, sticky dough out onto a well-floured surface. Pinch off a piece of dough the size of a walnut and roll it into a 6-inch-long log, ½ inch thick. Connect the ends to make a circle. It will resemble a little doughnut. Repeat with the remaining dough and place 1½ inches apart on buttered or parchment-lined baking sheets. Brush the tops with beaten egg.

Baking. Heat the oven to 350° F. Bake until lightly golden, 12 to 15 minutes. Cool on racks.

Inglesine

Round Buttery Cookies with Rum-soaked Raisins

Once they discovered Italy, the English came in droves, settling in Florence and the hills of Fiesole, bringing with them their tradition of tea and teatime. The Italians, who love a snack in mid-afternoon, were influenced by some of the English tastes and created this round buttery cookie with rum-soaked raisins in their honor.

Makes 3 dozen cookies

Scant ½ cup (65 grams) raisins, soaked in rum to cover
½ stick (55 grams) unsalted butter, room temperature
¼ cup plus 2 tablespoons (75 grams) sugar
½ teaspoon salt
1 egg
2 tablespoons milk
1 teaspoon vanilla extract
¾ teaspoon lemon extract
1 cup plus 1 tablespoon (150 grams) all-purpose flour
3½ tablespoons (50 grams) potato starch
1 teaspoon baking powder
Pinch salt

Soak the raisins in the rum for at least 30 minutes. Drain but reserve 1 teaspoon of the rum.

Cream the butter, sugar, and salt in a mixer bowl until light and fluffy. Add the egg, milk, reserved rum, the vanilla and lemon extracts and mix until well blended. Sift in the flour, potato starch, baking powder and salt and mix until smooth. Fold in the raisins. Drop the dough by teaspoons 2 inches apart onto buttered or parchment-lined baking sheets.

Baking. Heat the oven to 375° F. Bake until lightly golden, 12 to 15 minutes. Cool on racks.

Variation. Substitute 1½ to 2 teaspoons crushed anise seeds for the 1 teaspoon rum.

Buranelli
Butter Cookies from Burano

Close your eyes and picture the water stretching away from Venice, past the palazzi and gondolas on the Grand Canal, and think about finding your way to the little island of Burano that lies beyond Venice, where these S-shaped buttery cookies are made.

Makes about 4 dozen cookies

1 stick plus 2 teaspoons (125 grams) unsalted butter, room temperature
1 cup plus 3 tablespoons (240 grams) sugar
5 egg yolks
2 teaspoons vanilla extract
¾ teaspoon lemon extract or grated zest of 2 lemons
3 cups (400 grams) all-purpose flour
1 teaspoon (5 grams) salt

Cream the butter and sugar in a mixer bowl until light and fluffy. Add the egg yolks, one at a time, beating thoroughly after each addition. Mix in the vanilla and lemon extracts. Sift the flour and salt over the mixture and mix until blended.

Shaping. Roll the dough on a floured surface into a 2-inch-wide log. Slice the log at ⅜-inch intervals. Roll each piece into a 4-inch-long rod between the palms of your hands. Shape each rod into an inverted S and place 1½ inches apart on buttered or parchment-lined baking sheets.

Baking. Heat the oven to 375° F. Bake until pale blond and just golden at the edges, 20 to 25 minutes. Carefully remove to racks to cool.

Fregolata Veneziana

Fregolata from Venice

Fregolata means crumbly or friable, and this buttery rich, slightly coarse cornmeal shortbread is baked as a nut-covered flat cake and is cut into wedges after it has cooled.

Makes 10 to 12 cookie wedges

Scant 1 cup (100 grams) raw almonds
½ cup (100 grams) granulated sugar
7 tablespoons (100 grams) unsalted butter, melted and cooled
2 egg yolks
2 teaspoons lemon juice
Grated zest of 1 lemon
1 teaspoon vanilla extract
¼ teaspoon almond extract
⅞ cup (100 grams) fine yellow cornmeal
Scant ¾ cup (100 grams) all-purpose flour
Pinch salt
¼ cup (25 grams) raw almonds or skinned toasted hazelnuts (page 52), coarsely chopped
1 to 2 tablespoons turbinado sugar

Grind the almonds to a coarse powder in a nut grinder or a mortar and pestle, or grind them and 2 to 3 tablespoons of the granulated sugar in a blender or food processor fitted with the steel blade to a coarse powder. Add the remaining sugar and process to a very fine powder. Transfer to a mixer or a large mixing bowl and beat in the butter until blended. Add the egg yolks, lemon juice, lemon zest, and vanilla and almond extracts and mix until well blended. Sift the cornmeal, flour, and salt over the almond mixture and stir just until the dough comes together. It is important not to overwork the dough.

Assembling. Butter an 8- or 9-inch pie plate. Spread the dough in the pan, using your fingers to distribute the dough to the edge. Sprinkle with the almonds and the turbinado sugar.

Baking. Heat the oven to 350° F. Bake for 20 minutes. Reduce the heat to 300° F and bake 20 minutes longer. Cool completely on a rack and cut into wedges to serve.

Ungheresi

Hungarian
Cookies, Italian
Style

Makes about 80 little cookies

1 stick plus 3 tablespoons (160 grams) unsalted butter, room temperature
1 cup (140 grams) confectioners' sugar
2½ hard-cooked egg yolks (45 grams) very finely sieved
1 cup plus 1 tablespoon (150 grams) all-purpose flour
Scant ⅓ cup (40 grams) potato starch
6 ounces (170 grams) semisweet chocolate
Pinch salt

Cream the butter and sugar in a mixer bowl until light and fluffy. Add the egg yolks, a bit at a time, beating thoroughly after each addition. Place the flour, potato starch and salt in a sifter and sift over the butter mixture, while stirring by hand or mixing at the lowest speed of an electric mixer. Stir just until the dough is consistent.

Chilling. Wrap the dough tightly in plastic wrap and refrigerate 1 hour.

Shaping. Roll small pieces of the dough into logs 3½ inches long and ⅜ inch thick; shape each log into a horseshoe. Place 1½ inches apart on buttered or parchment-lined baking sheets.

Baking. Heat the oven to 375° F. Bake just until blond and sand colored but not golden, 10 to 15 minutes. Cool completely on racks.

Glazing. Melt the chocolate in the top of a double boiler over simmering water. Dip the ends of the cooled cookies in the melted chocolate. Place on baking sheets lined with waxed paper and refrigerate to set the chocolate.

Onde
Waves

Little ruffly cookies dotted with a candied cherry or a single almond.

Makes 2 dozen cookies

1 stick plus 3 tablespoons (150 grams) unsalted butter, room temperature
⅓ cup plus 1 tablespoon (80 grams) sugar
1 egg white
1 teaspoon vanilla extract
½ teaspoon lemon extract or grated zest of 1 lemon
1½ cups (200 grams) all-purpose flour
Pinch salt
24 candied cherries or raw whole almonds
1 egg white, lightly beaten (optional)

Cream the butter and sugar in a mixer bowl until light and fluffy. Beat in 1 egg white and the vanilla and lemon extracts. Sift the flour and salt over the mixture and fold in with a rubber spatula until combined. The dough should be moist and dense but soft enough to be piped.

Shaping. Spoon the dough into a pastry bag fitted with a ⅜-inch star-shaped tip. Place the pastry tip almost on a buttered or parchment-lined baking sheet and squeeze hard to make a 1½-inch-wide mound; release pressure gradually and pull forward 3 inches so that the cookies are 3 inches wide at the top but narrow to a finer point, like a fat teardrop. The star tip will give a lovely wavy appearance. Repeat with the remaining dough, spacing the cookies about 1½ inches apart. Finish by setting a candied cherry or almond at the narrow end of each cookie; you can paint the narrow tip of dough with a little of the beaten egg white to hold the cherry or almond in place, if you want.

Baking. Heat the oven to 350° F. Bake until lightly golden, 15 to 20 minutes. Cool on racks.

Tegole d'Aosta
Tile-shaped Cookies from the Val d'Aosta

These thin, round hazelnut cookies are named for the fine slate tiles that line the roofs of houses in the valley of Aosta. You can either shape the warm cookies on a rolling pin or wine bottle or let them cool flat. This dough also makes wonderful *Lingue di Gatto* (page 406). These are wonderful tea and after-dinner cookies, but they don't keep well—especially the lighter and more delicate variety—because the humidity in the air affects them so that they tend to lose their slight crunch.

Makes 4 dozen cookies

1 stick plus 3 tablespoons (150 grams) unsalted butter, room temper-ature
¾ cup plus 3 tablespoons (195 grams) sugar
½ teaspoon vanilla extract
⅔ cup (100 grams) skinned toasted hazelnuts (page 52)
3½ ounces (100 grams) leftover cookies, preferably butter or sugar
¼ cup (30 to 35 grams) all-purpose flour
Pinch salt
Scant ½ cup (105 grams) egg whites

Cream the butter and sugar in a mixer bowl until light and fluffy. Add the vanilla and mix well. Grind the hazelnuts to a coarse powder in a nut grinder or food processor fitted with the steel blade; remove and set aside. Grind the leftover cookies to crumbs. Add the hazelnuts to the crumbs and process to a fine powder. Add to the butter mixture and mix until thoroughly blended. Stir in the flour and salt and fold until blended. Beat in the egg whites. The batter should be light and almost runny.

Shaping. You can shape these cookies either with a pastry bag or by hand. Spoon the batter into a pastry bag fitted with a ½-inch plain tip and pipe 2½-inch circles onto buttered and floured or parchment-lined baking sheets. Smooth the tops with the back of a spoon without flattening them. The cookies will spread during baking, so leave at least 3 inches between the circles. To shape by hand, drop 2 teaspoons of the dough onto prepared baking sheets without flattening them, and smooth into 2½-inch circles using the back of a spoon dipped in cool water.

Baking. Heat the oven to 375° F. Bake until the edges of the cookies are evenly browned, 7 to 10 minutes. Let cool on the baking sheets 3 to 4 minutes and then gently dislodge and transfer to racks to cool. You may shape the warm cookies over a rolling pin or wine bottle if you wish.

Variation. For a slightly less delicate cookie, use ⅓ cup plus 1 tablespoon egg white (80 grams) in the dough.

Lingue di Gatto
Cat's Tongues

A *lingue de chat* becomes a *lingue di gatto* in Italy, a delicate crispy little cookie, long and narrow and curled like a cat's tongue.

Makes 5 dozen cookies

1 stick (115 grams) butter, room temperature
½ cup (110 grams) sugar
Grated zest of 1 lemon
1 teaspoon vanilla extract
5 tablespoons (100 grams) egg whites
¾ cup (110 grams) all-purpose flour
⅛ teaspoon salt

Cream the butter and sugar in a mixer bowl until light and fluffy. Mix in the lemon zest and vanilla. Add the egg whites, one at a time, beating thoroughly after each addition. Sift the flour and salt together three times. Sift the flour mixture, a third at a time, over the batter, beating thoroughly after each addition.

Shaping. Butter and flour or line a baking sheet with parchment paper. Spoon the batter into a pastry bag fitted with a ¼-inch flat tip. Pipe 1½- to 2-inch-long strips about 1 inch apart onto the prepared baking sheet.

Baking. Heat the oven to 350° F. Bake until the edges are crispy brown but the centers are still pale, about 10 minutes. Let cool for a moment or two and then place each cookie over a rolling pin or wine bottle; immediately press the cookie to the rolling pin or bottle, so that the cookie conforms to its shape. Remove when the shape is set. If the last cookies on the baking sheet are hard before you can mold them, return to the warm oven for a minute to soften.

Variation. To make *Lingue di Suocera* (Mother-in-law's Tongues) melt 5 ounces (140 grams) semisweet chocolate in the top of a double boiler over simmering water while the cookies are baking. Remove a just-baked cookie from the baking sheet with a spatula. Spread a little melted chocolate on the bottom with a knife. Remove another cookie and sandwich the chocolate between them. Immediately place over a rolling pin or wine bottle to mold as directed for *Lingue di Gatto.* Repeat with the remaining cookies and chocolate.

Biscotti

Biscotti al Latte

Vanilla-scented Tea Biscuits

Another one of those familiar vanilla-scented, slightly dry cookies so redolent of Italy, this tea biscuit is delicate, buttery, and resembles a wreath-shaped sugar cookie.

Makes 6 dozen cookies

1 stick plus 3 tablespoons (160 grams) unsalted butter, room temperature
1 cup (200 grams) sugar
1 tablespoon honey
3 or 4 eggs, room temperature
½ cup plus 3 tablespoons milk
1 teaspoon vanilla extract
½ teaspoon orange extract or grated zest of ½ orange
½ teaspoon lemon extract or grated zest of 1 lemon
3¾ cups (500 grams) all-purpose flour or 1 cup (125 grams) cake flour and 2¾ cups (375 grams) all-purpose flour
2 teaspoons baking powder
Pinch salt
1½ tablespoons coarsely ground raw almonds

Cream the butter, sugar, and honey in a mixer bowl until light and fluffy. Add 2 of the eggs, one at a time, beating thoroughly after each addition. Mix in the milk and vanilla, orange and lemon extracts. The batter may look curdled at this point, but don't worry, for it will smooth out later. Sift the flour, baking powder and salt over the batter; mix well.

Shaping. Transfer the dough to a floured surface. Break off pieces of dough the size of fat cherries; roll each piece into a thin 6-inch rod, and connect the ends to form a 3-inch ring. Place 1 inch apart on buttered or parchment-lined baking sheets. Beat 1 egg in a small bowl and brush the tops of the rings with the beaten egg. Sprinkle lightly with the ground almonds. Use the remaining egg if you run out of egg wash.

Baking. Heat the oven to 325° F. Bake until lightly browned, 20 minutes. Cool on racks.

Biscotti d'Anice
Anise Cookies

These anise-flavored cookies puff up like little spongecakes in the oven and have the delicate airy texture of ladyfingers when first cooked; cut them in diagonal slices and bake them a second time to make the traditional anise-scented crunchy cookies of Sardinia.

Makes 2 dozen cookies

4 eggs, room temperature
¾ cup (180 grams) sugar
1 teaspoon vanilla extract
Grated zest of ½ lemon
1½ cups (200 grams) all-purpose flour
Pinch salt
¼ teaspoon baking powder
2 teaspoons anise seeds, crushed

Beat the eggs and sugar in a mixer bowl until the mixture forms a slowly dissolving ribbon when the beaters are lifted, about 5 to 10 minutes. Mix in the vanilla and lemon zest. Sift the flour and salt and sift again with the baking powder over the egg mixture; fold in gently. Stir in the anise seeds.

Shaping. Spoon the batter into a pastry bag fitted with a plain tip. Pipe the batter in strips, 4 inches long and 1 inch wide, onto buttered or parchment-lined baking sheets. The piped batter should look like large ladyfingers.

Baking. Heat the oven to 375° F. Bake until slightly crisp and brown on the edges, 20 minutes. Remove from the oven. If you want drier, crunchier biscotti, reduce the heat to 325° F. Cut each strip in half on the diagonal and bake on the baking sheet 5 to 10 minutes longer. Cool on racks.

Biscotti di Prato

Diagonally Cut Almond Bars from Prato

These nut-studded bars are dry, crunchy and could even be called hard, because they are baked not once, but twice, to give them their texture. Tuscans serve them after dinner with Vin Santo, the sweet dessert wine kept for special occasions. Keep the biscotti in a cookie tin and they will last for a long time, but, if you let them dry out at room temperature, the flavor gets even better, and they will soften up immediately when dipped in a late harvest wine or port, if you can't find the special Vin Santo of Tuscany.

Makes about 4 dozen cookies

3¾ cups (500 grams) all-purpose flour
2½ cups (500 grams) sugar
4 eggs, room temperature
2 egg yolks, room temperature
1 teaspoon baking powder
Pinch salt
1 teaspoon vanilla extract
1⅔ cups (200 grams) raw almonds, toasted (page 52) and roughly chopped

Pour the flour in a mound on a work surface or in a big bowl. Make a well in the center and place the sugar, 3 of the eggs, the egg yolks, baking powder, salt, and vanilla in the well. Gradually work the flour into the ingredients in the well and mix with your hands until smooth. Knead in the almonds thoroughly and keep kneading, sprinkling with additional flour if needed, 4 to 5 minutes in all.

Shaping. Butter and flour 2 baking sheets that are at least 15 inches long. Divide the dough into quarters. Roll each piece of the dough on a floured surface into a 2- to 2½-inch-wide log and place the logs at least 2 inches apart on the prepared baking sheets. Beat the remaining egg and brush it over the tops of the dough logs.

Baking. Heat the oven to 350° F. Bake for 35 minutes. Remove from the oven and reduce the temperature to 325° F. Cut the logs diagonally into ¾- to 1-inch slices and lay them cut side up on the sheets. Return to the oven for another 15 minutes. Cool on racks.

Variation. In Pistoia, these biscotti are made with a mixture of almonds and hazelnuts.

Tozzetti

These glossy little blond bars with their shiny tops from Venice look as squat and chunky as the name implies. But bite into one and you'll find a pale, soft interior with big chunks of hazelnut and hints of orange—a delicious, elegant surprise.

Makes twenty 4½-inch × 1½-inch bars, twenty-four 2¼-inch squares, or sixty 1½-inch squares

1 stick plus 1 tablespoon (130 grams) unsalted butter, room temperature
½ cup plus 2 tablespoons (125 grams) sugar
2 eggs, room temperature
1 egg yolk, room temperature
¾ teaspoon vanilla extract
½ teaspoon lemon extract or the juice of ½ lemon
½ teaspoon orange extract or the juice of ½ orange
About 2 cups (250 grams) all-purpose flour
¼ teaspoon salt
1⅔ cups (250 grams) toasted and skinned hazelnuts, each roughly chopped into 2 or 3 pieces
⅓ cup (55 grams) finely chopped candied orange peel

Cream the butter and sugar in a mixer bowl until light and fluffy. Beat in 1 of the eggs and then the egg yolk. Mix in the vanilla, lemon, and orange extracts. Sift the flour and salt over the butter mixture, sprinkle with the nuts and orange peel, and gently fold in. If the dough seems too soft to be rolled out, refrigerate covered 1 to 1½ hours.

Shaping. Transfer the dough to a lightly floured surface and roll into a 15 × 9-inch rectangle. Roll up the dough on the rolling pin and unroll on a buttered and floured or parchment-lined baking sheet. Beat the remaining egg and brush over the dough.

Baking. Heat the oven to 375° F. Bake until shiny and blond but not golden, 15 to 20 minutes. It should still be slightly soft inside. Remove from the oven and let stand 10 to 15 minutes. While still warm, cut into 4½ × 1½-inch bars or 2¼-inch or 1½-inch squares. Transfer to racks to cool.

Various-Grain Cookies

Zaletti

*Raisin Cornmeal
Cookies from
Venice*

There are probably as many recipes for this diamond-shaped cornmeal cookie as there are Venetian bakeries and families, but they all feature raisins, the same shape, and the golden color (*gialletti*) from which the dialect name comes.

Makes about 5 dozen cookies

¾ cup dark seedless raisins or currants, soaked in rum to cover
1 stick plus 3 tablespoons (160 grams) unsalted butter, room temperature
½ cup plus 1½ tablespoons (120 grams) sugar
2 eggs, room temperature
1½ cups (220 grams) all-purpose flour, plus 1 to 2 tablespoons for the raisins
1 cup plus 3 tablespoons (200 grams) fine yellow cornmeal
2 teaspoons baking powder
¾ teaspoon salt

Soak the raisins in the rum at least 30 minutes and drain. Beat the butter and sugar together in a mixer bowl until light and fluffy. Add the eggs, one at a time, beating thoroughly after each addition. Sift in 1½ cups flour, the cornmeal, baking powder, and salt and mix well. Toss the raisins with 1 to 2 tablespoons flour and stir into the dough.

Shaping. Transfer the dough to a lightly floured surface. Roll into an 18-inch log, about 1¾ inches thick, and slice the log at ⅜-inch intervals. Using your fingers, pat and shape each piece into a diamond or oval, about 3 inches long. Place about 2 inches apart on buttered baking sheets because they puff and spread as they bake.

Baking. Heat the oven to 375° F. Bake until lightly browned, about 20 minutes. Cool on baking sheets for a few minutes and then transfer to racks.

Crumiri

*Buttery
Horseshoe-shaped
Cookies from
Piedmont*

These delicate, crumbly horseshoe-shaped cookies come from Piedmont where the oldest families of the region traditionally made them every Saturday. They are rich and surprisingly tender and get their special taste from the slightly crunchy cornmeal.

Makes 2 dozen cookies (the recipe can easily be doubled)

1½ sticks plus 2 tablespoons (200 grams) unsalted butter, room
   temperature
¾ cup (150 grams) sugar
2 eggs, room temperature
1¾ cups (240 grams) all-purpose flour
Pinch salt
⅔ cup plus 1 tablespoon (120 grams) fine yellow cornmeal

Cream the butter and sugar in a mixer bowl until very light and fluffy. Add the eggs, one at a time, beating thoroughly after each addition. Sift the flour, salt and cornmeal together and sift again over the batter; mix well.

Shaping. You can shape these cookies either with a pastry bag or by hand (I think the latter is easier). If using the pastry bag, spoon the dough into the bag fitted with a ⅜-inch star-shaped tip (the traditional cookies are ribbed). Pipe 4-inch-long logs, ½ inch thick, about 2 inches apart on buttered and floured or parchment-lined baking sheets. Or, roll pieces of the dough, each about the size of a walnut, into long thin logs of the same dimensions. Place 2 inches apart on the prepared baking sheets. Bend each piped or rolled log into a horseshoe.

Baking. Heat the oven to 325° F. Bake until lightly golden, about 12 minutes. Cool on racks.

Variation. To make *Lunette Siciliane,* another polenta cookie of the same dough and shape, brush the tops of the unbaked cookies with beaten egg and coat with sesame seeds. Place seed side up on the baking sheets and bake as directed for *Crumiri.*

Biscotti di Crusca

Bran Cookies Spiked with Rum

Part of the new Italian concern with health is apparent in this cookie, which bakes to granola-like crunchiness.

Makes about 3½ dozen cookies

1 stick plus 1 tablespoon (125 grams) unsalted butter, room temperature
¼ cup (50 grams) sugar
¼ cup plus 2 tablespoons (125 grams) packed light brown sugar
1 egg, room temperature
2 tablespoons rum
½ teaspoon vanilla extract
Scant 1½ cups (175 grams) pastry flour
1 cup (75 grams) bran
1 teaspoon baking powder
Pinch salt

Cream the butter and sugars in a mixer bowl until light and fluffy. Add the egg, rum, and vanilla and mix at medium speed for 1 minute. Sift the flour, bran, baking powder, and salt over the batter and mix until thoroughly blended, 30 seconds to 1 minute. The dough should be fairly stiff and easy to roll; the trick is to use as little flour as possible to roll out the dough so that it doesn't dry out. Transfer the dough to a very lightly floured surface and dust the top with a minimal amount of flour. Roll out ¼ inch thick and prick all over with a fork. Cut out 2½-inch scalloped circles with a cookie cutter. Place 1 inch apart on buttered or parchment-lined baking sheets. Gather and reroll the scraps; cut out as many circles as possible.

Baking. Heat the oven to 350° F. Bake just until firm, 8 to 10 minutes. If overbaked, the cookies will be dry and will have lost their appealing moistness. Cool on racks.

Biscotti Integrali

Whole-Wheat Cookies Spiked with Rum

These little cookies have a wonderful nutty, crunchy taste that is enhanced by a lacing of rum. The Mediterranean diet, which is being so heartily promoted as a healthy way of living, depends on whole grains in part, so you might even feel virtuous consuming these.

Makes about 3½ dozen cookies

1 stick plus 2 tablespoons (145 grams) unsalted butter, room temperature
½ cup plus 2 tablespoons (125 grams) sugar
1 egg, room temperature
2 tablespoons rum
½ teaspoon vanilla extract
1¾ to 2 cups (250 grams) whole-wheat flour
1 teaspoon baking powder
Pinch salt

Cream the butter and sugar in a mixer bowl until light and fluffy. Add the egg, rum, and vanilla and beat 2 minutes. Sift the flour and baking powder over the batter and mix until thoroughly blended. The dough should be fairly stiff and very easy to roll. Transfer the dough to a lightly floured surface and dust the top of the dough with a minimal amount of flour. Roll out ¼ inch thick and prick all over with a fork. Cut out 2½-inch scalloped circles with a cookie cutter. Place 1½ inches apart on buttered or parchment-lined baking sheets. Gather and reroll the scraps for more circles.

Baking. Heat the oven to 350° F. Bake for 8 to 12 minutes until firm. Cool on racks.

Sweet Pastry Dough Cookies

Savoiardi

*Ladyfingers,
Italian Style*

Savoiardi are one of the most basic Italian cookies. We call them ladyfingers, but they got their name and their popularity in the seventeenth century when the house of Savoy, the most powerful dynasty in northern Italy, ruled Piedmont. They are often used for desserts with and without fillings. *Pasticcio della nonna* from Piacenza, for example, alternates layers of *savoiardi* bathed in rum with amaretti dipped in maraschino.

Makes 30 cookies

5 eggs, separated, room temperature
¾ cup (160 grams) granulated sugar
2 drops vinegar
1 teaspoon vanilla extract
¾ cup plus 2 tablespoons (125 grams) all-purpose flour
⅓ cup (40 grams) potato starch
Pinch salt
Confectioners' sugar

Beat the egg yolks and 3 tablespoons of the granulated sugar in a large mixer bowl until the mixture is light, thick, and forms a slowly dissolving ribbon when the beater is lifted, 7 to 10 minutes. Beat the egg whites in a warmed bowl at high speed with clean beaters until foamy. Gradually beat in the remaining granulated sugar and continue beating at high speed until the peaks are stiff and shiny. Beat in the vinegar and vanilla. Sift the flour, potato starch and salt together. Fold a quarter of the egg yolks into the whites; then alternately fold the flour mixture and the egg whites into the egg yolks.

Shaping. Spoon the batter into a pastry bag fitted with a ½-inch plain tip. Pipe 5-inch-long strips of the batter about 1 inch apart on greased and floured or parchment-lined baking sheets. Sift confectioners' sugar generously over the tops.

Baking. Heat the oven to 425° F. Bake until lightly golden, 10 to 15 minutes. Cool on racks. Ladyfingers keep 2 to 3 weeks in an airtight container.

Garibaldi
Buttery Raisin-filled Bars

This delicious buttery raisin-filled cookie is simplicity itself. A layer of sweet pastry dough is covered with a thick carpet of raisins, topped with another layer of pastry, and glazed lightly with caramel.

Makes 88 bars

Pasta Frolla I (page 339) made through chilling
1 or 2 eggs, beaten
4 cups (600 grams) raisins

Divide the cold dough into 2 pieces, one twice as large as the other (two-thirds and one-third). Roll out the large piece into a 17 × 11-inch rectangle on a lightly floured work surface. Roll up the dough onto the rolling pin and then unroll it on a 17 × 11-inch baking sheet lined with parchment or waxed paper. Brush the surface with beaten egg and scatter the raisins evenly on top. Press the raisins firmly into the dough with the rolling pin and brush again with beaten egg. Roll the remaining dough into the same size rectangle. Roll it up onto the rolling pin and then unroll it over the raisins. Don't worry if it rips and tears a bit, for it's easily patched. Trim the dough and brush the surface with beaten egg.

CARAMEL GLAZE
½ cup (100 grams) sugar
¼ cup water, plus additional for thinning
1 tablespoon corn syrup

Stir the sugar, ¼ cup water, and the corn syrup in a small heavy saucepan until the sugar is dissolved, 3 to 4 minutes. Clean the side of the pan with a rubber spatula. Cook over medium heat without stirring until the bubbles get thicker and thicker and the mixture begins to caramelize. *Do not* stir again with the same spoon since it has sugar crystals on it that will cause the mixture to harden. Reduce the heat and cook to a dark caramel color, about 320° F on a candy thermometer. Remove immediately from the heat and swirl the pan to mix it evenly. Stirring constantly with a clean wooden spoon, very gradually and very carefully add water a tablespoon at a time, until the caramel is thin enough to be spread. Spread the dough with half the caramel glaze, smoothing it with a spatula or knife. Decorate the top with a squiggly pattern made with the tines of a fork or, better yet, with a cake-decorating comb made especially for this purpose. Refrigerate 15 minutes to 4 hours. Brush again with beaten egg and spread with the remaining glaze. Decorate the glaze as before.

Refrigerate 15 to 30 minutes to make sure that the dough is cold so that it can be cut cleanly into 1½ × 1-inch bars.

Baking. Heat the oven to 350° F. Bake until golden brown, 20 to 22 minutes. Cool in the pan.

Cake decorating comb

Fagottini
Little Jam-filled Pockets

The perfect snack: little buttery pockets of pastry dough filled with apricot or raspberry jam.

Makes about 2½ dozen cookies

Pasta Frolla I (page 339), made through chilling
1 or 2 eggs, beaten
6 to 8 tablespoons apricot or raspberry jam

Roll out the cold dough ¼ inch thick on a floured surface. Cut out 3-inch plain or scalloped ovals with a cookie cutter. Gather and reroll scraps and cut out as many ovals as possible. Brush the top of each one with the beaten egg and spoon a little less than 1 teaspoon of the jam in the center of each. Fold the ovals in half and seal the edges securely using the tines of a fork or the tips of your fingers. Place 1½ inches apart on buttered or parchment-lined baking sheets. Brush the tops with beaten egg.

Baking. Heat the oven to 350° F. Bake until golden, 20 minutes. Cool on racks.

Buccellati

Fig-and-Almond-filled Cookies from Sicily

Imagine, if you can, a Fig Newton Sicilian-style with figs and nuts rolled inside sweet pastry dough and topped with a dusting of powdered sugar. These fat little nougats look more like *pfeffernüsse* than Fig Newtons, but wait until you bite into them.

Makes 3 dozen cookies

⅔ cup (100 grams) finely chopped Calmyrna or light figs
Scant cup (100 grams) walnuts, toasted (page 52) and chopped
Scant cup (100 grams) blanched almonds, chopped
Grated zest of 1 orange
½ to ¾ teaspoon unsweetened cocoa powder, preferably Dutch process
¾ cup plus 1 tablespoon plus 1 teaspoon red wine
2½ teaspoons honey
1 tablespoon granulated sugar
Pasta Frolla I (page 339), made through chilling
Confectioners' sugar

Combine the figs, walnuts, and almonds in a saucepan. Add the orange zest, cocoa, wine, honey, and granulated sugar and stir to combine. Cook, stirring occasionally, over a medium heat to a rather dry paste. Remove from the heat. Pinch off 1 piece of the cold pastry dough about the size of a walnut, roll between your palms into a ball, and then flatten to a circle. Place 1 teaspoon nut paste in the center and wrap the pastry over the paste, enclosing it completely. Roll into a ball. Repeat with the remaining pastry and paste and place 1½ inches apart on buttered or parchment-lined baking sheets.

Baking. Heat the oven to 350° F. Bake until lightly browned, 25 minutes. Transfer to racks and immediately sift confectioners' sugar over the tops. Let cool completely.

Variation. Unorthodox but delicious—substitute *Pasta Frolla Integrale* (page 343) for the *Pasta Frolla I.*

Chocolate Nut Cookies

Baci d'Alassio

*Chocolate Kisses
from Alassio*

These chewy, nutty, pebble-shaped cookies look as if they may have come right off the beach of a Ligurian seaside town. The secret to making them is getting the dough the right consistency and allowing them to dry overnight before baking.

Makes 15 doubled cookies fused with chocolate

1½ cups (150 grams) hazelnuts, toasted and skinned (page 52)
1½ cups (150 grams) superfine sugar
11 ounces (300 grams) almond paste
1 teaspoon honey
4 egg whites, room temperature
3 to 4 tablespoons (30 grams) unsweetened cocoa powder, preferably Dutch process
Leftover cookies, such as butter, sugar, or chocolate, if needed
2 ounces (60 grams) semisweet chocolate

Grind the hazelnuts with 2 tablespoons of the sugar to a coarse powder in a food processor fitted with the steel blade. Add the remaining sugar and process to a fine powder. Add the almond paste and process to a smooth paste, or mix the nut mixture and the almond paste with an electric mixer until smooth. Transfer the mixture from the food processor to a mixer bowl if necessary. Mix in the honey. Stir in the egg whites with a wooden spoon and then stir in the cocoa. The dough should be gooey and sticky but definitely not runny. When you pull a piece between your hands, it should stretch to a ribbon. If the dough is runny, grind leftover cookies to fine crumbs and stir a bit at a time into the dough to correct the consistency.

Shaping. Spoon the dough into a pastry bag fitted with a ⅜-inch star tip. Pipe small button stars 1½ inches apart on buttered or parchment-lined baking sheets. Let stand uncovered overnight at room temperature to dry.

Baking. Heat the oven to 375° F. Bake 8 to 10 minutes. The cookies should be chewy inside and look almost a bit undercooked. Cool completely on racks. While the cookies are cooling, melt the chocolate in the top of a double boiler over simmering water. Join cookies together with melted chocolate. They should rest on their sides and be refrigerated 15 to 30 minutes to set the chocolate.

Ossi da Mordere

These crunchy, chocolatey cookies, with unexpected air pockets in their centers, are traditionally shaped like a human bone. This recipe is only one variation of the cookie, which can be found from Venice and Piedmont in the north all the way south to Sicily, where they are sometimes shaped to resemble skeletons, the infant Jesus, and even grape clusters. These cookies keep very well and, in fact, are actually better the second day.

Makes 2 dozen cookies

¾ cup plus 2 tablespoons (100 grams) blanched almonds
1⅓ cups (200 grams) confectioners' sugar
Scant ¼ cup (20 grams) unsweetened cocoa powder, preferably
  Dutch process
3 to 3½ tablespoons egg whites
1 tablespoon milk

Grind the almonds to a coarse powder in a food processor fitted with the steel blade. Add the sugar and cocoa and process to a fine powder. Add 3 tablespoons egg whites and process to a stiff, solid paste. Add the additional egg white if necessary.

Shaping. Pinch off pieces of dough the size of a fat cherry and roll between your hands into balls. Place 2 inches apart on buttered or parchment-lined baking sheets. Lightly brush the tops with milk.

Baking. Heat the oven to 325° F. Bake for 20 to 22 minutes. At first the cookies will flatten out and look like nothing at all, but, given a few more minutes, each of these little cookies will puff up and their tops will become cracked and shiny. Cool on racks.

APPENDIX

Source Guide to Ingredients and Equipment

Now that Italian food is so much in vogue, it has become remarkably easy to locate what used to be hopelessly recherché ingredients. I remember when searching out extra virgin olive oil meant special trips to a handful of ethnic markets, but these days olive oils are like wines and there are so many bottles with so many beautiful labels that sometimes I think the only logical response is total bewilderment. I'm not complaining, though. I used to have to carry home from Italy the ingredients I wanted, perfuming my suitcase with the most extraordinary aromas, but now specialty and gourmet shops have popped up all over, bringing Italy to America, and they seem to have booked first-class airplane passage for any number of Italian mushrooms, cheeses, olive pastes, sun-dried tomatoes, and exotic liqueurs. Still, some of the ingredients called for in these recipes may be difficult to find in smaller communities, and you may need to order them by mail.

Flours

INGREDIENTS

Most of the breads in this book are made with unbleached flour, which doesn't vary dramatically in its gluten content or texture from region to region the way bleached all-purpose flour does. But please don't feel that you have to buy specially milled flours or unusual brands; use any standard brand available in markets and supermarkets and you'll be fine. Of course, some recipes do call for special stone-ground flours or indicate specialties like semolina or durum flour, pastry flours, or unusual grain flours. Many of them can be found at health-food stores, and some even turn up in larger supermarket chains that have responded to the recent American fascination with health and baking by stocking new sections with these more exotic ingredients. (Among the brands of semolina flour to look for are Antoine's, Pasta Perfect, Estus Gourmet, and La Rinascente.) If you want to try baking with the "00" Italian flour just to see what it's like (and it is different, I promise you), you can mail-order a package of Tre Grazie brand from Dean and Deluca (see page 424). If you have trouble finding any of the flours in the recipes, there are several excellent sources that will send what you want by mail.

Arrowhead Mills
Box 866
Hereford, TX 79045

Arrowhead Mills, the famous mill in Deaf Smith County, has a list of all its stone-ground flours milled from organically grown grains. They include durum flour, rice flour, pastry flour, and cornmeals.

El Molino
P.O. Box 2250
City of Industry, CA 91746

El Molino makes an excellent yeast that is available in packages and in bulk, as well as unbleached white and whole-wheat pastry flours, and stone-ground natural-grain flours.

Giusto's
241 East Harris Avenue
South San Francisco, CA 94080

It would be hard to think of a grain or flour that Giusto's doesn't have among their forty organically grown, freshly ground whole-grain flours. Their selection includes corn flour; silky semolina and durum flours; graham, oat, brown rice; several grinds of whole wheat and rye; and pastry flour.

Great Valley Mills
687 Mill Road
Telford, PA 18969

Write for their list of stone-ground flours; it includes semolina, graham, rye, and oatmeal, as well as whites and whole wheats.

The Vermont Country Store
Weston, VT 05161

You can send for the store's mail-order catalogue, which lists graham flour, cornmeal, whole-wheat pastry flour, rye flour, and sea salt, along with wonderful kitchen equipment.

Vivande
2215 Fillmore Street
San Francisco, CA 94115

Vivande is a wonderful shop filled with Italian food, which will send a silky durum flour all over the country.

White Lily Flour Co.
Box 871
Knoxville, TN 37901

An excellent source of soft wheat pastry flour.

Malt Extract

Malt extract is a wonderful additive that gives bloom and color to the crust of a loaf of bread, but it is getting harder and harder to find. You may be able to get it in health-food stores as malted syrup, malted grain syrup, or a variant thereof, and it may come in a can or you may have to serve yourself from a big bottle with a spigot. If you can't find it, write or phone the best and what may be the only source of supply in America:

Premier Malt Products Inc.
Milwaukee, WI 53201
800-521-1057

Italian Products from Italy

If specialty shops and gourmet stores in your area haven't got the dried mushrooms, the fresh creamy cheeses, or the olives you need, here are excellent sources of supply:

Balducci's
424 Sixth Avenue
New York, NY 10011

Balducci's publishes a catalogue that includes imported ingredients and is available for $3.00.

Dean and Deluca
121 Prince Street
New York, NY 10012

Dean and Deluca have an unerring eye for the finest quality. The fabulous range of Italian products that they have brought to America includes dried porcini mushrooms; olives and olive oils; wonderful anchovies packed in olive oil; sun-dried tomatoes; olive paste; an outstanding pesto from Crespi in San Remo; Originario rice; herbs and spices; Pagani tomato paste.

Manganaro's
488 Ninth Avenue
New York, NY 10018

Yet another wonderful New York source of Italian cheeses, salamis, and olive oils.

Todaro Bros.
557 Second Avenue
New York, NY 10016

Todaro Bros. brings in all manner of Italian ingredients—cheeses, olives, olive oils, porcini mushrooms, and prosciutto—as well as *colombe, pandori, panettoni,* and *gubane,* all baked in Italy and imported to America, so you can know what the real Italian product tastes like.

Williams-Sonoma
P.O. Box 7456
San Francisco, CA 94120

Williams-Sonoma is primarily known as a kitchen equipment shop, but one look at its catalogue makes it clear that among the fine ingredients available by mail are durum flour, Nielsen-Massey vanilla, Blue Diamond ground blanched almonds, Callebaut chocolate, Dutch-process Dark Jersey cocoa, Dittman's lemon extract, and various olive oils and vinegars.

Nuts

Torn Ranch Grove
1122 Fourth Street
San Rafael, CA 94901

If it's a nut or a raisin, they have it: walnuts, almonds, hazelnuts, pine nuts, and every possible variety of raisin, including monnukas, currants, and seeded muscats.

Special Sugars and Flavorings

H. Roth and Sons
1577 First Avenue
New York, NY 10028

Has crystallized baking sugar, vanilla sugar, all kinds of flours, flavorings and essences, as well as baking equipment.

Spices

Select Origins
670 West End Avenue, Suite 10 E
New York, NY 10025

Select Origins scours the earth for the best spices and herbs grown and will mail them anywhere in the country. Their catalogue also offers garlic, cheeses, Crespi pesto and sun-dried tomatoes, and olives, all of the same high quality.

EQUIPMENT

Hammarplast
212 Fifth Avenue
New York, NY 10010

Hammarplast makes a special container for dough that is designed around the properties of yeast, and I have found it very helpful on especially hot or cold days. I particularly like the large 5-quart bowl for big doughs.

Maid of Scandinavia
3244 Raleigh Avenue
Minneapolis, MN 55416

A wonderful source of both equipment and ingredients special to the baker, Maid of Scandinavia publishes a fat catalogue that fully describes its products.

Old Stone Corporation
616 Davis Terrace
Glen Ellyn, IL 60137

Old Stone makes round baking stones.

Sassafras
P.O. Box 1366
Evanston, IL 60604

Sassafras makes round and rectangular baking stones as well as pizza peels and the La Cloche bread oven.

Williams-Sonoma
P.O. Box 7456
San Francisco, CA 94120

The Williams-Sonoma catalogue carries a phenomenal selection of kitchen equipment. Almost all of the special pans and molds needed for the specialty breads and sweets in these recipes can be bought there, including *pandoro* molds, Pullman loaf pans, nut grinders, baking and pizza stones, the La Cloche bread oven, bannetons, saddle pans, special thermometers, and metric and pound scales.

GLOSSARY

Acciughe (ah-CHEW-gay)   Anchovies

Amarene (ah-ma-RAY-nay)   Wild cherries

Anice (AH-knee-chay)   Anise

Arancia (ar-RAN-cha)   Orange

Baci d'Alassio (BAH-chee dah-LAHS-ee-oh)   Chocolate kisses from the seaside town of Alassio

Basilico (bah-SEE-lee-ko)   Basil

Biga (BEE-ga)   A starter dough of yeast, water, and flour. It gives force to the dough and allows it to mature slowly, bringing out the flavor of the wheat. Bakers sometimes call it old dough, *pasta vecchia,* when the *biga* is dough left from the previous day's bake

Bigio (BE-joe)   Mixed whole-wheat and white flour loaf

Binario (been-ARE-ee-oh)   Shaped like a railroad track

Biscotti (bees-SCOT-tee)   Literally "twice cooked" these cookies have been baked once, taken out of the oven and cooked again to a crisp hardness; they are meant to be dipped into *vin santo,* a sweet dessert wine

Bruschetta (brews-KAYT-tah)   Bread grilled or toasted, rubbed with garlic and spread with fruity green olive oil

Brutti ma buoni (BREWT-tea mah BWO-nee)   Cookies so called because they are "ugly but good"

Burro (BUR-row)   Butter

Cacao (ca-COW)   Cocoa

Calzone (cal-TZONE-nay)   Pizza dough folded to a half-moon shape enclosing a filling

Cannella (can-NELL-la)   Cinnamon

Cannoncini (can-non-CHEE-knee)   Little spiral-shaped cannons of puff pastry

Canoe (ca-NO-ay)   Canoe-shaped pastries

Capperi (CAP-pair-ee)   Capers

Carciofo (car-CHO-fo)   Artichoke

Carta da musica (car-ta da MOO-zee-ka)   An extremely fine bread from Sardinia made in an 8- to 10-inch disk. Its fine veining of lines gives it the name "sheet music" bread

Cassata (cas-SAH-ta)   A Sicilian cake, essentially made from layers of sponge cake filled with a ricotta cream and iced. Not to be confused with the industrially produced ice cream dessert

Cedro (CHEY-dro)   Citron

Cereali (chair-e-AL-ee)   Grains

Chiavari (key-AH-vah-ree)   A town on the Ligurian coast where olive paste
  bread is made
Chiodo di garofano (key-OH-dough dee gar-RO-fa-no)   Clove
Ciabatta (cha-BAHT-tah)   A slipper-shaped bread from Lake Como
Ciambella (chahm-BELL-lah)   Wreath shaped
Cioccolata (chee-oo-ko-LA-ta)   Chocolate
Ciliege (chill-ee-AY-jay)   Cherries
Cipolle (chee-POLE-lay)   Onions
Colomba (co-LOWM-bah)   Easter bread baked in the shape of a dove
Companatico (com-pah-NAH-tee-ko)   Something that goes with bread (from
  com: with and *pane:* bread)
Cornetti (core-NET-tee)   Croissants, Italian style
Crescenza (creche-EN-za)   Fresh semi-soft medium-fat cheese, used for *focaccia
  di Recco*
Crescia (CRECHE-shhah)   *Crescia* means "to grow," as Easter cheese bread
  does dramatically in the oven
Crostata (cros-TA-ta)   Tart
Crostini (cros-TEE-nee)   Tuscan specialty of saltless bread lightly sautéed,
  toasted, or grilled and spread with a soft topping, which usually includes
  chicken liver
Crostone (cros-TOE-nay)   Big slices of bread sautéed with oil and butter, then
  baked in the oven with cheese on top
Crumiri (crew-ME-ree)   Corn cookies from Piedmont shaped like an arch
Crusca (CROO-ska)   Bran
Dolci (DOL-chee)   Sweets
Erbe (AIR-bay)   Herbs
Ermelline (air-mel-LEAN-nay)   Bitter almonds
Farina (fah-REE-na)   Flour
Fazzoletti (faht-zo-LAYT-tee)   Turnovers
Fichi (FEE-key)   Figs
Focaccia, Focacce (fo-KA-cha; fo-KA-chay)   A kind of leavened dough which
  can be as dramatically high as the domed Focaccia Veneziana, although it
  usually refers to flat breads that are dimpled to keep them low
Formaggio, Formaggi (for-MAHG-gee-oh; for-MAHG-gee)   Cheese; cheeses
Funghi secchi (FOON-ghee SECK-kee)   Dried mushrooms, usually referring to
  porcini, the wild mushrooms of Italy
Genovese (je-no-VAY-say)   From Genoa
Giallo (JAHL-low)   Yellow; as in *pane giallo,* corn bread
Girelle (gee-REL-lay)   Spiral breakfast pastries
Gorgonzola (gor-gon-ZO-la)   Semi-soft blue cheese
Grano duro (GRAN-o DUR-o)   Durum flour made from gold-colored hard
  wheat and used in breads
Grissini (grees-SEE-knee)   Breadsticks
Gubana (goo-BAH-na)   This Easter sweet of the Friuli region near the
  Yugoslavian border is encased in a sweetened bread dough (in some places

puff pastry is used) filled with various nuts and raisins and flavored with grappa and citrus

In carrozza (een kar-ROTZ-zah)   "In a carriage"—usually a sandwich from Naples of cheese baked between two slices of bread

Integrale (in-tay-GRAH-lay)   Whole wheat

Latte (LAT-tay)   Milk

Lievito (lee-YEA-vee-to)   Yeast

Limone (lee-MO-nay)   Lemon

Mandorle (MAHN-door-lay)   Almonds

Maritozzi (ma-ree-TOTE-see)   Sweet rolls from Rome, from the dialect word for "big husband"

Marmellata (mar-mel-LA-ta)   Jam

Mascarpone (mahs-car-POH-nay)   Thick fresh cheese made from sweet cream

Mele (MAY-lay)   Apples

Miele (me-EL-ay)   Honey

Milanese (mi-la-NAY-say)   From Milan

Minestra (mi-NE-stra)   Soup with a slice of bread in it

Mozzarella (mots-za-REL-lah)   The classic pizza cheese

Napoletana (na-po-lay-TAH-nah)   From Naples

Nocciole (no-CHO-lay)   Hazelnuts

Noce moscata (NO-chay mo-SCAT-tah)   Nutmeg

Noci (NO-chee)   Walnuts

Olive (oh-LEE-vay)   Olives

Origano (or-REE-ga-no)   Oregano

Pancetta (pahn-CHET-ta)   Italian unsmoked bacon

Pan di Spagna (pahn dee SPAH-nya)   A cake, although literally "a bread of Spain"

Pandoro (pahn-DO-roh)   Tall star-shaped sweet Christmas bread of Verona, covered with a light layer of powdered sugar

Pane, pani (PA-nay; PA-nee)   Bread; breads

Panforte (pan-FOR-tay)   Honey- and spice-flavored sweet from Siena

Panino, Panini (pa-NEE-no; pa-NEE-nee)   Roll; rolls

Panzanella (pahn-tza-NELL-lah)   A bread salad

Parmigiano-Reggiano (par-mee-JAH-no reg-gee-AH-no)   Finest grating cheese of northern Italy

Pasquale (pah-SQUA-lay)   Easter

Pasta di mandorle (PAHS-ta dee MAHN-door-lay)   Almond paste

Pasta frolla (PAH-stah FROL-la)   Sweet pastry dough

Pasta sfogliata (PAH-sta Sfo-LYAH-tah)   Puff pastry

Pasticceria (pah-stee-chair-REE-ah)   Pastry in general

Pastiera (pah-STEE-AIR-ah)   An Easter pie from Naples made with ricotta cheese

Patate (pa-TAH-tay)   Potatoes

Pecorino (pe-co-REE-no)   Most popular hard grating cheese of southern Italy

Pepe (PAY-pay)   Pepper

Pere (PAY-ray) Pears

Pignoli (pee-GNO-lee) Pine nuts

Pizza (PEE-tza) Pizza is really a leavened dough, which, if allowed to rise, can become as dramatic and high as a *pizza Civitavecchia* bread with its glossy domed top

Pomodori secchi (pom-o-DOR-ee SECK-ee) Dried tomatoes

Pomodoro (pom-o-DOR-o) Tomato

Prezzemolo (praytz-SAY-mo-lo) Parsley

Prosciutto (pro-SHOOT-toh) Cured ham

Pugliese (pool-yee-AY-say) A type of country bread from Puglia in southern Italy

Ricotta (ree-COAT-tah) "Recooked"—a cheese made by boiling skimmed milk

Riso (REE-so) Rice

Rosmarino (rose-ma-REE-no) Rosemary

Ruota (rue-AW-ta) A big wheel of bread

Rustici (roo-STEE-chee) Savory puff pastry appetizer

Salatini (Sa-la-TEA-knee) Savory puff pastry appetizers

Sale (SAH-lay) Salt

Salvia (SAL-veeya) Sage

Sambuca (sahm-BOO-ka) A sweet anise-flavored liqueur from Lazio

Schiacciata (ski-ah-CHAH-tah) Flat bread, usually savory, but not always; Tuscan word for *focaccia* (they also use the term *stiacciata*)

Segale (say-GAH-lay) Rye

Semi di anice (SAY-me dee AH-nee-chay) Anise seeds

Semolina (say-mo-LEE-nah) Finely ground durum wheat

Siciliano (see-chill-LEEAH-noh) Sicilian

Spagna (SPAH-nyah) From Spain

Spezie (SPET-zeeay) Spices

Spinaci (spee-NAH-chee) Spinach

Stracchino (stra-KEY-noh) Creamy rindless fresh cheese

Strutto (STROOT-toh) Lard

Stuzzichini (stoo-tsee-KEY-knee) Something to whet the appetite, an appetizer

Taleggio (tah-LAY-joe) Rich, semi-soft fresh cheese with butter flavor

Torinese (to-ree-NAY-say) From Turin

Torta (TORE-tah) Cake

Toscani (toe-SKA-knee) From Tuscany

Uva (OOH-va) Grape

Uva passa (OOH-va PAHS-sa) Raisin

Vaniglia (van-KNEE-leeah) Vanilla

Verdura (ver-DOO-rah) Vegetables

Zabaione (za-buy-YO-nay) A rum- or marsala-flavored custard

Zaletti (zah-LET-tea) Cornmeal cookies from Venice

Zucca (ZOO-ka) Pumpkin

Zucchero (zook-CARE-oh) Sugar

Zuppa (ZOOP-pa) Soup

INDEX

Provolone, 47
in *pizza Pugliese* topping, 282
Pudding, bread, 195
Puff pastry, 318–22
little handkerchiefs of, 328–29
treats from Lecce, little, 332–33
Puglia
bread of, 122–24
olive-studded, 124
half-moon-shaped filled pizza
from, 286–87
potato flatbread from, 300–1
Pugliese topping, for *pizza alla
Romana*, 282
Pullman loaf pan, covered, 68
Pumpkin tart, 353
Puppola, Giorgio, 13–14

Quarry tiles, 65, 86

Raisin(s), 55
bread, 203–5
Milan sweet bread, 206–7
panettone, 220–23
Tuscan sweet bread, 210–11
breakfast pastries (*girelle*), 309
buns
Roman, 260–61
rosemary and, 262–63
cookies with rum-soaked,
round buttery, 400–1
cookie wreaths dotted with,
399–400
-cornmeal cookies from Venice,
411
Ramerino, pan di, 262–63
Razor blade, 70
Recco, cheese *focaccia* from, 317
Recipes, about, 32–33
Red pepper bread, sweet, 158–59
Regional and rustic breads, 99–
147
about, 99–100
Calabrian bread, 142–43
Chiavari bread, 140–41
Como bread, 102–3
corn bread from Lombardy,
130–31
crocodile bread, 116–17
dark Tuscan bread, 112–13
durum-flour bread from
Altamura, 120–21
Easter cheese bread, 146–47

Regional and rustic breads (*cont.*)
Genzano bread, 118–19
little rye rounds from the
Valtellina, 135–37
olive bread, 138–39
olive oil bread, 108–9
Puglia bread, 122–24
olive-studded, 124
rye bread
from Bolzano, 132–33
from Merano, 134–35
saltless Tuscan bread, 110–12
Sicilian bread, 124–27
slipper-shaped bread from Lake
Como, 106–7
spicy cheese bread, 144–45
starter for, 100–1
Terni bread, 114–15
whole-wheat bread, 128–29
Rehrücken molds, 75
Rendering fat, 50
Ribollita, 186–87
Ricciarelli, 396–97
Rice, 63
flour, 38
tart, 370–71
Ricotta
binario di, 322–24
binario di frolla alla, 369–70
cassata, 372–73
cheesecake in a flat strip of
pastry, 369–70
crostata di, 368–69
Easter cake
of Naples, 366–68
of Sicily, 372–73
focaccia with, 294
little handkerchiefs of puff
pastry filled with (*fazzoletti
dolci*), 328–29
pastiera, 366–68
pastry tart filled with, 322–24
and prosciutto and cheese
filling, 314–15
tart or cheesecake from
Tuscany, 368–69
Ring mold, 70
Rising, 81–82
second, 84–85, 90
timing of, 82, 90
Riso, 63
torta di, 370–71
Rocco, Sir Emanuele, 271
Rolling pin, 72, 92

Rolls, 246–58
cleft, little, 255
from Emilia Romagna, 247–51
artichoke shape, 251
coppietta shape, 249
little trunk from Mantua,
250–51
mustafa, 250
scroll shape, 250
from Florence, 252–53
from Piedmont, plump, 256–57
rosettes of Venice, 253–54
tomato, 257–58
Rome
ancient, 24–27, 56, 269, 270
Easter bread of, 238–39
Easter pizza of, 240–41
pizza of, 278–82
basic recipe, 279–80
bianca, about, 278
bianca (olive oil and garlic)
topping, 281
pugliese topping, 282
rossa (tomato and mozzarella)
topping, 282
sweet buns of, 260–61
Rosemary, 49
bread, 161–63
focaccia with, 291
and raisin buns, 262–63
whole-wheat bread with, 175–
76
Rosettes of Venice, (*Rosette
Veneziane*), 253–54
Rosmarino, 49
focaccia al, 291
pan di ramerino, 262–63
pane integrale con erbe, 175–76
panmarino, 161–63
Rossa topping, for *pizza alla
romana*, 282
Rum
bran cookies spiked with, 413
whole-wheat cookies spiked
with, 414
Rustic breads. See Regional and
rustic breads
Rustici, 332–33
Rustic whole-wheat pillows, 173–
74
Rye
bread
about, 132
from Bolzano, 132–33